CHRISTIAN DEMOCRACY IN FRANCE

R. E. M. Irving

LONDON. GEORGE ALLEN & UNWIN LTD
RUSKIN HOUSE MUSEUM STREET

ISBN 0 04 320085 0

Printed in Great Britain
in 10/11 point Times New Roman type
by Unwin Brothers Limited
Woking and London

To My Parents

Preface

Christian Democracy, which may be briefly defined as organized political action by Catholic democrats, has been a major political force in Western Europe since the war. But, unlike Socialism and Communism, it has attracted the attention of relatively few scholars. When M. P. Fogarty wrote *Christian Democracy in Western Europe* (Routledge and Kegan Paul, 1957), he emphasized the need for more studies of Christian Democratic political parties (his own book being concerned primarily with the social aspects of Christian Democracy). Since then a number of important books have been published in this field.[1] But major gaps—one such being France—have remained. François Goguel and Maurice Vaussard wrote useful introductory studies in the 1950s,[2] but both are now somewhat dated. Since then nothing substantial has appeared. It may, of course, be argued that this is not surprising in view of the decline and fall of the Mouvement Républician Populaire (MRP) in the mid-1960s. It certainly cannot be denied that, as an *organized* political force, Christian Democracy is now less important in France than it is in Germany or Italy. But this is not the whole story, for many politicians, who would be called Christian Democrats in other Western European countries, are active in the French Gaullist and Centre parties. Indeed many observers would consider the Gaullist party to be as much (or as little) a 'Christian Democratic' party as the German CDU. Be that as it may, the fact remains that the political activism of French Catholics since the war, together with their general reconciliation to the Republic, are parts of the continuing legacy of Christian Democracy. In that sense Christian Democracy is not dead in France, and no study of French politics or recent history can be complete without some understanding of Christian Democratic theory and practice.

My interest in French history and politics was first stimulated at Oxford in the late 1950s when I read Modern History at St Edmund

---

[1] For example, A. J. Heidenheimer, *Adenauer and the CDU* (Nijhoff, 1960) and J.-P. Chasseriaud, *Le Parti Démocrate Chrétien en Italie* (Colin, 1965).

(The first time a book is cited, its author and title will be given in full. Thereafter only the author's name will be given unless there is a possibilty of confusion, in which case the book's full or short title will also be given. For a full list of books, see the Bibliography, pp. 271–8)

[2] M. Vaussard, *Histoire de la Démocratie Chrétienne—France, Belgique, Italie* (Seuil, 1956).

M. Einaudi and F. Goguel, *Christian Democracy in Italy and France* (University of Notre Dame Press, 1952).

Hall, and my study of MRP began in 1965 when I returned to Oxford as a postgraduate. After completing a rather specialized doctoral thesis on MRP's colonial policy, I was able to extend my research to French Christian Democracy as a whole thanks to a grant from the Nuffield Foundation and financial help from the University of Edinburgh.

The bulk of my research was done at the Fondation Nationale des Sciences Politiques, Paris, and I would like to express my thanks to the Librarian and his assistants (particularly those in the Centre de Documentation) for much help during the past seven years. I am likewise indebted to the archivists and party officials at MRP's old headquarters in the rue de Poissy and at the Centre Démocrate's headquarters in the Boulevard St Germain. I would also like to thank the Librarians of St Antony's College, Oxford, Nuffield College, Oxford, and the Centre of European Governmental Studies, Edinburgh, for their assistance over the years. Amongst the many French scholars and politicians who have been kind enough to discuss Christian Democracy with me, I am particularly grateful to the following: Pierre Abelin, Robert Buron, André Colin, Pierre Corval, Paul Coste-Floret, Pierre de Chevigné, Philippe Devillers, François Goguel, Léo Hamon, Georges Hourdin, Jean-Jacques Juglas, Jean Lacouture, Georges Le Brun-Kéris, Jean Lecanuet, Robert Lecourt, Francine Lefebvre, Jean Letourneau, André Monteil, Pierre Pflimlin, Alain Poher, Maurice Schumann, Pierre-Henri Teitgen and Paul Vignaux. I would also like to thank Dr Malcom Anderson, Professor James Cornford, Mrs Sheila Gordon, Lady Anne Mackenzie Stuart, Mr Stephen Maxwell and Professor J. D. B. Mitchell for reading all or parts of the manuscript; Mr Peter McIntyre for helping to draw up the Index; and my wife for cheerfully tolerating many 'absentee' weekends and evenings during the last few years. But my principal debt of gratitude is to Mr Philip Williams of Nuffield College, Oxford, who has not only encouraged my work over the years but also read and criticized the whole draft with his usual thoroughness and perspicacity.

The Centre of European Governmental Studies
University of Edinburgh
December 1972

Contents

Introduction

Christian Democracy may be defined as organized political action by Catholics—and their sympathizers—within a democratic framework. Christian Democracy is closely connected with, but distinct from, Catholic Action, whose main concern is social, not political, action. Although Catholics have been the backbone of the Christian Democratic parties, the Christian Democrats have striven—with some success in Northern Europe (notably in Germany and Holland)—to avoid a 'confessional' image; in other words, Christian Democratic parties are not simply the political arm of the Catholic Church (even if at times the Italian Christian Democratic party has tended to belie this generalization). However, the Catholic 'view of life' is certainly an integral part of Christian Democratic political thinking. Christian Democratic parties thus have a tendency to be conservative in their emphasis on individualism, but they have abandoned the tenets of nineteenth century Liberalism, realizing that social and economic justice require intervention by the State. The German Christlich Demokratische Union (CDU) has an important labour wing, whilst the Italian Democrazia Cristiana (DC) has a small but active trade union faction; in France, too, a significant number of Christian Democratic militants always wanted to liaise, or even fuse, with the Socialists. But, broadly speaking, Christian Democratic parties have tended to act in a rather conservative manner when faced with the responsibilities of power. Indeed, one of their most important political achievements has been that they have helped to integrate conservatives[1] into the democratic system.

Although Christian Democracy was essentially a post-war phenomenon in France, the same cannot be said of Germany where the Catholic Zentrum had been a major party from 1870–1933 or of Italy where Don Sturzo's Partito Popolare was the second largest party (after the Socialists) from 1919–22. Christian Democracy, however, grew rapidly after the Second World War to fill the political void created by the collapse of Nazism and Fascism. German Catholics and (many) Protestants agreed to sink their differences in order to defend the democratic and Christian values rejected by Hitler. Italian Catholics joined together in a loose

---

[1] I shall use conservative with a small 'c' when referring to social, economic and political attitudes, and with a large 'C' when referring to political parties. In France there has never been a 'Conservative Party' as such, but the various parties and groups formed, for example, by the Independents and Peasants in the Fourth Republic can appropriately be described as Conservative.

11

confederation whose main cohesive force was aversion to Fascism. Many French Catholics, particularly those of left-wing tendencies, had been prominent in the Resistance, and they too were able to take advantage of the reaction against Vichy. Within five years of the end of the Second World War approximately two-fifths of the members of parliament of the lower houses of the six founding members of the first European Community (the Coal and Steel Community) were Christian Democrats. And the largest single group in the Assembly of the Coal and Steel Community, as well as in its successor the European Parliament, has always been Christian Democratic. But, important though Christian Democracy has been in numerical terms, its real significance is political. After a century and a half of indecision, Catholics have reconciled themselves to political democracy. The Papacy did not accept the democratic implications of the French Revolution until the pontificate of Leo XIII (1878–1903), and it took another fifty years for Catholic politicians to convince agnostics and Protestants that they could be genuine democrats. On the continent of Europe, in contrast to Britain, there was a great divide between Catholics and democrats. Until the Second World War Catholics were held by their political opponents to be reactionaries, whose real desire was a hierarchical, authoritarian State modelled on their Church. Democrats (in particular Socialists), on the other hand, were often seen by Catholics (and conservatives in general) as anti-clerical atheists, whose main objective was to destroy the whole basis of society for the sake of an egalitarian, materialistic utopia.

In France the quarrel between Catholics and Republicans had been particularly bitter. It began with the State's expropriation of the Church's property in 1790. Napoleon succeeded in patching up a truce ten years later, and this lasted (more or less) until about 1850. The quarrel was then exacerbated first by Catholic intransigence during the Second Empire and then by the Republican reaction in the early years of the Third Republic. It reached a crescendo at the turn of the century, culminating in the disestablishment of the Catholic Church in 1905. Thereafter the way was open for reconciliation, and Christian Democracy emerged as the chief vehicle by which Catholics were reconciled to the Republic.

French Christian Democracy has its political origin in the ideas propounded by Lamennais and Lacordaire in the 1830s. It owes much of its social doctrine to Montalembert, Harmel and de Mun, the 'Social Catholics' of the late nineteenth century. But Christian Democracy, in the sense of organized political action by republican Catholics to achieve social and economic reforms, is a twentieth-century phenomenon. Marc Sangnier's Sillon (1899–1910) was an embryo Christian Democratic political party, but it was never represented in the Chamber and was condemned by the Pope in 1910. Since then there have been four Christian Democratic parties: the Parti Démocrate Populaire (PDP) and Jeune République (JR) in the inter-war years; the Mouvement Républicain Populaire (MRP) from 1944–67; and the Centre Démocrate (CD), which was founded in 1966 and is, in effect, the rump of MRP.

Of these four Christian Democratic parties, MRP alone was really important in French politics. The PDP never had more than nineteen deputies, whilst the CD had a similar number in the early 1970s. The JR representation in the Chamber never exceeded four. MRP, on the other hand, was the largest party in the National Assembly from June to November 1946 with 169 deputies, and the second largest (after the Communists) from 1946–51 with 167. Although much less successful in the elections of 1951 and 1956, MRP never had less than eighty-five deputies in the National Assembly of the Fourth Republic. Approximately one registered elector in four voted MRP for the first legislature of the Fourth Republic (1946–1951), and one in eight thereafter.

MRP was to the Fourth Republic what the Radicals had been to the Third, the fulcrum within the parliamentary system. The Christian Democrats participated in twenty-three of the twenty-seven governments from 1944–58 and supported all but that of Pierre Mendès-France (June 1954–February 1955). There were three MRP Prime Ministers (Schuman, Bidault, Pflimlin) and seven deputy Prime Ministers (Schuman, Bidault, Teitgen, Gay, Letourneau, Coste-Floret, Pflimlin). MRP controlled the Ministry of Foreign Affairs from 1944–54 in the persons of Schuman and Bidault, and the Ministry of Overseas France (Colonies) was another MRP fief (Coste-Floret, Letourneau, Pflimlin, Buron, Juglas, Colin). The Ministry of Defence also had important MRP incumbents (Bidault, Teitgen, Chevigné). Strangely enough, MRP, which regarded itself primarily as a party of social and economic reform, was rather less important in the domestic Ministries. Significantly it never held the Ministries of Education and the Interior. Schuman and Pflimlin, however, each had a year at the Ministry of Finance, whilst Louvel was responsible for Industry for four years, Bacon for Labour and Social Security for almost five, Schneiter for Health for three, and Pflimlin for Agriculture for four. Not surprisingly MRP, like the Radicals, gained a reputation as a party of *ministrables*.[1]

---

[1] *ministrable* means 'capable of holding office', but is inclined to be a rather pejorative term implying excessive enthusiasm for gaining and holding office.

13

One result of this constant MRP participation in government was that the governments of the Fourth Republic were coalitions of the Centre. This might have been expected to have pleased the Christian Democrats, who were very critical of the 'outdated' quarrels of Right and Left. But it did not. For the Christian Democrats wanted either a stable left-of-centre coalition or a large reforming party attractive both to the Centre and to the non-Communist Left. The former, however, was impossible, partly owing to the fact that French voters persistently elected a National Assembly which was incapable of producing a stable majority, and partly because the end of tripartism (*tripartisme*) and the rise of Gaullism ensured that any majority which did emerge was, in the last analysis, dependent on conservative votes.[1] And a large reforming party (*un parti travailliste*) was unrealizable owing to France's basic political divisions. The old quarrel between Catholics and Republicans, still focused on *le problème scolaire*, was not dead: and so long as this was the case, a moderate party of reform could not emerge, for neither Socialists nor Radicals would contemplate a 'marriage' with any Catholic party, however strong its republican and left-wing credentials might be. With the foundation of the Gaullist RPF in 1947, MRP's dream of reconciliation between the moderate Right and Left became even more of a chimera, for the Gaullist movement provided a vehicle for the revival of conservatism, brought to a head the issue of Catholic schools (in 1951), and cut incisively into MRP's electoral base. Moreover, this base, even in MRP's heyday, was too limited. Like the Italian and German Christian Democratic parties, MRP was stronger in some regions than in others, but unlike the DC and CDU, MRP was *essentially* a regional party. It was also, *malgré soi*, a 'confessional' party, but unlike the Christian Democratic parties of Italy and Belgium, it was not *the* Catholic party. Its attempt to attract non-Catholics, unlike that of the German CDU, was unsuccessful. So MRP was caught between two stools. It was too Catholic to attract *laïc* Republican votes, but insufficiently Catholic (in the sense of having direct links with the Hierarchy) to appeal to the Catholic electorate as a whole.

This dilemma, apparent as early as 1947, came to a head at the 1951 General Election when MRP's vote was halved (to 2,500,000), mainly owing to desertions to de Gaulle's RPF, which was both Catholic and conservative. In the Fifth Republic the Gaullist party

---

[1] *Tripartisme*, government by a coalition of the three largest parties (Communists, Socialists and MRP), ended with the eviction of the Communists in May 1947. De Gaulle's Rassemblement du Peuple Français (RPF) was founded in April 1947.

won over not only the old RPF electorate but also many moderates and former Christian Democrats. MRP went into voluntary liquidation in the hope that a new, broad-based Christian Democratic party (the Centre Démocrate) would appeal to the Centre electorate. But the General Election of 1967 showed the extent to which the Gaullists were already entrenched in the Centre. In consequence, the importance of Lecanuet's refusal to co-operate with Defferre in establishing an anti-Gaullist, anti-Communist alliance in 1965 became fully apparent. Unwilling to co-operate with the Gaullists whose style of government they abhorred, and unable to ally with the Socialists who had turned to the Communists with a view to forming a Popular Front, the tiny Christian Democratic party appeared to have little future. Indeed, it really became anomalous after the fall of de Gaulle (1969), for Pompidou soon showed that he was prepared to take further steps towards integrating Western Europe. No longer able to claim that it was *the* 'European' party, the CD had little to distinguish it from the moderate wing of the Gaullist party. If Christian Democracy has a future in France, it would appear to lie either in the Centre Démocratie et Progrès (CDP), a small right-of-centre party which works in liaison with the Gaullists, or in the Gaullist Union des Démocrates pour la République (UDR), which has already acquired many of the characteristics of the moderate, conservative German CDU. The UDR, of course, is not a left-of-centre reforming party of the type advocated by MRP's early militants, but the history of Christian Democracy in France seems to indicate that, whilst a moderate, conservative Catholic party is a feasible proposition, a moderate, social-reforming Catholic party, which is what MRP wanted to be, is not.

Abbreviations

Aube	*L'Aube*
ACJF	Association Catholique de la Jeunesse Française
AP	*L'Année Politique*
APEL	Association des Parents d'Elèves et de l'Enseignement Libre
APSR	*American Political Science Review*
ARS	Action Républicaine et Sociale
CD	Centre Démocrate
CGA	Confédération Générale de l'Agriculture
CDP	Centre Démocratie et Progrès
CFDT	Confédération Française Démocratique du Travail
CFTC	Confédération Française des Travailleurs Chrétiens
CNI (P)	Centre National des Indépendants (et Paysans)
(CG) PME	(Confédération Générale des) Petites et Moyennes Entreprises
CGT	Confédération Générale du Travail
CNJA	Centre National des Jeunes Agriculteurs
CNPF	Conseil National du Patronat Français
CODER	Commission de Développement Economique Régional
CUMA	Coopérative pour l'Utilisation des Machines Agricoles
ECSC	European Coal and Steel Community
EDC	European Defence Community
EEC	European Economic Community
ENA	Ecole Nationale d'Administration
FGDS	Fédération de la Gauche Démocrate et Socialiste
FLN	Front de Libération Nationale
FNSEA	Fédération Nationale des Syndicats d'Exploitants Agricoles
FO	Force Ouvrière
GPRA	Gouvernement Provisoire de la République Algérienne
IVCC	Institut des Vins de Consommation Courant
JAC	Jeunesse Agricole Chrétienne
JOC	Jeunesse Ouvrière Chrétienne
JO (AN)	*Journal Officiel* (Débats de l'Assemblée Nationale)
JO (CR)	*Journal Officiel* (Débats du Conseil de la République)
JO (Sénat)	*Journal Officiel* (Débats du Sénat)
MRP	Mouvement Républicain Populaire
Monde	*Le Monde*
NATO	North Atlantic Treaty Organization
OAS	Organisation de l'Armée Secrète
ORTF	Office de Radiodiffusion—Télévision Française
Parl. Aff.	*Parliamentary Affairs*
PCF	Parti Communiste Français
PDM	Progrès et Démocratie Moderne
PDP	Parti Démocrate Populaire
PR	Proportional Representation
PRL	Parti Républicain de la Liberté
PSU	Parti Socialiste Unifié
RDA	Rassemblement Démocratique Africain
RDP	*Revue du Droit Public et de la Science Politique*
RFD	Rassemblement des Forces Démocratiques
RFSP	*Revue Française de Science Politique*

17

RGR	Rassemblement des Gauches Républicaines
RI	Républicains Indépendants
RPF	Rassemblement du Peuple Français
RS	Républicains Sociaux (Gaullists)
SAFER	Sociétés d'Aménagement Foncier et d'Etablissement Rural
SFIO	Section Française de l'Internationale Ouvrière
SIBEV	Société Interprofessionnelle du Bétail et des Viandes
SICA	Sociétés d'Intérêts Collectifs Agricoles
SOFRES	Société Française d'Enquêtes par Sondages
TC	*Témoignage Chrétien*
UDCA	Union de Defénse des Commerçants et des Artisans (Poujadists)
UDR	Union des Démocrates pour la République
UDSR	Union Démocratique et Socialiste de la Résistance
UDT	Union Démocratique du Travail
UFF	Union et Fraternité Française (Poujadist deputies)
UNR	Union pour la Nouvelle République

Chapter 1

ORIGINS OF CHRISTIAN DEMOCRACY IN FRANCE

THE CATHOLIC-REPUBLICAN CONFLICT

No realistic assessment of the importance of Christian Democracy in France can be made without reference to the conflict between Church and State which plagued France from the Revolution of 1789 until the Debré Educational Reforms of 1959. And, even today, the scars have not finally disappeared.

Before the Second World War French Catholicism was generally equated with conservatism, often of the most reactionary kind. The Republic had been the enemy of the Church since the Civil Constitution of the Clergy (1792). Under the *ancien régime* Church and Monarchy had been so closely linked that when the latter was deprived of its privileges, the former was inevitably attacked as well. But the expropriation of the Church's property in 1790 would not necessarily have put the ecclesiastical hierarchy at permanent odds with the revolutionaries, had it not been for the fact that it was followed by the Civil Constitution of the Clergy, which converted the Church into little more than a department of State. The Civil Constitution divided the Church, precipitated the flight of Louis XVI and provoked the revolt in La Vendée. The Church began a campaign of civil disobedience against a State which refused to recognize it, and in one important respect the Revolution was thus unacceptable to the vast majority of Catholics. It was not surprising that one of Napoleon's first acts was to try to breach the gap between Church and State. The Concordat of 1801 was to have an important influence on Church-State relations for over a century, but its apparent restoration of the *status quo*, i.e. an Established Church, was offset by the Organic Articles, which gave the Government more control over ecclesiastical appointments than had been the case before the Revolution. Moreover, when Napoleon crowned himself Emperor in the presence of the Pope in 1804, it was clear who was master and who servant. Later, as Napoleon's demands became more rigorous, the Pope realized that his submissive attitude was not necessarily to the advantage of the Church. He began to resist Napoleon's demands, and after refusing to annul Jerome Bonaparte's marriage, he was imprisoned at Savona, from where he was released just prior to Napoleon's fall in 1814.

The return of the Bourbons, accompanied by priests and nobles, showed on whose side the Church was fighting, and it was not surprising that when Napoleon escaped from Elba he was greeted with cries of 'Vive l'Empereur! A bas la calotte!'[1] The Papacy was against the Revolution, the Republic, the Empire, against 'liberty, equality and fraternity'; France must go to Canossa, confess her Republican sins, and, like Charles X at his Coronation, be purified with holy water from Rome. Some Frenchmen (devout Catholics) agreed to this submission; others (less devout) wanted to experiment further with Republicanism. Thus the underlying tension between Church and State continued.

Until the First World War the gulf between Republicans and Catholics was wide and unbridgeable. At the turn of the century the supporters of Waldeck-Rousseau and Combes were no more conspicuous for their moderation than were the members of Action Française. The *Union Sacrée* of the Great War provided a temporary truce, but Action Française was as active after the war as it had been before, and although Maurras's movement was condemned by the Papacy in 1926, the majority of its anti-Republican, anti-Semitic members continued to be right-wing Catholics. One hopeful sign, however, was the growth of Catholic Action groups and the foundation of the Parti Démocrate Populaire, both committed to Catholic-Republican reconciliation.

The Second World War gave those Catholics who professed to be sincere Republicans a chance to stand up and be counted, and many took the chance despite the hierarchy's widespread support for Vichy. Men like Georges Bidault, Pierre-Henri Teitgen and François de Menthon were in the vanguard of the Resistance, and the outcome of their efforts, allied to the preparatory work of Catholic Action, was the foundation of the Mouvement Républicain Populaire (MRP) in 1944. MRP was to be the great new 'bridge' between Catholics and Republicans. In practice, it developed into a 'cushion' rather than a 'bridge'. No French 'Labour Party' came into being, for neither side could escape from its history. The Catholic-Republican quarrel continued to bedevil French politics, and although it was now less vicious, it was no less damaging.

The Schools Question

The kernel of the problem was the schools question (*le problème*
___
[1] 'Down with the clerical party' (*Lit. calotte* = skull cap).

scolaire), which remained 'the Maginot Line between the Left and the Right'.[1] In a very real sense the schools question was *the* test for Christian Democracy in France. If progressive Catholics and moderate Socialists could get over this hurdle, it might be possible to develop a non-sectarian party of reform—like the British Labour Party. If not, Catholics would be under increasing pressure to return to their traditional place on the right wing of the political spectrum. The immediate post-war period provided a unique opportunity to tackle *le problème scolaire*, but, like the broader issue of Church-State relations, it was a problem with a long and bitter history.

Before the Revolution of 1789 education had been the prerogative of the Church, but as the Church was very closely linked with the State, education was in practice a public service entrusted to the Church. Under Napoleon the State officially took control of education with the establishment of *l'Université*, although the Concordat of 1801 permitted the clergy to teach in State schools. This relatively satisfactory situation continued after the Restoration despite the anti-clerical atmosphere of the 1820s, but a law of 1828 forbidding Jesuits to teach in State schools put the Catholics on the defensive, and they began to demand recognition of their own schools. This demand was not made purely for educational reasons. The Church was well aware that the political future belonged to the party which could 'convert' the greatest number of potential voters.

Even under the Orleans monarchy, when there were only 200,000 bourgeois voters, men like the Liberal Catholic, Montalembert, and the Intransigent, Veuillot, realized that the voting habits of electors would be influenced by their schooling. The question was, of course, not formulated so bluntly by Montalembert and Veuillot. Pious slogans were used to cover up political aims, but when the Catholics began to demand 'freedom of education' in the 1840s, they were clearly thinking as much in political as in educational terms. And the 'free schools' issue became even more critical after the introduction of universal manhood suffrage in 1848. Philip Spencer has convincingly argued that the late 1840s were crucial years in the history of Church and State in France,[2] since, although the campaign for 'freedom of education' united Liberal and Intransigent Catholics, it sowed the seeds for a new politico-religious quarrel between Churchmen and freethinkers at a time when the two sides appeared to be drawing together. For the 1830s and 1840s had witnessed a revival in the fortunes of the Catholic Church in France. In the 1848 Revolution, for example, churches were not attacked as they had

[1] G. Suffert, *Les Catholiques et la Gauche*, p. 71.
[2] P. Spencer, *The Politics of Belief in Nineteenth Century France*.

been in 1789 and 1830, and were to be again in 1871. But no sooner had this Catholic revival got under way than the Church embarked on the issue of 'freedom of education', which, as Tocqueville observed in 1850, was a major tactical mistake:

> When I think of the attitude to religion shown by public opinion and the press scarcely three years ago, and compare it with the attitude today, I cannot help seeing that the clergy must have committed huge blunders to reach their present position. By violent personalities and exaggerated accusations they have continued to spoil an excellent cause. Instead of restricting themselves to common law and claiming their elementary rights, they have revealed their intention of dominating and even controlling all forms of education.[1]

The Catholic campaign was successful, the Falloux Law of 1850 allowing the establishment of Catholic secondary schools. Over two hundred and fifty new Catholic schools opened within a year, and between 1850 and 1866 the percentage of boys in Church primary schools rose from $15 \cdot 7$ to $20 \cdot 9$ and of girls from $44 \cdot 6$ to $55 \cdot 4$. The proportion educated in Catholic secondary schools also rose dramatically, and by the end of the Second Empire there were more secondary school children in Church than in State schools.[2]

The trend towards Catholicism in education continued in the early years of the Third Republic, because the first Chamber was clerical and monarchical. An 1875 law, for example, authorized the establishment of Catholic universities. But the Left won the 1876 Election, polling 4,000,000 votes to 3,200,000 for the Right, and the new Chamber was not only Republican but also distinctly anti-clerical.[3] It was not long before the prescience of Tocqueville's remarks of 1850 became apparent. It had indeed been a 'huge blunder' on the part of the Catholics to try to dominate education. When in the ascendant the Catholics had pushed their case too hard. They were soon to reap a whirlwind from the seeds they had sown.

After President MacMahon's dissolution of the Chamber (16 May 1877), both the President and the hierarchy campaigned for a majority of the Right, but the Republicans again won and proceeded, in Brogan's phrase, 'to take over the Republic'.[4] Part of their policy was to eliminate the anti-Republican influence of the Church. The

---

[1] A. de Tocqueville, *Oeuvres et Correspondances Inédites*, vol. II, pp. 121–3.

[2] D. W. Brogan, *The Development of Modern France, 1870–1939*, p. 147.

[3] A. Coutrot and F. Dreyfus, *Les Forces Religieuses dans la Société Française*, p. 18.

[4] Brogan, p. 149.

Republic would be secure only when clerical influence was removed from education. In 1880 the Jesuits were expelled and other religious orders forbidden to teach without a licence. In 1882 free elementary education was introduced and religious instruction in schools was abolished, although Thursday was made a holiday so that parents could, if they wished, arrange for extra-curricular religious instruction. At the same time the two great *Ecoles Normales* at Saint-Cloud and Fontenay-les-Roses were established to train men and women to go out to the provincial *écoles normales* to instruct the country's elementary school teachers. *Lycées* for girls were also established at this time, and by the late 1880s there were more boys and girls at State *lycées* than at Catholic 'free' schools.

After these laws, for which Jules Ferry and Camille Sée were largely responsible, there was a period of truce until Waldeck-Rousseau's 1901 Law forbade teaching by religious orders without individual authorization by Act of Parliament (a considerable tightening up of the Ferry Law of 1880). However, Waldeck-Rousseau's next bill proposing that those educated in 'free' schools be disqualified for State service was buried in committee—doubtless a wise move in view of the fact that many ardent Republicans had been brought up in zealously Catholic homes. Nevertheless, even if Republicans in the Chamber had doubts about Waldeck-Rousseau's policy, the electorate apparently did not, for at the General Election of 1902 5,500,000 votes were cast for candidates of the Left and only 2,500,000 for those of the Right (350 of the 600 deputies were 'Republican'). Emile Combes, one-time candidate for the priesthood, former country doctor and extreme anti-clerical, became Prime Minister. Combes applied the Waldeck-Rousseau Law of 1901 with great rigour, 125 girls' 'free' elementary schools being immediately closed, and in 1904 religious orders were forbidden to teach under any circumstances. The battle between Republicans and Catholics culminated in the separation of Church and State in 1905. The disestablishment of the Church, regarded at the time by most Catholics as a disaster, in fact opened the way to reconciliation. Now that the quarrelling couple had been legally separated, they could start to think in terms of peaceful coexistence, if not yet of harmony. The growth of the Sillon in the first decade of the century indicated that some Catholics understood the possibilities offered by the new situation.[1] The First World War, and even more the Second, helped to take the bitterness out of the Catholic-Republican quarrel by showing that Catholics could be loyal Frenchmen, but the schools question remained a running sore in French politics; so

[1] See pp. 36–40.

much so that it may be regarded as one of the chief reasons for the limited success of Christian Democracy in France.

In the last fifty years the Republicans have retreated from the extreme position of 1905, whilst many Catholics have proved their Republicanism. The Republicans never repealed that part of the 1801 Concordat allowing 'free' schools (whose teachers were paid by the State) in Alsace and Lorraine. The Astier Law of 1919 gave State aid to 'free' technical schools, and State subsidies were made available to Catholic youth organizations. The Poinso-Chapuis Decree of 1948, empowering family associations to underwrite the education of deprived children at Catholic schools, and the Barangé Law of 1951, granting subsidies to children at 'free' schools, were further steps towards a compromise position, although their enactment took place amid much bitterness. Finally, the Debré Law of 1959, by which Catholic teachers are paid by the State (provided the schools in which they work are State-registered), is the last in a long line of laws which have tended to alleviate, if not to solve, the schools problem.[1]

Writing in 1962, William Bosworth was sceptical about the long-term effectiveness of the Debré Law,[2] but in 1970 François Goguel was prepared to go so far as to say 'le problème scolaire est mort'.[3] This may be true in the narrower sense (i.e. in so far as the schools are concerned), but in the wider sense (the whole problem of clericalism versus Republicanism) it is clear that the old quarrels are not dead. The failure of Defferre's Presidential initiative in 1965 and the refusal of the Centre Démocrate (CD) to join the Federation of the Left in 1967 were due in part to the old clerical issue, whilst more recently Mitterrand's Socialist party has shunned Lecanuet's Christian Democrats in its bid to regroup the non-Communist Left. No doubt the main reason for this is the conservatism of the CD, but Socialists still feel that they cannot risk being labelled 'clerical'.[4]

Despite today's partial reconciliation between the two sides, it is important to emphasize from a historical point of view the fundamental differences between Catholics and Republicans which affected French politics from the Revolution to the Fifth Republic. They were quarrelling not about political means but about ends. The Boulangists (if not Boulanger himself), the followers of Charles Maurras, and the Vichyites wanted to overthrow the Republic, not merely to

---

[1] Of the 1,900,000 children being educated in private schools in 1969, 1,600,000 were at 'registered' schools, i.e. those which are recognized by the Ministry of National Education. *Monde*, 2 July 1970.

[2] W. Bosworth, *Catholicism and Crisis in Modern France*, pp. 283–4.

[3] Interview with Goguel, 21 March 1970.   [4] Cf. *Combat*, 26 June 1971.

change it. In trying to achieve their ends both sides ruled out compromise. Because of their basic differences, political in-fighting was more bitter in France than in England. Passion weighed more heavily than reason. Hence the deep hatred of Dreyfusards and anti-Dreyfusards, of Popular Front and Action Française, of Clericals and Republicans. Under the Fourth Republic the quarrelling was less bitter, partly owing to the presence of MRP, but MRP's arrival on the political scene did not signify the disappearance of those fundamental politico-religious divisions which centred for so long on the schools question.

CHRISTIAN DEMOCRACY AND SOCIAL CATHOLICISM

Most of those who have written about the origins of Christian Democracy in France have distinguished between 'Social Catholicism' and 'Christian Democracy'.[1] The ideas of Lamennais, Ozanam, Lacordaire, de Mun and Harmel are said to have been essentially social (although it is conceded that Lacordaire and de Mun had political ideas as well). From this distinction between social and political Catholicism it follows that, whilst the term 'Christian Democracy' was used before the end of the nineteenth century, there was, in fact, no genuine Christian Democracy in the sense of organized political action by progressive Catholics before Marc Sangnier's Sillon (founded in 1899), for, in so far as the ideas of Lacordaire and de Mun were political, they were insufficiently democratic to qualify for the epithet 'Christian Democratic'. Social Catholicism, on the other hand, is accepted as a valid nineteenth-century phenomenon, although, after its first flourish under the Orleans Monarchy, it virtually disappeared for a generation after 1848, and cannot be said to have reached full fruition until the emergence of Catholic Action in the twentieth century.

It is probably a mistake to try to compartmentalize social and political concepts when discussing Christian Democracy. Some of the ideas expressed in L'Avenir in 1830–31 were social, although more were political. The Cercles Catholiques of the 1880s were concerned primarily with social matters, but leaders of the Cercles, such as de Mun and Harmel, were also actively engaged in politics. And later, members of Catholic Action found a natural political outlet in

---

[1] E.g. J. B. Duroselle, *Débuts du Catholicisme Social en France, 1822–70*; H. Rollet, *L'Action Sociale des Catholiques en France*, 1871–1914 (2 vols.). The statement is less true of M. Vaussard, *Histoire de la Démocratie Chrétienne*.

MRP. The distinction between Social Catholicism and Christian Democracy can be useful, but should not be applied too rigidly.

The social aspects of Christian Democracy may be said to date from the Sermon on the Mount, the political ones from the American and French Revolutions. Until the Industrial Revolution there was no particular reason why the two should come together. Private charity had served Europe adequately for two and a half thousand years, whilst the new political concept of popular sovereignty had no inevitable connection with social policy. But at the same time as Europeans were moving towards greater political freedom, they were being increasingly subjected to another so-called 'freedom'— economic liberalism—which, in practice, meant not freedom but a form of enslavement for the vast majority of those employed in manufacturing industry. Machines began to dominate men. The old guilds, in so far as they still existed, were powerless to deal with the new market forces. Political and social 'Darwinism' was the accepted creed long before (and after) Darwin's observations on the natural world.

Although the Industrial Revolution came to France later and on a smaller scale than in England, its effects were similar. Villeneuve-Bargemont's Report on conditions in the Department of Nord in 1828, followed by Villermé's in 1840, give some idea of the intolerable conditions prevailing in industrial areas. A working day of thirteen to seventeen hours was normal for both men and women, whilst small children worked for up to twelve hours a day. Half the children born in the Department of Haut-Rhin died before they were two years old. Almost half of Lille's population of 70,000 lived in conditions of extreme poverty. And 55 per cent of those examined for military service in Amiens between 1820 and 1834 were rejected as unfit.[1] The 1841 Factory Law forbidding the employment of 8- to 12-year-olds for more than eight hours a day and of 12- to 16-year-olds for more than twelve hours a day was widely ignored, partly because there were no inspectors to enforce it.

LACORDAIRE: A VOICE CRYING IN THE WILDERNESS

In these circumstances it was not surprising that certain Catholics began to question political and economic liberalism. From the point of view of the future development of Christian Democracy, the most important were men like Lamennais, Lacordaire and Buchez— above all Lacordaire, because he seems to have understood most clearly that social reform could be achieved only through political

[1] Vaussard, pp. 23-5.

action. Moreover, unlike Buchez, he was a man of considerable influence. Although J. B. Duroselle's thesis that the Catholic reformers of the 1830s and 1840s were more concerned with social than political change is a valid one, his conclusion that they should be placed in the mainstream of Social Catholicism rather than of Christian Democracy requires qualification. It is true, for example, that Frédéric Ozanam who founded the Society of St Vincent-de-Paul in 1841 was essentially a social reformer and that the Society was a charitable organization, but Lacordaire, despite his confused political ideas, cannot be categorized so precisely. Indeed, Lacordaire could be described as the father of French Christian Democracy.

Lacordaire inherited many of his ideas from Lamennais, but it was he who developed them into some of the basic tenets of what later came to be known as Christian Democracy. Lacordaire first met Lamennais in 1830 when he was almost thirty and Lamennais fifty. Although the two were to go their separate ways a few years later (Lamennais left the Church in 1834), their meeting was important, especially for Lacordaire. Lamennais was a rather scatter-brained idealist. Lacordaire was a more practical man, capable of synthesizing and developing Lamennais's ideas and in some cases of applying them.

Lamennais was not cut out to be the leader of a movement. Although he had a small group of disciples, this headstrong Breton priest had no interest in their views. He expected them to agree with his constantly changing opinions. If they did not, he ignored them. Caring as little about his personal appearance as he did about his friends, Lamennais has nevertheless been justifiably described as a 'visionary genius':

> He foresaw with uncanny precision the collapse of temporal power, the declaration of Papal Infallibility, the separation of Church and State, the triumph of democracy and its ultimate reconciliation with the Church; and what he foresaw, he declared with a ruthless and intimidating clarity.[1]

Lamennais had originally been a Gallican and a Monarchist, but in the 1820s he became an Ultramontane, asserting the Pope's authority over both Church and monarchy in France. Finding himself under attack from the Royalists for putting the Bourbons in second place, he turned against the monarchy as an institution and proposed a new ally for the Pope—the People. It was this proposal which attracted Lacordaire, although, unlike Lamennais, he did not become a convinced Republican until the Revolution of 1848. Both

[1] Spencer, p. 39.

men, however, were delighted when Charles X fell in 1830, seeing this as an opportunity to put into practice their proposed alliance of Pope and People, unencumbered by a backward-looking legitimist dynasty. As one of their friends put it, 'Did the Son of God die on a gibbet eighteen hundred years ago in order to set the Bourbon family back on the throne?'[1]

With this end in view, Lacordaire, Lamennais and a young nobleman, Charles de Montalembert, founded *L'Avenir* in 1830. This publication, which came out erratically for a year, may be regarded as the first Christian Democratic journal. Certainly many of the ideas put forward in *L'Avenir* were taken up again seventy years later by the Christian Democrats of the Sillon. *L'Avenir* advocated the separation of Church and State, which was to be accepted by the Sillonists, although not at first by the vast majority of Catholics; it favoured universal suffrage and a free press; it proposed the development of intermediary bodies such as trade unions, another concept which was revived at the turn of the century, reaching fulfilment in 1919 with the establishment of the Confédération Française des Travailleurs Chrétiens (CFTC).

Lacordaire hoped that the Pope would support the ideas of *L'Avenir*, but, after his visit to Rome in 1831, Pope Gregory XVI condemned his views in the encyclical *Mirari Vos* (1832), which pronounced against the separation of Church and State, against any alliance with 'liberal revolutionaries', against freedom of opinion. Lacordaire, Lamennais and Montalembert formally made their submission to the Pope in September 1832 (although two years later Lamennais gave up the Catholic faith). This looked like the failure of a movement which seemed to be opening up a new horizon for the Church in France, giving it a chance to come to terms with the Revolution of 1789 and, in some measure, with the Industrial Revolution. But although it is true that the three reformers had failed to get any practical changes, their ideas did not die. One group which propagated them centred round Philippe Buchez, a Republican who had been converted to Catholicism in 1829. Buchez and his friends, Feugueray, Rampal and Bastide, wanted to reconcile Catholicism with the ideas of 1789. Buchez had little success, partly, Duroselle suggests, because he and his friends were very 'introverted'.[2]

Lacordaire, however, was much more successful in getting his ideas across, not least because he was a brilliant orator. At first he fell foul of Monseigneur de Quelen, Archbishop of Paris, but after

---

[1] Cited in A. Dansette, *Histoire Religeuse de la France Contemporaine*, vol. 1 p. 296.
[2] Duroselle, p. 700.

1835 Quelen decided to try to influence Lacordaire as a friend rather than treat him as an enemy. He gave Lacordaire permission to deliver a series of lectures at Notre Dame. These lectures aroused great interest, attracting crowds of five thousand, including such distinguished figures as Lamartine, Berryer and Chateaubriand. Lacordaire's appeal lay not only in his powers of oratory, but also in his novel approach to Christianity. He addressed his audience as 'Gentlemen' not 'Brothers'. He related the Church to his own world, showing his interest in contemporary problems—so much so that one of his listeners remarked 'Lui aussi, il a connu cela'.[1]

Although Lacordaire became a Dominican in 1839, and thereafter spent much of his time in a monastery near Grenoble, he remained an outstanding figure in the Church until 1845. Little was heard of him for the next three years, but in 1848 he came out of his 'retirement' to welcome the Republic—'Who in France today thinks of defending the Monarchy? Who *can* think of it? France imagined that she was still Royalist when already she was Republican. Yesterday she was surprised; today she is no longer.'[2] Hoping that the 1848 Revolution would succeed where those of 1789 and 1830 had failed, namely in economic and social reforms, Lacordaire started a daily newspaper, *L'Ere Nouvelle*, which was to all intents and purposes a new *L'Avenir*. Lacordaire used phrases like 'Christian socialism' and 'Christian economy', and the paper was supported by Archbishop Affre of Paris. But the majority of the hierarchy condemned Lacordaire's ideas. It was one thing to link the Church with the Republic, quite another to link it with socialism.

Lacordaire became a deputy in the Assembly elected in April 1848 and sat well to the Left, but he was deeply disappointed by the mob's invasion of the Assembly on 15 May, resigning his seat a few days later, and was even more distressed when his friend Archbishop Affre was murdered in the June days. The closing of the national workshops and the bloody suppression of the workers symbolized the economic and social failure of the 1848 Revolution. Once again the changes had been political only. Lacordaire and his friends of *L'Ere Nouvelle* realized that a political revolution without social reorganization and economic redistribution of wealth could hardly be permanent. With his hope of Church and People united under a revolutionary banner frustrated, Lacordaire left *L'Ere Nouvelle* (which soon collapsed) and retired to Grenoble.

The Church's reaction to the 1848 Revolution was the very opposite of Lacordaire's. In the face of social revolution, the Church

---

[1] Delpech, cited in Fosset, *Vie du R. P. Lacordaire*, vol. II, p. 523.
[2] Quoted by J. D'Almeras, *La Vie Parisienne sous la République de 1848*, p. 159.

sided with the forces of reaction and conservatism. And when Louis Napoleon was elected President (December 1848), the Church openly supported him because he promised to release the Pope and grant freedom of education:

> In their anxiety to gain immediate political ends, the Catholics forfeited the friendship of all who cared for personal freedom, democratic government and social reform. The loss did not seem serious at the time, for democratic ideas were at a discount. But, at a remove of a hundred years, it assumed the proportions of a disaster.[1]

Ultramontanism and conservatism were in the ascendant. Pius IX's *Syllabus Errorum* (1864), condemning 'progress, liberalism and modern civilization',[2] symbolized the triumph of reaction in the Church as a whole. Veuillot's biting criticisms of liberalism in *L'Univers* played the same role within France. Even Montalembert, Lacordaire's friend of *L'Avenir* days, wrote: 'My choice is made. I am for authority against revolt, for conservatism against destruction, for society against socialism.'[3] Less surprisingly, Pius IX told a group of priests and laymen in 1871:

> What I fear for you is not that miserable band of Communards—demons escaped from Hell—but Catholic liberalism. I do not mean those Catholics once called Liberal (they have often deserved well of the Holy See), but that fatal system which dreams of reconciling two irreconcilables—Church and Revolution. I have already condemned it, but, if need be, I would condemn it forty times more.[4]

The Social Catholic, indeed Christian Democratic, ideals of Lacordaire could not be fulfilled in these circumstances. In a sense he had tried to combine two incompatibles—progressive liberalism and Ultramontanism. Lacordaire's ideas, like his character, were, in fact, full of contradictions. He was 'medieval' and 'modern' at the same time, being a fanatical flagellant as well as a progressive Catholic. He wanted to believe both in the sovereignty of the People and in that of the Church, but Papal Infallibility could hardly be reconciled with democratic principles. Perhaps, as Philip Spencer claims, Lacordaire's outstanding feature was his sincerity: 'He had no hesitation in proclaiming his belief in progress, affirming his faith in the people (were not they the poor of the New Testament?),

1 Spencer, p. 130.
2 H. Bettenson, *Documents of the Christian Church*, p. 381.
3 Cited in Spencer, p. 134.   4 ibid., p. 244.

and welcoming the advance of science.'[1] At the same time he seems to have been equally sincere in his (contradictory) belief in Papal supremacy.

Lacordaire did not achieve his aim of reconciling Church and People, but he stands out as one of the fathers of Christian Democracy, and his bold progressive liberalism must be seen in contrast to the negative, reactionary attitudes of the Church until the arrival of Leo XIII at the Holy See in 1878.

THE RALLIEMENT

The stormy pontificate of Pius IX ended in 1878. His successor Leo XIII (1878–1903) abandoned the purely negative attitude of the *Syllabus Errorum*. He adopted a Thomist position, attempting to reconcile faith with reason. In a series of encyclicals—*Immortale Dei* (1885), *Libertas* (1888), *Rerum Novarum* (1891), *Au Milieu des Sollicitudes* (1891)—he defined Roman Catholic doctrines of State and society more realistically than any other Pope between 1789 and the First World War. He continued to condemn materialism, socialism and secularism, but he conceded that democracy and liberalism would not disappear under Papal condemnation. The solution was to infuse Christian values into democracy and liberalism. Thus, in *Rerum Novarum*, capitalist exploitation was as roundly condemned as Marxist materialism. Governments should legislate to prevent social and economic oppression, and workers should form associations to defend their interests. In *Libertas* he had declared that it was 'a vain and baseless calumny to allege that the Church looks unfavourably on most modern political systems and rejects all the discoveries of contemporary genius'.[2] In *Au Milieu des Sollicitudes* (written in French) he declared that all established governments were legitimate. French Catholics should therefore co-operate with the Republic whilst opposing doctrinaire anticlericals. He made it clear that he wanted Catholics to co-operate with moderate Republicans in a broadly based, non-confessional political formation.

Leo XIII's successor Pius X (1903–19), whilst accepting the Republic, was bitterly opposed to the separation of Church and State in France (1905), and in some ways his pontificate must be seen as a step backwards after the progressive policies of Leo XIII. For instance, Pius X condemned Sangnier's Sillon in 1910. Nevertheless, Pius X did not attempt to return to the purely negative position of

[1] Spencer, p. 248.
[2] Cited in *Cambridge Modern History*, vol. XI, p. 314.

Pius IX, and, although the separation of Church and State in France was not officially accepted until after the First World War by Pius XI, the work of Leo XIII was not undone. A new climate of opinion had developed, and progressive Catholics began to adapt themselves to democracy and to the Republic. There was a revival of Social Catholicism in the Oeuvre des Cercles organized by Albert de Mun and René de La Tour du Pin. This was accompanied by the growth of political Catholicism both in the moderate Ralliement of de Mun and in the more progressive Sillon of Sangnier. At the same time, Harmel's Cercle d'Etudes, which indirectly gave birth to Démocratie Chrétienne in 1896, may be regarded as an attempt to fuse the political and social objectives of those Catholics who were beginning to rally to the Republic.

The success of the Ralliement and of the Cercles should not be exaggerated. Political events such as the Panama scandal (1892) and the Dreyfus Affair (1894–1903), were sufficient to rock the boat of reconciliation. Nevertheless, the Ralliement of the 1890s was of some importance. In 1893 thirty-five Ralliement candidates were elected to the Chamber, and, although the hierarchy was slow to accept the Republic, even after *Au Milieu des Sollicitudes*, some senior members of the French Church, such as Cardinal Lavigerie of Algiers who had proposed a toast to the Republic when receiving naval officers in 1890, gave full support to Albert de Mun and his small band of Catholic Republicans.

Albert de Mun had started life as a Catholic Royalist. He had been a regular army officer, but was so shocked by the social conditions he found in Paris after the suppression of the Commune that he decided that the State ought to intervene. He entered the Chamber in 1881 and remained a prominent member for the next thirty years, rallying to the Republic at the time of *Au Milieu des Sollicitudes*. De Mun always sat on the Right in the Chamber, and his attitude was certainly paternalistic, but at least he advocated legislation to improve social conditions. Indeed he was the French counterpart of Disraeli or Bismarck. Socialism could be undermined by conservative paternalism. As early as 1884 he proposed an international labour code, but without success, whilst in 1890 he proposed an 'English' working week (i.e. the abolition of Sunday work), but this proposal was rejected by 304 votes to 210.[1] Like the Socialists he also favoured an eight-hour working day, but had no success in achieving it.

Albert de Mun's Ralliement group was virtually destroyed by the Dreyfus Affair, but in 1901 de Mun and Jacques Piou formed

[1] Vaussard, p. 52.

Action Libérale Populaire (ALP), which was a loose parliamentary grouping of Catholics who were determined to protect the interests of the Church (they were strongly opposed to the separation of Church and State in 1905), and at the same time to defeat revolutionary socialism by a programme of social reforms. Amongst other things the ALP favoured the extension of trade union rights, the introduction of insurance schemes to cover sickness, unemployment and old age, and the promulgation of factory legislation, notably on hours, safety and health. The ALP reached a maximum of about eighty deputies in the decade before the First World War, but in the face of criticism by both the *patronat* and the hierarchy (especially after 1910 in the case of the latter),[1] the ALP made little impact in the Chamber.

Albert de Mun cannot be described as a Christian Democrat. Indeed, he criticized Harmel for his 'radicalism' and specifically rejected the abortive Christian Democratic party established by the *abbé démocrates* in 1896.[2] He and his friends of the Ralliement and ALP were sincere Republicans but paternalistic conservatives. Nevertheless it would be wrong to omit their contribution, albeit unintentional, to the emergence of Christian Democracy in France. The Ralliement and ALP accustomed Catholics to accepting the Republic and facing up to the need for State action to solve social problems. Without de Mun it would have been much more difficult for the Sillon and the Jeune République to have emerged before the First World War, although de Mun himself was much too conservative to support either of these movements.

De Mun's greatest achievement was to awaken the social conscience of Catholics. The same is true of René de La Tour du Pin, who, like de Mun, had been a regular army officer who was equally appalled by the social conditions revealed at the suppression of the Commune. The two men founded an organization called L'Oeuvre des Cercles in 1871. These Cercles were working men's clubs run by employers and members of the Catholic bourgeoisie. The Cercles reached a peak membership of about 45,000 in 1878,[3] but of these 45,000 at least 10,000 were employers. Most of the members were skilled workmen, and their main activities were to run hostels for apprentices and to conduct evening classes. But the Cercles were not embryo trade unions nor in any real sense the precursors of the

[1] Some members of the ALP approved the activities of Sangnier's Sillon, which was condemned by the Pope in 1910 (see p. 38). As a result the ALP tended to be tarred with the same brush as the Sillon when the latter was criticized by the hierarchy. Cf. Rollet, vol. II, pp. 52–9, especially pp. 57–9.
[2] See p. 35.   [3] Rollet, vol. I, p. 35.

Catholic Action organizations of the twentieth century. Throughout they were run on a very paternalistic basis.

Also paternalistic, at least at the outset, were the Cercles d'Etudes of Léon Harmel.[1] The Cercles d'Etudes, whose full name significantly was Cercles Chrétiens d'Etudes Sociales, were first established by Harmel in the Rheims region in 1891. Harmel was himself a wealthy Catholic employer. Originally a member of L'Oeuvre des Cercles of de Mun and La Tour du Pin, he decided these organizations did not go far enough. Harmel's Cercles aimed not only to educate their members but also to press for political action, but Harmel was against a proposal made at the 1896 Congress to form a political party out of the Cercles. The first Congress of Harmel's Cercles had taken place in 1893, when ninety members were present, mainly from the Department of Nord. No definite proposals were made at this Congress, but discussion ranged over topics such as the education of workers and the establishment of workers' and family associations—ideas which were to be developed by Christian Democrats in the twentieth century. It is also interesting that the Congress discussed the possibility of establishing a Christian trade union.[2] This idea was pursued in the 1890s with the establishment of several 'mixed' (i.e. combined employers and workers) unions in the north.

At the second Cercles Congress at Rheims in 1894 a definite programme was drawn up. It demanded an extension and improvement of insurance schemes; statutory holidays on Sundays; the development of co-operatives; a policy for housing and the establishment of 'mixed' trade unions. Harmel's Cercles reached a peak between 1896 and 1902. In 1896, for example, delegates from 133 branches, representing over 20,000 members, attended the annual Congress.[3] This Congress was also important in that it drew up a programme which can justly be called Christian Democratic, and came near to founding a Christian Democratic political party.

The programme of the 1896 Congress brought together many of the ideas expressed in the review *Démocratie Chrétienne*, founded in 1894. The programme emphasized that the family was the basic unit in society; hence, the State should promote measures to help the family, such as laws regulating the employment of children, implementing the 'English' week and establishing family insurance schemes. Work was seen as a basic human right. Trade unions (preferably 'mixed' employers—workers unions) should be established to defend this right, and these unions should be organized on a regional basis to

[1] Rollet, vol. I, pp. 338–89.   [2] ibid., p. 347.   [3] ibid., p. 384.

form Chambres de Travail for industry and Chambres d'Agriculture for farming.[1] Such ideas as these were to be developed by the Sillon and came to fruition through Catholic Action after the First World War.

Some of the delegates at the 1896 Congress wanted to found a Christian Democratic political party. Indeed the *abbés démocrates*, abbots Naudet, Lemire and Garnier, did set up such a party, Démocratie Chrétienne, but it had disintegrated by 1898.[2] Harmel, although personally attracted by the proposal of the *abbés démocrates*, was too orthodox a Catholic to accept a proposal which ran counter to the ideas of Leo XIII. In this he was supported by the majority of the delegates at the 1896 Congress, where he argued that the main task of the Cercles was social, and that the best way to achieve a more equitable society was to appeal to employers to accept their social obligations rather than to force them to change by political means.[3] This type of argument suggests that Harmel was, after all, a rather impractical idealist—a French Robert Owen.

Nevertheless, the Cercles movement of the 1890s brought social and political Catholicism to the verge of Christian Democracy, although it did not result in a fully Christian Democratic movement or political party. This was partly due to the fact that Albert de Mun and Léon Harmel did not get on well together. Harmel even called L'Oeuvre des Cercles '*la Contre-Révolution*'[4] when de Mun refused to fuse his Cercles with those of Harmel in 1896. Harmel also lacked the personality of a great leader. Moreover, in the last analysis, he was opposed to creating a political party out of his own movement. And this was understandable in view of the fact that de Mun's group of Republican Catholics in the Chamber was small enough without being further split. Probably the most important reason, however, for the non-emergence of a fully-fledged Christian Democratic movement was the general political situation in France. Until the Dreyfus Affair was forgotten and the problem of the separation of Church and State finally solved, there were simply not enough progressive, Republican Catholics to establish a definitive Christian Democratic movement, fully committed to the achievement of social and economic reform by political means.

[1] For the full Cercles programme of 1896, see ibid., p. 387.
[2] Démocratie Chrétienne held a second and final Congress in 1897. It disintegrated partly on account of condemnation by the hierarchy, partly on account of organizational weakness, but above all, according to J. Raymond-Laurent, it was killed by 'les déchirements de l'Affaire Dreyfus'—*Le Parti Démocrate Populaire*, 1924–44, p. 18.
[3] Rollet, vol. I, p. 384.   [4] ibid., p. 355.

THE SILLON

Despite the political climate in France and despite the unfavourable reaction of the French hierarchy and of Pius X to progressive, Republican Catholicism, the seeds sown by various 'social' and 'political' Catholics from Lacordaire to Harmel came to fruition before the First World War. The Sillon of Marc Sangnier and its successor, the Jeune République, can justifiably be described as Christian Democratic. Sangnier and his friends were Catholics, but they fully accepted the Republic and democracy. They wanted to educate and convert the masses, but they were not as paternalistic as the leaders of the Cercles of de Mun and Harmel. *Tutoiement* was normal for Sillonists, whatever their social background.[1] They wanted to create 'un plus grand Sillon' (a phrase used by Sangnier in 1907) as a broad-based political movement, attracting Protestants and, if possible, non-Christians. Indeed, this desire of the Sillonists was doubtless the main reason for their undoing, because by 1909 Sangnier had decided that such a political movement would be ineffective unless it were embodied in the structures of a political party.[2] But the Papacy of 1909 was even less willing to accept the establishment of a formal Christian Democratic political party than it had been under Leo XIII. In practical terms the Sillonists did not have much more success than their nineteenth century precursors, but their attitude and objectives were sufficiently novel for them to merit the epithet Christian Democratic, because by 1910 they were on the verge of transforming their movement into a political party specifically committed to achieving political reconciliation and economic and social reforms.

Marc Sangnier, founder of the Sillon, member of the *grande bourgeoisie*,[3] *Polytechnicien*, life-long Catholic and sincere Republican, first entered 'politics' as a schoolboy. In 1891 he started organizing meetings between upper-middle-class Catholic schoolboys and boys from Catholic working-class homes. These gatherings took place in the crypt of the chapel of Sangnier's school, the Collège

[1] Raymond-Laurent, p. 23; see also Rollet, vol. II, pp. 18–30, on the whole Sillon movement.

[2] Ernest Pezet, *Chrétiens au Service de la Cité; du Sillon . . . au MRP*, pp. 8–10, 40.

[3] Sangnier's maternal grandfather was a famous Paris *avocat*, Lachaud, a native of Corrèze. His father died when Sangnier was a boy, but he was brought up by his mother, who was apparently not only a very gifted woman but, more remarkable for *une grande bourgeoise*, was quite willing to accept all her son's friends, whatever their social origin, at her home in the Boulevard Raspail. Sangnier was born in 1874 and died in 1950.

Stanislas in Paris. The contacts established at school continued when the middle-class boys were students and the working-class boys were in industry. The main purpose of the meetings was to discuss the practical implications of the encyclical *Rerum Novarum* (1891), and to pray and meditate, but, according to two former Sillonists, Sangnier's Cercles d'Etudes, unlike those of de Mun and Harmel, were run in a very egalitarian manner with everyone being encouraged to contribute to the discussions.[1]

The Sillonists carried the educational work of the Cercles d'Etudes a stage further with the establishment of Instituts Populaires in country towns as well as in the larger cities. Workers, peasants and their wives could take educational courses and discuss their problems at the Instituts. Perhaps Vaussard exaggerated when he called the Instituts Populaires 'Universités Populaires',[2] but there can be little doubt that the Instituts Populaires, run by Louis Rolland, later a Law Professor at Nancy and a Jeune République deputy, touched a far wider spectrum of society than the Cercles of de Mun and Harmel. The Sillonists also held an annual Semaine Silloniste, a week of meditation and discussion for the more important people within the movement. J. Raymond-Laurent was present at the 1907 Semaine at Saisy-sur-Ecole, a small Seine-et-Marne village: 'A hundred odd militants from all over France lived together for a week like an early Christian community. They listened to "Marc"—for that is what all the Sillonists called Sangnier; they prayed, they discussed, and they returned home refreshed.'[3]

The climax of the Sillonist year was the annual congress, when as many as 2,000 would gather from all over France to hear Sangnier and other leading personalities such as Canon Desgranges of Limoges and Louis Rolland. The congresses were not always entirely peaceful —in 1906 a group of Socialist intruders who tried to disrupt the proceedings by singing the Internationale had to be evicted.

Sangnier's aim was simple—to persuade people that it was possible to be both 'chrétien sans peur et républicain démocrate sans équivoque', not an easy task in the days of Combism and reactionary Catholicism. The Sillon had no specific programme, but its objectives were made clear at the various types of meeting and through its publications. Sangnier had sufficient private means to buy a review, *Le Sillon*,[4] in 1897—he had originally joined its staff in 1894. Articles

[1] Pezet, p. 10; Raymond-Laurent, p. 23.
[2] Vaussard, p. 72.   [3] Raymond-Laurent, p. 26.
[4] Each copy of *Le Sillon* carried a small picture of St Francis of Assisi ploughing a furrow (*sillon*). The name of the review was adopted by the movement in 1899.

were written not only by three regular contributors, Sangnier himself, Paul Renaudin, the review's founder, and Jean Lerolle, a Paris advocate, but also by young Sillonists and by unorthodox *abbés démocrates* such as Abbé Naudet of Bordeaux (who ran his own review, *La Justice Sociale*) and Abbé Six of Nord (who helped to establish a Catholic railwaymen's union). From 1905 to 1910 the Sillonists also had a weekly newspaper, *L'Eveil Démocratique*, edited by Henry du Roure and distributed throughout France. In 1910 Sangnier decided that a daily was needed. *Démocratie*, which replaced *L'Eveil Démocratique*, was due to begin publication in August 1910, the month in which the Sillon was condemned by Pius X. As a result the first issue of *Démocratie* was delayed, but it appeared regularly from late 1910 until 1914 and was the 'official' newspaper of the ex-Sillonists and, from 1912, of the movement which they founded, the Jeune République.[1] The most important newspaper which propagated Sillonist ideas was *Ouest-Eclair*, predecessor of *Ouest-France*, the Rennes daily which still has a wide circulation throughout Normandy and Brittany. Founded in 1899 by Emmanuel Desgrées du Lou, a young naval officer who had given up his career at sea to preach reconciliation between Catholics and Republicans, *Ouest-Eclair* had the largest circulation of any provincial daily by 1914. Edited in the pre-war years by Henri Teitgen, later president of the Bar at Nancy, and father of Pierre-Henri Teitgen, a future President of MRP, *Ouest-Eclair* probably played a greater role in spreading Sillonist ideas than the publications more closely associated with Sangnier.

French Christian Democrats were to look back on the Sillon period as a Golden Age, but it is doubtful whether 'les beaux temps du Sillon'[2] were as idyllic as later apologists implied, for the movement appears to have been disintegrating prior to the Papal condemnation of 1910. In 1904 Sangnier had been warmly welcomed in Rome by Pius X, but three years later the Sillon underwent an internal crisis and six years later it went into liquidation on Papal orders. What went wrong?

Part of the trouble was Sangnier himself. He was a fine orator and debater—he was quite able to hold his own in debates with men such as Jules Guesde, the Socialist leader, and Jean Lapicque, a Sorbonne Professor of Logic. He attracted many gifted men into the Sillon—Louis Rolland, organizer of the Instituts Populaires, Marius Gonin, responsible for the Sillon in the Lyons area, Maurice Guérin, a young trade unionist from Limoges, later a prominent figure in the

[1] See p. 49 for details about the Jeune République.
[2] A phrase cited by Vaussard, p. 76; Raymond-Laurent, p. 31; Pezet, p. 10.

CFTC, and Henry du Roure, editor of the weekly *Eveil Démocratique*, and its successor, the daily *Démocratie*. But the young Sangnier became increasingly autocratic in his dealings with his colleagues. After the 1905 Sillon Congress several leaders from the South broke away from the movement, including Marius Gonin who complained of the dominant role played by Sangnier and his Parisian friends.[1] In 1906 the Limousin group, led by Abbé Desgranges, and including men such as Pierre Poyet, a well-known publisher, and the trade unionist Maurice Guérin, followed suit. Desgranges justified his break with the Sillon in a letter to the *Populaire du Centre* in 1907:

> The Sillon has become an absolute monarchy, subject only to the authority of Marc Sangnier, the sole proprietor of the review and the movement's newspaper, and the dominant figure at the movement's headquarters. The provincial groups have gradually been deprived of any means of control of the movement.[2]

Personal differences, however, were probably the least important reason for the failure of the Sillon. Much more important was the fact that nearly every member of the French hierarchy was opposed to it. Influential bishops like Monseigneur Gieure of Bayonne, Monseigneur de Cabrière of Montpellier and Monseigneur Delamamaire of Cambrai were outspoken critics of Sangnier's movement. Only a few bishops gave the Sillon their tentative approval—Monseigneur Gibier of Versailles, Monseigneur Herscher of Langres, Monseigneur Chapon of Nice—but they were a tiny minority. The hierarchy was far too bitter about the 1905 separation of Church and State to consider the possibility of full reconciliation with the Republic, and in this they were supported by Pius X, who not only condemned the 1905 separation but also considered Sangnier's proposal for 'un plus grand Sillon', including Protestants and non-believers, repugnant and dangerous. The Papal condemnation of the Sillon was couched in doctrinal terms—Sangnier was accused of propounding a 'new Gospel'[3]—but the real reason for the ban was political. Sangnier and his friends realized that a Christian Democratic political party would have to be created if they were to achieve their ends, but, as Pezet emphasizes,[4] Pius had already shown in the encyclical *Motu Proprio* (1903) that he was opposed to such a development. So long as the Sillonists concentrated on social work

---

[1] Pezet, p. 37. [2] Cited in Vaussard, p. 74. [3] Vaussard, p. 75.
[4] Pezet, p. 8.

and preached reconciliation with the Republic they were in no danger, but once they began to think in terms of achieving their ends by political action in the Chamber they were almost bound to encounter papal opposition.

It would, indeed, have been almost impossible for Christian Democracy, with all that the phrase implies in terms of political action as well as of social change, to have flourished before 1914. The political atmosphere in France in the era of Dreyfus and Combes was not one in which the voices of reconciliation could easily be heard. But the flame lit by the Sillon was not extinguished by Pius X's decision of 1910. It was kept alight, if only just, by the Jeune République. And even if politically Christian Democracy achieved little before the First World War, at least the necessary social infrastructure was firmly established before 1914. The preparatory work done by the Cercles of Albert de Mun and Léon Harmel and of the Instituts Populaires of the Sillon has already been discussed. There were also various other organizations which helped to prepare the way for the emergence of Christian Democracy in France. The Association Catholique de la Jeunesse Française (ACJF), established by de Mun in 1886, had 26 trade union branches, 150 farmers' branches, 20 co-operative societies, 118 friendly societies and 8 social service bureaux by 1911.[1] In the pre-war period the ACJF was almost exclusively a middle-class organization, and in this sense it was less important from the point of view of emergent Christian Democracy than the various types of Cercles and the Sillon, which, whatever their mode of organization, were socially heterogeneous. More important were the Semaines Sociales, founded in 1904 by Marius Gonin, a Lyons silk foreman, and Adéodat Boissard, a Professor at the Catholic Law Faculty in Paris. The Semaines Sociales are still functioning today,[2] and now, as then, Catholic employers, trade unionists, teachers and others interested in social problems meet for an annual conference.

Without the preparatory work done by such organizations, Catholic Action would not have flourished in the inter-war years and the Confédération Française des Travailleurs Chrétiens would not have been set up in 1919. The full harvest of Christian Democracy was not ripe until after Hitler's War, but the seeds were sown before the Kaiser's War.

---

[1] For further information about ACJF, see pp. 63 and 79. For the above statistics see *L'ACJF*, 1939, p. 467. For Catholic Action in general see W. Bosworth, *Catholicism and Crisis in Modern France*.

[2] E.g. the 1970 Semaine Sociale was held in Dijon—*Monde*, 5 July 1970.

THE PARTI DEMOCRATE POPULAIRE (PDP)

Prior to the First World War the political and religious climate in France was such that a Christian Democratic party would have been unlikely to have survived if it had been created. But the bitterness of the Catholic-Republican conflict was diminished by the passage of time, by Poincaré's *Union Sacrée* of 1914 and by the death of one and a half million Frenchmen, both Catholics and Republicans, in the war. The post-war circumstances appeared to be suitable for the launching of a Christian Democratic party.

Marc Sangnier and several other former Sillonists were returned to the Chamber in November 1919. Apart from Sangnier himself, elected on a Bloc National list in Paris, the other deputies of Christian Democratic background were Paul Simon from Finistère, later President of the PDP Parliamentary group; Alfred Bour and Georges Thibout, the former being President of the Société des Jardins Ouvriers of Pantin-Aubervilliers and the latter Mayor of Epinay; Adéodat Boissard from Côte d'Or, one of the founders of the Semaines Sociales; and finally, François-Xavier Reille-Soult, a Tarn landowner and prominent Christian Democratic personality for the next forty years. Robert Schuman and Joseph Dufos du Rau were also elected in 1919, but neither was closely associated with Sangnier at this time, although both were later to play prominent roles in the Mouvement Républicain Populaire. Sangnier himself seems to have considered establishing a Jeune République parliamentary group,[1] but the others would not agree, so the idea was dropped and no specifically Christian Democratic group came into being until 1924.

Meanwhile, although there was no Christian Democratic parliamentary party, two important Christian Democratic groups were active in the country. These were the Fédérations des Républicains Démocrates of Finistère and of Paris. The former had been founded in 1912 and was revived after the war. Its first outstanding achievement had been the election of Paul Simon in a by-election at Brest in 1912, and although Simon alone was returned from the Finistère Federation in 1919, success followed in 1924 with the election of

---

[1] Raymond-Laurent, p. 38. Sangnier had founded the Jeune République (JR) in 1912 to further the ideas of the Sillon. JR functioned in a desultory fashion in the inter-war years, a handful of deputies being elected to the Chamber. Its members favoured more progressive economic and social policies than those of the PDP. In 1944 JR merged itself with MRP, although outside Parliament it continued to function autonomously for a few more years. For further details, see p. 49.

four deputies, all of whom were to join the PDP parliamentary group. The Paris Federation was a more recent creation, not having been officially established until June 1919, although its origin has been traced by one writer to 1917, the year in which two wounded former Sillonists, Abbé Jean de Saint-André (later killed at the Front) and Emmanuel Rivière founded a new Christian Democratic review, *L'Ame Française*.[1] This review was important because it brought together Catholics of 'political' (i.e. Sillon) and 'social' (i.e. Cercles, Semaines Sociales, ACJF) background, those whom Pezet described as 'les démocrates et républicains populaires d'inspiration chrétienne et catholique'[2]: men like Paul Simon and Paul Archambault, both former Sillonists, and Jean Lerolle and Adolphe Delmasure of ACJF. Several of these men belonged to the Paris Federation presided over by Georges Thibout of Epinay. Other members were Alfred Bour from Pantin and Robert Cornilleau, founder of the Christian Democratic newspaper, *Le Petit Démocrate de St Denis* (established in 1912). Apart from the important Finistère and Paris Federations there were local Christian Democratic groups in Limoges, led by the trade unionist Maurice Guérin; in Rouen, led by two trade unionists, Etienne Touré and René Dragon, both of whom were later to die in German concentration camps; in Clermont-Ferrand, led by the ex-Sillonist Eugène Laudouze, also a future concentration camp victim; and in Le Havre, led by Louis Siefridt, later an MRP deputy.

The next logical step was to set up a national Christian Democratic political party. This occurred in 1924 as a result of a proposal made in August 1922 by Gaston Tessier at a Semaines Sociales conference at Strasbourg. Tessier, the first Secretary General of the Confédération Française des Travailleurs Chrétiens (CFTC), proposed that the various Christian Democratic groups should unite to defend themselves against the attacks of Action Française. The resulting Bureau d'Action Civique, whose leading members were Gaston Tessier (CFTC), Charles Flory (ACJF) and Adéodat Boissard (Semaines Sociales), acted as an organ of liaison between the various Christian Democratic groups, who held a conference in Paris in January 1924 at which it was decided that a Christian Democratic political party should be created. However, such a party was not officially set up until after the General Election of May 1924, when Christian Democratic candidates stood under various labels and mostly did rather badly. Sangnier, Reille-Soult, Thibout and Bour were defeated, but Paul Simon found a sufficient number of sympathetic deputies to organize a parliamentary group called the Groupe des Démocrates.

[1] Pezet, p. 60.   [2] ibid., p. 14.

Table 1: The Parti Démocrate Populaire (PDP) 1924–40

The PDP formed the Groupe des Démocrates, 1924–28 (14 members, increasing to 15 in 1927); the Groupe des Démocrates Populaires, 1928–32 (19 members); and the Groupe Démocrates Populaires, 1932–40 (16 members from 1932–36, 11 from 1936–38, 12 from 1938–40).

	1924	1928	1932	1936
FINISTERE:				
Victor Balamant	*			
Jean Jadé	*	*		
Paul Simon	*	*	*	*
Pierre Trémintin	*	*	*	*
COTES-DU-NORD:				
Alfred Dualt				*
MORBIHAN:				
André Bahier		*		
Ernest Pezet		*	*	*
ILLE-ET-VILAINE:				
Armand Le Douarec	*			
Etienne Pinault		*	*	*
MANCHE:				
Léon Vaur				*
MAINE-ET-LOIRE:				
Louis Rolland			*	
SARTHE:				
Paul Goussu				*
François Saudubray	*1			*
VENDEE:				
Charles Gallet		*	*	
Auguste Durand		*	*	
LOIRET:				
Maurice Berger		*		
ARDENNES:				
Edmond Petitfils	*			
MOSELLE:				
Jean Labach		*		
Gaston Louis	*			
Louis Meyer	*			
Emile Peter			*	
Robert Schuman		*	*	*
BAS-RHIN:				
Michel Walter	*			
Henri Meck		*	*	
Thomas Seltz	*	*	*	
HAUT-RHIN:				
Camille Bilger	*	*		
Joseph Brom	*	*	*	

1 Joined the group after winning a Sarthe by-election in February 1927.

Table 1—continued

HAUTE-SAVOIE:				
Louis Martel			*	
HAUTE-LOIRE:				
Joseph Antier		*		
LOIRE:				
Jean Raymond-Laurent				*1
TARN:				
François-Xavier Reille-Soult		*	*	*
BASSES-PYRENEES:				
Auguste Champetier de Ribes	*	*	*	*
Pierre Lamazou-Betbeder	*			
SEINE:				
Jean Lerolle		*	*	

1 Joined the group after winning a Loire by-election in June 1938.

The new parliamentary group had fourteen members, the minimum for such a group being thirteen.[1] Already there was evidence of the regional tendency of Christian Democracy in France, for five of the deputies were from Brittany (including four from Finistère, the western-most department) and six from Alsace-Lorraine. Two others were from the south-western department of Basses-Pyrénées, where there were strong Catholic pockets despite Radical control of most of the south-west. The same regional pattern was apparent during the remaining years of the Third Republic, although the 1928 Election seemed to hold out the promise of a more successful electoral future, for there were signs of progress in regions other than the north-east, west and extreme south-west. Fifteen of the new Christian Democratic deputies, who now called themselves the Groupe des Démocrates Populaires, were from these 'traditional' areas, but four seats were won in less peripheral parts. One deputy was elected in Seine and one in Loiret (a department lying sixty miles south of Paris), whilst two others were elected in central-southern France, one in the Massif Central department of Haute-Loire and one in Tarn, a largely rural department west of Toulouse. One notable addition to the Christian Democratic parliamentary group was Robert Schuman. He had been elected in Moselle in 1919 and 1924, but prior to 1928 belonged to the Independent parliamentary group. Probably the main reason for Schuman's decision to join the PDP was his support for the party's declared foreign policy of international reconciliation rather than sympathy

1 See the table on p. 43, for details about the PDP in the Chamber of Deputies.

for the economic and social policies proposed by the more progressive PDP members.[1]

The Elections of 1932 and 1936 were disappointing for the PDP. In 1932 the parliamentary group was reduced to sixteen and in 1936 it declined to eleven. No electoral progress was made outside traditionally Catholic and conservative regions. The only new department to be represented by a PDP deputy in the 1930s was Haute-Savoie, a Catholic highland area which was later an MRP stronghold. The electoral laws of 1928, 1932 and 1936 discouraged the growth of centre parties like the PDP, because *scrutin d'arrondissement à deux tours*, the system then in operation, encouraged electoral alliances and polarization between Right and Left. The PDP, like its successor MRP, favoured proportional representation for the simple reason that Christian Democrats did not like being forced into electoral alliances with the anti-Republican Right or the anti-clerical Left. However, although Bidault justifiably compared the PDP to 'grain being crushed between two mill-stones',[2] it is doubtful whether a different electoral system would have changed the fortunes of the PDP. Despite improving relations between Catholics and Republicans, no party which could be labelled clerical by its opponents had much hope of electoral success outside traditionally Catholic areas. The PDP did well in 1928 *despite* an electoral system which it disliked, simply because there was a general swing to the Right,[3] the only occasion on which this happened between 1900 and 1940 except for the 'khaki' Election of 1919. Without the traumatic experiences of Vichy and the Resistance no significant Christian Democratic breakthrough could have been expected, whatever the electoral system.

PDP ORGANIZATION AND POLICIES

Although the Paris congress of Christian Democrats held in January 1924 had decided on the creation of a political party and the parliamentary Groupe des Démocrates had been organized in May, the Parti Démocrate Populaire (PDP) was not officially constituted until November after a meeting of Christian Democratic deputies and other militants in Paris. The PDP's headquarters were installed at 26 rue Pigalle, the office of the Christian Democratic weekly *Le Petit Démocrate*, which had begun publication in 1923. In 1926 they

[1] Robert Rochefort, *Robert Schuman*, p. 72.

[2] Quoted in Raymond-Laurent, p. 97.

[3] F. Goguel, *Géographie des Elections Françaises sous la Troisième et la Quatrième République*, p. 40.

both moved to the rue Palatine beside St Sulpice on the Left Bank.

The PDP was organized nationally and locally, but, unlike its successor MRP, it was essentially a party of 'cadres' and not a mass party.[1] Neither its organization nor its doctrine were as coherent as those of MRP. The PDP never had a precise programme, although the press was informed of its principles on the day after the party's foundation. These were:

1. Full support for the Republic and for political liberties, i.e. freedom of conscience, freedom of education, freedom of the press and freedom of association;
2. Determination to realize a genuine democracy by reforming economic and social conditions and by sincere co-operation between employers and workers;
3. Promotion of civic and moral education through respect for religious convictions;
4. Implementation of a foreign policy which not only takes account of French national interests but also of all means of international co-operation.

The communiqué went on to say: 'Until now these four principles have not been found in the programme of any nationwide political party. Hence our decision to found the Parti Démocrate Populaire.'[2]

These principles were rather vague, but certain characteristic ideas which run through French Christian Democratic thinking can be detected in them. The idea that democracy is not just political but also social and economic is one such characteristic. So is the emphasis on international co-operation. Another important Christian Democratic idea is contained in the phrase 'sincere co-operation between employers and workers'. The Christian Democrats wanted reform but not revolution. Sangnier argued that reform was necessary because France was not a 'genuine' democracy. He defined democracy as 'a system in which the individual can play a maximum civic role'; thus, democracy was not a set of institutions but a constantly evolving 'way of life'.[3] Everything which tended to associate the individual with the State and the worker with his firm was thus 'democratic'. Conversely, everything which alienated the citizen from the State and the worker from his firm was 'undemocratic'. But in a modern society the individual could only be associated with the State and with his employers through intermediary bodies. Hence the emphasis on what a PDP pamphlet of 1934 called

---

[1] See pp. 91–105 for MRP organization.   [2] Raymond-Laurent, pp. 47–8.
[3] Quoted in Raymond-Laurent, p. 69.

'les forces vives de la nation'.[1] The most important of these was the family, described by Sangnier as 'la véritable cellule de la nation', but trade unions, family associations and communes were also on Sangnier's list of *forces vives*.[2] The pre-war Christian Democrats, like their post-war successors, were thus traditionalists and reformers at the same time. They were traditionalists, or conservatives, in their emphasis on political liberty, the family and Christian morality. but they also advocated economic and social changes in so far as these fitted in with their rather individualistic principles—a contradiction which afflicted MRP even more than the PDP, because MRP, unlike its predecessor, found itself as a powerful force in government.[3]

It has often been asserted that the PDP was a rather conservative party.[4] It is true that the party did not distinguish itself by proposing radical social and economic reforms, and that it did not participate in Blum's Popular Front Government in 1936, but it should not be forgotten that Jean Lerolle was *rapporteur* for the 1930 bill which extended family allowances to all social categories. It is also arguable that insufficient effort was made to come to terms with the Republic. Indeed Paul Simon's demand for the re-establishment of diplomatic relations with the Vatican probably exacerbated the situation, although Simon tried to distinguish between *laïcisme*, which he defined as a fundamentally anti-religious attitude, and *laïcité*, seen as a sincere belief in a lay State combined with respect for religious faith. The PDP, he contended, had nothing against *laïcité* defined in this way.[5]

In foreign affairs, on the other hand, the PDP adopted a progressive and liberal stance. Paul Simon and the PDP group supported Briand's efforts to improve Franco-German relations after the French occupation of the Ruhr. In the debate on the Locarno Treaty Briand was criticized by Poincaré for 'surrendering' French national interests, but Simon spoke in favour of the Locarno terms.[6] The PDP also supported Briand's proposal at the League of Nations in 1929 for a European Federal Union.[7] The party was consistently hostile to Fascism. Ernest Pezet advocated the implementation of

---

[1] Quoted in Raymond-Laurent, p. 72.   [2] ibid., p. 70.

[3] Cf. Francisque Gay, *Les Démocrates d'Inspiration Chrétienne à l'Epreuve du Pouvoir.*

[4] E.g. M. Einaudi and F. Goguel, *Christian Democracy in Italy and France*, pp. 114–15; P. M. Williams, *Crisis and Compromise, Politics in the Fourth Republic*, p. 103. Henceforth cited as Williams. References to other books and articles by Philip Williams will include their full or short title.

[5] JO (Chambre), 26 January 1925, pp. 297–305, especially p. 301.

[6] JO (Chambre), 2 March 1926, p. 1139.   [7] Raymond-Laurent, p. 83.

sanctions against Italy in 1935.[1] Georges Bidault was very critical of the Munich agreement in 1938,[2] whilst François Saudubray, on behalf of the PDP group, attacked the agreement in the Chamber on 4 October.[3] In 1939 Raymond-Laurent criticized Franco amidst constant interruptions from the Right and Centre.[4] And *Le Petit Démocrate* was as consistently anti-Fascist as *L'Aube* despite physical attacks on its premises by Action Française supporters. On 10 July 1940 only three out of the twelve PDP deputies voted against handing over power to Pétain (Champetier de Ribes, Paul Simon and Pierre Trémintin), but no former PDP members became prominent members of the Vichy régime.

The PDP probably achieved as much as could be expected of a new Christian Democratic party, given the political and religious climate in which it operated. Raymond-Laurent attributes its relative failure to lack of money, lack of personalities and the electoral system. It is true that the party lacked men of the national status of, for example, Georges Bidault at the end of the Second World War, but it is unlikely that personalities or money would have had any profound effect on French voting habits and political sociology in the inter-war years. At least the PDP appears to have had an effective national organization. Besides the party's annual congress, there was a National Council which met every three months; an Executive Committee which met monthly; and a permanent Bureau selected from members of the Executive Committee. In practice the last two bodies were the key organs of the PDP. In contrast to MRP there was no suggestion that the annual congress should have a decisive influence on the party's policy. The PDP Executive Committee had twenty-four members, selected on an *ad hoc* basis from Christian Democrats of all backgrounds. The first Executive Committee, for example, consisted of deputies such as Paul Simon and Joseph Brom, men of social Catholic background such as Alfred Bour and Georges Thibout, journalists such as Robert Cornilleau, editor of *Le Petit Démocrate*, and Emmanuel Desgrées du Lou, proprietor of *Ouest-Eclair*, and a trade unionist, Léon Viellefon. The Bureau of the party was similarly heterogeneous in background. Nevertheless, one of the great weaknesses of the PDP was its failure to attract the support of *all* Christian Democratic sympathizers despite the heterogeneity of its membership. After the Second World War both

[1] Raymond-Laurent, p. 84.

[2] E.g. *Aube*, 29 September 1938; 30 September 1938; 1 October 1938; 4 October 1938; 5 October 1938.

[3] JO (Chambre), 4 October 1938, p. 1542.

[4] JO (Chambre), 28 January 1939, pp. 221–5.

the PDP and Jeune République merged into MRP, but before the War Marc Sangnier and the Jeune République remained apart from the PDP.

The Jeune République had been created in December 1912 by Marc Sangnier to further the ideas of the banned Sillon. It was revived after the Great War, and in 1936 four Jeune République candidates were returned to the Chamber.[1] The Jeune République deputies supported the Popular Front Government and were more left-wing than those of the PDP. The difference between the two Christian Democratic groups does not appear to have been merely tactical, as maintained by Raymond-Laurent.[2] There was a fundamental political difference between those who wanted to involve themselves wholeheartedly with the Left (as did the Jeune République) and those whose main aim was to win formerly reactionary Catholics to support the Republic (the chief objective of the PDP). One group was of the Left, the other of the Centre. The overt split between the Jeune République and the PDP foreshadowed the dilemma later faced, but never resolved, by MRP—a dilemma analysed with such clarity by Francisque Gay in his book, *Les Démocrates d'Inspiration Chrétienne à l'Epreuve du Pouvoir* (1951). The Jeune République was, to use post-war terminology, *pure et dure*. Half measures were worse than no measures. Principles were not commodities for bartering in the market-place of politics. The PDP, and later the majority of MRP, thought that occupying the middle ground and making package deals was preferable to inaction. One might almost say that the Jeune République was *Guesdiste* and the PDP *Jaurrèsien* in their respective attitudes.

The PDP did not succeed in fusing the various Christian Democratic organizations, although it made some progress in this field. Not did it make a notable political contribution in the Chamber. Probably its most important achievement was at the level of grass-roots politics, where steps were taken which undoubtedly facilitated the emergence of MRP after the war. The Instituts Démocrates Populaires, working closely with the Association Catholique de la Jeunesse Française (ACJF), carried on the work of political education begun by the Sillonist Instituts Populaires. The PDP Commission Rurale, run by Emile Blocquet, worked in liaison with the Jeunesse Agricole Chrétienne (JAC), the Catholic Action young farmers' association founded in 1929. The PDP Commission de l'Industrie likewise worked closely with the Jeunesse Ouvrière

---

[1] They were Paul Boulet (Hérault), Alain Blanchoin (Maine-et-Loire), Philippe Serre (Meurthe-et-Moselle), Jean Leroy (Vosges).

[2] Raymond-Laurent, p. 45.

Chrétienne (JOC), founded in 1926, as well as with the Confédération Française des Travailleurs Chrétiens (CFTC), whose Secretary General, Gaston Tessier, was one of those who had proposed a Christian Democratic party in 1922. PDP departmental federations were established in sixty-four departments, including important ones in Nord, Pas-de-Calais, Paris, Seine, Seine-et-Oise, Isère and Tarn, as well as in the various departments of Brittany and Alsace-Lorraine. The Fédération des Elus Municipaux et Cantonaux helped to maintain contact between Christian Democratic local government officials. The PDP Fédération Féminine brought together several young women who were later prominent in MRP, including Germaine Peyroles, Solange Lamblin and Germaine Poinso-Chapuis. Many future MRP deputies came from a Catholic Action background. Often their first experience of political action was in the PDP youth organization, Jeunesse Démocrate Populaire, or in Jeunesse Etudiante Chrétienne (JEC), the student section of ACJF. Robert Lecourt was the President of Jeunesse Démocrate Populaire in 1938 and Pierre-Henri Teitgen, Robert Buron, the Coste-Floret twins, André Colin and Jean Letourneau all 'graduated' from ACJF or Jeunesse Démocrate Populaire.

The PDP also played an important role in propagating Christian Democratic ideas. The PDP Association des Journalistes Démocrates, run by Louis-Alfred Pages of *Ouest-Eclair*, distributed press releases to newspapers such as *L'Etoile de la Vendée*, *Le Mémorial de la Loire*, *Le Courrier du Pas-de-Calais*, *Le Journal du Tarn*, *L'Alsacien* and *L'Echo du Mulhouse*. Many of these press releases were prepared by the PDP Bureau d'Etudes run by Georges Hourdin and Charles d'Hellencourt. Both of these men contributed articles to *Le Petit Démocrate*, the PDP's weekly newspaper edited by Robert Cornilleau. *Le Petit Démocrate*, which began publication in 1923, attained a maximum circulation of around 20,000 in the 1930s (although the edition which came out immediately after the riots of 6 February 1934 sold over 100,000 copies). From 1932 there was also a Christian Democratic daily, *L'Aube*, founded by Francisque Gay and sympathetic to the PDP and Jeune République without being specifically committed to either.[1]

It cannot be asserted that there would have been no MRP without the PDP. Indeed MRP owed much more to the war and the Resistance than it did to the PDP. Nevertheless, there can be little doubt that

[1] For a full discussion of *L'Aube* in the 1930s see Françoise Mayeur, *L'Aube Etude d'un Journal d'Opinion 1932–1940*. For *L'Aube's* independence from both PDP and JR see especially p. 164 ff. For *L'Aube* in the Fourth Republic, see pp. 84–6 below.

MRP's birthpangs would have been much more severe without the preparatory work done by Catholic Action, the CFTC and various Christian Democratic newspapers in the inter-war years. The PDP was not responsible for the growth of Catholic Action, the rising influence of the CFTC or the increasing number of Christian Democratic publications, but it helped to bring together people from various backgrounds and movements broadly interested in Christian Democratic ideas. The PDP endowed French Christian Democracy with a political structure for the first time, and this was no small achievement in itself.

Chapter 2

CHRISTIAN DEMOCRATIC DOCTRINE
AND CONSTITUTIONAL THEORY

Christian Democratic ideas cover such a wide spectrum that Bernard Georges has argued that there is no such thing as Christian Democratic doctrine.[1] It is true that in the immediate post-war period (which Georges was discussing) there did not appear to be much in common between the neo-liberal German CDU and the neo-socialist MRP, whilst the Italian DC had deliberately avoided drawing up a political programme in reaction to the over-precise manifesto of Don Sturzo's Popular Party in 1919. But, whilst it cannot be denied that the practical policies pursued by Christian Democratic parties have varied widely, these policies have emanated from a number of common ideas which do form a solid core of Christian Democratic doctrine. Even if parties do not have a fully developed doctrine, they have ideas or at least *an* ideal. This is as true of conservative as of progressive parties. It is particularly true of French parties, which, like pre-war German parties, consider themselves incomplete without a *Weltanschauung* or all-embracing doctrine. It is perhaps significant that even the Radicals, whose ideas were incoherent or non-existent, contributed through Alain a corpus of doctrine which stands as a testimonial to the Third Republic.

Unlike the Radicals, the Christian Democrats regarded doctrine as a basic factor in their political engagement.[2] Indeed MRP's great dilemma was one faced by many reforming parties. Should the party try to maintain doctrinal purity, or should it involve itself in government and accept compromises? Or, as Jacques Fauvet once put it: 'Is it better to withdraw the colours from battle or to let them become bloodstained in the pursuit of success?'[3] Francisque Gay argued in *Les Démocrates d'Inspiration Chrétienne à l'Epreuve du Pouvoir* that MRP did great harm to itself by remaining in power after 1947, when it was incapable of putting into practice its original proposals for *une révolution par la loi*. The MRP leaders (of whom Francisque Gay

---

[1] Bernard Georges, *Problèmes du Catholicisme Français*, 1953, p. 145.

[2] Cf. Einaudi and Goguel, p. 123.

[3] Jacques Fauvet, *De Thorez à de Gaulle: Les Forces Politiques en France*, p. 170 (henceforth cited as Fauvet, *Forces Politiques*).

was no longer one after 1947) decided otherwise on the ground that, even if the governmental majority had moved to the Right, it was necessary to remain within it to defend the institutions of the Republic against the Communists and Gaullists. For MRP political democracy was as important as economic or social democracy. Raymond Barrillon argued that MRP's great failing was not that it abandoned its doctrine, but that it failed either to modify it or to explain its inability to implement it to the party militants.[1] And yet this analysis of MRP's failure is not entirely fair, for men like Etienne Borne and Maurice Byé were still putting forward new Christian Democratic ideas in the 1960s, whilst at annual congresses party leaders regularly emphasized the constraints imposed by governing within coalitions.

MRP doctrine had its origins in the ideas of Social Catholicism (Lamennais, Ozanam, Harmel, de Mun) and in those of embryo and nascent Christian Democracy (Lacordaire, the Sillon, PDP, Jeune République).[2] But these ideas were given an important fillip during the Second World War by Gilbert Dru, a young Catholic philosophy student who drew up a manifesto for post-war Christian Democratic action shortly before being shot by the Gestapo in Lyons in July 1944. The ideas of Dru were developed into a coherent body of doctrine by Etienne Gilson and Etienne Borne, both men of considerable intellect and originality. Gilson was the 'philosopher' of the MRP newspaper *L'Aube*, and played a particularly important role in developing MRP doctrine in the immediate post-war period. Borne was also involved in MRP from its foundation, but his greatest contribution came later with his unceasing efforts to modify and modernize Christian Democratic theory, both in *Terre Humaine* (1951–57) and in its successor *France-Forum*, which he edited from 1957–68. As late as 1970 Borne, although over eighty, was still taking a lively interest in *France-Forum*, which may be described as a periodical of progressive Christian Democratic tendency. The only other important MRP theorist was Maurice Byé, a Professor of Economics at Paris, who, although less well-known than Gilson or Borne, was largely responsible, with Borne, for an unpublished collection of articles on Christian Democratic doctrine in 1961.[3] Although never an MRP deputy or senator,[4] Byé was a much respected

[1] *Monde*, 9 January 1954.   [2] See chapter 1.

[3] *Le MRP, Cet Inconnu*, Maurice Byé, Etienne Borne, Alfred Coste-Floret, Pierre Dhers, Jean Raymond-Laurent, Pierre-Henri Teitgen. Henceforth cited as *Cet Inconnu*. I am indebted to Mme Francine Lefebvre, the former MRP deputy, for a copy of this collection of articles.

[4] Byé was a member of the Economic Council in the Fourth Republic and of the Economic and Social Council in the Fifth Republic.

member of the party who spoke frequently at MRP congresses, usually on subjects such as 'La vie du Mouvement', when he had the opportunity to develop his economic and social theories.

MRP's doctrine was revolutionary in the sense that the Christian Democrats were aiming at nothing less than a complete metamorphosis of man and society by political action. Gilson argued that the Revolutions of 1789 and 1848 had been abortive, resulting only in political democracy.[1] These Revolutions must now be completed by the development of economic and social democracy. Dru doubted whether even political democracy had been created. In his view the politicians of the Third Republic had been so self-seeking and the State so much under the control of capitalists and civil servants that pre-war France had been no more than a sham political democracy.[2] MRP's aim was to construct a 'genuine democracy'[3] for the first time, to be achieved not by violent methods (they were liable to be counter-productive, argued Gilson, citing 1789 and 1848), but by legal means, *la révolution par la loi*, a phrase reputedly coined by Georges Bidault, head of the Conseil National de la Résistance (CNR) and a founder member of MRP.[4]

But what was this 'genuine democracy'? The MRP definition was based on an interpretation of history and a concept of religion. Both were important, particularly the latter. Gilson and Borne, whilst referring rarely to Christianity by name, always based their doctrinal arguments on a Christian interpretation of the value of the individual. Democracy, the family, the school, the trade union—even the Church—were important only in so far as they made it possible for the individual to develop his capacities to the maximum.[5] As regards their interpretation of history, Gilson and Borne, like Sangnier before them, accepted unequivocally the two great Revolutions of the modern age, the Political and the Industrial. Both had opened the way for undreamt-of possibilities for the individual, but both had gone astray. The Political Revolution had led to a centralized, elitist form of government. Although this elite had widened a little in the Third Republic, it had remained narrow and unrepresentative.[6] The Industrial Revolution had given wealth and freedom to a few but slavery to the majority. Large-scale capitalism had devalued the importance of the individual whilst preaching the merits of individualism. In these circumstances it was not surprising, as Borne put it, that the 'dehumanized masses' turned to Marxism, which

---

[1] Borne, *Cet Inconnu*, p. 26.   [2] Dru Manifesto, 1943, MRP docs no. 1.
[3] Gilson, *Aube*, 2 May 1948.   [4] ibid.
[5] Gilson, *Aube*, 2 May 1948; Borne, *Cet Inconnu*, p. 24.
[6] Dru Manifesto, 1943, MRP docs. no. 1.

promised to take all power from the Capitalists and Liberals and give it to the proletariat.[1] But Marxism in practice meant not government by the majority but dictatorship by the State; Marxism merely replaced a number of petty tyrants with one overriding tyrant, and the individual was worse off than ever before.

MRP's answer was to choose a middle way between Liberalism and Marxism, or, as their theorists put it, a combination of freedom and justice. It is important to emphasize the word 'combination', because justice without freedom, or vice versa, was liable to result in tyranny:

> The originality of our doctrine lies in the fact that we hold on to both ends of the rope at the same time. Justice and freedom must be pursued together and with equal vigour. Freedom without justice is artificial, deceptive and hypocritical; it can be used to justify the mechanism of the free market and the servitude of the proletariat; such freedom is, in fact, the antithesis of freedom. Likewise, justice without freedom leads to tyranny and to the totalitarianism of Soviet communism or Fascist corporatism.[2]

Borne went on to argue that the Christian Democratic definitions of freedom and justice were wider than those used by the Liberals and Marxists respectively. For the Liberals, freedom meant freedom to act within the limits of the law; for Christian Democrats freedom 'from' (in the Atlantic Charter sense) was as important as freedom 'to'.[3] Justice, in Marxist or socialist doctrine, meant 'from each according to his capacities to each according to his needs', but the Christian Democratic definition of justice was a fuller one which took account of the fact that Marxist redistributive theory could lead to injustice to individuals. The annihilation of a class, or even of one human being, could never be anything but injustice:

> Thus we believe in a more comprehensive definition of justice based on the absolute respect which a man owes to his fellow human beings. This makes it impossible for him to treat them as pawns or as a means to an end, even if it is a question of the well-being and survival of the majority.[4]

MRP doctrine was thus very individualistic, not in a nineteenth-century Liberal sense but in a Christian sense. Man as an individual

---

[1] Borne, *Cet Inconnu*, p. 35.   [2] ibid., p. 32.
[3] Borne makes the contrast between *liberté libre-arbitre* and *liberté-libération*, *Cet Inconnu*, p. 23. The four freedoms of the Atlantic Charter were freedom from want and from fear, and freedom of expression and of religion.
[4] ibid., p. 24.

was always regarded as more important than society as a whole, but it was necessary for society and the State to provide a combination of freedom and justice so that man could develop his full potential both spiritually and materially.

Of course, in the real world of politics, freedom and justice were often difficult to reconcile. But the Christian Democrats, nevertheless, aimed at this reconciliation. Borne described this idealistic aim as an 'act of faith':

> An act of faith, however, has no meaning unless it leads to action. Faith must generate thought and political engagement. Because we believe that freedom and justice are ultimately reconcilable, we must try to bring this about. Political engagement entails a passion for freedom and a passion for justice.[1]

In practice this dual emphasis on freedom and justice produced what Christian Democrats called a synthesis and their critics often called a compromise. Christian Democrats of all countries have had a tendency to poach from the political theories of others,[2] but they do not mind admitting this. Borne once wrote that Liberalism, Marxism and Positivism were individually anathema to Christian Democrats; yet he could not but admire the Liberal emphasis on the individual, the Marxist emphasis on justice and the Positivist emphasis on pluralism. All three, however, had gone astray by taking their ideas to extremes—thus, for example, Comte's Positivism carried pluralism to the point where society was so hierarchical that Comte should be regarded as a direct precursor of Maurras and Action Française.[3]

The Christian Democratic approach, Gilson maintained, was pragmatic and empirical. Christian Democrats aimed to 'transform enemies into partners',[4] even if this strategy was open to misunderstanding or misrepresentation. Thus MRP worked in government with the Communists from 1944–47, fulfilling one of Gilbert Dru's hopes.[5] Gilson emphasized the similarity of Christian Democratic and Communist social aims at a time when the MRP and PCF were very much at loggerheads (1948);[6] and Maurice Byé made the same point about economic policy at the 1954 MRP Congress.[7] MRP's

---

[1] Borne, *Cet Inconnu*, p. 25.
[2] Cf. M. P. Fogarty, *Christian Democracy in Western Europe, 1820–1953*, p. 114 'Over the years the Christian Democrats have learnt Liberalism from the Liberals and Socialism from the Socialists'.
[3] *Cet Inconnu*, p. 29.   [4] *Aube*, 5 May 1948.
[5] Dru Manifesto, 1943, MRP docs no. 1.   [6] *Aube* 5 May 1948.
[7] MRP National Congress, 1954, Lille; report on 'La politique économique et

desire to synthesize and its opposition to polarization and blocs was apparent in the party's determined advocacy of proportional representation (PR), which (it was hoped) would save the Christian Democrats from having to make electoral alliances with parties of the Right or Left.[1] It was equally apparent in foreign policy, for in the immediate post-war period Bidault strove as hard as anyone to prevent the emergence of Communist and Capitalist blocs.[2] He hoped that France could play a bridging role between East and West similar to that being attempted by MRP between the political Right and Left. For various reasons neither stratagem succeeded. Nevertheless, 'bridge-building' remained an essential part of MRP doctrine even if the Christian Democratic attitude to the Communists in the 1950s tended to belie this fact.

Before analysing MRP's doctrine in more detail, one final general point should be made. Although MRP documents of 1944–46 speak constantly of 'revolution', Christian Democrats not only rejected Marxist methodology, i.e. violence, which they thought would be counter-productive, they also rejected the Marxist concept of the 'final' revolution. Owing to the diversity of historical influences, the difference between one generation and the next, and the changing pattern of international relations, 'the nature of democracy, i.e. the need to give man the greatest possible amount of freedom and justice, is constantly evolving. The revolution, therefore, is permanent.'[3]

MAN AND SOCIETY

The first article of our faith is the freedom of man, a freedom which is constantly threatened and constantly evolving.[4]

sociale'. (MRP National Congresses will in future be referred to simply as MRP Congr., followed by the date and venue of the Congress and the title of the report or debate.)

[1] MRP's hopes suffered a blow with the introduction of *apparentements* in 1951 (under this system of 'bastardized PR' parties which made an alliance before the Election and received over 50 per cent of the votes cast took all the seats in their constituency. It was a system devised to reduce 'anti-Republican', i.e. Gaullist and Communist membership of the Assembly, for the RPF and PCF were most unlikely to make alliances with other parties). With the coming of the Fifth Republic and the introduction of *scrutin d'arrondissement à deux tours*, MRP's hopes suffered a further blow although the party accepted the new system with surprisingly good grace and at first did quite well under it; see pp. 233–6. For a full discussion of French electoral systems see Peter Campbell, *French Electoral Systems and Elections since 1789.*

[2] See pp. 160–2.   [3] Borne, *Cet Inconnu*, p. 34.
[4] Borne, *Cet Inconnu*, p. 32.

Man, as has already been emphasized, is at the centre of the Christian Democratic universe. Etienne Gilson argued that whereas 'our enemies of the Right and Left recognize that the human race consists of a large number of individuals, the Christian Democrat sees man not only as an individual but also as a human being' ('chaque homme n'est pas seulement un individu, mais aussi une personne').[1] Gilson goes on to explain what he means by this apparently spurious distinction. Animals, he says, are individuals grouped in herds or flocks. Man is an individual in this sense too, but his unique feature is that he alone is also 'une personne' capable of making rational decisions and assuming responsibility for his own actions. Conservatives, with their elitist view of society, implicitly reject this concept of man, at least for the majority, while Marxists, with their emphasis on the mass rather than the individual, do likewise:

> For a democrat of the MRP the word 'mass', when applied to human beings, is repugnant, because every human being is different . . . the role of the State is to contribute to the full development of all the human beings who make up society.[2]

The Christian Democratic view of man is not unlike Aristotle's concept of the ideal citizen—a responsible, educated human being, fully involved in the life of his community, society and State. But although political engagement is essential for the Christian Democrat, it is not his whole life: he has a duty to participate actively in the 'natural structures' of society—the family, the community, the youth group, the trade union.[3] This view of man as a responsible human being owes something to Emmanuel Mounier's Personalist philosophy, as expounded in the 1930s in the periodical *Esprit*.[4] Mounier emphasized the importance of man as an individual, but he developed this simple Christian axiom further. Man is only a full personality when he is wholly *engagé* in the sense outlined by Gilbert Dru in his 1943 Manifesto (Dru was well known as a disciple of Mounier). Dru makes it clear that he himself had become *engagé* rather reluctantly. He refers to the politics of the 1930s with disgust, but then goes on to describe the new form of political life which he hopes will emerge. This new type of politics will centre on a movement, not a traditional party. And the essence of the movement will be that those engaged within it will not just be cogs in the party machine but responsible militants striving to build a new France through community action and political engagement.[5]

---

[1] *Aube*, 2 May 1948.   [2] ibid.
[3] Borne, *Cet Inconnu*, p. 33; and see below, section on Pluralism, pp. 60–5.
[4] Cf. Borne, *Cet Inconnu*, p. 31   [5] Dru Manifesto, 1943, MRP docs no. 1.

Having defined man's nature and role in this way, it is not surprising to find that

Man is not a tool of production, nor may he be reduced to being a mere servant of society. He is a free and reasonable being, endowed by God with an eternal destiny, and equipped to that end with supreme value as a person, with inalienable rights, and with high responsibilities.[1]

Work is more than just the pursuit of wealth. Both Borne and Byé emphasized the dangerous effect on man as a spiritual being if materialism were regarded as the chief goal of political action.[2] Borne, however, realized perfectly well that man could hardly be expected to develop his full personality whilst constantly worrying about food, wages and housing. And Byé made it clear at the 1954 MRP Congress that the French worker must be able to see decisive improvements in his living conditions if he were going to be wooed away from the Communist party. Hence, for example, MRP frequently criticized the level of SMIG (Salaire Minimum Interprofessionnel Garanti) and the inadequacies of the housing programme.[3] Nevertheless, the long-term aim was to encourage the development of responsible, self-sufficient human beings. Thus, family allowances should be seen as a temporary expedient; the ultimate ideal was a living wage for the head of the household. The MRP attitude to works' councils (comités d'entreprise) also illustrates the Christian Democratic concept of man as a responsible human being. A worker is not just a 'tool of production'; therefore he should be associated with the running of his factory, and, because he is a responsible person, he should elect representatives to the works council and not simply let them be appointed by his trade union.

Every effort should also be made to humanize work. Work should be adjusted to the worker and not vice versa. Science and technology should be used wherever possible to achieve this end.[4] Thus Robert Schuman, describing a new steel factory in Lorraine, wrote:

Here the roles are happily reversed as compared with old-style steel strip mills. Man resumes his place as the being who observes and reflects. Teachers and other intellectuals have taken up this work in place of their old profession, and have no feeling of constriction of their personality or of loss of social status.[5]

1 CFTC Workers' Action Programme, 1945, p. 5.
2 Byé, MRP Congr. 1954, Lille; report on 'La politique économique et sociale'.
3 See pp. 129–37 for details.   4 Borne, Cet Inconnu, p. 30.
5 Tour d'Horizon, no. 13, 1954; quoted in Fogarty, p. 33.

59

The Christian Democrat was also inclined to take a long-term view of the economy, calculating that patience would bring real material advantages to the individual worker. Byé argued that economic planning and investment would result in a growth in production and an increase in overall prosperity. Ideally, the worker should realize that this was more to his advantage than a quick wage rise.

But, in all their discussion of politics, economics and society, the Christian Democratic theorists always come back to man. In a passage which starts with the words 'il y a l'homme lui-même', Borne compares man to Prometheus at the time when Jupiter had decided to release him from his bondage in the Caucasian mountains. Likewise, the great struggle to free man from his chains has begun. As Prometheus returned to the world of the gods, so man, through political involvement and social action, could aspire to his true destiny as a free and responsible being.

PLURALISM

> Pluralism is an essential feature of democracy. A free and just society, i.e. a democracy, is one which recognizes and gives institutional form to pluralism, which is part of the natural destiny of man.[1]

It is appropriate to discuss the Christian Democratic doctrine of pluralism before the doctrine of the State, for the Christian Democratic view of life puts man first, society next and the State last. The State is artificial; it has meaning only in so far as it helps to make possible the full development of man. Society, on the other hand, consists of 'natural social structures': 'From birth to death each man is involved in a plurality of natural social structures (*structures sociales naturelles*), outside which he can neither live nor achieve his full potential.'[2]

Borne, using the phrase 'natural social groups' instead of 'natural social structures', develops Gilson's theme:

> A people is not really a people and certainly does not live in freedom unless the natural social groups (*communautés naturelles*) which compose it accept each other, and unless the State recognizes their differences and ensures that their interests are represented. There can be no justice unless the rights of individuals and natural social groups are protected and encouraged. For a people is not really a people when it consists of a crowd of unassociated individuals or a mass of characterless pawns. A genuine people's democracy,

[1] Borne, *Cet Inconnu*, pp. 34–5.   [2] Gilson, *Aube*, 4 May 1948.

using this phrase correctly and not hypocritically, is neither an individualistic democracy nor a totalitarian democracy.[1]

The natural social groups, 'outside which the perfection of human beings is impossible',[2] are based on those of the Church. A man is born into a family, and the Church, itself a natural social group, consists of the whole family of Christians. A man lives in a commune, his parish. The region is his diocese. Less traditional, but equally important, natural social groups are those associated with Catholic Action—young workers groups (JOC), young farmers (JAC), young students (JEC), family and women's organizations. Then there are trade unions (the CFTC for Christian Democrats) and, most important, the Movement itself, not, it should be emphasized again, a traditional party but a mass movement, almost a way of life. These autonomous social groups are important not only because they help man to develop his full potential but also because they provide 'a guarantee against the spontaneous totalitarianism of the State'.[3]

The most important of these natural groups is the family. The first two MRP manifestos contain prominent sections on the family:

> Without a satisfactory family life no nation can prosper. True education and freedom can flourish only within families. The legislator, therefore, has a duty to do all that is necessary for the family.
>
> Amongst other things, he ought to give the family positive help by marriage loans to help young families to set up house; by the maintenance of family allowances; by a vigorous housing policy; by encouraging mothers to stay at home and bring up their families; by a campaign against social vices (abortion, alcoholism, prostitution); by ensuring that family organizations are represented in public bodies.[4]

These basic demands were developed over the years into an elaborate doctrine of the family. The most important point for the family, as for the individual, was to develop a sense of responsibility. The first objective was to achieve justice for the family, but ultimately the open, creative responsible family would be able to stand on its own feet. Family allowances were necessary owing to the economic conditions produced by the Industrial Revolution, but in time they would wither away when the bread-winner could support his family without them. In the meantime they should be related to income, and distributed not by the State, but by intermediary organizations

---

[1] Borne, *Cet Inconnu*, p. 35.   [2] ibid.   [3] ibid.
[4] Declaration of MRP National Committee, 25–26 August 1945.

run by natural social groups, such as trade unions and family organizations. It is typical of the Christian Democratic approach that they have organizations *of* the family, not *for* the family. By 1960 there were approximately 50,000 families affiliated to the Association Familiale Catholique. And many women were also members of the Union Féminine Civique et Sociale, for, although the Christian Democrats emphasized that a woman's main role was the traditional one of 'Kinder, Küche, Kirche', they had moved away from a patriarchal concept of the family. Old style paterfamilias could not be reconciled with Personalism. The unthinking, housebound woman could never become a fully responsible citizen.

It is appropriate to refer again briefly to the schools problem in the context of the family, because MRP frequently emphasized that education was the responsibility of the head of the family.[1] For the Christian Democrat the private (Catholic) school was an essential aspect of pluralism. If the State took pluralism seriously, it would accept the Christian Democratic solution of parallel public and private schools, equally subsidized by the State. If it were not, and insisted on instituting *laïcité*, it would not only encourage internal strife but also be acting undemocratically, for 'democracy and pluralism are indivisible'.[2]

The family is the most important of the natural social groups, but it is by no means the only one: 'The commune, like the family, is prior to the State; the politicians found it, they did not create it.'[3] Hamon goes on to say that this is equally true of schools, universities, hospitals, industrial companies and trade unions. The commune, however, is particularly important because 'it is both a public body concerned with the general interest, and therefore opposed to individualistic liberalism, and a sufficiently small unit for the individual to be able to express himself without being crushed by higher authority'.[4]

The commune is important for some of the Catholic Action organizations. Action Catholique Générale, Hommes (ACGH) and Action Catholique Générale, Femmes (ACGF) are organized on a communal or parish basis. Dansette estimated that ACGH had about 600,000 members in the early 1950s, whilst ACGF had branches in no less than three-quarters of French parishes (28,000 out of 36,000).[5] The Scouts, too, are organized on a parish basis. (In France the

---

[1] E.g. 1944 MRP Manifesto, and Borne, *Cet Inconnu*, p. 36.
[2] Borne, *Cet Inconnu*, p. 36.
[3] Léo Hamon, quoting Royer-Collard, *Aube*, 4 May 1948.   [4] ibid.
[5] Dansette, p. 413.

Scouting Movement is to all intents and purposes a junior branch of Catholic Action.)

It is true that some of the best known and most active sections of Catholic Action (ACJF and its offshoots, JOC, JAC, JIC and JEC) are organised on a national and regional base, but the region, too, is important in the Christian Democratic pluralist society. The departmental Federation for example was supposed to be the most important unit in the MRP organization, 'the nerve centre of political action within the Movement',[1] although, of course, in practice it usually fell far short of this ideal.

Apart from some of the Catholic Action groups, the most important nationwide pluralist organizations were the trade unions and the Mouvement Républicain Populaire itself. Indeed, from a political point of view, the CFTC and MRP were much more important than the Catholic Action groups. The desirability of a strong trade union federation, in which Christian Democratic opinion predominated, fitted well into the MRP doctrine of pluralism, but, equally, in accordance with that doctrine there was no demand for structural links between MRP and CFTC.

MRP, like other Christian Democratic parties, wanted to see the trade unions involved in industrial and economic planning at three levels—nationally through an economic and social council or, ideally, in a second chamber representing the natural social groups;[2] industrially, e.g. in some body representing the nation's whole cotton industry; and at the level of the individual firm. The distinctive feature of MRP doctrine was its emphasis on partnership rather than workers' control. The nationwide industry and the individual firm were both seen as natural working communities (*communautés naturels de travail*),[3] a notion also expressed in the CFTC's *Programme d'Action Ouvrière* (1945).[4] The management was as much a part of the natural community of the firm as the workers, and MRP was not afraid to emphasize that management must manage, even if elected representatives of the workers should help with running the firm. The long-term aim was joint control (*cogestion*), not just consultation, which was all that was achieved with the works' councils set up in 1946. The MRP objective of joint control was quite clearly stated, even if the party was uncertain how it was to be achieved. In the meantime it advocated a gradualist approach: 'There is no divine law by which authority in the firm should be exercised only by the

[1] Fonteneau, MRP Congr. 1951, Lyon; report on 'La vie du Mouvement'.
[2] See p. 116. [3] Teitgen, *Cet Inconnu*, p. 95.
[4] Cited in Fogarty, p. 68.

representatives of capital. It appears essential to us that labour should gradually be involved in the exercise of this authority.'[1]

Finally, there was the party itself, or, as Christian Democrats would prefer it, the movement. The Mouvement Républicain Populaire was seen both as a natural structure within a pluralist society and as an intermediary between the State and the other structures. For Gilbert Dru the party (movement) was not just an electoral machine, but a mass movement through which the militant engaged himself full-time in political action.[2] Pierre-Henri Teitgen wrote:

> Through political action a militant becomes a democrat in the fullest sense of the word. In the party and through the party the militants can exercise a permanent influence on the political orientation of the country. In their sections and in their federations they contribute not only to electoral success but to the policy of the party. . . . They are not only electors who vote every four or five years; they are citizens, who are well informed about contemporary problems, conscious of their importance and in a position to contribute to their solution. The militants of the party are the aristocrats of democracy.[3]

Ultimately the Christian Democratic doctrine of pluralism comes back to man as an individual. Gilson's 'natural structures' and Borne's 'natural communities' are important only in so far as through them man 'can attain the full development of which he is capable'.[4] Godin and Daniel wrote that the Christian Democratic ideal was:

> A Christian centre in this shop, another in that office; a Christian nucleus among those hikers, another in that group of actors. The leaven is working in that big family lodging house and in that block of workers' flats. Leaven in that technical college, leaven in that evening class. Leaven among the men on their allotments, leaven among the film actors. Leaven in the trade union branch and the social work committee. Leaven in the caretakers' union of the VIIth *arrondissement*, among the artists of Montmartre, among the girl assistants in department stores. . . .[5]

Pluralism was central to Christian Democratic thinking because

[1] Teitgen, *Cet Inconnu*, p. 94.
[2] Dru Manifesto, 1943, MRP docs no. 1; and cf. Henri Teitgen, quoted in Einaudi and Goguel, p. 125.
[3] Teitgen, *Cet Inconnu*, p. 91.   [4] Gilson, *Aube*, 2 May 1948.
[5] Godin and Daniel, *France, Pays de Mission*, cited in Fogarty, p. 125.

man could reach the ideal of individual responsibility only through participation in natural social groups.

In practice MRP was doctrinally isolated in French politics.[1] It was thus open to attack from all sides. The Conservatives were opposed to the welfare state, economic planning and workers' participation in management. The Radicals, broadly in agreement with the Conservatives, could not accept MRP's schools' policy. The Socialists and Communists, especially the latter, criticized MRP for its individualism and its lukewarm support for State intervention and control, as well as for its clericalism. Sangnier's appeal for a 'revolution in men's hearts'[2] may have been theologically sound but was politically naive. Mounier may have been right when he criticized Christian Democracy for the 'weakness' of its doctrine, a weakness which produced 'a sweet animal without a temper and addicted to mental confusions'.[3] It is difficult to disagree with Borne that the hardest doctrine to practise is a doctrine of the centre which is openly admitted to be constantly evolving.[4] In these circumstances it was not surprising that MRP militants, exposed to constant sniping from Right and Left, became increasingly uneasy about a party whose doctrinal position, like that of the pre-war *Times*, seemed always to coincide with the views of the Government of the day.

THE STATE AND THE CONSTITUTION

MRP, like all Christian Democratic parties, was instinctively suspicious of the power of the State. The party was afraid that the pendulum would swing from the tyranny of Liberalism to the tyranny of collectivism: 'The role of the State is to be the protector and regulator of the natural social groups, which alone permit the free development of human beings in the direction of their own interests as well as in those of the community.'[5]

MRP was not averse to State control of the economy or to the institutions of the welfare state. Indeed it showed more enthusiasm for nationalization than any other European Christian Democratic party. Nevertheless it held that the power of the State should be limited to clearly defined areas. Hence MRP's emphasis on human rights, bicameralism, devolution and limited presidential powers. It

[1] Gilson, *Aube*, 4 May 1948; Borne, MRP Congr. 1954, Lille; report on 'Le Sens de Notre Engagement Politique'; and Einaudi and Goguel, p. 138.
[2] Quoted in Fauvet, *Forces Politiques*, p. 198.
[3] Borne interpreting Mounier, *Terre Humaine*, February 1951, p. 67.
[4] MRP Congr. 1954, Lille; report on 'Le Sens de Notre Engagement Politique'.
[5] Gilson, *Aube*, 4 May 1948.

C

goes without saying that MRP favoured a democratic system of government, not out of any *a priori* conviction that democracy was an absolute ideal, but because in practical terms it seemed to offer the best climate in which men could develop as responsible human beings.

MRP's constitutional theory, as François Goguel has pointed out,[1] was most clearly stated in the debates on the first constitutional draft of the Fourth Republic. After its rejection in May 1946 and the Election of June 1946, Paul Coste-Floret became *rapporteur* of the constitutional committee, but the second draft, which in October 1946 became the Constitution of the Fourth Republic, represented a compromise between the constitutional theory of MRP and that of the Left.

In January 1946 Coste-Floret said, 'If the Constituent Assembly adopts a system of *gouvernement d'assemblée*, we will ask the country to vote No at the referendum'.[2] In place of *gouvernement d'assemblée*, advocated by the Left and entailing the concentration of virtually all political power in the National Assembly, MRP favoured a 'mixed' system, in which a second chamber would play an important, though subordinate, role in the legislative process.[3] The second chamber would have two main functions. It would ensure that legislation was carefully drafted, not only by examining bills in detail but also by means of suspensive veto. At the same time it would be able to represent the natural social groups:

> Are there not regional and local interests which must be defended? At the very moment when we are moving in the direction of tightening community bonds, it would be illogical to give a purely individualistic representative system to the country. The second assembly should represent these collective and community interests.[4]

Maurice Guérin, a former trade union official, developed this proposal by suggesting that the unions should be represented in the new second chamber.[5]

The first chamber would, of course, play the decisive role in legislation. It would be elected by proportional representation which would give responsible citizens the maximum opportunity to express their individual preferences. Voting would be compulsory. MRP also

---

[1] Einaudi and Goguel, p. 133.   [2] *Aube*, 15 January 1946.

[3] Coste-Floret called it *un régime parlementaire* in contrast to the Left's *gouvernement d'assemblée* and de Gaulle's *régime présidentiel*, JO (AN Constit.), 20 August 1946, p. 3184. Borne used the phrase *démocratie parlementaire*, MRP Congr. 1954, Lille; report on 'Le Sens de Notre Engagement Politique'.

[4] Henri Teitgen, quoted in Einaudi and Goguel, p. 134.   [5] ibid.

wanted a statute of parties written into the Constitution, because without organized, legally-defined parties, there could be no guarantee that the democratic system would not be abused:

> Universal suffrage is sovereign, but it is at present unsystematized; . . . to establish a statute of parties would be to give it a framework. The parties would then become what they should be, the intermediaries between the people and the executive and legislative powers. How can they play this role if they are not organized?[1]

Another important feature of MRP's 'mixed' system concerned the presidency. MRP wanted the President to have 'the power to dissolve the Assembly in order to achieve executive stability',[2] but opposed a presidential régime of the type advocated by General de Gaulle, i.e. one with complete separation of powers. The President would be elected by an electoral college consisting of the two houses of parliament and an equal number of representatives of the large cities, departments and overseas territories. He would be able to choose his Prime Minister without the latter requiring an investiture debate prior to the formation of a government.

MRP also proposed that a Declaration of Human Rights be an integral part of the Constitution. In order to protect the individual against the potentially overweening power of the State, it was essential that his rights should be constitutionally guaranteed, but it was also necessary to protect the natural social groups against a possible abuse of power by the State. MRP wanted the rights of trade unions, professional bodies and similar organizations to be written into the Constitution. The rights of the family should also be defined, including the right of the head of the family to choose his child's education and have it paid for by the State, whether he went to a religious or lay school.[3] Finally, MRP wanted a 'high council' for the national economy, a body which would be consulted about economic planning and whose members would be representative of business, trade unions and consumers.

In the political circumstances of the immediate post-war period it was inevitable that the Christian Democrats did not obtain their 'ideal' constitution. As Philip Williams has pointed out, 'The makers of the Fourth Republic gave themselves the impossible task of solving by constitutional arrangements a problem set, not by the

---

[1] Henri Teitgen, quoted in Einaudi and Goguel, p. 135.

[2] ibid.; and first MRP Manifesto, 1944.

[3] Henri Teitgen, quoted in Einaudi and Goguel, p. 135; and first MRP Manifesto, 1944.

forms of the law, but by the divisions of the people'.[1] The Communists and Socialists had an overall majority in the first Constituent Assembly (October 1945–May 1946), but their constitutional draft, essentially *gouvernement d'assemblée*, was rejected on MRP, Radical and Conservative advice in the referendum of 5 May 1946 by a million votes.[2] In the second Constituent Assembly the Left no longer had an overall majority, and the MRP point of view gained some ground, but only in a limited area. It was soon apparent that the Constitution of the Fourth Republic, which embodied neither the checks and balances advocated by MRP nor the powerful Assembly government advocated by the Left, was not unlike the system of the Third Republic except that the Senate (Council of the Republic) was now much weaker. And, as the old Conservative (Third Republic) parties revived, the Fourth Republic increasingly came to resemble its despised predecessor.

MRP succeeded in obtaining a certain number of concessions from the Left in the second constitutional draft, partly because the Socialists and Communists feared the possibility of a Gaullist backlash if the constitutional debate went on much longer. Changes in detail, however, outnumbered those of substance. MRP had wanted a Declaration of Human Rights, including the rights of various social groups, in the Constitution itself. They did not achieve their objective. Instead of an exhaustive Declaration there was a short Preamble, and although economic and social rights were briefly mentioned, those of the so-called natural social groups were not, nor did MRP succeed in getting the inclusion of free education at Catholic schools despite a close vote of 274–272 on 28 August. Coste-Floret justifiably described the Preamble as 'one step forward' from the 1789 Declaration of the Rights of Man, but he exaggerated when he said it marked 'the achievement of political, economic and social democracy'.[3]

The concessions made to MRP with regard to the presidency were quite substantial. In the first draft the President was to be elected publicly by the National Assembly; he was not to preside over the Council of Ministers or the Committee of National Defence, nor was he to retain the personal right of legal pardon; he could propose a Prime Minister only with the approval of the President of the National Assembly. In the second draft, the President was to be

[1] Williams, p. 188.

[2] The first draft was rejected by 10,273,000 to 9,110,000 votes on 5 May 1946; 20·4 per cent of the electorate of 24,657,000 abstained. The second draft was accepted by 9,039,000 to 7,830,000 votes on 13 October 1946; 30·9 per cent of the electorate of 25,073,000 abstained.

[3] JO (AN Constit.), 20 August 1946, p. 3184.

elected in secret by both houses of parliament (the Communists and Socialists agreed to secret election on 27 September 1946, although it was not written into the Constitution); he was to preside over the Council of Ministers, the High Council of the Judiciary and the Committee of National Defence; he regained the traditional right of pardon; finally, he was to appoint the Prime Minister, whose governmental programme had to be approved by the Assembly. Coste-Floret commented, 'It is up to the President to choose the head of government, but it is the duty of the National Assembly to say if he has chosen well.'[1] These changes in the powers of the President had an undoubted influence on the governmental system of the Fourth Republic, for they made it possible for the shrewd and determined Vincent Auriol to play a very much more important role than would have been possible under the first draft.

Twelve years later MRP showed that its basic attitude to the presidency had not changed. Pierre-Henri Teitgen, one of the three MRP members of the 1958 constitutional committee (the others being Paul Coste-Floret and Jacques Menditte) told the National Committee of the party:

> The President has been given formidable powers but he is neither the hierarchical superior nor the antagonist of the Prime Minister. The Prime Minister retains control of the policy of the government; he is responsible only to Parliament; this is a genuine parliamentary regime.[2]

Robert Schuman wondered whether 'the texts will be applied in the future',[3] and when they were not, MRP swung against the Gaullist concept of presidential government, regarded as excessive power in the hands of one man (*pouvoir personnel*). In 1962 MRP came out against direct election of the President, but Lecanuet's comparatively successful presidential bid of 1965 convinced most Christian Democrats that they had nothing to gain by opposing a system which existed and which had been approved by the electorate.

As regards Parliament itself, MRP's doctrinal position was contained in one word—bicameralism. The party did not want an overpowerful second chamber like the old Senate, but they did want a 'house of second thoughts'. In the discussions on the first draft of the Constitution MRP was adamantly against the single-chamber Parliament proposed by the Left, and the rejection of MRP's proposal that the Assembly of the French Union should at least be part of

[1] JO (AN Constit.), 20 August 1946, p. 3187.
[2] *Monde*, 9 September 1958.   [3] ibid.

Parliament was the last straw which swung the party decisively against the first draft.[1] In the course of the debates on the second draft some concessions were made to MRP. Bicameralism was introduced, albeit in a somewhat mutilated form. Coste-Floret called it *monocaméralisme tempéré* or *bicaméralisme incomplet*,[2] adding that it was up to the individual to decide which description was most apt. The Council of the Republic (a name chosen by MRP) was not, Coste-Floret claimed, merely a revised Senate. Its members would be elected for six years not nine, and they were to be elected by all the *collectivités communales*[3] in such a way as to represent the whole electorate and not just the rural communes. The Council of the Republic would be a 'chamber of reflection'.[4] Unfortunately it was not a very serious 'chamber of reflection' until the 1954 reforms, because at first it could not discuss bills until the National Assembly had done so. The effect of this was that the Council was underworked at the beginning of the session and overworked at the end. Moreover, bills classed as 'urgent' had to be passed by the Council in the time laid down by the National Assembly, which in practice usually meant that insufficient time was available for discussion. Even more debilitating was the absence of any delaying power (as distinct from the right to veto), so there was at first nothing to oblige the National Assembly to take any notice of the second chamber's views. Another flaw was that the Council had, to all intents and purposes, a veto in that if it rejected or amended a bill by an absolute majority in public ballot, the Assembly could overrule it only in the same manner. The importance of this was not realized until the 1948 electoral reform which resulted in the Council being much more reflective of rural, Radical and Conservative France than the 1946 Council, elected mainly by PR, had been.[5] It thus came into conflict with the National Assembly more frequently.

The procedural reforms of 1954, by which the Council dropped its veto in exchange for delaying power in the form of the *navette* (the Third Republic system of shuttling bills between the two houses until agreement had been reached on controversial amendments),

[1] The vote against MRP's proposal was 288–260 on 15 April 1946.

[2] JO (AN Constit.), 20 August 1946, p. 3184.

[3] Thanks to a Socialist concession to MRP, the phrase *collectivités communales* was included in the Constitution, AP 1946.

[4] JO (AN Constit.), 20 August 1946, p. 3186.

[5] Contrasting the 1946 and 1948 electoral procedures, Philip Williams comments: 'the 1946 system of thinly disguised direct election was replaced by an indirect method, which, as in the Third Republic, favoured small communities against large', Williams, p. 279. For detailed discussion of the Council of the Republic see Williams, pp. 276–91.

produced a second chamber more in line with that advocated by MRP, i.e. a 'chamber of reflection', whose powers were nevertheless clearly subordinate to those of the National Assembly. However, MRP's original hope that the second chamber should contain representatives of trade unions, business organizations and other 'natural social groups' was not achieved in the Fourth or Fifth Republics.

The powers attributed to the National Assembly of the Fourth Republic may be said to have coincided with MRP's doctrinal position. The way the National Assembly functioned did not, for there was no governmental stability and this discredited the Fourth Republic and with it the main new party of the Republic, MRP. The constitutional debates had little to do with this outcome. Indeed the only major difference between the first and second drafts was that the power of the committees was somewhat reduced. They could no longer pass bills on their own account,[1] nor could they sit in public. However, in practice, the specialized committees of the National Assembly were very powerful[2]—the sort of 'mini-parliaments' which MRP spokesmen had criticized in the debates on the first draft. In MRP's view the main legislative decisions should have been taken by the whole body of representatives of the sovereign people and not by committees.

It was the practice of the National Assembly which veered far away from MRP's early hopes. In August 1946 Paul Coste-Floret said that the Constitution would guarantee governmental stability through its rules on questions of confidence, censure motions and the right of dissolution. It was hoped that Governments would fall only if defeated by an absolute majority on questions of confidence or votes of censure. In fact the National Assembly never took the vote of censure seriously,[3] whilst the supposedly solemn question of confidence was used over-frequently, and Prime Ministers who were defeated, even by a relative majority, always resigned.[4] As regards dissolution, there were various constitutional rules which made it difficult to apply. Governments had to be defeated twice by an absolute majority in a vote of confidence or censure; these two defeats had to occur within an eighteen-month period, but this eighteen-month period did not include the first eighteen months of

[1] Under the first draft bills could have been passed in committee unless one-third of the National Assembly had asked for a debate.

[2] See Williams, pp. 245–6, for details.

[3] Only five of the twenty censure motions put down in the Fourth Republic were ever discussed and none was passed, Williams, p. 240.

[4] Except for Bidault who did not resign after a tied vote (which is negative in French procedure) in December 1949.

the life of a Parliament, nor did constitutional defeats occurring within the first fortnight of a Government's life count. The only dissolution which did occur was in 1955, and it did nothing to solve ministerial instability thanks to the decision of the electorate in January 1956.[1]

Right to the end the Fourth Republic's basic problem was that it could not produce a stable parliamentary majority. MRP had some ideas for reform, such as the proposals put forward at the 1956 party Congress in favour of a German-type constructive vote of no confidence or Coste-Floret's proposal that confidence issues should be deemed to have been passed by the National Assembly unless an opposition motion of censure was carried by an absolute majority. But these proposals would not in themselves have produced a stable majority, although they would have made it easier for a determined Government to stay in office. However, there was no point in a Government remaining in office when it could not legislate. The Fifth Republic may owe a small part of its governmental stability to constitutional devices such as the Coste-Floret proposal mentioned above, but much more is due to the emergence of a disciplined majority.[2]

Finally, MRP's hopes for a 'high council' for the economy were disappointed. MRP's ideal (not unlike that of de Gaulle in the Bayeux 'constitution') would have been an elected second chamber representing economic and social groups, regions and the overseas territories. This elected 'economic senate' would have had an important role in legislation and economic planning, whilst remaining subordinate to the National Assembly. Neither the Economic Council of the Fourth Republic nor the Economic and Social Council of the Fifth Republic fulfilled MRP's hopes. Although the latter has been more effective than the former, especially in the formulation of France's economic plans,[3] they have both been a far cry from the influential 'economic senate' proposed by MRP.

[1] It is significant that Pierre Schneiter, the MRP President of the Assembly, played an important part in influencing Faure to ask Coty for a dissolution (Williams, p. 239). Schneiter's action was in line with MRP's constitutional theory, namely that dissolution could help towards governmental stability. The National Assembly returned in January 1956 consisted of 150 Communists, 99 Socialists, 84 MRP, 75 Radicals, 18 UDSR, 97 Conservatives, 22 Gaullists, 42 Poujadists and 8 others (total 596).

[2] Robert Lecourt pointed out that most of the Fifth Republic's institutional devices had already been proposed by MRP between 1954–58; interview, 22 June 1970.

[3] J. E. S. Hayward, *Private Interests and Public Policy, the Experience of the French Economic and Social Council.* Hayward also emphasizes that throughout

In conclusion, it can be said that the Fourth Republic disappointed MRP's constitutional hopes because, owing to France's basic political divisions, the Fourth Republic, in constitution and in practice, ended up too like the Third. The Fifth Republic, on the other hand, looked as if it might be more in line with MRP's constitutional theory until it developed into a presidential rather than a parliamentary system.[1] Indeed, after the institution of direct election of the President in 1962, the Fifth Republican regime became almost as abhorrent to MRP as the proposed monocameralism of 1946, although it must be emphasized that this had more to do with the Gaullist style of government than with presidentialism as such. Nevertheless, Gilson's hope was not fulfilled. Neither in the parliamentary system of the Fourth Republic nor in the presidential regime of the Fifth Republic was the role of the State limited to 'protecting and regulating the natural social groups, which alone permit the free development of human beings'.[2]

its history the Council has been hampered by the hostility of Parliament and the contempt of the Civil Service, p. 86.

[1] See chapter 8 on 'Christian Democracy in the Fifth Republic'.

[2] *Aube*, 4 May 1948.

Chapter 3

THE MOUVEMENT REPUBLICAIN POPULAIRE (MRP)

EMERGENCE AND CHARACTERISTICS

MRP arrived spectacularly on the French political scene. In 1936 less than 3 per cent of the French electorate had voted for the Parti Démocrat Populaire and Jeune République; in 1945–46 no less than 25 per cent voted for MRP. Mushroom growth by French parties and political movements has not been uncommon, for example the Boulangists in the 1880s and Poujadists in the 1950s, but usually parties of this type have quickly been cut to size or disintegrated. To some extent MRP suffered from its rapid growth, but the party nevertheless settled down, after the 1947 desertions to the Gaullist RPF, to a position of major importance in the politics of the Fourth Republic. MRP's electorate of 5,000,000 in November 1946 was halved in 1951, but there was virtually no change in 1956. And, although the party's parliamentary representation dropped from over 170 to under 100, MRP continued to play an important governmental role owing to the continuing necessity for coalitions of the centre.[1]

Edmond Michelet, one of the few MRP deputies who left the party to join de Gaulle's RPF in 1947, said at the time that MRP was 'Catholic against its wishes and the child of the Resistance. . . . The party draws strength and weakness from its dual background'.[2]

[1] MRP's electoral performance in the Fourth Republic:

	Votes	% of electorate	% of votes	seats*
21 Oct. 1945	4,580,222	18·6	23·9	150
2 June 1946	5,589,213	22·6	28·2	166
10 Nov. 1946	4,988,609	19·9	25·9	173
17 June 1951	2,369,778	9·8	12·6	95
2 Jan. 1956	2,366,321	8·8	11·1	83

* includes seats won by overseas deputies of the group Indépendants d'Outre-Mer (IOM), affiliated to MRP. Figures from P. M. Williams *French Politicians and Elections*, 1951–1969, p. 293.

For details about MRP's electoral performance and geography in the Fourth Republic, see pp. 86–91.

For Fifth Republic, see Chapter 8, pp. 231–51.

[2] Quoted in Fauvet, *Forces Politiques*, p. 168.

MRP was certainly a Catholic party despite its attempt to embrace non-Catholics, and it became a major force on the French political scene owing to the Resistance record of its early leaders and militants.

The Resistance paved the way for the emergence of MRP in two important ways. It showed that Catholics, at least of the Left, could co-operate loyally with other Republicans, and it provided MRP with an élite of leaders, something which the PDP had always lacked. Henri Michel has pointed out that in the early days of the Resistance men of very different backgrounds, such as Freemasons and Catholics, worked closely together.[1] It was only later that groups such as Combat and Libération emerged as essentially Catholic and essentially Socialist, although the distinctions between the Catholic and Socialist membership of the two organizations remained blurred until the end of the war. Moreover, the creation of the Conseil National de la Résistance (CNR) in April 1943 helped to conceal the differences which were emerging. Jean Moulin, who set up the CNR, was de Gaulle's personal nominee, and de Gaulle was determined to keep the Resistance as united and non-partisan as possible. From the point of view of MRP's future emergence, it was significant that Georges Bidault was elected President of the CNR by the members of that body after the capture and execution of Jean Moulin in June 1943. (De Gaulle's uneasy relationship with Bidault doubtless owed something to the fact that he did not himself appoint Bidault to the Presidency of the CNR.) The unity of the Resistance can, of course, be exaggerated. The largely Communist Francs-Tireurs et Partisans (FTP) constituted an autonomous network within the nationally organized Forces Françaises de L'Intérieur (FFI—set up in February 1944). The CNR's Resistance Charter did not go much beyond the Popular Front ideas of 1936,[2] and was regarded as no more than a stepping-stone by the Communists, whilst conservative members of the CNR, such as Joseph Laniel, regarded it as too socialist. Nevertheless, the French Resistance, unlike that in Greece, did not split into distinct factions.

Catholics, including a number of priests, were prominent in the FFI. Former members of Catholic Action youth groups were particularly important in the Southern Maquis,[3] and in Normandy a young Catholic militant, Henri Bouret, later an MRP deputy, organized a major Resistance network whilst still in his twenties. Max André, a founder member of MRP, was Vice President of the Comité Parisien de la Libération, an organization led by the Com-

---

[1] H. Michel, *Histoire de la Résistance en France*, p. 231.
[2] J. Chapsal, *La Vie Politique en France Depuis 1940*, p. 71.
[3] Robert Aron, *Histoire de la Libération*, p. 124.

munist Georges Marrane. Three of the fourteen members of Bidault's CNR were future MRP Ministers—the President himself, François de Menthon and Pierre-Henri Teitgen. Many former PDP and JR members were prominent in their opposition to Pétain and the Germans, and the stand which they took during the war conferred prestige on MRP as well as preparing the way for their own political advancement.

Maurice Schumann, first President of MRP, had been the London 'Voice of France' for four years. Born a Jew and converted to Catholicism in the 1930s, Schumann's greatest assets were enthusiasm and affability. At times his enthusiasm verged on fanaticism, and it was thus that he acquired nicknames such as 'Savonarola' and 'the mad virgin of Carlton Gardens',[1] but his background as a Jeune République militant and *Résistant de la première heure* was an advantage to MRP. As a junior Minister in the Fourth Republic he showed a lack of political judgment, but as an orator at MRP congresses he could not be faulted, at least not by the faithful.

Georges Bidault, who succeeded Schumann as President of MRP, naturally was an important asset owing to his Presidency of the Resistance Council (CNR). He had been a PDP militant in the 1930s, but was never elected to the Chamber, although he was the party's foreign affairs expert. He contributed regularly to *L'Aube*, whilst continuing to teach history at the Lycée Louis Le Grand in Paris. His most famous articles were those in which he spoke out fearlessly against the Munich settlement.[2] Unfortunately Bidault developed a 'Munich complex' in the Fourth Republic, especially with reference to colonial policy, where every concession was seen as a surrender. This attitude led him finally to break with MRP in 1958 with the establishment of Démocratie Chrétienne as an *Algérie française* party, followed by his involvement in OAS in the early 1960s.[3] This tragic end to Bidault's career, however, cannot detract from his very real contribution to the emergence of MRP and to his country as Prime Minister and Foreign Minister in the decade after the war. François Goguel noted in 1952 that Bidault's 'greatest weakness' was that 'he has too high an opinion of himself'.[4] There is no need to qualify this judgment now, although it should be added that Bidault was frequently a sick man, partly as a result of his propensity for drinking. The combination of intellectual arrogance and poor

[1] Gordon Wright, *The Reshaping of French Democracy*, p. 74.
[2] *Aube*, 20, 22, 29 and 30 September 1939. And see Françoise Mayeur, p. 149.
[3] See 226. OAS = Organisation Armée Secrète, the fascist organization which was determined to keep Algeria French at any price.
[4] Einaudi and Goguel, p. 167.

health resulted in rather a disappointing career after a brilliant beginning.

Also prominent in the Resistance were Francisque Gay, friend of Marc Sangnier since the days of the Sillon and founder of *L'Aube*, which was the first Paris newspaper to be banned by the Germans in 1940; François de Menthon, a Professor of Law at Nancy, member of an ancient Savoy family and future MRP Minister; Peirre-Henri Teitgen, another lawyer, who had the good fortune to escape from a train carrying him to a concentration camp in Germany in 1944; like Menthon, Teitgen was to be an important MRP Minister in the Fourth Republic.

Another asset to MRP was Robert Schuman, for he was capable of reassuring those Conservatives who were contemplating voting MRP *faute de mieux* in the hope that the new party of the Fourth Republic would not be too iconoclastic, i.e. 'socialist'. Although he had voted for Pétain in 1940 and played almost no part in the Resistance compared with those mentioned above, Schuman had taken an unequivocal stand against the Germans after being briefly imprisoned by them in 1940. He escaped to the Vichy zone, where he was constantly sought by the Milice and Gestapo. According to his biographer, Schuman changed houses at least twelve times between August 1942 and the Liberation.[1] Schuman's Resistance seems to have been verbal rather than physical, but he had done enough to receive pardon for his vote of 10 July 1940. He could thus stand for the Constituent Assembly in 1945 and was successively Finance Minister, Prime Minister and Foreign Minister in the early years of the Fourth Republic. Schuman was immensely popular in MRP as a sincere Catholic, a moderate man and, above all, in the 1950s, as a European integrationist. Ironically, Schuman himself was not an MRP *inconditionnel*; once, when asked if he was fully committed to MRP, he replied, 'I am a Catholic from Moselle'.[2] He was such a poor speaker that Bidault compared him to 'an engine running on low grade petrol', to which Schuman retorted, 'Everyone cannot have an engine which runs on alcohol'.[3] Alain Poher said that MRP militants liked Schuman above all for his humility and sincerity.[4] This was no doubt why they gave him a standing ovation annually at Congress. It certainly was not on account of the type of classical rhetoric which earned standing ovations at Radical conferences.[5]

The Resistance provided MRP with prestige and a party élite, but

[1] Rochefort, pp. 128–34.   [2] J. Fauvet, *La IVe République*, p. 132.
[3] ibid., p. 131.   [4] Interview with Poher, 24 March 1970.
[5] Cf. F. de Tarr, *The French Radical Party from Herriot to Mendès-France*, pp. 16–17.

MRP's Resistance background was not an unmixed blessing. Many Conservatives and moderates got on to the MRP bandwagon in 1945–46. Their own parties had been discredited by their Vichy connections, and they voted MRP not because they wanted a 'new France' with greater economic and social justice, but because they wanted to clear their consciences or because they were anti-Communist. They were *with*, but not *of*, MRP. Like the Gaullists, who wrongly assumed that *le Parti de la Fidélité* would play follow-my-leader to the General whatever the circumstances, most left MRP in 1947. The desertion of MRP by these groups weakened the party numerically, but, like the Catholic Church after the Counter-Reformation, MRP emerged smaller but more united. Nevertheless, it is arguable that this early over-inflation did more harm than good. The party's organization was stretched to the limit, too many early deputies lacked political experience and, when the desertions came, the militants were more depressed than they might otherwise have been. MRP came near to being the spoilt child of the Resistance.

MRP's connections with Catholicism, like its Resistance inheritance, both helped and hindered the party. Unlike the German CDU, MRP made very little impression on the non-Catholic electorate. Robert Lecourt stated emphatically at the end of the war that MRP was not a Catholic party,[1] and former MRP leaders are fond of asserting that the party had non-Catholic members, but in fact the agnostic Max André, the Protestant Lagravière and the Jew Léo Hamon were very much exceptions to the rule.[2] The post-war Catholic revival, the strength of Catholic Action and the broad support of the Catholic trade union federation, CFTC, may be said to have benefited MRP. From almost every other point of view the party's failure to rid itself of a 'confessional' image was a disadvantage. Above all, it resulted in MRP being a regional party, in contrast to both the German CDU and the Italian DC.

William Bosworth has analysed the political and social importance of Catholic Action in post-war France, and there is no need to discuss it in depth here.[3] In the context of MRP, however, it should be emphasized that Catholic Action provided MRP with grass-roots support, and, perhaps even more important, with leaders at all levels. Catholic Action is a general term used to describe all Catholic lay groups approved by the Hierarchy. These groups had no specific

[1] *Aube*, 16 May 1945.
[2] See pp. 87–91 for details about MRP's Catholic electorate.
[3] For information on Catholic Action organizations contained in the next three paragraphs, see Bosworth, pp. 97–155, and A. Latreille and R. Rémond, *Histoire du Catholicisme en France*, pp. 592–609 and 651–7.

political role, but naturally many of their members were interested in politics. Catholic Action had its origin in the Association Catholique de la Jeunesse Française (ACJF), founded by Albert de Mun in 1886, but the movement received real impetus in the late 1920s and early 1930s with the establishment of Jeunesse Ouvrière Chrétienne (JOC), Jeunesse Agricole Chrétienne (JAC), Jeunesse Etudiante Chrétienne (JEC) and Jeunesse Indépendante Chrétienne (JIC). The young Christian Workers, Farmers, Students and Independents worked under the umbrella of ACJF until the early 1950s when ACJF, in trying to dominate the youth organizations, lost control of them completely, going into voluntary liquidation in 1956. Many MRP leaders had been active in the Catholic youth organizations before the war. André Colin and Jean Letourneau had presided over ACJF, Paul Bacon had led JOC and Robert Lecourt had been President of the Fédération Française des Etudiants Chrétiens (FFEC), to which JEC was affiliated. In 1959 seven out of the thirteen members of MRP's National Bureau had been in Catholic Action and all the others had been involved in other Catholic organizations. Thirty of the thirty-nine members of the National Executive Committee had also been active in Catholic organizations.[1]

After the war, Catholic Action spread amongst adults. Action Catholique Ouvrière (ACO), founded in 1950, was in effect the senior brand of JOC, and JAC, after raising its age limit from 18 to 30, grew to almost 300,000 in the mid-1950s, and by 1961 had won control of the Fédération Nationale des Syndicats d'Exploitants

---

[1] The members of the National Bureau (Catholic connections in brackets) were: A. Colin, President of MRP (ACJF), M. R. Simonnet, Secretary General of MRP (ACJF), C. Bosson (ACJF), A. Apirault (Semaines Sociales), A. Poher (FFEC), R. L'Helguen (JOC), P. Pflimlin (Institut Catholique, Paris), R. Schuman (Third Order Franciscan), L. Dubois (JAC), G. Hourdin (President, *La Vie Catholique Illustrée*), P-H Teitgen (PDP), M. Schumann (*Jeune République*), F. Lefebvre (ACO). National Executive Committee: R. Lecourt (FFEC), P. Bacon (JOC), R. Buron (Director, *La Vie Catholique Illustrée*), J. Fontanet (JEC), R. Charpentier (JAC), H. Dorey (CFTC), N. Rombeaut (CFTC), P. Gabelle (CFTC), M. Blin (JEC), G. Boulanger (JAC), C. Mont (JEC), A. Fosset (ACJF), M. Byé (Semaines Sociales), G. Le Brun-Kéris (JEC), J. de Montgascon (ACJF), Jean Catrice (ACJF), G. Touquet (UFCS), R. Poudouson (JOC), J-P. Prévost (JEC), P. Farine (JEC), M. Lucas (ACJF), P. Dhers (ACJF), J. Raymond-Laurent (Sillon, PDP), E. Grabouty (Coeurs Vaillants, Ames Vaillantes), C. Ferise (Editions du Cerf), E. Borne (CCIF), J. Fonteneau (JOC), G. Delfosse (JOC, CFTC), C. Flory (ACJF, Semaines Sociales), F. Bouxom (JOC, CFTC). The nine members without Catholic Action or other specifically Catholic connections were: M-M. Dienesch, L. Raymond-Clergue, J. Lecanuet, H. Claireaux, C. Barangé, G. Peyroles, A. Edot, R. Dorfliner, J. Teitgen.
Information given by J-P. Prévost, in Bosworth, p. 254.

Agricoles (FNSEA), the most important farmers' organization. JAC was complemented by the Mouvement Familial Rural (MFR), an organization which was similar to ACO but less class-bound. With the exception of MFR, however, Catholic Action for young people remained essentially a working-class phenomenon. The Young Students and Independents had a total membership of under 2,000 in the late 1950s, whereas JOC and JAC (including the females of JOCF and JACF) had about 350,000 members.

The general Catholic Action adult organizations, Action Catholique Générale, Hommes (ACGH) and Action Catholique Générale, Femmes (ACGF), founded in 1945, were less active than JOC, ACO, JAC and MFR, but had a total membership of over a million. The Associations Familiales Catholiques (AFC), a family organization with around 50,000 members, the 5,000 Catholic employers of the Centre Français du Patronat Chrétien (CFPC) and the small number of writers and academics of the Centre Catholique des Intellectuels Français (CCIF) were not, strictly speaking, part of Catholic Action. But all these organizations tended to strengthen the grass-roots support for MRP even if French Catholics voted less decisively for their Christian Democratic party than those of Holland, Germany and Italy. Moreover, although the Catholic Action organizations were not specifically committed to any form of political action, Bosworth has shown that some of them, notably JOC, ACO and JAC, made clear their progressive Catholic views on subjects as far apart as housing conditions in France and colonial policy in Indo-China, whilst other groups took up a political stance, albeit an equivocal one, in their various publications. This stance probably tended to favour MRP rather than the Conservatives and Gaullists, although its effect on the voting habits of the readers seems to have been limited.

The degree of trade union support for MRP is no easier to quantify than that of Catholic Action. The essentially Catholic trade union federation, Confédération Française des Travailleurs Chrétiens (CFTC), which had been set up in 1919, made a distinct break with the Hierarchy in the post-war period. Article I of its revised Statutes stated that CFTC welcomed all workers, 'whatever their personal, philosophical, moral and religious convictions, provided they are determined to struggle for a democratic society of free and responsible human beings'.[1] Like all French trade union federations, CFTC maintained a nominal independence of political parties, but in practice its relations with MRP were close, particularly in the

---

[1] *CFTC Statutes*, p. 5.

immediate post-war period.[1] With the failure of *la révolution par la loi* and MRP's movement to the Right over economic and colonial policy, CFTC's links with MRP became more tenuous. The growing importance of the Reconstruction group, who favoured a complete break with the Hierarchy and MRP, demonstrated CFTC's fears about direct association with the Church and Christian Democracy. By the late 1950s Reconstruction was commanding up to 40 per cent of the mandates at CFTC conferences, and its final triumph came at the special conference of 1964 when 90 per cent of the delegates voted to change CFTC's name to Confédération Française Démocratique du Travail (CFDT).[2] After 1964 CFDT's contacts with MRP were minimal, in contrast to the early post-war period and a brief interlude at the beginning of the Fifth Republic when trade union influence on MRP was quite important.[3]

Although CFTC shunned the Hierarchy, it was openly supported by the bishops in 1945:

> We earnestly remind all Catholics that their place is in the Christian trade unions which, truly professional and free, draw their inspiration from Christian morality and Christian social doctrine. Such unions must be preferred to the Socialist or Communist unions, inspired by materialist conceptions of life, of work, and of society.[4]

MRP was never supported in such a decisive manner either by the Hierarchy or by CFTC. Nevertheless, in the immediate post-war period no less than 31 of MRP's 173 deputies came directly from CFTC, although they had to resign their CFTC membership on election to the National Assembly.[5] Several of the 31 played an influential role in MRP. Paul Bacon and André Monteil both became Ministers, whilst Francine Lefebvre, Joseph Dumas, Maurice Guérin, Fernand Bouxom and Marcel Poimboeuf were prominent members of the National Assembly, all taking a particular interest in social and economic problems. Guérin and Poimboeuf lost their

[1] Interview with Vignaux, 14 January 1967. Vignaux was leader of the Reconstruction group in the CFTC.

[2] The minority continued as La CFTC Maintenue. It consisted essentially of the Catholic miners' union, which was strong in Lorraine and Alsace. Several progressive MRP deputies, notably Henri Meck, had close connections with the miners' union.

[3] Interview with Goguel, 23 March 1970.

[4] Romain, *Le Syndicalisme en France*, p. 137, quoted in Bosworth, p. 270.

[5] I am indebted to Paul Vignaux of CFTC (now CFDT) for figures on CFTC background of MRP deputies; interviews, 23 December 1966 and 14 January 1967.

seats in 1951, but the others remained as deputies throughout the Fourth Republic. The number of MRP deputies of trade union background was cut to 14 out of 95 in 1951 and 10 out of 83 in 1956. Nevertheless, an analysis of MRP deputies and the militants who attended National Congresses suggests that about 20 per cent of MRP's élite was working-class. Many members of CFTC, of course, did not vote MRP. The CFTC had about 700,000 members in 1958, of whom perhaps 150,000 voted MRP.[1] It has been shown that CFTC membership was highest in those Departments of the west, north-east and southern Massif Central, where MRP and Catholic Action were also well represented.[2] And, although it is impossible to correlate CFTC and Catholic Action membership with Christian Democratic voting, it seems clear that MRP gained more than it lost by its association with CFTC and Catholic Action.

The same cannot be said of MRP's other Catholic connections. After 1951 the Hierarchy did not openly support MRP, but its endorsement of the party in the immediate post-war period may well have done MRP more harm than good in a country where anti-clericalism remains a potent force despite the fact that at least 80 per cent of Frenchmen are baptised Catholics. The de-christianized regions of France and the religiously apathetic workers could not be expected to take much interest in a party which could so easily be labelled 'confessional'. Likewise, MRP found itself supported only by overtly Catholic newspapers, although in the early days *Le Monde* and a number of provincial papers were inclined to endorse MRP policies.[3]

In a discussion of the characteristics and structure of MRP it is necessary to say something about the Catholic press in France. In the immediate post-war period all newspapers suffered from a lack of newsprint, and many (especially Radical and Conservative) from the Provisional Government's refusal to grant a licence. As regards licences, MRP was fortunate in that Pierre-Henri Teitgen, de Gaulle's Minister of Information, was originally responsible for granting them. As a result, MRP developed a flourishing Parisian and provincial press. The party, however, was soon affected by national press trends. Party political dailies rapidly lost their popularity. Between January 1946 and March 1950 *L'Humanité* (Communist) lost 58 per cent of its readers, *Le Populaire* (Socialist) 85 per cent and *L'Aube* (MRP) 75 per cent. There was a tendency for provincial newspapers to gain at the expense of national newspapers; in 1939 the provincial press accounted for 46 per cent of the total, whereas in 1957 it

---

[1] Bosworth, p. 274.   [2] ibid., p. 373.

[3] Grosser, *La IVe République et sa Politique Extérieure*, p. 168.

accounted for 63 per cent. Paris papers were distributed less in the provinces than they had been before the war, and in Paris itself the number of dailies declined from thirty-two in 1945 to thirteen in 1957.[1] Provincial dailies tended to concentrate less on political comment and more on general, usually local, news. This had a particularly bad effect on MRP, which had to rely on provincial press support after the collapse of *L'Aube* in 1951. Some of these provincial papers were quite important, notably *Ouest-France* in Normandy and Brittany, *La Liberté du Centre* in the Limoges area, and *Nord-Eclair* in Nord, but, in the opinion of Jean-Pierre Prévost, they did little to help MRP owing to their superficial interest in national politics.[2]

Whilst it is true that Fourth Republican dailies, with the major exception of *Le Monde*, tended to avoid serious political coverage, the opposite is true of the weekly press. MRP fared better here, although none of the well-known Catholic weeklies were specifically committed to the party. Georges Hourdin's *La Vie Catholique Illustrée* (circulation 600,000 in 1957)[3] was closest to MRP but was the least political of the Catholic weeklies. In so far as it engaged in political comment, it tended to support the moderate leadership of MRP, although it was critical of MRP's colonial policy in the early 1950s. Georges Suffert's *Témoignage Chrétien* (circulation about 50,000)[4] represented the progressive wing of MRP. In 1951 it was concerned lest the schools question be allowed to disrupt the MRP-SFIO coalition. When the Barangé Law did just this, it attacked the party for participating in Pinay's Government and abandoning its social and economic objectives. *Témoignage Chrétien* was also bitter about MRP's colonial policy, being consistently ahead of the party over Indo-China, Tunisia and Morocco. It was so outspoken over Algeria that it was condemned by the Assemblée des Cardinaux et Archevêques in 1958. Although an important organ of the MRP Left, *Témoignage Chrétien* probably contributed little to a party whose electorate was basically conservative. At the other end of the political spectrum was the Gaullist weekly *Carrefour*. Although it was not specifically Catholic or Christian Democratic, it was important as the organ of the extreme right of MRP.[5] Its colonial opinions were similar to those of the Bidault faction, which in 1958 broke away to

[1] For above figures, see Grosser, p. 162; Einaudi and Goguel, p. 163.

[2] Interview with Prévost, 12 July 1966.

[3] Jacques Maître, *Le Fonctionnement de la Presse Catholique en France*, mimeographed study for Association Française de Science Politique, 1957, p. 6.

[4] ibid., p. 19.

[5] Interview with Prévost, 12 July 1966. Bidault and his friends quite often wrote for *Carrefour*.

form Démocratie Chrétienne, a right-wing Christian Democratic group whose main interest was the defence of Algeria.

Perhaps more important for MRP were three periodicals, *Terre Humaine, France-Forum* and *Esprit. France-Forum* was founded in 1957 as a monthly review of Christian Democratic inspiration. It has always contained a mixture of doctrinal articles and contemporary political comment. Although not specifically committed to MRP, nearly all its contributors were prominent Christian Democrats. *France-Forum's* predecessor, edited by Etienne Borne, was *Terre Humaine* (1951–57). More concerned with doctrine than with political comment, *Terre Humaine* had an important influence amongst Christian Democratic intellectuals despite its limited circulation of less than 4,000. *Esprit* was never an MRP periodical, but its influence on the party was considerable:

> Founded as an expression of Mounier's 'personalist' philosophy, *Esprit* has never claimed to be Catholic. But its major contributors are Catholics and its political position is very close to that of the Catholic left. In addition *Esprit* has had a decisive influence on an entire generation of left-wing Catholics.[1]

Esprit was critical of the Barangé Law and even more of the conservative Barangé majority which governed France from 1951–56. It adopted a position similar to that of *Témoignage Chrétien* over colonial policy, and was one of the first French publications to insist that Algeria had become a nation which deserved independence. With a circulation of about 15,000, *Esprit*,[2] which is almost as much an 'institution' as a periodical, undoubtedly influenced a minority of MRP intellectuals and militants, but, like the other Catholic weeklies and reviews mentioned above, its contribution to the growth of MRP as a broad political movement was limited.

MRP's own publications were, broadly speaking, a failure. *L'Aube* was MRP's national daily from 1945–51, although it was never accepted by the party as its official organ. If it had been, there is no reason to assume that its fate would have been different. *L'Aube's* circulation was 230,000 in June 1946; by June 1951 it was 45,000;[3] the last copy of the paper was sold on 20 October 1951. *L'Aube* collapsed partly for technical reasons such as escalating distribution costs, which multiplied twenty-five times between September 1944 and January 1948;[4] partly also on account of certain national tendencies, such as the decline of party political newspapers, especially those based on Paris. But this was not the whole story,

---

[1] Bosworth, p. 188. [2] Maître, p. 9.
[3] Einaudi and Goguel, p. 163. [4] Vaussard, p. 117.

for a newspaper like *Le Monde*, starting from scratch in 1944, survived and prospered. At the Liberation every authorized paper was given enough newsprint and paper for 150,000 copies per day. *Le Monde* decided to print only 75,000 copies, but on four pages. *L'Aube*, like most of the other newspapers, printed its full quota, but with only two pages. One result was that *Le Monde* won over a serious though limited readership. *L'Aube* failed to do this, partly because it had insufficient space for serious articles. By 1946 the newsprint shortage was less acute and *L'Aube's* circulation exceeded 200,000, but the policy of obtaining a high circulation at the cost of poor quality was mistaken. By 1947 René Guyomard was calling for more subscribers to *L'Aube*.[1] In the same year Francisque Gay, *L'Aube's* owner and Editor-in-Chief, who had run the paper in the 1930s when its circulation never exceeded 20,000, left Paris to become France's Ambassador in Canada. His successor in charge of *L'Aube* was Jean Letourneau, of whom Maurice Vaussard wrote, 'His only aspiration was to get back to being a Minister again.'[2] At the 1948 MRP Congress René Guyomard said, 'The press as a whole is going through a very difficult period; and *L'Aube* is no exception.'[3] Letourneau appealed for more sales, 'the indispensable condition for the survival of our national newspaper'.[4] In 1949 and 1950 Jean Fonteneau made similar appeals,[5] but *L'Aube* died in 1951. It had survived for its last two years only thanks to contributions from ministerial 'special funds'.[6]

L'Aube published a number of well-argued and thoughtful articles such as those by L. P. Aujoulat on the French Union in April 1946, and an excellent series on governmental and administrative reforms by Robert Lecourt in August 1950, but on the whole its political comment was superficial and bombastic, like Maurice Schumann's editorials on colonial policy between 1947 and 1951. Bidault, who contributed a weekly editorial after the fall of his Government in July 1950, seemed to be affected by the generally trivial style of *L'Aube*. Gone were the days of Bidault's thorough analyses of foreign policy, which had been one of the features of *L'Aube* in the 1930s. It is perfectly possible that by 1950 it was too late to save *L'Aube*, whatever the style of Bidault's articles or the extent of his prestige in MRP. *L'Aube* had fallen between two stools. It had

[1] MRP Congr. 1947, Paris; report on 'Le Mouvement'.
[2] Vaussard, p. 118.
[3] MRP Congr. 1948, Toulouse; report on 'La Vie du Mouvement'. [4] ibid.
[5] MRP Congresses, 1949 and 1950, Strasbourg and Nantes; reports on 'La Vie du Mouvement'.
[6] Vaussard, p. 118.

catered only for a mass readership, and when that readership abandoned it, *L'Aube* had nothing to fall back on.[1]

MRP's official publications included *Forces Nouvelles* and a number of tracts for distribution amongst militants. *Forces Nouvelles* was at first a weekly but became a fortnightly in 1947. It was the official organ of the party leadership and as such was full of deadly orthodoxy. It was not a publication in which policies were discussed, and André Denis was justified in his complaint that party members were never allowed to express dissenting views in *Forces Nouvelles*, a criticism later echoed by Pierre Corval with reference to MRP's North African policy.[2] *Forces Nouvelles's* most useful contribution to political debate was contained in its occasional special numbers, such as those by Georges Le Brun-Kéris on Indo-China and North Africa in 1954 and by Pierre-Henri Teitgen on the French colonies of Black Africa in 1956.[3]

MRP's tracts for militants included *Action Rurale* for farmers, *Pour Agir* for women, *Pour Servir* for youth, *Consignes d'Action* for workers and *MRP à l'Action*. Of these, the most widely distributed was the fortnightly *MRP à l'Action*, a simplified version of *Forces Nouvelles*, but, judging by the comments made annually at Congresses by *rapporteurs* such as Guyomard and Fonteneau,[4] the militants took little interest in reading or distributing the tracts published by the party. Overall, the failure of the MRP press was less a cause than a symptom of the failure of MRP to develop into a mass movement for political education and political action.

ELECTORAL GEOGRAPHY, PERFORMANCE AND SOCIOLOGY

With a limited press, 'confessional' image and artificially swollen electorate, it was not surprising that MRP had difficulty in maintaining its position outside traditionally Catholic regions.

Any student of French electoral geography is indebted to François Goguel and his colleagues at the Foundation Nationale des Sciences Politiques for the work they have done in this field.[5] The analysis of

---

[1] A certain number of *L'Aube's* readers no doubt changed to *La Croix*, a Paris Catholic daily with a circulation of about 150,000 in the late 1950s (Bosworth, p. 196), but *La Croix's* support for MRP was always very discreet (Rémond, p. 77).

[2] Denis in *Monde*, 5 February 1954 (Denis had been expelled from MRP in January 1954; see p. 103); Corval, interview, 7 February 1967.

[3] G. Le Brun-Kéris, *Indochine, Tunisie et Maroc*, June 1954; Pierre-Henri Teitgen, *Pour Sauver l'Afrique Francaise*, July 1956.

[4] E.g. Guyomard at 1948 Congr.; Fonteneau at those of 1949 and 1950; reports on 'La Vie du Mouvement'.

[5] See in particular F. Goguel, *Géographie des Elections Françaises Sous la*

MRP's electoral performance in this section makes no pretence to originality except in so far as some of the surveys of the Institut Français de l'Opinion Publique (IFOP) and MRP's own studies of electoral and party sociology help to fill in one or two gaps.

The first five years of the Fourth Republic are crucial in any study of MRP's electoral performance, for between 1946 and 1951 MRP's vote fluctuated considerably. Thereafter the percentage of votes cast for the party settled down to about 11 per cent until the General Election of 1962.[1] It is, therefore, appropriate to compare MRP's performance at the Election to the first legislature of the Fourth Republic (10 November 1946) with its performance at the Election to the second legislature (17 June 1951). Some account must also be taken of Council of the Republic elections, municipal and cantonal elections, and, of course, of the General Election of 2 January 1956, which largely confirmed the results of the 1951 General Election as far as MRP was concerned. The results of the Council of the Republic, municipal and cantonal elections are not strictly comparable with those of General Elections owing to different methods of election, the importance of individual candidates at local elections and MRP's failure to present candidates in all constituencies at local elections (this applies particularly to cantonal elections).

In November 1946 MRP polled almost 5,000,000 votes (20 per cent of the registered electorate, 26 per cent of votes cast), figures which were broadly in line with those of October 1945 and June 1946 (elections for the two Constituent Assemblies). In June 1951 the party obtained just under 2,500,000 votes (10 per cent of the registered electorate, 12·5 per cent of votes cast), and in January 1956 MRP polled the same number of votes, although its percentages of the registered electorate and of votes cast had now dropped to 9 per cent and 11 per cent respectively.[2]

Maps 1 and 2 (pp. 92–3) show the comparative strength of the MRP vote in 1946 and 1951. In both years MRP was strong in the west, particularly in the Departments of Finistère, Manche, Orne, Ille-et-

---

Troisème et la Quatrième Republique (revised edition, 1970) and *Cahiers de la Fondation Nationale des Sciences Politiques* (especially no. 82 on 1956 Election, no. 109 on 1958 Elections and Referendum, no. 142 on 1962 Elections and Referendum). See also F. Goguel, 'Géographie des Elections du 21 Oct. 1945', *Esprit* (December 1945); P. M. Williams, 'The French Elections', *The Fortnightly* (September 1951), and analyses in RFSP after various elections.

[1] This section concentrates on MRP's electoral performance in the Fourth Republic. See chapter 8 for a discussion of MRP's role and performance in the Fifth Republic.

[2] For MRP vote at General Elections in the Fourth Republic, see p. 74, n. 1.

Vilaine, Mayenne, Maine-et-Loire and Vendée, and to a lesser extent in Côtes-du-Nord, Loire Inférieure, Sarthe, Deux-Sèvres and Vienne.[1] The party also polled well in the north-east, especially in the Departments of Moselle, Bas-Rhin and Haut-Rhin, and in the mountainous country near Switzerland, especially in the Departments of Jura and Haute-Savoie. It also had isolated pockets of strength in the Departments of Nord, Basses-Pyrénées, Aveyron, Drôme and Loire. In sum, MRP was strong in the west, the north-east (plus the Department of Nord) and in a broken strip of territory running from Savoy to the western Pyrenees by way of the southern Massif Central. The regional characteristics of MRP were confirmed at the 1956 Election, when the party obtained the votes of over 15 per cent of the electorate in seventeen departments, of which six were in Normandy and Brittany and five in Alsace-Lorraine; four others were in the Savoy area (Map 3, p. 94).

The MRP electorate was mainly conservative and mainly Catholic. Goguel has shown the similarity between the areas of moderate-conservative strength in 1936 and MRP strength in 1946, a pattern which was confirmed in varying degrees by the Council of the Republic election of 1948, the cantonal elections of 1949 and the General Elections of 1951 and 1956.[2] After 1951 approximately half of MRP's deputies (37 out of 83) came from conservative departments in the north-east and Catholic west, and a quarter had held their seats in alliance with Conservatives against Socialists.[3] This pattern was repeated in 1956 when 44 out of 70 were elected from the same conservative departments, often in opposition to candidates of the left-wing Republican Front.[4]

MRP, however, did gain a foothold in a few Departments which had not had a strong moderate-conservative vote before the war. In 1946 MRP polled at least 10 per cent of the votes of the registered electorate in Aisne, Ardennes, Saône-et-Loire, Isère, Drôme, Tarn and Charente-Maritime, all of which had had a low moderate-conservative vote in 1936. MRP held its vote at over 10 per cent in all these Departments except Ardennes and Saône-et-Loire in 1951, to which Drôme and Charente-Maritime were added in 1956. Probably women's suffrage was the prime reason for MRP's con-

[1] For map of French Departments, see p. 95.

[2] Einaudi and Goguel, pp. 176–7, 182, 184; Goguel, *Elections*, pp. 123, 127, 145, 147, 175; Fauvet and Mendras *Les Paysans et la Politique*, pp. 123–7; Williams, p. 109 and 110, notes 19–22.

[3] Williams, p. 105.

[4] Not all the MRP votes in the west were conservative, in particular in the Departments of Finistère, Côtes-du-Nord and Mayenne. Nevertheless, the generalization about MRP's vote being essentially conservative is valid.

tinued penetration in these areas where the moderate-conservative electorate had been relatively weak.[1]

Whilst it is true that MRP's main support came from Departments which had been moderate-conservative before the war and from urban areas with a sizeable Catholic bourgeoisie, the party also won a significant number of working-class votes in certain industrial areas, notably in Alsace-Lorraine and in parts of Nord. According to an IFOP poll of June 1946, 34 per cent of workers voted Communist, 22 per cent Socialist and 18 per cent MRP.[2] In the municipal elections of October 1947 MRP's urban vote was cut by about 60 per cent. In the 344 cities with over 9,000 inhabitants, MRP's vote went down from 1,250,000 in November 1946 to 500,000, i.e. from 23·8 per cent of votes cast to 10·2 per cent; and in Paris MRP did even worse, receiving only 5·4 per cent of votes cast.[3] However, MRP recovered from this low point, and in 1949 Fonteneau claimed that one quarter of MRP's members were working class,[4] a figure which was put at 20 per cent in 1951.[5] Amongst MRP deputies 24 per cent were wage-earners in 1946, 19 per cent in 1951 and 18 per cent in 1956.[6] The percentage of working-class participation at National Congresses seems to have been even higher, at least in the 1940s. An analysis of the social categories of the 891 non-parliamentarian *congressistes* of 1947, 1948 and 1949 indicates that 38 per cent had a working-class background.[7] Of course, party membership and Congress attendance figures do not have a direct relationship to the social characteristics of a party's electorate, but they can be a useful pointer, as was shown by an IFOP poll of 1952 which indicated that 21 per cent of MRP voters were working-class.[8] The 1953 municipal elections confirmed MRP's relative strength in areas where the CFTC was strong.[9] MRP gained 208 seats in towns of over 9,000 compared with 1947. The party lost seats in some southern towns, notably Marseilles, Toulon and Lyon, but gained in Alsace, Ardennes, Nord, Pas de Calais, Seine-Inférieure and in Normandy

[1] Goguel, *Elections*, p. 108. And see p. 91, notes 1 and 2 below, on religious practice and female voting.

[2] *Sondages*, 16 July 1946.

[3] Einaudi and Goguel, p. 180.

[4] MRP Congr. 1949, Strasbourg; report on 'La Vie du Mouvement'.

[5] MRP Congr. 1951, Lyon; report on 'La Vie du Mouvement'.

[6] 1946 figure calculated from social categories of deputies as given in *Assemblée Nationale, 1re Législature, Notices et Portraits* (November 1946); 1951 and 1956 figures from M. Dogan, *Partis Politiques et Classes Sociales en France*.

[7] Calculated from details about *congressistes* given at end of reports on MRP Congresses.

[8] *Réalités*, May 1952.

[9] See Bosworth, p. 353, for map showing CFTC strength in 1955.

and Brittany. Studies of voting figures at polling stations (*bureaux de vote*) suggested that MRP was gaining ground amongst the working classes.[1] The gains were probably quite small, but MRP's working-class vote, apart from the 1947 municipal elections, seems to have been consistently around the 15 per cent mark in the Fourth Republic,[2] and in the early years of the Fifth Republic the working-class elements within the party, led by Bernard Lambert, Théo Braun and Nestor Rombeaut, were to play a significant part in trying to orientate the party to the Left.[3] MRP, as its progressive leaders were well aware,[4] failed to make a decisive break into the working-class vote, which remained predominantly Communist, but the party's electorate included a significant and loyal minority of wage-earners, even if it is true that most MRP voters were rural and conservative.

The other major characteristic of the MRP electorate was, of course, that it was Catholic. MRP was not a 'confessional' party in the sense that it favoured direct links with the Catholic Church and hierarchy. There was no reference to either in the party's Statutes, (unlike those of the CFTC until they were changed in 1964). Except in 1945–46 the hierarchy did not openly advise Catholics to vote MRP.[5] This contrasts with the decisive support given to the Italian DC by the hierarchy. MRP, nevertheless, remained a Catholic party in terms of sociology and electorate. There were close contacts between MRP ministers and Catholic bishops.[6] The party élite nearly all had a Catholic Action background.[7] And in the National Assembly MRP defended the attitudes and interests of the Church in debates on issues involving moral principles, such as family policy, education and censorship.

An IFOP poll of 1952 showed that 54 per cent of regular Catholic churchgoers voted for MRP, compared with 20 per cent for Conservatives (Moderates and Independents) and 18 per cent for RPF.[8] Forty-three per cent of MRP voters claimed they were con-

---

[1] According to Fonteneau at MRP Congr. 1953, Paris; report on 'Les Elections Municipales et la Vie du Mouvement'.

[2] On the basis of electoral studies and opinion polls, Williams estimates that about 360,000 industrial workers voted MRP, p. 109, note 14.

[3] See chapter 8, p. 244, note 1.

[4] Interview with Buron, 23 December 1966; and with Monteil, 30 June 1970.

[5] In 1951 *Osservatore Romano* advised Catholics to vote against parties which advocated *laïcité*, but did not propose a specific vote for MRP. This advice may well have benefited Gaullists and Conservatives more than MRP (see Bosworth, p. 285).

[6] Rémond, *Forces Religieuses et Attitudes Politiques*, p. 77; and interview with Buron, 23 December 1966.

[7] See p. 79, note 1.   [8] *Réalités*, November 1952.

siderably influenced by the Church in their voting habits, compared with 26 per cent of Conservatives and 18 per cent of Gaullists.[1] Yet MRP probably obtained the votes of only a minority of the practising Catholic electorate. Although 54 per cent of those who went regularly to Mass in 1952 claimed to vote MRP, Fogarty has calculated that if this had in fact happened in 1951, MRP would have obtained at least 15 per cent of votes cast and not just 12 per cent.[2] It seems clear that it was the male practising Catholics who let MRP down, for 66 per cent of the females claimed to have voted for MRP in 1951.[3] MRP's problem was that it was not 'confessional' enough to obtain all the Catholic votes, but too 'confessional' to obtain anything but Catholic votes.

In conclusion, MRP was a regional party, although it made a partial break-out from the pre-war confines of the PDP; a rural party, although it had a sizeable urban working-class electorate in Alsace-Lorraine and Nord; a conservative party, although many militants and a few leaders were determined not to be shackled by their conservative electorate; and a Catholic party, although its founders had striven hard to avoid a 'confessional' image.

ORGANIZATION, DISCIPLINE, LEADERSHIP

We are a Movement, not an electoral machine. . . . Through our Movement we must realize an ever closer union between the people in their diverse social groupings and the Government. . . . We must make contact with the social, professional and economic organizations, listen to their suggestions, and win them over to our Movement.[4]

Jean Fonteneau's remarks at the 1951 party Congress were fundamental to MRP thinking, but not original. Year after year those who reported to the Congress on 'La Vie du Mouvement' pointed out that the aim of MRP was to be a great *rassemblement* of ordinary men and women, inspired by their political doctrine and humanitarian ideals to reform the republican regime. Aiming at political education as much as electoral success, MRP laid great emphasis on its grass-roots organization.

---

[1] ibid. Goguel has also shown the striking similarity between areas of 'satisfactory religious practice' and of MRP strength, *Elections*, p. 175.

[2] Fogarty, p. 358; a conclusion supported by Rémond, p. 79.

[3] *Réalités*, November 1952. Forty-six per cent of the Gaullist vote was female, 41 per cent of the Conservative, 32 per cent of the Socialist, 30 per cent of the Communist and 27 per cent of the Radical.

[4] MRP Congr. 1951, Lyon; report on 'La Vie du Mouvement'.

Map 1: National Assembly Elections of 10 November 1946

MRP vote (as percentage of registered electorate).
From Goguel, *Géographie des Elections Françaises*, p. 109.

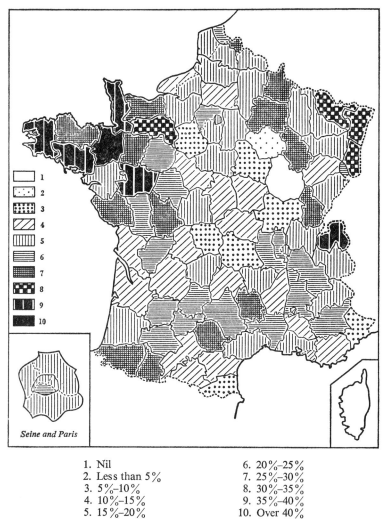

1. Nil
2. Less than 5%
3. 5%–10%
4. 10%–15%
5. 15%–20%
6. 20%–25%
7. 25%–30%
8. 30%–35%
9. 35%–40%
10. Over 40%

Map 2: National Assembly Elections of 17 June 1951

MRP vote (as percentage of registered electorate).

From Goguel, p. 127.

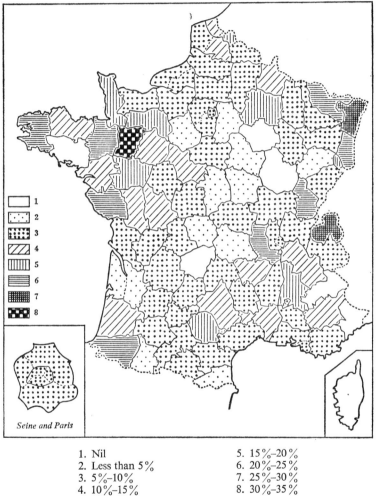

1. Nil
2. Less than 5%
3. 5%–10%
4. 10%–15%
5. 15%–20%
6. 20%–25%
7. 25%–30%
8. 30%–35%

Map 3: National Assembly Elections of 2 January 1956

MRP vote (as percentage of registered electorate).

From Goguel, p. 147.

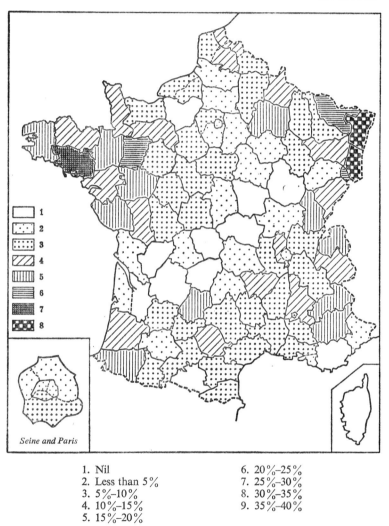

Seine and Paris

1. Nil
2. Less than 5%
3. 5%–10%
4. 10%–15%
5. 15%–20%
6. 20%–25%
7. 25%–30%
8. 30%–35%
9. 35%–40%

Map 4: French Departments

In the original party Statutes of 1944 the Federations, together with the Sections and specialized teams (*équipes*), were seen as the most important elements within the Movement. The role and organization of the departmental Federations was outlined before that of the national organs.[1] MRP was to be a democratic movement with ideas flowing from base to summit and vice-versa. In practice, although the research teams did much valuable work, the Federations

[1] The MRP Statutes consisted of eight chapters: I Objectives; II Organization; III Federations; IV National Congress; V National Committee; VI National Executive Committee; VII Discipline; VIII Revision of Statutes.

95

and Sections did not fulfil the dynamic role envisaged for them. This was partly due to the decreasing enthusiasm of the militants, who soon found that political education was much less exciting than clandestine Resistance had been. Some militants were disillusioned by the Fourth Republic's apparent failure to achieve a profound social and economic revolution, others by MRP's tendency to become more and more like an 'ordinary' political party. They saw their great new Movement succumbing to Robert Michels's 'oligarchic' tendencies and becoming what Duverger calls a 'caucus party'.[1]

The failure of democracy within MRP doubtless owed more to human lethargy than to anything else. Nevertheless, the party's organization did not help. The original party Statutes were decisively weighted in favour of the leadership despite the important role apparently assigned to the militants. The amendments of 1950 and 1955 did nothing to increase militant influence. The important structural reforms of 1959, on the other hand, helped to produce a more democratic party, but they came too late. This minor injection of blood could not revive the ailing patient. MRP's organizational structure outwardly resembled that of the SFIO, but, unlike SFIO, MRP suffered from too little, not too much, militant influence. Neither party succeeded in striking a balance between leadership and participation.

Within the MRP structure the departmental Federation was supposed to play a vital co-ordinating role. All MRP members had to be members of a Federation, composed of at least five Sections with a total membership of not less than one hundred. The Federation ran its own specialized teams for women, workers, young people and professional groups. It elected its own bureau consisting of a President, two Vice-Presidents (one of whom had to be a woman), Secretary and Treasurer. All over eighteen could vote at Federation and Section meetings; secret voting was obligatory for the election of officials and for all other matters at the request of one quarter of those present. Federations could group together on a provincial basis, for example the departmental Federations of Calvados, Eure, Manche, Seine-Inférieure and Orne formed the Regional Council of Normandy.[2]

Despite the apparent possibility for vigorous action by the

[1] R. Michels, *Political Parties*; M. Duverger, *Political Parties*, especially pp. 17–23.
[2] There were ten such regional councils: Région du Nord, Alsace-Lorraine, Bretagne, Normandie, Poitou, Limousin, Massif Central, Provence, Région Bordelaise, Région Toulousaine.

Federations, they were in practice constrained by the party leadership, under-represented on the national organs, limited by financial weakness, and debilitated by the members' apathy. The party Statutes laid down that each Federation's statutes should be approved by the national Executive Committee; that reports of all meetings should be sent to the national Secretariat; that candidates for parliamentary elections, selected by the Federations, should be endorsed by the national Executive Committee. In addition, the reports of the departmental Congresses held immediately prior to the national Congresses were apparently often ignored by the party Secretariat,[1] although these reports were supposed to be the basis for the reports discussed at the annual Congresses. Equally frustrating was the tendency to ignore militant opinion in the National Committee and the Executive Committee, although this was less easy after 1959.[2]

The financial weakness of the Federations was chronic, partly through their own fault. The 1947 Congress agreed that each member of the party should give one day's pay to his Federation; in 1948 Guyomard reported that the results of the appeal for a day's pay had been 'far from what was expected';[3] in 1949 Fonteneau pointed out that three-quarters of the Federations could not employ any full-time officials. He reminded members of their promises of 1947 and 1948, and told them that only one Federation (Eure) had, in fact, taken the trouble to hold a campaign to raise the money. He castigated the Federations for their lack of initiative. If the Federation of Basses-Pyrénées could cover its annual expenses by running a fête, and that of Loire-Inférieure by investing in a children's playpark, why should the others be in a permanent state of financial crisis?[4]

Above all, the Federations suffered from lack of commitment by the militants. There may have been good reasons for this, such as the depressing effect of Communist and Gaullist attacks and the general disappointment at the failure of *la révolution par la loi*. Whatever the reasons, the fact remains that the militants were largely inactive—with one important exception, those who worked in the specialized teams.[5] Fonteneau told the 1949 Congress that MRP was democratically organized but lacked democratic 'life';

---

[1] E.g. at MRP Congr. 1953, Paris, complaints to this effect were made by several militants in the debate on 'La Vie du Mouvement'.

[2] See pp. 100–1.

[3] MRP Congr. 1948, Toulouse; report on 'La Vie du Mouvement'.

[4] MRP Congr. 1949, Strasbourg; report on 'La Vie du Mouvement'.

[5] See pp. 98–9.

Federations and Sections were not meeting enough, they were slack about distributing party leaflets, too few ideas were being sent up to party headquarters.[1] In 1950 Fonteneau said that the Federations, and especially their secretariats, were the key to electoral success in 1951, and yet a recent inquiry by the Executive Committee had indicated that there was insufficient contact between Federations and Sections and that the Federations were failing in their task of co-ordinating the work of the Sections.[2] These criticisms were echoed in the 1950s. Borne told the 1954 Congress that unless MRP militants devoted more time to political education and propaganda, 'the Republic of militants is in danger of becoming the Republic of notables'.[3] In 1956 Fonteneau appealed again for more effort:

May our Federations and Sections develop into true forces for democracy! May serious thought and reflection impregnate all levels of the Movement, so that each person can contribute to its decisions . . . In the solitude of politics, we need to work as a team.[4]

Such emotive appeals drew forth the applause of Congress, but were no more effective in obtaining grass-roots commitment than the 1959 reforms.[5] After the first flush of enthusiasm, the vast majority of MRP converts, like most French Catholics, were non-practising.

The specialized teams (*équipes*) were an exception, although even they were not free from criticism at party Congresses. The first specialized teams functioned in the departments under the supervision of the Federation. Later there were special research teams who worked under the national Secretariat. The departmental teams were organized by social category under six headings: women, youth, workers, peasants, managers and liberal professions. They were supposed to be the shock-troops of the Movement, and, in so far as MRP had an élite, it consisted of the members of the specialized teams. Jacques Fauvet described the departmental teams as the key to MRP success in 1945.[6] Seventeen years later an inquiry in *L'Express* came to a similar conclusion, emphasizing that many members of the specialized teams had learned enthusiasm and discipline in Catholic Action groups before joining MRP.[7] The specialized teams made inquiries into specific problems such as housing. Their reports

[1] MRP Congr. 1949, Strasbourg; report on 'La Vie du Mouvement'.

[2] MRP Congr. 1950, Nantes; report on 'La Vie du Mouvement et la Propagande'.

[3] MRP Congr. 1954, Lille; report on 'Le Sens de Notre Engagement Politique'.

[4] MRP Congr. 1956, Montrouge (Paris); report on 'La Vie du Mouvement'.

[5] See p. 100.   [6] *Monde* 13 December 1945.

[7] *Express*, 12 April 1962.

were sent to party headquarters in Paris, and often formed the basis of a national report such as Georges Coudray's on *La Politique du Logement* (1951). The success of reports such as these led to the establishment of a permanent team of national specialists, who either made their own inquiries and reports or co-ordinated the work done by the Federation teams. The Federation teams also held spasmodic national congresses of their own, usually in election years, although the Equipes Ouvrières, led by the energetic Georges Delfosse, had an annual congress from 1950.[1] At national Congresses, too, there were special meetings for representatives of the teams, whose leaders occasionally had a chance to report to the whole Congress on their work. Jean Gilibert reported in this way on behalf of the Equipe des Jeunes in 1949. The Equipes Ouvrières were constantly prodding the party with their critical motions, and in 1953 and 1956 defeated the party platform on workers' control and on day-release for young workers.[2] The Catholic farmers were also very active, and by 1961 progressive Catholics were in control of the main farmers' union, FNSEA.[3]

Fonteneau, in his various reports on 'La Vie du Mouvement', was inclined to praise the specialized teams whilst criticizing the Federations and Sections,[4] and René Plantade agreed that some of the most important work done at the Rue de Poissy (MRP Headquarters) was that of the national specialized teams.[5] There can be no doubt that the various teams were an essential, and original, part of MRP, but at times they made MRP look rather like an army which has cavalry but no infantry. MRP seemed to have an élite corps but all too few troops on the ground.

The national organs of MRP were the National Committee,[6] the Executive Committee,[7] the National Bureau[8] and the National

---

[1] Other *équipes* held irregular national congresses, e.g. the Equipes Féminines held one such on 3–4 February 1951 in Paris; *Aube*, 5 February 1951.

[2] MRP Congr. 1953, Paris; see also Williams, p. 108. MRP Congr. 1956, Montrouge (Paris).

[3] See chapter 5 on Agriculture.

[4] E.g. MRP Congr. 1948, Toulouse, praise for Equipes Féminines and Equipes des Jeunes, and 1951 Congr., again praise for Equipes Féminines. On both occasions, as in many other years, the Federations were criticized for their apathy; reports on 'La Vie du Mouvement'.

[5] Interview with Plantade, 24 April 1967.

[6] Called Conseil National, 1944–50; then Comité National after revision of party Statutes at Nantes Congress. It will be referred to in the text as the National Committee.

[7] Called Comité Directeur, 1944–50; then Commission Exécutive. It will be referred to in the text as the Executive Committee.

[8] Called Commission Exécutive Permanente, 1944–50; then Bureau National. It will be referred to in the text as the National Bureau.

Congress. All four were dominated by the party leadership, i.e. leading parliamentarians, even after the 1959 reforms. The National Committee was charged with 'representing MRP, . . . executing the decisions of Congress and controlling the Federations'.[1] Its 200-odd members met three times a year until 1950 and six times thereafter. Up to one-third of the membership came from the parliamentary groups (National Assembly, Council of the Republic and Assembly of the French Union). The President and Secretary of MRP, the Presidents of the three parliamentary groups and the Presidents of the three parliamentary chambers (if they happened to be in MRP), together with members of the Government, were *ex officio* members; the Federations were represented by elected militants;[2] the specialized teams elected twelve members, and the Executive Committee itself appointed ten more militants 'in recognition of their functions, position or services'.[3] At any given time well over half the National Committee were *ex officio* members, parliamentarians or government ministers.

As a result of the 1959 reforms, which were designed to give greater scope to *les forces vives* within the Movement, the number of militants on the National Committee was increased by twenty-nine (twelve representatives of the specialized teams, two representatives of town councillors and fifteen representatives of the Federations, including five from Federations without parliamentary representation). At the same time this increase in grass-roots representation on the National Committee was offset by the decision to include all parliamentarians, not just one third, as *ex officio* members.[4] The 1959 reforms produced a larger National Committee (about 200 instead of 150, to which it had dropped in the 1950s), and militant representation went up from about 30 per cent to 40 per cent, but the militants never came near to a majority on the National Committee, which in any case was a less important body than the Executive Committee or the National Bureau.

One important new task of the enlarged National Committee was to elect the National Bureau, hitherto elected by the Executive

[1] MRP Statutes, Art. 31.

[2] On the basis of 1 representative per 1,000 members, and 1 for each fraction of 1,000 over 100, i.e. a Federation with 3,200 members sent as many representatives (4) as a Federation with 3,900 members. This system benefited the smaller Federations, although it did not favour them as decisively as the sliding scale used for selecting delegates for National Congresses; see p. 102, note 1.

[3] MRP Statutes, Art. 32.

[4] The National Treasurer and his assistant also became *ex officio* members of the National Committee. For full details of the 1959 reforms, see report of MRP Extraordinary Congr. 31 January–1 February 1959, Clichy (Paris).

Committee. The Bureau, a key permanent organ responsible for the everyday running of MRP, now had eight elected members out of thirteen, instead of seven.[1] The Bureau was a skeleton of the Executive Committee. After the 1959 reforms the membership of the Executive Committee, totalling about forty-five, was unchanged except that it was now elected by a larger, more representative National Committee. The Executive Committee, which met fortnightly, was the most important central organ in MRP. It was large enough, and met with sufficient regularity, to become the party's main decision-making body,[2] and, although the *ex officio* members of the Executive Committee could not exceed one-quarter of its total membership, their influence was out of all proportion to their numbers owing to their own political experience and the militants' deference and loyalty.[3]

As early as 1944 a Cher militant, M. Leloup, suggested that it was a mistake to give the party leadership such influence in the three main national organs,[4] but his criticisms were ignored. One of the results was that by 1947 other militants were complaining that the party leadership had already lost touch with the rank-and-file. M. Thébaud of Charente called on MRP ministers and deputies 'to behave like militants, and not like Radical-Socialists'.[5] Criticisms of this type were repeated in the 1950s by men like Francisque Gay and André Denis, and later still by Robert Buron.[6]

In theory the supreme national authority of MRP lay neither with the local organizations nor at party headquarters, but with the annual party Congress. In practice, this Congress, like that of the annual

---

[1] Prior to 1959 the six *ex officio* members of the Bureau were the President, Secretary General and Treasurer of MRP, together with the Presidents of the MRP groups in the National Assembly, Council of the Republic and Assembly of the French Union. Honorary Presidents, of whom there had been three (Sangnier, Bidault and M. Schumann), had also been *ex officio* members. Now they were dropped, in order, it seems, to save the party the embarrassment of officially expelling Bidault. After 1959 the Bureau had five *ex officio* members: the President, Secretary General and Treasurer of MRP, and the Presidents of the MRP groups in the National Assembly and Senate. No more than five of the eight elected members were to be parliamentarians (in fact, only three of the eight elected at Clichy were—R. Schuman, M. Schumann and A. Poher).

[2] At the inaugural MRP Congr., November 1944, Jean Catrice called it 'le moteur . . . qui animera l'action du MRP'.

[3] Cf. Duverger, p. 137; and interviews with Mme Lefebvre, 7 June 1967, and Hourdin, 6 June 1967.

[4] MRP Congr. 1944, Paris; debate on 'L'Organisation du Mouvement'.

[5] MRP Congr. 1947, Paris; debate on 'La Vie du Mouvement'.

[6] Gay in *Les Démocrates d'Inspiration Chrétienne à l'Epreuve du Pouvoir*; Denis in *Monde*, 5 February 1954; Buron, interview, 23 December 1966.

conference of the British Labour Party, was dominated not by the party delegates but by the leaders of the parliamentary party. And the parliamentary leaders, as *ex officio* members of the National Committee and Executive Committee, naturally continued to control party policy between Congresses. Even at the Congress itself the voting procedure favoured the parliamentarians. Members of the National Committee, the National Assembly, the Council of the Republic and the Assembly of the French Union were given personal votes. Apart from parliamentarians, the only other voting members of Congress were the official departmental delegates, but they were selected on a sliding scale which reduced the influence of the largest Federations.[1] In 1947 four of the seven largest Federations were in Brittany and Alsace, essentially regions of Catholic and conservative strength.[2] If MRP had allowed the big Federations more influence, it would probably have developed even faster as a regional party, although, paradoxically, not necessarily as such a conservative party, because the two biggest Federations, Nord and Seine, were inclined to be the most progressive. However, the main reason for the sliding scale was to strengthen the party leadership *vis-à-vis* the big Federations, thus avoiding the type of clash which characterized relationships within SFIO.[3]

Nearly all the speeches at Congresses were made by leading party members. The same major *rapporteurs* appeared year after year— André Colin, Albert Gortais, Jean-Jacques Juglas, Jean Fonteneau, Georges Le Brun-Kéris—not necessarily the most prominent MRP politicians, but men of great influence within the party. MRP's parliamentary leaders—Robert Schuman, Georges Bidault, Maurice Schumann, Jean Letourneau, Pierre Pflimlin—were more likely to give an opening or closing address (usually the latter) than to make specific policy statements. Robert Schuman, despite his incompetence as a speaker, received a standing ovation almost every time he spoke. So did Jean Letourneau, even when his Indo-China policy was clearly a failure. So did Georges Bidault, even at his last Congress in 1957,

---

[1] The Federations had one representative per fifty members for the first two hundred; one per hundred from two hundred to five thousand; and one per two hundred thereafter. MRP Statutes, Article 25. Williams, p. 107, draws the contrast between MRP and SFIO—'whereas a Socialist Federation with two hundred members had nine delegates and one with two thousand had eighty-one, MRP allotted them four and twenty-two respectively'.

[2] The seven largest Federations were Nord (20,500 members), Seine (17,075), Pas de Calais (6,000), Finistère (6,000), Ille-et-Vilaine (4,400), Morbihan (3,100), Bas-Rhin (3,000); MRP Congr. 1947, Paris.

[3] Duverger, p. 144; Williams, p. 107.

when his extreme *Algérie française* position was totally opposed to the views of the vast majority of the delegates.[1]

General debates on policy tended to be limited, although they could be lively, especially when economic and social policies were being discussed. At Nantes in 1950 there was considerable criticism of the party's failure to obtain progressive social legislation, and Joseph Dumas, one of the main critics, received a surprising number of votes when he challenged André Colin for the party Secretary-ship (Colin 314, Dumas 212). Occasionally motions were passed against the wishes of the platform, but they were usually ignored by the leadership. In 1952 François de Menthon proposed that MRP should leave the Government in protest against Pinay's economic policy; in one of the longest debates at a National Congress he was supported by many others, including the respected André Monteil and Joseph Dumas, but Bidault, at his last Congress as President of MRP, successfully defended the party's continued participation in the Government.[2]

MRP, of course, had its disciplinary problems, but they did not normally lead to expulsion from the party. Charles d'Aragon, Paul Boulet and Abbé Pierre might well have been expelled for their opposition to the Atlantic Alliance (amongst other things), but they resigned in 1950 before the party leadership had to act. André Denis was an exception, but his misdemeanours would have resulted in expulsion from most parties. In October 1953 he sent a circular to all the Federations criticizing the party's policies and leadership; he spoke against his own party at public meetings; and he was an open critic of the European Defence Community (EDC). Despite this indiscipline, Denis was only finally expelled by a 71–30 vote in the National Committee.[3] Léo Hamon and Henri Bouret lost the

[1] MRP Congr. 1957, Paris; debate on Colin's report on 'La France d'Outre Mer'.

[2] MRP Congr. 1952, Bordeaux. Pinay eventually resigned in December 1952 without waiting for a vote when MRP decided as a party to abstain over family allowances in a budget vote. MRP 'mutinies' have been succinctly summarized by Philip Williams (p. 105): 'In 1950 a third of MRP deputies frustrated Queuille's attempt to form a conservative ministry. Two years later the same proportion withheld their support from Pinay, whose administration (detested by the militants) was brought down in December 1952 by an MRP revolt. In the long ministerial crisis of the following summer half the deputies opposed Reynaud, three-fifths supported Mendès-France, almost all repudiated Marie, and only with extreme reluctance did they resign themselves to Laniel. At the beginning of Mendès-France's government in 1954 most of them voted him special economic powers, and on his fall they did their best to recover a left-wing reputation by supporting a Socialist, Christian Pineau, for the premiership.' See also Williams, p. 246, note 20, and p. 397, note 3.

[3] *Monde*, 10 January 1954.

party whip at the end of 1954 for voting against EDC, and André Monteil, Jean-Jacques Juglas and Robert Buron were temporarily expelled for joining Mendès-France's Government in 1954–55. At the 1955 Congress Jean Fonteneau emphasized the importance of party discipline, and Congress unanimously passed a new disciplinary clause by which members participating in a Government opposed by the party were automatically expelled.[1] MRP was the most disciplined party in the Fourth Republic apart from the PCF, but it relied less on disciplinary techniques than on loyalty, based on common doctrinal objectives and Resistance memories. Monteil, Juglas and Buron were all welcomed back into the party before the end of 1955, and Bidault, despite his setting up of Démocratie Chrétienne,[2] was never officially expelled from MRP. When this was proposed at the special Congress at Clichy in 1959, Maurice-René Simonnet, the party's Secretary General, said it was unnecessary to expel Bidault, because 'he has placed himself outside the Movement'.[3]

The MRP leadership also showed skill in controlling its followers. Criticism of colonial policy was allayed by references to 'conciliating' North African nationalism and granting 'independence' to the Associated States of Indo-China.[4] Although men like Kenneth Vignes and Pierre Corval criticized the North African policies of Bidault and Maurice Schumann,[5] most members of MRP accepted their leaders' statements at face value.[6] It was only after MRP left the Government in 1954 that party leaders such as Pierre-Henri Teitgen spoke out decisively in favour of concessions to the nationalist parties, the Tunisian Néo-Destour and the Moroccan Istiqlal. From the mid-1950s party members and militants constantly argued that French policy in North Africa was incompatible with the ideals of Christian Democracy. The war in Indo-China, on the other hand, had been opposed (by a small group), not on moral but on economic grounds.[7] Like the Mendésists, the MRP liberals, who favoured a negotiated peace with Ho Chi Minh, criticized the war chiefly because it was retarding economic and social recovery in the Métropole. But their voice was largely unheard. Loyalty to the party

---

[1] MRP Congr. 1955, Marseilles.   [2] See chapter 7, p. 226.

[3] MRP Extraordinary Congr. January 1959, Clichy (Paris).

[4] Cf. final declarations at MRP Congresses, 1951, Lyon, and 1953, Paris.

[5] W. S. Lee, *French Policy and the Tunisian National Movement* (Oxford D. Phil., 1963) pp. 85–90, and interview with Corval, 7 February 1967.

[6] Interview with Hourdin, 6 June 1967. After the deposition of the Sultan of Morocco, August 1953, Hourdin paid a special but ineffective call on Bidault to protest that the deposition was in direct conflict with MRP policy as laid down at successive Congresses.

[7] See chapter 7 on Colonial Policy.

leaders precluded effective criticism of their disastrous policy in Indo-China.

Indeed, party unity, both in terms of disciplined voting and loyalty to the leaders, was one of the most important characteristics of MRP. The schisms which occurred at the time of the Pinay and Mendès-France Governments were exceptions to the rule. MRP soon closed ranks again. Even the foundation of de Gaulle's RPF did not really affect the unity of the party,[1] although it affected its electoral support. Whenever MRP's progressives were over-critical of the party leadership, appeals were made for loyalty such as had been given to MRP leaders when they were in the Resistance. J-M. Domenach once compared an MRP Congress to an Old Comrades' Meeting,[2] whilst Robert Buron said Congresses were like religious services; instead of political issues being discussed, delegates were given a spiritual uplift.[3] Francine Lefebvre pointed out that the leaders of MRP nearly all knew each other from pre-war Catholic Action groups.[4] André Colin, Robert Lecourt, Georges Bidault and Jean Letourneau had all been prominent members of such groups, and the vast majority of MRP deputies and militants also came from a Catholic Action background, where they had learned to respect those in authority. In Georges Hourdin's opinion this common religious and wartime experience of the MRP rank-and-file was the most important single reason for the party's continued loyalty to its leaders after their drift to the Right.[5] Whatever the reasons, MRP, like the British Conservative Party, tended to think critically about its policies only in times of crisis.

[1] At the 1948 Congr., Toulouse, René Guyomard pointed out that no MRP Federation had followed its deputy in supporting the Gaullist RPF, although eleven MRP deputies left the party in 1947 to join the RPF (the most prominent figures being Edmond Michelet and Louis Terrenoire).

[2] *Observateur*, 22 June 1950.   [3] Interview with Buron, 23 December 1966.

[4] Interview with Lefebvre, 7 June 1967.

[5] Interview with Hourdin, 6 June 1967.

Chapter 4

ECONOMIC AND SOCIAL POLICY

MRP, like the other parties of government in the post-Liberation period, was determined to change France's traditional economic and social patterns. MRP advocated the implementation of the Resistance Charter, whose main economic proposals were:

> ... the introduction of genuine economic and social democracy, entailing the eviction of the economic and financial monopolists from their control of the economy;
> ... increased national production in accordance with a plan drawn up by the Government after consultation with all those concerned in the processes of production;
> ... the return to the nation of the large industrial monopolies, the sources of energy, the natural resources, the insurance companies, the large banks;
> ... the right of workers to have access within their firms to the functions of control and management, and the participation of workers in the running of the economy.

Equally important were the social provisions of the Charter:

> ... the improvement of the system of work contracts;
> ... the guarantee of a wage and pensions which can assure security, dignity and the possibility of a full life to each worker and his family;
> ... restoration of free and independent trade unions, endowed with the right to play an important role in economic and social life;
> ... a comprehensive social security system, ensuring that all citizens who cannot earn a living are looked after, with joint control of social security by the State and the insured.[1]

With the Conservative parties in disarray, it was not difficult to introduce changes which were meant to be revolutionary. The leading banks and insurance companies and the coal, gas and electricity industries were taken over by the State in 1945–46. A nationwide system of social security was introduced by the Laws of 4 October 1945 and 22 May 1946. A national Planning Commission was

[1] AP, 1944–45, pp. 430–1.

established in January 1946 (the Commissariat du Plan under Jean Monnet). Government intervention in the economy was not new in France, but in the Fourth Republic the State began to play a positive role, stimulating and guiding, rather than merely protecting, French industry and agriculture.

MRP always found itself in a slight dilemma over national economic and social planning. Basically the Christian Democrats favoured planning in depth, but at the same time they were always suspicious of the powers of the State. They were as critical of collectivism as of individualism. Thus, they wanted a nationwide social security system, but the beneficiaries, not the State, should administer it. They favoured State control of monopolies and a degree of nationalization, but trade unions and employers should be allowed to negotiate their own wage agreements (at least in the private sector). Workers should be allowed to participate in the management of companies, but workers' control was not advocated. Some members of the party were outspokenly 'interventionist'; others adopted a more *laisser faire* approach. These nuances within MRP exposed the party to criticisms from Right and Left. It was not difficult to accuse the self-styled reconcilers of MRP as hypocrites, or to contend that a party which adopted some of the arguments of both sides was sitting on the fence. Nevertheless, there can be little doubt that the majority of Christian Democrats were genuinely committed to *la révolution par la loi* in social and economic policy, particularly in the early years of the Fourth Republic.

MRP always saw economic and social policy as complementary: economic and social democracy were as essential as political democracy for man's development as a responsible and 'whole' human being. Thus, it is appropriate to discuss social and economic policy in the same chapter, but, for the sake of clarity, some attempt has been made to differentiate between the two. And, for the sake of brevity, no attempt has been made to cover all aspects of economic and social policy in the Fourth and Fifth Republics. Instead, three 'case studies' have been chosen, because they are particularly illustrative of Christian Democratic attitudes in these areas.

PLANNING AND NATIONALIZATION

MRP's first manifesto (1944) called for 'an economy controlled by the State' and 'an economic plan to increase the wealth of all by the rational exploitation of the nation's resources and by the organization of production in such a way that it benefits society as a whole and not just the capitalists'.[1] Pierre-Henri Teitgen said that the first step towards a planned economy was 'the nationalization of the key industries, in particular mines, electricity, banks and insurance, . . . because the French nation can no longer work for capitalism'.[2] For MRP, nationalization was not an end in itself. The party had no *a priori* conviction that nationalization was an economic panacea, but Joseph Dumas contended that the Government could not run the economy for the benefit of all if the large monopolies and service industries were not in the hands of the State.[3] And Marcel Poimboeuf, one of MRP's trade union deputies, made the same point in the National Assembly, emphasizing the State's role as 'promoter and arbiter of the common good',[4] which meant that the State should take over private concerns only where they threatened a large number of people through their monopolistic and financial strength. In other words, MRP's advocacy of nationalization was a by-product of its enthusiasm for national planning. 'Nationalization', said André Colin, MRP's first Secretary General,

> is not an end in itself, but a means by which the pressure of private interests on the State can be reduced. What we need is not so much individual 'nationalizations' as the 'nationalization' of the economy as a whole, that is the planning of the economy as a whole, so that all national resources can be put at the service of the nation.[5]

Pierre Pflimlin, one of MRP's more conservative spokesmen, announced as early as 1947 that, although he fully supported the nationalizations which had already taken place, it would be a mistake to nationalize any other industries:

> I say this quite emphatically. It must be made clear to industrial firms that there is no question of further nationalization. If a firm has to live under the threat of nationalization, it cannot be expected to develop its own initiatives for modernization and progress.[6]

At the 1949 Congress there was a proposal for the nationalization of the chemical industry, but Paul Bacon said that what was needed was more effective control of the present nationalized industries rather than the extension of nationalization.[7] Thereafter MRP, for

[1] MRP Docs no. 2.
[2] MRP Congr. 1944, Paris; report on 'La Politique Générale du Mouvement'.
[3] ibid.   [4] JO (AN), 4 July 1945, p. 1301.
[5] MRP Congr. 1945; report on 'La Politique Générale'.
[6] MRP Congr. 1947, Paris; report on 'La Politique Economique et Sociale'.
[7] MRP Congr. 1949, Toulouse; report on 'La Politique Economique'.

whom State ownership had never been a doctrinaire issue, gave up all interest in further nationalization. The party showed much greater concern for national planning than for nationalization, perhaps principally because they saw a certain 'moral' purpose underlying the plan: man could be liberalized and humanized through economic growth and social progress. It was important that the government should plan for such growth and progress, but State ownership of industry was relevant only in so far as it made national planning possible. This pragmatic attitude towards nationalization was justified by the course of events, because nationalization did not prove to be such a revolutionary step as had been anticipated (or feared). The publicly-owned industries were no less profit-conscious than private companies. Some proved to be extremely progressive, others were less enterprising. Electricité de France and the Société Nationale des Chemins de Fer (nationalized in 1936) gained a world reputation for the high standard of their technical analysis as well as for their efficiency. The nationalized coal industry and telephone service, on the other hand, never succeeded in operating profitably or efficiently, although the former was in a particularly difficult situation owing to poor coal seams and antiquated machinery. The nationalized banks soon came under the influence of traditional financiers, a development criticized by François de Menthon at the 1951 Congress.[1] The nationalized car company, Renault, set high standards in labour relations as well as in exporting, but the privately owned Peugeot, unlike Citroën, was also a successful exporter. There was little to choose between two very competent aircraft firms, Sud Aviation (nationalized) and Dassault (privately owned).

If nationalization soon became a non-issue, planning did not, or at least the degree and control of planning did not. Broadly speaking, there were two main tendencies in MRP. Pierre Pflimlin, Robert Schuman and Robert Lecourt represented the more conservative approach. Like all Christian Democrats they believed in some degree of State planning, but they saw the Plan primarily as a guide and indicator, not as a precise instrument of government policy. François de Menthon, Pierre-Henri Teitgen and Maurice Byé, on the other hand, were firm believers in interventionist planning, although they did not go as far as some CFTC leaders in 1959. Paul Bacon and Charles Barangé, although advocates of workers' participation and profit-sharing, were inclined to adopt a minimalist position with regard to State intervention. They were, therefore, representative of

[1] See p. 111.

another tendency in MRP, being more progressive in social than in economic affairs.

In his Report on Economic Reform at the 1947 Congress, Bacon said that he favoured *une économie d'entreprise*, defined as one in which employers and employees could develop their own initiative to the maximum for the benefit of all members of the company concerned: 'The State should intervene only to stimulate initiative where it is lacking and to co-ordinate effort so that over-production is avoided in one sector of the economy whilst there is under-production in another'.[1] At the same Congress Pflimlin said that 'planning' had been a dirty word before the war because at that time it had been completely negative, providing France only with a 'protective corset'. He went on:

> The Monnet Plan is quite different. It is *dirigiste*, not in a protective, but in a stimulative sense. The Plan will give the economy the possibility of expansion and revival, . . . it can and must stimulate and guide production, but there is no question of direct intervention *vis-à-vis* manufacturers. . . . What we want is a mixed economy, which is quite different from a controlled economy of bureaucratic or corporatist character. The Government will see that the civil service and the nationalized industries fulfil their obligations under the Plan, but in the private sector it will rely mainly on the goodwill of manufacturers.[2]

The principles outlined by Pflimlin in 1947, and largely repeated by Barangé in 1951, were in fact those on which the Plan operated, for French plans, although they have varied in their objectives, have all consisted of a series of general indicators. Although economic growth rates are outlined, and particular emphasis is given to specific sectors of the economy, French plans are not precise 'target' plans like those of the Soviet Union. The Government encourages particular areas of the economy by granting favourable credit facilities but it does not normally use coercive measures to implement its outline objectives, and the latter have often not been achieved, as in the Third (1954–57) and Fifth (1966–70) plans, which were well wide of the mark. The one exception to the rule was the First Plan (1946–50, extended to 1953), which concentrated on six basic industries, coal, electricity, public transport, agricultural machinery, steel and

[1] MRP Congr. 1947, Paris; report on 'La Réforme de l'Economie et de l'Entreprise'.

[2] ibid.; report on 'La Politique Economique, Financière et Sociale'. Cf. Pflimlin's report on 'Une Politique de Productivité' at 1953 Congr. for similar view.

cement, setting specific targets for each. And, when the Planning Commission did not agree with the rather conservative proposals put forward by the privately owned steel companies, it rejected them out of hand and set new targets for production and modernization, the acceptance of which was made a condition for the grant of government loans.

In general, however, the minimum intervention policy, advocated by men like Pflimlin and Schuman, was followed, but there were many Christian Democrats who would have liked a more global and interventionist approach to planning. In 1949, for example, Bacon, after admitting the slowness of economic and social progress (despite the relative success of the re-equipment programme), called for the establishment of a 'Ministry of the National Economy', which would control speculators and ensure a fairer distribution of the national income, as well as implementing the Monnet Plan.[1] Bacon also said that social policy must be linked to economic planning, a theme developed by Menthon in 1951 and 1952 and by Byé in 1954 and 1960. Menthon told the 1951 Congress that governments should not be afraid to intervene directly in the economy, and that 'une veritable administration économique' was required to co-ordinate all France's economic policies.[2] He said that the Conseil National du Crédit, in practice run by the Governors of the Bank of France, was deciding the Government's credit policy instead of vice versa: 'We did not nationalize the banks for the sake of installing State capitalism in place of private capitalism. We nationalized the banks, so that credit would be used exclusively for the nation.' Menthon went on to advocate a more active role for the State:

The State's role is to stimulate, orientate and co-ordinate a dynamic policy of economic expansion, which demands precise objectives and means of action . . . MRP fully supports the Planning Commission, but the State should help not only the basic industries, the main object of the Plan, but also small and medium-sized companies. . . . We, therefore, demand that a second plan for the modernization, equipment and co-ordination of the manufacturing industries succeed the Monnet Plan.[3]

The Second Plan (1954–57) did in fact give greater emphasis to manufacturing industry and consumer goods, but Maurice Byé was very critical, not so much of the objectives of the Second Plan, as of

[1] MRP Congr. 1949, Strasbourg; report on 'La Politique Economique et Sociale'.
[2] MRP Congr. 1951, Lyon; report on 'La Politique Economique et Sociale'.
[3] ibid.

111

the means for its implementation. He argued that it had not been too difficult to implement the First Plan, because three of the six industries on which it concentrated were nationalized, but now it was much more difficult when the Plan was dealing with 'uncontrolled' private companies. In Byé's view the Government should not hesitate to intervene in order to harmonize production in the various sectors of the economy; moreover, it should see that wages were linked to rises in productivity, and that agricultural and industrial wages were kept in line with each other. On the subject of investment, Byé emphasized the importance of public investment in the implementation of the Plan, although he also favoured as much private investment as possible, but 'We must take all the necessary measures to see that private investment is directed where it is needed, that is into the sectors of the economy which can contribute most to the growth of social justice'.[1] In this context he wanted to see the development of a regional policy by means of selective investment by the Government, a revised tax system with a more equitable place being given to income tax and, in industry, the development of works councils. Six years later Byé also emphasized the importance of linking social to economic planning. He said that the Debré Government had almost succeeded in stabilizing the economy, but warned that 'good financial planning is of no value unless it improves the well-being of society as a whole'.[2]

The differences between the 'liberals' (Pflimlin and his followers) and the 'interventionists' (Menthon and his followers) were also apparent in the extent to which they advocated democratic control of planning. The 'liberals' in theory emphasized the importance of democratic planning as much as the 'interventionists', but in practice they tended to favour the *status quo* of the Monnet system, whilst the 'interventionists' were much more critical of that system, agreeing with the CFTC's 1959 Declerq Report that the degree of democratic participation and control of the Plan was far from satisfactory.[3] Planning, of course, raised important political questions. How far should there be democratic control of such a technical operation? Which objectives should be given the greatest emphasis? Should the Plan be drawn up by Parliament and implemented by a Planning Ministry subject to parliamentary control? Or was it better to leave the Plan to technocrats, provided interest groups and politicians were given some say in its formulation?

---

[1] MRP Congr. 1954, Lille; report on 'La Politique Economique et Sociale'. See also article by Byé in *France-Forum*, February 1957, 'Qui Dirige l'Economie?'.
[2] MRP Congr. 1960, Evian; report on 'La Politique Economique et Sociale'.
[3] See p. 115.

In the 1950's these problems were solved by default. The First and Third Plans were never discussed in the National Assembly, and the Second Plan was only briefly debated in its third year of operation (1956); even then there was only a vote on a short three-clause bill, whilst the details of the Plan, which were not debated, were contained in a separate appendix. Shonfield has commented:

> In some ways the development of French planning in the 1950s can be viewed as an act of voluntary collusion between senior civil servants and the senior managers of big business. The politicians and the representatives of organized labour were both largely passed by.[1]

The Fourth Plan (1962–65), a series of major options, was debated by the Economic and Social Council and by Parliament, but the options were not very great, being essentially three different growth rates with a predetermined package of programmes attached to each. The Fifth Plan (1966–70) was also debated, but no major concessions were made to the critics, who produced a counter-plan, criticizing the original document's priorities and arguing that it would produce greater unemployment than indicated. In the end the majority of MRP's successor, the Centre Démocrate, joined the left-wing opposition in voting against the Fifth Plan.[2]

The Christian Democratic 'liberals' advocated improvements in the system of drawing up the Plan, but were opposed to fundamental changes. Robert Lecourt's basic contention was that, whatever the drawbacks of the planning system, it worked. This was the underlying theme of his long speech in the National Assembly in 1951.[3] Fourteen years later Pflimlin made a similar speech in the debate on the Fifth Plan. He argued that the system by which the Plan was drawn up (i.e. by specialized committees, of which twenty-two were 'vertical' committees, responsible for particular industries, and five were 'horizontal', co-ordinating the work of the 'vertical' committees), was essentially democratic, because over 3,000 representatives of industry, trade unions, universities and the civil service had been consulted, and the Plan had also been debated by the Economic and Social Council. Nevertheless, despite his broad approval of the planning system, Pflimlin would have liked to have seen more consultation in depth and a parliamentary debate on the objectives of the Plan before the specialized committees set to work in drawing it up. In particular he would have liked to have seen more broadly-based specialized committees, in which trade union and consumer

---

[1] Andrew Shonfield, *Modern Capitalism*, p. 128.
[2] See p. 118.   [3] JO (AN), 17 April 1951, pp. 3393–95.

interests were properly represented. And, not surprisingly for an Alsatian, he was critical of the planners' failure to listen to the arguments put forward by the Alsace-Lorraine Regional Council in favour of top priority emphasis on the Rhône-Rhine canal link-up.[1] The basic contention of the MRP 'liberal' economists was that, although more people should be involved in the planning process, there was no need for fundamental changes. The 'technocrats' should be controlled, but the details should be worked out by experts, not politicians. Barangé argued that if Parliament drew up the Plan, it would be infected by the political demagoguery of the extreme left and right. It was, therefore, better to leave it to the Planning Commission, although Parliament should debate the final document. The ideas of MRP's 'liberal' economists were, in practice, not unlike those of de Gaulle. Planning should be left to the experts, although it should be subject to political approval. One major difference, however, was that all MRP spokesmen, whether 'liberals' or 'interventionists', paid lip service to the idea of European planning, a topic conspicuously omitted by the General.

MRP's 'interventionist' economists were outspokenly critical of the whole planning system, especially in the Fifth Republic. Like the conservative members of the party, they favoured greater participation by the trade unions. In 1944 Pierre-Henri Teitgen had advocated 'active participation by the trade unions in the control of the economy',[2] a theme repeated many times over the years from Buron in 1948 to Abelin in 1965. But the 'interventionists' carried their arguments for participation and democratic control much further than the 'liberals'. In 1950 Reille-Soult said that the Plan was beginning to work, but that wage-earners were not benefiting fully from increased production; indeed, their real incomes had actually declined by $3 \cdot 1$ per cent since 1938.[3] In the same debate André Denis said that indirect taxation had increased from $49 \cdot 5$ per cent of the total in 1938 to $62 \cdot 6$ per cent in 1949.[4] Both men went on to advocate a full-scale Ministry of Economic Planning, which would promulgate a Plan concerned with social and fiscal justice and not just with growth rates and industrial modernization. Menthon said that he agreed with Reille-Soult's proposal, but pointed out that MRP could not get it implemented in a coalition in which their voice had become weaker since the departure of the Socialists.

[1] JO (AN), 4 November 1965, pp. 4464–6.

[2] MRP Congr. 1944, Paris; report on 'La Politique Générale du Mouvement'.

[3] MRP Congr. 1950, Nantes; debate on Barangé's report on 'La Politique Economique et Sociale'.

[4] ibid.

Nevertheless, he would like to see an overall Plan, concentrating on such social objectives as housing (240,000 houses per annum were needed, not just 70,000) as well as on increased production. The ideal would be a 'real Ministry of Planning', but in the meantime this was politically impossible.[1] In 1959 a special number of *France-Forum* repeated the arguments for a global Plan, emphasizing that politicians should be involved at each stage of planning, particularly in the specialized committees: 'The Third Plan is being elaborated at a crucial moment in the economic development of France and Europe without any part being played by parliamentarians.'[2]

With the coming of the Fifth Republic, and the emasculation of Parliament's powers,[3] the issue of democratic planning became even more important. The debate was opened with the CFTC's Declerq Report in 1959:

We are the convinced supporters of a planned economy, that is, in our view, an economy that functions both effectively *and* democratically. The present modernization plans, drawn up within a capitalist framework, are certainly very far from the organization we should like to establish. Nevertheless, they do represent an advance . . . and a point of departure for a planned economy in the true sense of the term.[4]

The Report criticized the Planning Commission for its failure to consider ends as fully as means. Trade unionists opposed the planners' tendency to emphasize production rather than consumption. The workers felt alienated by not getting their share of increasing prosperity. The solution was to bring the unions into the planning operation from an early stage, instead of continuing with a system in which everything was fixed behind the scenes and the tiny number of trade unionists on the specialized committees of the Plan could exercise no influence. The Declerq Report also complained that big firms concealed their true profits and even their plans from the specialized committees, and proposed that wages and prices should also be included in the national plan. Free collective bargaining in private industry resulted in excessive influence for employers, whilst the determination of wages in the public sector by the Government

[1] MRP Congr. 1950, Nantes; debate on Barangé's report on 'La Politique Economique et Sociale'.

[2] *France-Forum*, December 1959.

[3] For a full discussion of the role of Parliament in the Fifth Republic, see P. M. Williams, *The French Parliament, 1958–67*.

[4] *Rapport sur le Programme Economique de la CFTC*, 1959, p. 12, quoted in M. MacLennan, *French Planning: Some Lessons for Britain*, PEP, p. 348.

was producing an ever-widening gulf between wages in the two sectors, private and public.

At a 1962 conference on democratic planning, attended by MRP, André Jeanson, Vice-President of the CFTC, proposed an 'Economic Senate', an idea supported by men like Michel Debatisse, the farmers' leader, as well as by Maurice Duverger, the well-known political scientist. Jeanson's basic idea was that the Economic and Social Council should become the auxiliary of the National Assembly in economic and social matters:[1]

> Its task will be to form and inform the decisions of this body in three ways: by collaborating in the preparation of the Plan; by giving its advice in advance of all economic legislation submitted to Parliament; by putting questions to the Government (which will be obliged to reply) and even itself proposing economic legislation to the National Assembly.

The ideas of Duverger, Debatisse and Jeanson were spelt out even more clearly by Bloch-Lainé in 1963.[2] The Economic and Social Council should be given the power of a second chamber, and, aided by regional Economic and Social Councils, it would become the nerve centre of economic planning. The specialized committees of the Plan would work within the framework of the Economic and Social Council.

Although MRP's 'interventionist' economists agreed with many of these ideas, they did not give them their full support. Maurice Byé, a strong advocate of more democratic planning, insisted that the second chamber should continue to be elected on a geographical basis; otherwise there was a danger of growing corporatism.[3] Pierre-Henri Teitgen called for more democratic planning, but went on to say that he meant by this more information available to the public and greater participation by 'economic, social and professional groups' in the formulation of the Plan.[4] Teitgen was very critical of the fact that the Fourth Plan was being drawn up without thorough consultation, but he did not go so far as to support the ideas of Duverger and Bloch-Lainé. Maurice Guérin, on the other hand, one of MRP's trade union deputies, whilst not specifically advocating a combined Economic and Social Council and Senate, favoured a new-style Senate, consisting of 'family, professional, economic and social

[1] *Cahiers de la République*, June 1962, p. 486, Special No. on the conference; cited in J. E. S. Hayward, *Private Interests and Public Policy*, pp. 92–3.

[2] F. Bloch-Lainé, *Pour une Réforme de l'Entreprise*.

[3] *Revue Economique*, November 1962, p. 909, cited in Hayward, p. 100.

[4] MRP Congr. 1962, Dijon; report on 'La Démocratie Moderne'.

representatives',[1] and Marcel Gonin of the CFTC proposed that a reformed Senate of this type should have an important planning role, for 'there will be no true industrial democracy in this country until there is genuine participation in determining the ends and means of the Plan'.[2] Joseph Fontanet, in contrast, maintained that the present institutional machinery was adequate if it were properly used; the preparation of the Fifth Plan had seen 'an improvement in democratic practices, and it is not unreasonable to hope that this will develop further'.[3] The debates on the Fourth and Fifth Plans, however, showed that many Christian Democrats were more sceptical than Fontanet. The critics did not advocate a new-style economic second chamber, like that proposed by the Declerq Report, Bloch-Lainé and Duverger; what they wanted was thorough consultation about the Plan before its promulgation, and, above all, a Plan concerned with social justice and the 'quality of life', not merely with economic growth rates.[4]

In the debate on the Fourth Plan, Nestor Rombeaut, a former shipbuilding trade union official and deputy for Loire-Atlantique, agreed with the four main principles of the Plan as outlined by Pompidou, namely increased economic growth to provide more jobs for the young, improved living conditions for all Frenchmen, continued participation by France in the Common Market and other international trading organizations, and more aid for developing countries. But he doubted whether the domestic objectives of the Plan could be achieved without a proper regional policy. His own region, the west, had a high rate of unemployment and had been allowed to decline despite the promises in the Third Plan. Moreover, it was useless to talk about more jobs for the young if nothing were done to improve educational facilities, particularly technical education. He also would have liked to have seen a policy for the old, such as retirement at sixty and improved pensions: 'If the Plan is to succeed it must be the affair of *all* Frenchmen'.[5] Maurice Blin criticized the Plan for its timidity; it made no proposals for a more equitable distribution of national income, and its provisions on employment and regional policy were inadequate.[6] Georges Coudray said the Plan's greatest weakness was its failure to put forward an emergency programme to deal with the housing crisis.[7] Despite these criticisms, however, MRP voted for the Fourth Plan, Rombeaut explaining that the party was sufficiently satisfied with the Plan's

[1] *France-Forum*, April 1961. [2] *France-Forum*, February 1963.
[3] *France-Forum*, January 1965. [4] See pp. 117–18.
[5] JO (AN), 20 June 1962, pp. 1824–5. [6] JO (AN), 30 May 1962, pp. 1360–1.
[7] ibid., p. 1364.

objectives despite its doubts about the method by which it had been drawn up and its limitations in social and regional policy.

In the debate on the Fifth Plan many of the criticisms voiced in 1962 were repeated. Joseph Schaff and Paul Ihuel were particularly worried about the lack of a regional policy, the former with reference to Lorraine, which had a high birth rate and declining steel industry, the latter with reference to Brittany, where educational and employment opportunities were much more limited than in most other parts of France.[1] But the main Christian Democratic criticism came from Pierre Abelin, who said that the Plan had three major failings. Firstly, he contended that the economists had not done their sums properly and that insufficient funds had been allotted to implement the Plan. Secondly, the Plan should have been worked out in a European context, as national plans were becoming less relevant with the development of the Common Market. But, above all, he was critical of the 'lack of social content' in the Plan. It was essential to implement a regional policy, including the direction of advanced technological industries such as electronics to areas like Brittany; firms should be forbidden to develop further in the Paris region; there must be a national housing programme; more money should be devoted to education to deal with the effect of the post-war demographic bulge.[2] In all these matters the Plan was deficient, and Abelin, therefore, advocated voting against it. In the event thirty-four out of the fifty-five members of the Centre Démocratique group voted against the Fifth Plan, including all MRP members except Pflimlin, Schumann, Halbout, Meck and Rivière, who supported the Government, and Schaff, who abstained.

A discussion of the Christian Democratic approach to planning brings into focus one of the basic dilemmas faced by MRP and the Centre Démocrate. Christian Democrats favour State planning but dislike too much intervention by the State. The dilemma resulting from this attitude could equally well be illustrated by a study of MRP's policies with regard to collective bargaining and minimum wages. Thus, Bidault's Government was responsible for the return to free collective bargaining in February 1950, but at the same time MRP insisted that the State should fix a minimum wage, operating on a sliding scale related to prices.[3] Workers and unions should be

[1] Ihuel, JO (AN), 3 November 1965, p. 4399; Schaff, ibid., 5 November 1965, p. 4537.

[2] JO (AN), 4 November 1965, pp. 4445–7.

[3] The sliding scale (*échelle mobile*), which applied only to SMIG (Salaire Minimum Interprofessionnel Garanti), not to all wages, was introduced on 8 July 1952. In 1953 *Année Politique* described the 8 July 1952 Law as one of the

given the chance to bargain for wages, but the State had a duty to prevent the type of hardship resulting from the uncontrolled operation of market forces. The majority of MRP militants, encouraged by party leaders like Menthon and Teitgen, leant towards a 'socialist-interventionist' concept of the economy without having any doctrinaire belief in the merits of nationalization. The main criticisms of the planning system, as of the Pinay experiment in economic liberalism, came from the party's 'interventionists'. But despite the preponderance of 'interventionist' militants, they were usually outgunned by the 'liberal' economists, men like Pflimlin and Schuman, and later Fontanet, who had the advantage of the sympathy of a largely conservative electorate.

Another dilemma facing the Christian Democrats, equally apparent in their attitude to planning, was that they supported both traditional democratic representation (on a geographical basis) and representation for 'natural social groups' (family organizations, regional groups, trade unions). If they emphasized the latter too much, they could easily be accused of corporatism, something which a Resistance party inevitably resented. If, on the other hand, they failed to support the claims of the 'natural social groups', they could be accused of betraying one of the fundamental aspects of Christian Democratic doctrine. This dilemma came to a head in 1969 when the vast majority of Christian Democrats followed Poher in voting against de Gaulle's proposals for regional assemblies, although Christian Democrats had advocated the setting up of such bodies for many years.[1]

MRP may be said to have reflected the unresolved conflict in France between *dirigisme* and liberalism, between centralization and devolution. Planning helped to increase freedom of choice and mobility, but it did not create as much educational opportunity as was hoped for by the early Christian Democrats, nor did it produce an economic and social democracy devoid of the old class conflicts. Planning inevitably resulted in some curtailment of individual freedom, but for MRP this was preferable to the social injustice caused by economic liberalism. Nevertheless, the Christian Democrats were ultimately no more successful than Western societies as a whole in finding a happy medium between justice and freedom.

most important pieces of social legislation since the war (p. 139); MRP and SFIO were both firm supporters of the *échelle mobile*.

[1] Most voters in the April 1969 referendum, of course, voted for or against de Gaulle, not for or against regional and Senate reforms; cf. J. E. S. Hayward, 'Presidential Suicide by Plebiscite: de Gaulle's Exit, April 1969', *Parliamentary Affairs*, Autumn 1969.

COMITES D'ENTREPRISE

French Christian Democrats from Bacon in the immediate post-war period to Abelin in 1970 have been consistent advocates of workers' participation in the running of industry.[1] They have never proposed workers' control, but they have tended to favour some degree of participation. Likewise they have supported schemes for profit-sharing.[2] They would also like to see trade union participation both at the level of national planning and in individual industries and factories. But this has been difficult to achieve, partly because French workers are badly and divisively organized, and partly because the *patronat*, at least until 1968, generally refused to co-operate with the trade unions and adopted a very negative attitude towards the *comités d'entreprise* (works' councils). At the same time it was difficult for the trade unions to produce a united front in collective bargaining or in the *comités d'entreprise* so long as they were divided into three major confederations, of which the largest was Communist and therefore sceptical about all forms of co-operation, and so long as no more than a quarter of workers were unionized.[3]

Despite the difficulties Christian Democrats have stuck to their ideal of workers' participation and profit-sharing from the institution of the *comités d'entreprise* in 1945–46, through Bacon's proposed Sociétés de Travail et d'Epargne, to the 1967 Vallon 'amendment' and the 1968 trade union and *comité d'entreprise* reforms. Christian Democrats would agree with Bloch-Lainé that economic efficiency, and they would add social justice, owes as much to democracy and participation within the firm as to national planning.

In December 1944 *L'Aube* argued that, although economic conditions in industry were far from ideal, the basic reform needed was social rather than economic, namely the reintegration of the working class into society:

> The real social problem is to bring the workers out of the isolated proletarian situation into which they were driven by nineteenth century capitalism, to re-establish them as full members of the firm instead of continuing to regard them as interchangeable elements in an impersonal system of production.

[1] *Aube* 14 December 1944; interview with Abelin, 8 July 1970.

[2] MRP Congr. 1947, Paris; Bacon report on 'La Réforme de l'Economie et de l'Entreprise'. And *Forces Nouvelles*, 30 September 1966, article by Georges Delfosse.

[3] Cf. Hubert Lesire-Ogrel, *Le Syndicat dans l'Entreprise*, 1967, for the difficulties encountered by trade unions in the face of *patronat* hostility. Lesire-Ogrel was *chef du service juridique* of the CFDT prior to the publication of his book.

The solution was not to hand over complete control to the workers, as this would upset 'a system which has given incomparable material prosperity to the Western world', but to ensure that the workers benefited from their efforts through profit-sharing formulae and 'particularly by the establishment within firms of institutions through which the workers will be able to control their own social interests and receive full information about the general situation of the firm'.[1]

De Gaulle's Provisional Government of 1944–45 took the first step towards giving workers a greater say in the running of industry with the ordinance of 22 February 1945 setting up *comités d'entreprise*. This ordinance was elaborated into the Law of 16 May 1946, which was complemented by the Law of 16 April 1946, establishing a system for the election of workers' representatives (*délégués du personnel*).[2]

The *comités d'entreprise* were to be established in all firms employing at least fifty wage earners (the figure had been 100 in the ordinance of 22 February 1945). The *comité* consisted of the head of the firm together with representatives of the wage-earners in firms of up to 500, and representatives of wage-earners and junior management in firms of over 500.[3] The candidates were selected by the most representative trade unions and all over eighteen could vote provided they had worked in the firm for at least six months. Candidates had to be at least twenty-one, and were elected on a two ballot system (over 50 per cent of votes cast resulted in election after one ballot; a simple plurality sufficed on the second ballot). The *comité* was given full responsibility for social matters within the firm (recreation facilities, workers' gardens, children's nurseries, etc.), but was allotted only a consultative role in economic matters. Nevertheless, the Law of May 1946, in contrast to the 1945 ordinance, laid down that the *comité must* be consulted (*consulté obligatoirement*) on all matters concerned with the management and general financial policy of the firm. The *comité* also had the right to discuss working conditions with the management and to meet for twenty hours a month during working hours on full pay in accommodation provided by the company. It could not, however, put forward pay claims.

Délégués du personnel were elected on a similar basis to the

[1] *Aube*, 14 December 1944.
[2] Cf. *Ordonnance* No. 45–280, JO, 22 February 1945 and *Loi* No. 46–1065, JO, 16 May 1946, for details about *comités d'entreprise*. And *Loi* No. 46–730, JO 16 April 1946, *Statut des Délégués du Personnel dans les Entreprises*.
[3] 2 delegates for 50 workers; 3 for 51–75; 4 for 76–100; 5 for 101–500; 6 for 501–1,000; 7 for 1,001–2,000; 8 for any figure above 2,000. In firms with over 500 employees at least 1 representative of junior management was also to be elected to the *comité d'entreprise*.

comités d'entreprise. They had the right to meet for fifteen hours per month during working hours and to meet the management monthly to discuss working conditions. If these were unsatisfactory, they could request a visit from a Ministry of Labour inspector, and the management could be fined for failure to comply with the orders of the inspector. Unlike the *comités d'entreprise,* however, the *délégués du personnel* did not have to be consulted about company policy, nor did they have access to company financial information. In firms which had both *comités d'entreprise* and *délégués du personnel,* the latter had the right to put forward 'suggestions and observations' to the former in matters with which they were competent to deal. (The *comités d'entreprise* and *délégués du personnel* were not mutually exclusive, although generally the *comités* functioned within larger firms and the *délégués* in smaller ones.)

MRP was decisively in favour of the steps taken at the Liberation period to institute some degree of workers' participation. Marcel Poimboeuf, one of MRP's trade union deputies, spoke enthusiastically of the proposed *comités d'entreprise* in the Provisional Assembly in December 1944, contrasting them with the sham works' councils established by Vichy, to which workers were nominated and in which the *patron* had the right of veto. He saw the proposed *comités d'entreprise* as 'the beginning of genuine collaboration between the various elements responsible for production, which have been at loggerheads for so long'.[1] After the promulgation of the May 1946 Law Maurice Guérin, another former CFTC official, said

The Law of 16 May 1946 marks an important step in the evolution of the social policy of our country. The compulsory establishment of *comités* in firms with 50 to 100 wage earners, the right of the *comités* to make proposals to the management not only in technical matters but about the general running of the business, and the increasingly prominent role being assigned to trade unionists, particularly in the *comités d'entreprise,* are evidence of the extent of the reform.[2]

Moreover, the Law of 16 April 1946 (*délégués du personnel*), extending workers' participation, even if in a limited way, to firms with under fifty employeees, was directly attributable to MRP as the bill was put forward by members of the MRP group. And in July 1947 MRP registered another success when a bill altering the mode of

1 JO (Assemblée Provisoire), 12 December 1944, pp. 496–7.
2 *Aube,* 22 June 1946.

election to the *comités d'entreprise* from majority voting to proportional representation was passed by the National Assembly.[1]

Enthusiasm for the reforms instituting a measure of workers' participation was, however, of no particular value in itself. Most companies paid no attention to the legislation of 1945–46. Decisions on finance, marketing and production continued to be taken by management without reference to the workers' representatives. This applied to nationalized industries almost as much as to private companies. When the *comités d'entreprise* were allowed to play a role, it was limited to discussion of working conditions. In some companies, such as the Lafarge cement firm, these discussions led to substantial improvements in such matters as safety regulations for workers and specially organized holidays for their children. But, in general, French employers ignored the 'participation' laws, or, worse still, victimized employees who tried to implement them.[2] As early as May 1945 *Le Figaro* had wisely commented:

> The tool is there . . . the question is, how will it be used? In this sense the *comités d'entreprise* are an act of faith. A radical change in habits is required: one can only hope for fair dealing from the management and loyal co-operation by the workers. Up till now, at least in France, these conditions have rarely been met. There is a tradition of excessive secrecy on the side of the *patronat* and of distrust on the side of the workers.[3]

These words could equally well have been written twenty-five years later. But, in the euphoria of the immediate post-war period, MRP was inclined to be rather over-optimistic about the possibility of changing ingrained habits by legislation. By early 1947 it was clear that a number of companies were evading the provisions of the bill, either by subdividing themselves or by reducing their employees to just under fifty. Mme Lefebvre and members of the MRP group put forward a bill, proposing to replace the words 'normally employing 50 persons' (Article 1, Law of 16 May 1946) with 'employing 50 persons on 16 May 1946'[4], in an attempt to prevent firms from getting round the law, but Mme Lefebvre's bill disappeared in committee. In any case, it would have affected the evasion of the law in only one respect.

The main problem was that most firms simply ignored the law altogether. Paul Bacon said as much in his report on 'La Réforme de

---

[1] *Loi* No. 47–1234, 7 July 1947; *Aube*, 6 July 1947, described the new election procedure as 'a great MRP achievement'.

[2] Cf. Lesire-Ogrel, pp. 65–87.   [3] *Figaro*, 15 May 1945.

[4] *Proposition du Loi*, no. 1214, JO (AN) *Docs. Parl.* 2 May 1947.

l'Economie et de l'Entreprise' at the 1947 MRP Congress, and the subsequent motion on economic and social policy demanded the implementation of the 1945–46 legislation, so that those 'who devote their labour to a firm may also have the right to participate in its management as well as in the fruits of its success'.[1] The CFTC journal *Syndicalisme* complained that firms refused to allow *comités d'entreprise* and *délégués du personnel* to carry out their duties in working hours, although the Laws of April and May 1946 entitled them to twenty and fifteen hours per month respectively.[2] *L'Aube* called for 'a workers offensive against the capitalist citadel' to persuade the *patronat* to fulfil its side of the bargain with regard to the *comités d'entreprise*; the latter should not be seen as 'soviets or as instruments of collaboration, but as the means by which capitalist firms can be transformed into genuine *communautés du travail*'.[3]

L'Aube did not attempt to define a *communauté du travail*, but it was clear from MRP's proposals for the Berliet company in 1949 and from Bacon's ideas about Sociétés de Travail et d'Epargne what was meant. For, although MRP consistently advocated *comités d'entreprise*, they were not seen as an end in themselves. Rather they were one means to achieve the final end of a just society in which employers and workers participated jointly in running industry and in sharing its profits.

The case of the Berliet company has been discussed in detail by Goguel,[4] but it seems worthwhile to outline again MRP's ideas about the structure of Berliet, as they show the extent to which Christian Democratic ideas about industry differ from those of Marxists and traditional Liberals. Very briefly, the management of the Berliet lorry company had collaborated so closely with the Germans, that at the end of the war the Commissioner of the Republic in the Lyons area had replaced them with a board of management consisting of workers. A cabinet decree of 1946 provisionally accepted this arrangement, but it was later annulled by the Conseil d'Etat, which could find no constitutional justification for what amounted to workers' control. The Berliet company, therefore, reverted to its traditional form of management, in which the board of the company was responsible to the shareholders. But, before the Conseil d'Etat announced its decision, there was a debate in the National Assembly, in which MRP showed that it was opposed to the outright nationalization of the company proposed by the

---

[1] MRP Congr. 1947, Paris. André Colin also called for proper application of the *comité d'entreprise* legislation at the 1948 Congress; report on 'La Politique Générale'.
[2] *Syndicalisme*, 21 October 1948. [3] *Aube*, 22 April 1949.
[4] Einaudi and Goguel, pp. 141–3.

Communists and to the straightforward workers' control advocated by the Socialists.[1] Instead, MRP proposed that the company's shares should be partially owned by the workers, who would therefore be involved in the management and control of the company. MRP's proposal passed its first reading in the National Assembly on 6 December 1949 by 261 to 247, with the support of the Socialists and some Radicals, but before it emerged from committee the Conseil d'Etat had made its decision and Berliet went back to management by a board responsible to the company's shareholders.

The above ideas were spelt out in more detail by Paul Bacon both in a bill submitted to the National Assembly in December 1946 and in his report on 'La Réforme de l'Economie et de l'Entreprise' at the 1947 MRP Congress. Bacon began his report by emphasizing that MRP was determined to free man not only from the economic but also from the social limitations of capitalist society. The worker must participate in the running of his firm through *comités d'entreprise* in order to make his work more understandable, and therefore tolerable and human. But, he must also be allowed to benefit from the work he did; otherwise he was a 'stranger' in his own firm. The simple answer was to distribute profits amongst the workers. Bacon was opposed to the State taking over any more firms or intervening directly in the affairs of the company. He realized that in the absence of nationalization, private capital would be needed and that it would be attracted only if shareholders could be assured of dividends. He, therefore, proposed a new type of company, the Société de Travail et d'Epargne, in which the board would consist of one third workers, one third managers and one third shareholders. All three groups would be elected to the board by their respective constituents, and the managing director of the company would be responsible to the board. Profits would be distributed in such a way that at least 50 per cent went to the workers: 'The realization of this change would constitute a revolution; it would therefore be a mistake to try to carry it through all at once;' instead, a start should be made with companies employing more than 500 people (less than 25 per cent of French companies at that time), and even then the new status should not be forced upon them; rather, firms should be encouraged to become Sociétés de Travail et d'Epargne by fiscal advantages. The new-style companies would liberate the worker both economically and 'spiritually', and so family life would reach a new plane of fulfilment (*épanouissement*).[2]

[1] JO (AN), 15 November 1949, pp. 6105–12 (speeches by André Denis, Maurice Guérin and Francine Lefebvre).
[2] MRP Congr. 1947, Paris; report on 'La Réforme de l'Economie et de

These extremely far-reaching proposals for participation and profit-sharing came to nothing. Bacon's bill of December 1946 was buried in committee, whilst his proposals for new-style companies associating capital, labour and management, were only mentioned once again at an MRP Congress. During the 1950s the idea of workers' participation almost disappeared from French politics, no doubt mainly owing to the economic boom which followed Pinay's year of restraint. Nevertheless, the Christian Democrats never quite lost sight of their ideal. In 1953, for example, the MRP Congress decided, after hearing Pflimlin's report on economic policy, to amend his motion by adding a demand for 'the participation of the workers not only in the results of increased productivity, but also in the management of their companies'.[1] This amendment was carried by 201 to 151 against the wishes of Pflimlin and the platform. MRP also supported a 1955 decree providing tax relief for companies which instituted profit-sharing schemes. And at the 1957 Congress Bacon revived his idea of Sociétés de Travail et d'Epargne after making a scathing attack on employers for their refusal to implement the 1946 Law instituting *comités d'entreprise*. He also said that those who were elected to the *comités* should be sent on training courses in economics and administration so that they could take full advantage of their position.[2] But, in general, the controversy about participation and profit-sharing lay dormant between the late 1940s and the middle 1960s, when it came to a head again, partly because improved economic conditions had not removed the sense of alienation of unions and workers, partly because of the interest shown for a long time by left-wing Gaullists such as Louis Vallon and René Capitant in schemes to associate capital and labour.

In 1965–66 a series of articles in the MRP weekly, *Forces Nouvelles*, discussed the state of the *comités d'entreprise* and assessed the importance of the Law of 25 June 1966 reforming the *comités*.[3] The main reason for the new Law, for which Gilbert Grandval, Pompidou's Minister of Labour, was largely responsible, was that the 1945–46 legislation was still not being applied. A 1961 inquiry by the Ministry of Labour showed that very few firms with under 500 employees had a *comité d'entreprise*, although the statutory figure

l'Entreprise'. And see Einaudi and Goguel, p. 140, for brief summary of Bacon bill of December 1946 (*Annexe au Procès-verbal de la Séance du 12 déc. 1946*, no. 96).

[1] MRP Congr. 1953, Paris; report on 'Une Politique de Productivité'.

[2] MRP Congr. 1957, Biarritz; report on 'La Démocratie Economique et Sociale'.

[3] *Forces Nouvelles*, 4 March 1965; 1 April 1965; 8 July 1965; 30 September 1966.

was 50; that *comités* existed in less than 50 per cent of firms with over 500 employees; and that in certain parts of the country, notably Alsace and Loire-Atlantique, *comités* were virtually non-existent.[1] Georges Delfosse, one of MRP's labour experts, reckoned that no more than 3,000 of the 10,000 *comités* in existence in 1966 played the sort of role they should have done by law.[2]

The Grandval Law of 25 June 1966 was welcomed by Delfosse as a step in the right direction. In Delfosse's view, its most important provision was that the *ex officio* trade union representative on the *comité d'entreprise* should henceforth be properly recognized by the firm and should not lose pay by attending the *comité* for up to twenty hours per month (the 1945–46 legislation had not been clear on this point). The Grandval Law also laid down that all firms with over fifty employees must report the fact to the Ministry of Labour, who could send an inspector at any time to see that the firm had a properly constituted *comité d'entreprise*. Finally, the management was to present the *comité* with a detailed report of its activities, number of employees and investment situation every three months. The second and third points were less important than they appeared to be, as there were too few inspectors to check up on the 25,000-odd firms which were supposed to have *comités d'entreprise* and companies could still keep 'confidential information' to themselves (this had been one of the main points of contention between *patronat* and trade unions when Grandval's proposed legislation was discussed in the Economic and Social Council in March 1965). *Témoignage Chrétien* called the Grandval Law 'a victory for the *patronat*',[3] and the CFDT said it did not go far enough in recognizing the role of trade unions in firms.[4] The young Catholic businessmen's organization found the reforms 'timid',[5] and in the spring of 1967 Yves Lagarde said that nothing had been done to improve the position of trade unions in firms,[6] an impression confirmed by Lesire-Ogrel's book on the subject published later that year.[7]

One of the many causes of the Events of May–June 1968 was the frustration of workers and unions at the high-handed action of Gaullist technocrats, who, like the *patronat*, seemed determined to ignore their claims. Thus the new social security package of October 1967, by which workers' contributions were increased and benefits reduced, was pushed through without any consultation with the unions. It is significant that the CFDT, who reacted more positively

---

[1] *Perspectives*, 8 May 1965.   [2] *Forces Nouvelles*, 30 September 1966.
[3] *TC*, 8 July 1965.   [4] ibid.   [5] *Monde*, 28 July 1966.
[6] *France-Forum*, April 1967.
[7] H. Lesire-Ogrel, *Le Syndicat dans l'Entreprise*.

127

to the Events of 1968 than the other two trade union confederations, showed as much interest in demanding increased workers' participation and proper recognition of trade unions as in wage rises *per se*. In this way the CFDT continued the old theme of MRP's labour leaders such as Bacon, Delfosse and Mme Lefebvre. And in December 1968 they gained some of their objectives with the trade union reforms introduced by Maurice Schumann.[1] *Témoignage Chrétien* hailed the full recognition of trade unions within firms as the most important trade union legislation since the Law of 1884 recognized the right of workers to form trade unions.[2] From a union point of view the most important gain was that henceforth shop stewards could do trade union work in the firm's time, and *comités d'entreprise* were to be provided with an office in the factory. On the other hand, the fact that the new legislation applied only to firms with at least fifty employees excluded more than 3,000,000 workers. The Schumann Law, however, was welcomed by all the major trade union confederations, who realized that proper recognition of trade union rights was the *quid quo pro* for improved industrial relations.

De Gaulle's watchword after the events of 1968 was 'participation', reviving an old idea which he had shared with MRP in the early post-war period. The trade union reforms of December 1968 were one step towards greater participation. Another was the accelerated implementation of the 1967 profit-sharing scheme, originally put forward by Louis Vallon in July 1965. The profit-sharing regulations of 1967–68[3] laid down that companies with more than 100 employees should set aside any profit exceeding a return of 5 per cent on the company's capital. This 'super-profit' was to be shared on a 50–50 basis between shareholders and employees, but only after it had been kept in a special fund run by the firm for five or eight years, depending on the contract. The scheme is quite complex but is unlikely to cost the firm very much; for example, if a firm increases its investment by an amount equal to that paid into the fund, it can deduct the whole payment from its tax bill. And, by skilful management of the fund, the firm may gain more for itself and its shareholders than for its employees, whose bonus money is only earning interest at a fixed rate.[4] Nevertheless, the scheme, although watered down from the original Vallon proposals, is a step towards profit-sharing, and,

[1] JO (*Lois et Décrets*), 27 December 1968, *Loi* No. 68–1179. Schumann was *Ministre d'Etat* responsible for Social Affairs at the time.

[2] *TC*, 28 November 1968. The new measures were also welcomed by *Démocratie Moderne* (official organ of the Centre *Démocrate*), 21 November 1968.

[3] *Ordonnance* no. 67–694, 17 August 1967, and *Décret* no. 68–528, 30 May 1968.

[4] *Monde* (*Sélection Hebdomadaire*), 10–16 August 1967.

as such, was welcomed by the Centre Démocrate.[1] By March 1971, 5,778 such profit-sharing agreements, involving almost 3,000,000 workers, had been signed.[2]

And yet, so long as so much of French labour is unrepresented in the political process owing to the isolation of the Communist Party, and so long as the unions remain weak and divided, with the CGT fundamentally opposed to the capitalist system, it is unlikely that there will be any real progress towards meaningful workers' participation and profit-sharing in France. The ideals of the Christian Democratic labour leaders remain almost a dead letter, although there is some evidence that the reaction of the *patronat* to the events of 1968 has been less negative than their reaction to the Popular Front legislation of 1936 or the *comité d'entreprise* legislation of 1946. Nevertheless, the present situation is a far cry from the new type of industrial partnership between capital and labour envisaged by the more progressive Christian Democrats.

HOUSING

In 1965 *Le Monde's* housing expert, Gilbert Mathieu, described France's housing policy since the war as a 'national scandal'.[3] Throughout the years MRP had been acutely aware of deficiencies in this sector. In 1947 *L'Aube* maintained that the right to a house ought to have been written into the Constitution.[4] MRP claimed to be the first French party to devote a major Congress report to housing policy (Coudray's in 1948). The party saw housing as an essential aspect of their family policy, demanding year after year a national housing plan, the development of mortgage schemes, increased investment in council houses (Habitations à Loyer Modéré —HLM), a national rent system and special housing loans for young married couples. Overall, their demands met with limited success, although the Christian Democrats could claim some credit for the Grimaud Rent Law of 1948, the Epargne Logement (housing loans) scheme of 1951 and the *cités d'urgence* scheme of the mid-1950s, whilst the most successful Housing Minister of the Fifth Republic, Pierre Sudreau, was a left-wing Catholic technocrat sympathetic to Christian Democracy, although never a member of MRP or the Centre Démocrate.[5]

[1] *Démocratie Moderne*, 21 November 1968.
[2] *Monde*, 28–29 March 1971.
[3] *Monde*, 19 November 1965; and see G. Mathieu, *Peut-on Loger les Français?*
[4] *Aube*, 29 March 1947.
[5] Sudreau was asked to stand as a Centre presidential candidate in 1965; it was only after he declined that Lecanuet decided to stand.

France's post-war housing problem is partly a historical legacy, but it has frequently been aggravated by other factors, of which the most important has been the failure to implement any coherent housing policy. The basic problem was created by the 1914 decision to freeze rents. This was a laudable decision at the time; it would have been unreasonable for landlords to raise rents when their tenants were fighting in the trenches. But, for electoral reasons, the 1914 Law was not repealed until 1948, and even then it was only partially repealed. The result of frozen rents was that only 1,800,000 houses were built between 1919–39, about 90,000 a year, compared with an average of over 200,000 a year in the 'golden age' for housing, 1900–1914. By 1945 approximately 1,500,000 houses had been destroyed or severely damaged in the war, whilst an estimated 1,500,000 were unfit for habitation owing to old age. L'Aube may have exaggerated when it maintained that France had not had a proper housing programme since Louis XIV's reign, but it was not far off the mark when it described France as 'a huge bombed-out building'[1] In 1948 Georges Coudray said that the average age of a French house was 120 years, that 35,000 families of three to five persons in Paris were living in one room, that only 6 per cent of workers' houses in St Etienne received any sunlight, and that only 20 per cent of French houses had running water and gas or electricity.[2] 5,000,000 new houses, he said, were needed to solve the housing crisis. The Congress called for 240,000 per annum, of which the majority should be HBM.[3] In 1950 L'Aube contended that 300,000 houses a year would be needed for thirty years to solve the housing problem.[4] In 1951 the MRP Congress called for 250,000 per annum.[5] In 1956 the Equipes Ouvrières called for 320,000,[6] and in 1962 the Congress called for 400,000.[7]

In fact the house-building record of the Fourth Republic was dismal. Only 500,000 housing units were completed in the decade 1944–54. Thereafter there was a considerable improvement, with a record number of 274,000 units being completed in 1957. Over 300,000 houses have been built in each year of the Fifth Republic, with a peak of 467,000 in 1967. Nevertheless, the problem is far from solved. The 1962 census showed that 62 per cent of all French houses were built before 1914 (75 per cent in the rural communes);

[1] *Aube*, 29 March 1947.

[2] MRP Congr. 1948, Toulouse; report on 'La Politique du Logement'.

[3] Habitations à Bon Marché. The name HBM was changed to HLM (Habitations à Loyer Modéré) in 1951. The HBM scheme was started in 1906.

[4] *Aube*, 21 March 1950.   [5] MRP Congr. 1951, Lyon; housing motion.

[6] MRP Congr. 1956, Paris; motion of Equipes Ouvrières.

[7] MRP Congr. 1962, Dijon; housing motion.

22·5 per cent were without running water (42 per cent in rural communes); 60 per cent lacked an inside lavatory (80 per cent in rural communes).[1] Frances's population increased from 40 million in 1946 to 50 million in 1968, so that there has been a growing demand for new houses. The accelerated building programme of the 1960s did little more than keep abreast with rising population. The fundamental problems of city slums and sub-standard rural housing have not been solved. *Le Nouvel Observateur* produced a mass of evidence in 1965 showing that, amongst other things, half a million Parisians had to live in furnished rooms owing to the housing shortage, and that the average French house was smaller, less comfortable and more expensive than in Britain and in all the Common Market countries except Italy.[2] In 1967 an IRCOM (Institut de Recherches Economiques et Commerciales Appliqués) survey confirmed these findings.[3]

MRP played a role in tackling, if not in solving, the rent problem. At the 1948 Congress Georges Coudray emphasized the need for higher, more realistic rents, even if these were unpopular. Without higher rents landlords would not improve buildings and there would be no incentive to build more houses. Coudray contended that higher rents would help to prevent the sort of tragedy which had recently occurred in Metz when twenty people had been killed when an old block of flats had collapsed,[4] and the motion on housing recognized the need for unfreezing rents. Unfortunately the 1948 Rent Act, the Grimaud Law, named after its MRP *rapporteur*, Henri-Louis Grimaud, was only a half-measure. Henceforth, gradual increases in rents were permitted, provided some of the increase was spent on repairs, and new houses were not subject to rent control. However, one important clause of the 1914 Act, giving tenants complete security of tenure even after the lease expired, was not repealed. The result of this has been that many families in pre-1948 flats and houses continue to pay uneconomic rents, handing their houses down to the next generation, whilst families in post-1948 houses often have to pay very high rents. As early as 1950 *L'Aube* complained that landlords were failing to apply the Grimaud Law, because they refused to carry out repairs which might cost more than the total realized by gradually increasing rents.[5] At the 1952 MRP Congress Coudray contended that far too many wealthy

---

[1] *TC*, 29 April 1965, Special number on housing.
[2] *Nouvel Observateur*, 11 March 1965.
[3] Cited in M. Anderson, *Government in France*, p. 139.
[4] MRP Congr. 1948, Toulouse; report on 'La Politique du Logement'.
[5] *Aube*, 21 March 1950.

tenants were still not paying realistic rents,[1] and in 1953 Henri Amiot wrote that the 1948 Law was simply being ignored, because it suited neither landlords nor tenants to raise rents.[2] The building committee of the Planning Commission followed this up by maintaining that pre-1948 rents should be doubled if more houses were not to be allowed to fall into disrepair,[3] and three years later Paul Legatte, a *maître de requêtes* at the Conseil d'Etat, argued that the only way to attract more capital to the building industry was to repeal the Grimaud Law and allow completely free rents on all property.[4] Later still Joseph Fontanet praised the Grimaud Law for having taken a step in the right direction, but said that the time had come to repeal it; he went on to assert (unconvincingly) that if all rents were freed, the excessively high rents in the free sector would tend to come down as the pre-1948 rents rose. At the same time, however, he insisted that the Government should spend far more on HLM.[5] There can be little doubt that the 1948 Law did not go far enough in freeing rents, for it helped to produce a situation in which the rents of some tenants remained uneconomically low whilst others were exorbitantly high. Nevertheless, without a national housing policy, the repeal of the 1948 Law would not of itself have solved the problem of wide variations in rents; in particular, it would not have touched the problem caused by the reluctance of most Frenchmen to allot a reasonable proportion of their income to housing. Between 1946–67 the figure rose from 3·4 per cent to 7 per cent of average family income, but in Britain and the United States the comparable figures were approximately 10 per cent and 12 per cent.

Another major problem in the housing sector has been the lack of funds available for borrowers who wish to build or repair their own houses. There are still no private building societies in France. As with rents, MRP could claim some credit for having tried to solve this problem. A bill put forward by Lionel de Tinguy and the MRP group in 1951, which became law in 1952, set up a national savings scheme for housing, Epargne Logement. Under this scheme a Caisse National d'Epargne Logement was set up under the Crédit Foncier de France. A savings account could be opened at any Caisse d'Epargne (Savings Bank), and when an amount totalling 20 per cent of the purchase price of a new house had been saved, a mortgage could be obtained from the Caisse National d'Epargne Logement, which ran a central fund for this purpose. Georges Coudray optimistically told the 1952 MRP Congress that the scheme would make

---

[1] MRP Congr. 1952, Bordeaux; report on 'La Politique du Logement'.
[2] *Monde*, 11 July 1953. [3] *Monde*, 5 August 1953.
[4] *Monde*, 30 June 1956. [5] *Forces Nouvelles*, 19 November 1964.

it possible for young couples to buy a new house,[1] and Tinguy described it as a major step towards the solution of the housing problem.[2] But the scheme had obvious drawbacks. The CFTC newspaper, *Syndicalisme*, pointed out that loans could not be obtained for the improvement of existing buildings,[3] an omission which was eventually put right in 1965 with the extension of Epargne Logement to all buildings. A more serious criticism was made by the Socialist newspaper *Le Populaire*, which said that, although it favoured the Tinguy Law, the fact of the matter was that very few young married couples could save the necessary amount to obtain a mortgage.[4] MRP was aware of this drawback. In 1951 François de Menthon had proposed that there should be a national mortgage scheme, under which borrowers could obtain a loan repayable over twenty years without having to put down an initial deposit. This idea was revived in a bill put forward by Fernand Bouxom and the MRP group in 1956, proposing that the Bank of France should establish a mortgage fund of 300 million francs, from which borrowers could obtain a loan, repayable over a period of from thirty to sixty-five years at interest rates varying from 0·5 per cent to a maximum of 10 per cent.[5] However, nothing came of this bill, and it was not until 1966 that banks and insurance companies were authorized to grant twenty-year building loans at 8–9 per cent, thus at last implementing the proposal made by Menthon fifteen years previously.

Probably the greatest failing in post-war French housing policy has been the lack of a national housing plan. In the Fourth Republic the Planning Commission concentrated at first on basic industries, and in the 1950s on consumer goods. In the Fifth Republic higher priority has been given to national prestige and productivity than to social policy. Since the Fourth Plan (1962–65), however, more attention has been paid to housing, but even at the beginning of the 1970s the Government could be criticized for its failure to invest more in HLM, for the red tape which still permeates the administration of building, and for its failure to deal with land speculation.

As early as 1947 Mme Perrot of Grenoble told the MRP Congress that housing should be included in the National Plan,[6] whilst *L'Aube*, citing Le Corbusier, contended that France required a

---

[1] MRP Congr. 1952, Bordeaux; report on 'La Politique du Logement'.
[2] *Forces Nouvelles*, 17 May 1952.   [3] *Syndicalisme*, 18 March 1953.
[4] *Populaire*, 25 November 1953.
[5] *Proposition du Loi* no. 1980, 29 May 1956.
[6] MRP Congr. 1947, Paris; debate on 'La Politique Financière, Economique et Sociale'.

national housing plan: uncontrolled reconstruction of bombed-out buildings would simply create another housing problem within a few years.[1] In 1948 Coudray said that if France did not adopt a housing plan, she would repeat the errors of the inter-war period, when far too few houses had been built,[2] and in 1952, after pointing out that the Grimaud Rent Law had been only a limited success, Coudray said that the only solution to the housing problem was 'a real Monnet Plan for Construction';[3] indeed, such a plan should be a condition for MRP's contined support of the Pinay Government (MRP had been particularly annoyed in April 1952 when Pinay had cut the HLM credits from 42 milliard to 35 milliard francs; 7 members of the party voted against this decision and 4 abstained).[4] L'Aube argued that only a national plan orientated towards social housing would prevent the building of luxury flats costing between 4,500,000–7,500,000 francs at a time when there was an acute national housing shortage.[5] In 1955 L'Observateur pointed out that an average of only 10,000 HLM had been built annually since the war, a 'scandalously low' figure which was an indictment of the laisser faire housing policies of successive governments,[6] and L'Express wondered why there was a National Assembly committee which specialized in alcohol but none which specialized in housing.[7]

In an attempt to obtain a more coherent housing policy, Georges Coudray and members of the MRP group put forward a bill in 1955 to establish a Conseil Supérieur du Logement et de l'Habitation. Amongst other things, this body would

promote a national housing policy, concentrating on the construction of social housing (i.e. HLM), . . . determine the necessary fiscal measures to encourage an acceleration of the building programme, . . . and study all means to reduce the cost of building, in particular by the use of prefabricated materials.[8]

But, like many other bills in the Third and Fourth Republics, it never emerged from committee, and almost ten years later Eugène

1 Aube, 29 March 1947.

2 MRP Congr. 1948, Toulouse; report on 'La Politique du Logement'.

3 MRP Congr. 1952, Bordeaux; report on 'La Politique du Logement'.

4 H. Bouret, P. Coste-Floret, A. Denis, J. Dumas, E. Fouyet, F. Lefebvre, A. Monteil voted against; P. Bacon, A. Coste-Floret, A. Gau and P. H. Teitgen abstained. JO (AN), 2 April 1952, p. 1794.

5 Aube, 21 February 1951.   6 Observateur, 14 April 1955.

7 Express, 4 June 1955.

8 Proposition du Loi no. 10743, 13 May 1955. The MRP Equipes Ouvrières also called for 'the realization of a national housing policy under the auspices of a Conseil Supérieur du Logement' at the 1956 Congress.

Claudius-Petit,[1] who had been Minister of Housing from late 1948 to early 1952, again criticized French housing policy for its incoherence. He maintained that the building of HLM should be the chief priority of a national housing plan, for HLM should be seen not as a charity but as an essential aspect of social justice. He pointed out that in 1963 car production had risen by 19 per cent and housing by only 4 per cent; the roads were crowded with cars belonging to people who lived in slums. A modern state like France could solve its housing problem; all that was needed was a national housing plan and the will to implement it.[2]

Neither the Fourth nor the Fifth Republic has produced such a national plan, although considerable progress in house-building occurred in the 1960s. Despairing of any possibility of decisive governmental action in the 1950s, Abbé Pierre, an MRP deputy from 1946–50, had led a one-man campaign to obtain better housing for the poor. In several articles in Le Monde in May and June 1951, Abbé Pierre showed that families of up to seven were living in one room, that others had to carry out a constant campaign against rats and fleas, that many families lived in basement rooms without light or gas. Abbé Pierre's campaign resulted in a Pyrrhic victory, the Law of 31 March 1954 establishing cités d'urgence.[3] These cités were set up on waste ground; the houses were prefabricated and were built to last for no more than ten years. It was a crash programme to deal with a desperate situation.

Unfortunately the cités d'urgence were a failure. In June 1955 L'Observateur reported that the cité d'urgence in Plessis-Trévise, a Paris suburb, consisted of badly-built, leaky prefabs; there was only one school for forty children, although there were 950 school-age children in the cité; moreover, many of the workers had to spend a total of four hours travelling to and from work.[4] Six months later L'Observateur concluded that the cités d'urgence had no future; those at Pontoise, Conflans, Aulnay-sous-Bois and Chaville, as well as that at Plessis-Trévise, had become slums; it was clear that houses could not be built at 600,000 francs apiece.[5]

The nearest the Fourth Republic came to a national housing

---

[1] Claudius-Petit was a member of the UDSR. In 1969 he joined the Centre Démocratie et Progrès (CDP), a centre party which counts several Christian Democrats amongst its members; see chapter 8.

[2] Express, 16 July 1964.

[3] The cités owed something to MRP, for Robert Buron and the MRP group had put forward a bill for a similar scheme. It was withdrawn when the Government decided to implement Abbé Pierre's scheme; cf. R. Buron, Les Dernières Années de la IVe République, pp. 91–5.

[4] Observateur, 30 June 1955.   [5] Observateur, 8 December 1956.

policy was the Loi Cadre put forward by Bernard Chochoy, the Minister of State responsible for Housing in Guy Mollet's Government (February 1956–June 1957). The three main features of Chochoy's Loi Cadre were priority for HLM building, rationalization of the administration of housing, and concentration on industrialized building. MRP devoted a special pamphlet to the Loi Cadre, fully supporting its objectives, whilst wondering whether it might have an adverse effect on small building firms, who would be unable to win HLM contracts owing to the size of buildings involved.[1] However, the Loi Cadre could not be translated into concrete decrees, because the Mollet Government fell within a fortnight of its second reading on 17 May 1957.

The first Housing Minister of the Fifth Republic, the left-wing Catholic Pierre Sudreau (Minister from 1958–62), attempted to introduce a more rational policy, but, like Edgard Pisani in agriculture,[2] he was partially frustrated by the resistance of established interest groups and by the conservatism of his Ministry. In an attempt to obtain more land for development and to prevent speculation, a Law was passed in 1959 empowering the Ministry to mark out Zones à Urbaniser par Priorité (ZUPS) and Zones d'Aménagement Différé (ZADS). The Ministry had the right to make compulsory purchases in these areas and to use them for the construction of publicly financed buildings such as HLM. However, the scheme was only applied on a relatively small scale, and up to 1965 only 81 square miles had been purchased and 50,000 flats built. Sudreau's successors, in particular Albin Chalandon, Chaban-Delmas's Minister of Equipment, opted for a more 'liberal' approach, and the concept of a national housing plan became a dead letter once again. In the early 1970s land speculation, one of the major obstacles to cheaper and more plentiful housing, continued unabated.

Other factors besides rents, mortgages and planning, which have contributed to France's housing problems, have been the constantly changing administrative regulations which have made long-term planning very difficult,[3] and the unwillingness of the French building industry to use prefabricated materials and standard plans.[4] But

[1] 'Construction: Essor ou Stagnation'; MRP Docs, February 1957.

[2] See chapter 5 on Agriculture.

[3] *Monde*, 29 May 1954; and see Report of Economic and Social Council, JO (Conseil Economique et Sociale) 14 December 1963.

[4] *Monde*, 18 December 1956, estimated that only 20,000 of the 250,000 houses completed in 1956 would be 'industrially built'; *Express*, 20 September 1964, said that 35,000 different plans had been used in the construction of 330,000 houses in 1963.

the most important reasons for the prolonged post-war housing crisis have been the failures to plan nationally, to charge economic rents on pre-1948 property, and to develop mortgage schemes. In all these areas the Christian Democrats could claim some credit for having put forward constructive proposals for reform, even if the outcome was disappointing. The 1966 national mortgage scheme is the direct heir of Tinguy's Epargne Logement of 1951. The relative importance attached to housing in the Fourth and Fifth Plans can be ascribed in part to constant MRP demands for a national housing plan, even though no such plan ever materialized. And the partial unfreezing of rents, resulting from the Grimaud Law of 1948, has helped to prevent the growth of even more slum property, even if the problem of widely disparate rents has scarcely been touched.

Chapter 5

AGRICULTURE

It is appropriate to devote a whole chapter to agriculture, because in spite of the existence of the Peasant Party, MRP was in a very real sense *the* farmers' party, especially in the early years of the Fifth Republic. (The extent to which MRP was a rural party has already been discussed in the chapter on elections.)[1] It was therefore natural that the Christian Democrats should be deeply involved in agricultural politics, both in government, especially in the Fourth Republic, and through their rural organizations, especially in the early years of the Fifth Republic. Pierre Pflimlin was both Minister of Agriculture in the formative years of the Fourth Republic and one of the fathers of the common agricultural market of the European Community. Then in the late 1950s and early 1960s the young Catholic farmers of Jeunesse Agricole Chrétienne (JAC) won control of the two most important agricultural organizations, the Centre National des Jeunes Agriculteurs (CNJA) and the Fédération Nationale des Syndicats d'Exploitants Agricoles (FNSEA), a development which opened the way for what has been described as the 'rural revolution'[2] of the 1960s.

Pierre Pflimlin was Minister of Agriculture from November 1947 to June 1951, with a break of seven months in 1949–50 when he was replaced by another Christian Democrat, Gabriel Valay. In the Fourth Republic approximately one-seventh of MRP's deputies were farmers (*agriculteurs, cultivateurs, viticulteurs*) and at the first two elections of the Fifth Republic (when MRP still put up candidates) the proportion of farmers elected was almost a quarter.[3] These figures were reflected in party membership. At the 1951 Congress it was claimed that 15 per cent of MRP members were farmers, whilst in 1960 the figure was put at 22 per cent. The second figure coincides with the growing importance of JAC, whose members or ex-members, often standing on MRP tickets, won approximately 4,000 seats at the

1 See chapter 3, especially pp. 86–91.
2 Gordon Wright, *Rural Revolution in France*.
3 31 out of 159 metropolitan deputies in November 1946 (19 per cent); 12 out of 84 in 1951 (14 per cent); 11 out of 72 in 1956 (15 per cent); 13 out of 54 in 1958 (24 per cent); 12 out of 51 in 1962 (24 per cent).

138

municipal elections of 1959.[1] The proportion of MRP rural members and deputies also inevitably rose as the party was pushed back into agricultural (and Catholic) strongholds such as Brittany.

MRP's agricultural policy, as might be expected, was neither collectivist nor individualist. The party favoured the continuation of peasant family farming, as shown by the agricultural motion at the 1949 Congress and speeches by Pflimlin at the same Congress and by François de Menthon in 1951 and Maurice Byé in 1954. MRP might be criticized for having paid too much attention to the family farm; indeed Pflimlin conceded as much in 1971.[2] But, on the other hand, MRP, unlike the Communists, did not limit itself only to the defence of the small farmer. Robert Buron in 1948, Gabriel Valay in 1949, François de Menthon in 1951, Maurice Byé in 1954, Jean Lecanuet in 1957, and Pierre Pflimlin, year after year, emphasized the importance of structural reforms, co-operation, mechanization and improved marketing. Only in the field of mechanization, how-ever, did MRP contribute much towards agricultural restructuring in the Fourth Republic. The twin pillars of MRP's agricultural policy in this period were increased production and greater exports, the latter to be achieved through Pflimlin's (abortive) Green Pool[3] and later through the Common Market. The first problem to be solved after the war was that of production, and there can be no doubt that Pflimlin was right to emphasize this aspect, but it is arguable that he put the cart before the horse by orientating his policy towards exports before the internal marketing system had been organized, and before the basic structures had been modernized. Pflimlin later defended himself on the ground that he did lay con-siderable emphasis on restructuring.[4] In fact MRP *talked* a great deal about restructuring agriculture, but achieved little. Probably the main reason for inaction was the power of the conservative agri-cultural pressure groups throughout the Fourth Republic. Pflimlin discounted the influence of these agricultural pressure groups,[5] but the French economic historian, Alfred Sauvy, produced convincing evidence of their retrogressive influence in a series of articles in *Le Monde* in 1957.[6]

Although it is true that MRP may have stressed exporting too much and restructuring too little in the Fourth Republic, the party's

[1] Wright, p. 159. Cf. R. Buron, *Le Plus Beau des Métiers*, p. 28, for importance of the agricultural vote from the point of view of an MRP deputy from a western Department, Mayenne.

[2] Interview with Pflimlin, 3 April 1971.

[3] The original proposal for a European agricultural market; see pp. 153–5.

[4] Interview with Pflimlin, 3 April 1971.

[5] ibid.   [6] *Monde*, 19/20/21 September 1957.

genuine interest in restructuring was shown in the early years of the Fifth Republic, when it supported Henri Rochereau's reforms of 1960 and voted against Edgard Pisani's reforms of 1962 only because they did not go far enough in strengthening the Sociétés d'Aménagement Foncier et d'Etablissement Rural (SAFER). The structural and social reforms of the early 1960s were important, but less revolutionary than implied by Gordon Wright. Nevertheless, there is no reason to disagree with Wright's conclusion that the Pisani reforms, limited though they were in some ways, would never have gone through at all without the support of the young Catholic farmers of JAC, 'the most dynamic force for rural change in post-war France'.[1]

France's agricultural problems have not been solved by the early 1970s, but the positive reforms which have been implemented owe a considerable amount to the Christian Democrats. Pflimlin, Buron, Valay and Menthon may not have done much to restructure agriculture, but they helped to create a climate conducive to reform by their advocacy of planning. They helped to change the psychology of the French farmer, even if it is true that the really concrete proposals for reform came from below, especially from the young Catholic farmers of CNJA, who by 1961 had taken over FNSEA, and thus opened the way for a breakthrough which may give France a rational and prosperous agriculture by the 1980s.

It is impossible to appreciate the achievement of the Christian Democrats (and, of course, of other advocates of reform) without some realization of the magnitude of the agriculture problem, which is essentially a historical legacy.

Since the eighteenth century there have been 'two agricultures' in France, one essentially north of Paris, where there were large tenant farms before the Great Revolution; the other consisting of the rest of France, i.e. the west, the Massif Central, the Midi and the south-west, where the farms were small and the peasants illiterate, immobile and poor. The Napoleonic inheritance laws encouraged *parcellement* (the subdivision of farms), and the inefficient marketing system, which benefited no one but the middlemen, encouraged *polyculture* (the production of a little of everything) and hoarding.

The opening up of the American West, which brought cheap wheat to Europe from the late 1870s, the growth of elementary education in the 1880s, and the construction of rural railways in the same decade, might have had a catalytic effect on French agriculture south of the Loire. Among the many reasons it did not, perhaps the most important was that throughout the Third Republic politicians

[1] Wright, p. 150.

and writers were almost unanimous in extolling the virtues of the peasant farmer. France's 'yeomen', therefore, must be protected from the cold wind blowing from the New World. Jules Méline's tariff law of 1892 gave just such protection, but at the cost of internal stagnation. In 1900 45 per cent of the working population was engaged in agriculture; by the end of the Second World War approximately 35 per cent were still engaged in agriculture, compared with about 5 per cent in Great Britain and 12 per cent in West Germany. France had excluded outside influences which might have forced modernization, but she, unlike her neighbours, had faced no internal pressure for reform because her birthrate was stagnant or declining from 1880–1914.[1] A rising birthrate would have encouraged industrialization and migration from the land, which would in turn have encouraged more efficient agricultural methods. But the birthrate did not rise; as Jean Jaurès, the great Socialist leader remarked, 'the only way to make the peasants fertile is rape'.[2]

The First World War left an indelible mark on the French peasantry. Those who stayed at home prospered, and those who went to the Front, and were lucky enough to return, had at least widened their experience by meeting other Frenchmen and seeing other parts of France. But the rural population was embittered by the facts that three-fifths of France's active peasants fought in the front line, most of them in the infantry, and that over a million (53 per cent of those killed) were peasants: 'the deeper effects of the wartime experience seem to have been . . . resentment, an increased hostility towards the politicians and the urban world, a sense of being victimized and misunderstood'.[3] At the very time when it was becoming essential for the peasants to face up to the need for modernization they buried their heads in the sand. In the inter-war years there was, to all intents and purposes, no agricultural policy in France. The politicians gave no lead and the peasants had no wish to be led. However, there were one or two significant developments. In 1919 the Confédération Nationale des Associations Agricoles (CNAA) was set up. It was controlled by large-scale northern farmers and took few initiatives, but may be regarded as the precursor of the post-war farmers' organizations, the Confédération Générale de l'Agriculture (CGA) and the Fédération Nationale des Syndicats d'Exploitants Agricoles (FNSEA). The CNAA was conservative throughout, and so were the specialized agricultural organizations of the inter-war period, such as the Association Générale des

[1] See J. Sheahan, *An Introduction to the French Economy*, p. 4, for birthrate figures.
[2] Cited in Wright, p. 2. [3] Cited in Wright, p. 30.

Producteurs de Blé (AGPB), the Confédération Générale des Betteraviers (CGB) and the Fédération des Associations Viticoles (FAV).

The economic depression of the 1930s affected the peasants slowly but decisively. Overproduction of wheat and wine was a problem before and after the depression, but it was in the 1930s that the State began to control some agricultural prices for the first time. The agricultural lobby in the Chamber refused to countenance government intervention in production quotas or marketing methods, but the peasants began to see that a measure of government intervention, such as that exercised over prices by the Popular Front's Wheat Office, could work to their advantage. The Popular Front's other agricultural reforms, such as a modified eight-hour day and collective bargaining for farm labourers, were buried in the Senate, which by the end of the Third Republic had become the symbol of stagnant France. Overall, the Popular Front's attempt to grasp the nettle of France's agricultural problems was a failure.

The Vichy period was important, because the Peasant Corporation, with its nominated leaders, encouraged the emergence of a new peasant élite and really impressed on small farmers the value of organization. The idea of peasant unity survived in the post-war CGA (actually founded in 1943), and even more in the CGA's obstreperous offspring, the FNSEA. Moreover, Vichy introduced several reforms which survived the Liberation, notably the 1941 *remembrement* decree (government aid to do away with *parcellement*), the relaxation of the Napoleonic inheritance laws and the grant of loans for the improvement of rural property (more than 100,000 homes had been improved in this way by the Liberation). Basically, however, the peasants did rather well under Vichy, selling even poor quality produce at inflated prices, so there was no incentive for fundamental reforms.

The Liberation period, indeed the Fourth Republic as a whole, was a disappointing time for root and branch reformers. This was especially true of agriculture. The first Minister of Agriculture, the Socialist Pierre Tanguy-Prigent, was more interested in sectarian politics than in major reforms. He seems to have spent too much time trying to infiltrate the CGA, which he had founded, and the FNSEA with Socialists (failing in both cases), and too little on structural reforms. Although he favoured the development of co-operative farms and a national land office to buy up land for distribution to efficient peasants on favourable terms, he did nothing to achieve either. He set up *foyers ruraux* as agricultural education and youth centres, but they were soon superseded by JAC organizations. Tanguy's only major contribution was his establishment of

142

Coopératives pour l'Utilisation des Machines Agricoles (CUMA), which helped to make possible the tractor revolution of the Fourth Republic (56,500 tractors in 1946; 588,600 in 1958).[1]

By the time Pierre Pflimlin of MRP became Minister of Agriculture in Robert Schuman's Government in November 1947, it was perhaps already too late to implement radical reforms. Tripartism had ended in May 1947 with the dismissal of the Communists from the Government. Their replacement by Radicals strengthened the conservative forces within the Government, and these forces were further boosted with the growing influence of de Gaulle's RPF. Moreover, the chief farmers' organization, FNSEA, had already fallen under the influence of the conservative, protectionist, large-scale farmers of the north, who, under the leadership of René Blondelle, were to dominate FNSEA until challenged by the ex-JACists of CNJA in the late 1950s. The FNSEA under Blondelle worked hand in glove with the Peasant Party of Paul Antier and Camille Laurens, playing an obstructive, protectionist role throughout the Fourth Republic.[2] But even if the political climate had been more conducive to reform, it is doubtful whether Pflimlin, instinctively rather conservative, would have been the man to inaugurate fundamental changes.

Pflimlin, like MRP's other agricultural experts, was well aware of the problems created by France's historical legacy as well as by the contemporary political situation. He told *L'Aube* that the first requirement was to increase production after the dislocation caused by the war.[3] He supported the first Monnet Plan, which set an agricultural production target for 1950 equal to that of 1938. He persuaded Monnet to devote more money to restructuring in the revised Plan covering the years 1948–53, whilst proposing that the 1953 production target should be 25 per cent above the 1938 figure.[4] He favoured *remembrement* and re-equipment.[5] He emphasized the importance of exporting—'France ought to be the granary and cellar of Europe' he told *Le Monde*.[6] 'It would be imprudent to switch to a policy of massive exports', the deputies were informed, 'but they are our trump card if France is going to balance her external trade'.[7]

---

[1] INSEE, *Annuaire Statistique de la France: Retrospectif*, 1961, vol. 66, p. 99.

[2] The Peasants made an unlikely alliance with the Independents (mainly conservative northern businessmen) in 1950. At the 1951 Election over 100 CNIP (Centre National des Indépendants et Paysans) deputies were elected. From 1951–56 the Ministry of Agriculture was held by two mutually hostile Peasants, Antier and Laurens.

[3] *Aube*, 24 March 1948. [4] Interview with Pflimlin, 3 April 1971.

[5] *Aube*, 24 March 1948; MRP Congr. 1947, Paris; report on 'La Politique Economique, Financière et Sociale'.

[6] *Monde*, 10 January 1949. [7] JO (AN), 26 February 1949, p. 976.

At the 1949 MRP Congress Gabriel Valay emphasized the importance of organized home markets as well as the growth of production and the development of export markets.[1] And in the debate which followed Valay's report, Pflimlin showed that he was already thinking in European terms: 'If France is going to export more, there must be more European co-operation which so far is non-existent. . . . Once Europe becomes a reality, French agriculture can play a vital role, for we are the one great agricultural producer of Western Europe'.[2] In summing up the debate, Valay praised Pflimlin's achievements as Minister of Agriculture, pointing out that expenditure on modernization had doubled in 1948 compared with 1947 and would double again in 1949, but he did not underestimate the problems still facing agriculture. More should be spent on agricultural training (he wanted to know why only 600 million francs had been spent on agricultural training in 1948, whilst 14 milliard had been spent on industrial training); co-operative farming should be developed (he suggested jointly-owned milking-machines which would increase profitability without putting farmers out of business); above all, however, 'it must be admitted that a considerable number of small farms are destined to disappear'.[3]

Buron in 1948, Menthon in 1951 and Pflimlin in 1953 all emphasized the importance of structural reforms, some of which would be unpalatable. Buron said that although MRP was opposed to compulsory co-operative farming, it was essential for peasants to participate voluntarily in co-operative projects.[4] He made the same point when he became Minister of Finance in Mendès-France's Government, and went on to say that 'Farmers must organize their production to suit internal and external consumption requirements, and . . . investment policy must be orientated towards sectors in need of expansion'.[5] In 1951 Menthon said that France was now producing enough. Two things, however, were still required—guaranteed prices and greater exports. Agricultural exports had totalled 115 milliard francs in 1950, a higher figure than in any previous year, but were still too low: 'it is above all in the organization of European agricultural markets, in which Pierre Pflimlin has taken the initiative, that we will be able to find permanent outlets for our agricultural produce'.[6] Like other MRP spokesmen Menthon

1 MRP Congr. 1949, Strasbourg; report on 'Les Questions Agricoles'.
2 ibid.
3 MRP Congr. 1949, Strasbourg; report on 'Les Questions Agricoles'.
4 MRP Congr. 1948, Paris; report on 'La Politique Economique'.
5 Monde, 25 January 1955.
6 MRP Congr. 1951, Lyon; report on 'La Politique Economique et Sociale'.

emphasized the importance of professional training, mechanization, co-operative farming and *remembrement*.

In 1953 Pflimlin—besides advocating more agricultural training (60 per cent of Danish farmers were trained compared with 5 per cent of French) and technical advice for practising farmers (there was one technical adviser for every 240 farmers in Holland compared with one per 6,000 in France)—tackled one of France's basic agricultural problems, the marketing system:

> We in MRP are resolute partisans of organized agricultural markets. . . . If it is true that the direct intervention of the State should be as limited as possible, it is also true that the Government should not abdicate from its responsibilities to the nation as a whole. If it is a question of achieving certain economic and social goals, it may be necessary for the State to intervene directly, for the deciding factor (*la loi suprême*) must be the general interest of the whole nation. The outworn structures of classical liberalism must be uprooted.[1]

He went on to say that it was iniquitous that 25 per cent of France's fruit and vegetables were allowed to perish every year owing to inefficient marketing. And then he attacked one of MRP's *bêtes noires*, the home distillers (*bouilleurs du cru*) and the whole alcohol lobby, whose policies led to 'the systematic and permanent over-production of alcohol',[2] paid for by the State, i.e. the tax-payer.

The Christian Democrats were clearly aware of the problems of French agriculture, but the extent of their contribution to their solution is difficult to assess. The twin pillars of Pflimlin's agricultural policy were increased production and greater exports. The former was largely achieved; the latter was only a partial success. The greatest failure of Pflimlin, however, was that he did not really tackle the fundamental structural problems of French agriculture, which had to be solved if farmers' incomes were going to keep pace with those being earned in industry.

As early as February 1949 Pierre Abelin expressed concern about the growing disparity between agricultural and industrial prices,[3] and in the early 1950s the gap widened. In 1953 René Charpentier pointed out that agricultural discontent could largely be explained by the fact that GNP had increased by 13 per cent since 1948, but farmers' incomes had gone down by 241 milliard francs.[4] And by 1958 average peasant incomes were only 25 per cent above those of

[1] MRP Congr. 1953, Paris; report on 'Une Politique de Productivité'.
[2] ibid.   [3] JO (AN), 25 February 1949, p. 954.
[4] JO (AN), 13 November 1953, p. 5035.

1938, whereas average industrial wages were 60–70 per cent higher. Moreover, the figure of 25 per cent was an average. Many farmers south of the Loire and in Brittany were living in debt and poverty. Although prices for agricultural products were rising, industrial prices were rising much faster, so that the peasants had to pay for increasingly expensive fertilisers and machinery out of relatively declining income. Their basic answer was to demand *indexation* (a sliding scale for agricultural prices related to inflation) and protection. So long as FNSEA was dominated by Blondelle and the National Assembly was under the influence of the Amicale Parlementaire Agricole (especially true of the years 1951–56), protectionism and price supports were the sole demands of the agricultural lobby. They cared little about structural reforms and modernization. Powerful lobbies, such as that representing the sugar-beet growers, were not concerned about over-production provided they lined their own pockets. This largely negative attitude did little to solve France's basic agricultural problems, especially those of the south and west, and it was not surprising that as inflation continued peasant frustration increased, culminating in major disturbances in the Midi in 1953 (mainly led by wine growers) and the growth of Poujadism in the mid-1950s.

MRP cannot be blamed for the negative attitude of FNSEA and the peasant lobby, but it is arguable that Pflimlin might have pressed harder for structural reforms in the late 1940s and early 1950s, because the FNSEA lobby, acting through the Amicale Parlementaire Agricole, only became really powerful after the CNIP successes at the 1951 General Election.[1] Even if Pflimlin's argument[2] that his time was fully occupied with achieving production targets and ending the black market is accepted, there is still a case for suggesting that he might have done more to orientate investment and to initiate structural reforms. As early as August 1948 Marcel Tardy criticized Pflimlin in *Le Monde* for just such failings, and in 1950 he said that Pflimlin had encouraged over-production of sugar-beet and alcohol by his policy of guaranteed prices and his subservience to the agricultural pressure groups: 'The system of guaranteed prices and monopolies leads to a vast coalition of those who produce wheat, sugar-beet, wine and alcohol, a sort of huge cartel run by the State'.[3] Pflimlin argued that a system of guaranteed prices was the only way to gain the confidence of the farmers, and that without this confidence no plans for modernization would be

---

[1] See p. 143, note 2, for details about CNIP.
[2] Interview with Pflimlin, 3 April 1971.   [3] *Monde*, 21 January 1950.

accepted by the agricultural community.[1] It was for this reason that he resigned in December 1949 when Bidault refused to agree to a higher guaranteed price for sugar-beet.[2] But a few years later the economist Alfred Sauvy criticized all post-war Ministers of Agriculture, not for guaranteeing prices, but for paying the same price in all parts of the country; thus, a wheat farmer in Lot, with a yield of 12 quintals to the acre, could scarcely make ends meet, whilst the Aisne farmer, with a yield of 38 quintals, made a very good profit.[3] Various members of MRP were well aware of the problems created by indiscriminate price guarantees and insufficiently controlled investment. Henri Bouret and René Charpentier both argued for price differentials and a special investment policy for areas such as Brittany.[4] Eugène Forget, the MRP President of FNSEA, maintained that the uncontrolled expansion of agriculture had led to overproduction in certain sectors, and that some farmers should be encouraged by government grants to change to other products.[5] Robert Buron said that 'there must be a clearly defined policy, so that farmers organize their production in accordance with internal and external consumption requirements'.[6] No steps, however, were taken during the Fourth Republic to deal with the underlying problem of over-production in some sectors, usually those with powerful pressure groups, and under-production in others.

MRP deserves credit for Jean-Marie Louvel's attempt to improve the internal marketing system by his decree of 30 September 1953, which established advisory committees and executive agencies in some of the agricultural sectors which had hitherto not been organized (unlike wheat and sugar-beet). The advisory committees were consulted by the Planning Commission, whilst the executive agencies dealt with the practical side of marketing. The advisory committees seem to have worked well, but only three executive agencies were set up, the Institut des Vins de Consommation Courante (IVCC) for wine, the Société Interprofessionnel du Bétail et des Viandes (SIBEV) for meat, and Interlait for milk. Overall, these organizations were hampered by lack of finance, whilst their powers to intervene were much less than those of British Marketing Boards: 'They

[1] Interview with Pflimlin, 3 April 1971.

[2] *Monde*, 3 December 1949; *Le Nouvel Alsacien*, 5 December 1949. Pflimlin returned to the Ministry of Agriculture in July 1950; Valay (MRP) was Minister in the interim period.

[3] *Monde*, 20 September 1957.

[4] JO (AN), 13 October 1953, pp. 4241–6 (Charpentier); 15 October 1953, pp. 4306–8 (Bouret).

[5] *Bulletin du Conseil Economique*, 10 November 1954, pp. 516–19.

[6] *Monde*, 25 January 1955.

provided little more than a palliative to prevent disastrous price fluctuation, rather than a first step towards a system of organized marketing under State control'.[1] Nevertheless, Louvel had at least taken a small step towards the organization of the market, and the executive agencies may be regarded as the precursors of the Sociétés d'Intérêt Collectif Agricole (SICA), producers' marketing groups set up in the early 1960s with the encouragement of men like Michel Debatisse, the ex-JACist Secretary General of CNJA. The *marchés gares*, marketing depots such as Rungis near Orly, were another example of increasing concern in the 1960s with the marketing situation. Louvel's inadequate decree of 1953 recognized the problems created by middlemen and archaic marketing, but it did not do much to solve them. The main developments came in the 1960s under the auspices of the Fonds de Régularisation et d'Orientation des Marchés Agricoles (FORMA), established by Edgard Pisani in 1962.

As regards migration from the land, MRP played a cautious but constructive role. Although Pflimlin was warmly applauded at the 1953 Congress when he said it would be wrong to 'tamper with the family structure of French agriculture',[2] he and numerous other MRP spokesmen emphasized the importance of agricultural rationalization, including a reduction in the number of those engaged in agriculture. Inevitably Christian Democrats were concerned about the social consequences of structural changes, but they were not opposed to change as such, provided it was implemented in a humane manner.

In 1945 35 per cent of France's working population was on the land; by 1958 the figure was 23 per cent; by 1970 it was down to about 14 per cent. This compared with 3 per cent in Great Britain. The number of farms was reduced from 2·5 million in 1945 to 2·2 million in 1958; by 1970 the figure was 1·9 million, compared with 300,000 in Great Britain. Allowing for the fact that France is more suited to agriculture (90 per cent of the land could be cultivated), there were still too many holdings and too many agricultural workers in the early 1970s. In 1968 48 per cent of French farms were under 25 acres in size and 25 per cent were between 25 and 50 acres. The average size was about one-third of the average in Britain. Meanwhile agricultural wages were lagging about 25 per cent behind industrial wages.[3] But, although there had been insufficient migration

[1] Wright, p. 133.

[2] MRP Congr. 1953, Paris; report on 'Une Politique de Productivité'.

[3] For detailed facts and figures on French agriculture (in 1968) see D. I. Scargil, *Economic Geography of France*, ch. 1, pp. 1–30.

from the land overall, it had gone through too quickly in some parts. The Southern department of Lozère lost 43 per cent of its population in ten years (up to 1968) with drastic consequences on the economic structure of the whole Department, whilst at the other end of the scale Morbihan, a Breton Department with a high birthrate, was suffering from excess population and unemployment despite a general drift from the land. In order to deal with the social problems created by this type of situation, the National Association for Migration and Rural Settlement had been established on the advice of Eugène Forget, the MRP President of FNSEA, in 1950. It was responsible for the resettlement of about 7,000 people in the 1950s, mostly moving from Brittany to less populated agricultural regions such as Aquitaine. In 1962 former JAC leaders, now in control of FNSEA, supported the establishment of the Fonds d'Action Sociale pour l'Amélioration des Structures Agricoles (FASASA) to do the same type of work as was done by Forget's National Association, but on a larger scale. The FASASA also trains rural workers for jobs outside agriculture and helps to pension off older farmers, usually in order to re-allocate their land.

MRP and JAC encouraged *remembrement* which had been going on under the Service du Remembrement since 1941.[1] In 1948 Pflimlin said that *remembrement* was required at the rate of 500,000 hectares per annum; in fact, only 110,000 hectares were reparcelled in 1947, 115,000 in 1948, 110,000 in 1949 and 185,000 in 1950.[2] And since then the work has progressed slowly, with only 7,300,000 hectares being reparcelled between 1941–1961, the work continuing at an average rate of 150,000 hectares in the 1960s.[3] Another important step towards restructuring, taken in 1960 with full MRP support, was the establishment of Sociétés d'Aménagement Foncier et d'Etablissement Rural (SAFER), which buy up land as it becomes available and sell it to competent individuals or co-operatives. MRP's only complaint was that the SAFERs were given insufficient powers to buy land as it became available. Thus, in the 1962 debate on Pisani's Loi Complémentaire, Louis Orvoën and Alexis Méhaignerie proposed that the SAFERs should have the right to make pre-emptive bids at fixed prices for farms coming on to the market,[4] and when the MRP amendment was rejected, 39 of the party's 57 deputies voted against the Loi Complémentaire. In explaining MRP's attitude M. Fourmond said his party would vote against the Law partly because of the SAFER clause and partly because the

[1] E.g. Pflimlin, *Aube*, 24 March 1948; Buron, *Monde*, 25 January 1955.
[2] *Aube*, 26 May 1951.   [3] Scargil, p. 21.
[4] JO (AN), 18 July 1962, pp. 2584, 2603.

Government had given insufficient time for proper discussion of the Law.[1] The real reason for MRP's hostile vote, however, was almost certainly less honourable. The fact of the matter was that rural parliamentarians of all parties were under pressure from the traditional farm lobbies to vote against the bill. MRP used the limitations of the SAFER clause as a pretext to avoid voting *for* a bill which they favoured but which might earn them dangerous enemies amongst their constituents.

No discussion of the Christian Democrats' contribution to French agricultural reforms would be complete without reference to the young Catholic farmers of JAC. Before the war JAC had been a very poor relation to the young Catholic workers of JOC, but René Colson succeeded in changing the movement from a priest-dominated to a peasant-dominated organization by 1951. In 1938 there had been 20,000 JACists; by 1959 there were 300,000.[2] By the mid-1950s former JACists were beginning to exert political influence. In 1957 Hubert Buchoi and Michel Debatisse became President and Secretary of the Centre National des Jeunes Agriculteurs (CNJA). Having gained a foothold in CNJA, they proceeded to take over FNSEA, hitherto dominated by the conservative René Blondelle. In 1961 Marcel Bruel, a former JACist, became Secretary General of FNSEA, and in 1964 he was succeeded by Michel Debatisse. As early as 1959 the former JACists had shown their strength by electing about 4,000 candidates at the municipal elections, whilst eight of the nine JACists returned to the National Assembly in 1958 were members of MRP, where they acted as a powerful ginger group under the leadership of Bernard Lambert, a Breton farmer who was one of the chief advocates of the Rassemblement des Forces Démocratiques (RFD) in the late 1950s.[3]

The important role played by the former JACists in the early years of the Fifth Republic can be seen by the fact that they accepted the Debré Government's Loi d'Orientation of April 1960, which was rejected three times by the Senate, where opposition was led by Blondelle, after which the Government overruled the Senate. The JACists also gave their support to Edgard Pisani's Loi Complémentaire of July 1962, although they did not think it went far enough in certain respects.

The aim of the 1960 Loi d'Orientation was to give the peasants a better deal in relation to other workers. Restructuring was emphasized more than price guarantees, which drew forth the wrath of Blondelle, but was conditionally welcomed by Debatisse, who

---

[1] JO (AN), 27 July 1962, p. 2905.   [2] Bosworth, p. 124.
[3] See p. 244, note 1. Lambert is now (1972) in the PSU.

told the CNJA Congress that he wanted fair prices as well as the development of viable agricultural units.[1] Léon Dubois, who presided over MRP's Equipes Rurales, welcomed the reforms, but deplored the Government's refusal to call a special session of the National Assembly to discuss the agricultural crisis.[2] Maurice-René Simonnet, MRP's Secretary General and a member of the party's progressive wing, gave more qualified approval, doubting whether the Law would bring social justice to the countryside.[3] René Charpentier hoped that the establishment of the Fonds de Régularisation et d'Orientation des Marchés Agricoles (FORMA) would help to solve the marketing problem, but he was doubtful whether the Government would promulgate the necessary decrees to implement the rest of the programme, principally *remembrement* and improvements to rural electricity and water supplies.[4] Debré assured him that the Government would act soon.[5] But in fact it failed to do so. Bernard Lambert and Louis Orvoën both praised the FORMA, whilst calling for the extension of full family allowances and social security benefits to the agricultural community.[6] And Marie-Madeleine Dienesch, reporting on behalf of the Cultural, Family and Social Affairs Committee, called for more expenditure on agricultural training; there would be radical changes in French agriculture in the next ten years, she said, yet 96 per cent of French farmers were untrained.[7] Mlle Dienesch's appeal remained unanswered until the Pisani Loi Complémentaire two years later, when a large programme for agricultural training, including the building of fifty agricultural colleges, was outlined.

After passing the Loi d'Orientation the Government failed to issue decrees implementing it, partly because of the influence of pressure groups acting in the Ministry of Agriculture,[8] and partly because Henri Rochereau, the Minister of Agriculture, was not a very forceful personality. The peasants soon became restive, as they were bearing the brunt of the inflation without any compensation, and major riots occurred in Brittany and the Midi in May 1961. In Brittany they were led by the former JACist, Alex Gourvennec. The Government's reaction was to promise short-term price supports and long-term restructuring. Edgard Pisani, one of the most lively Gaullist technocrats, became Minister of Agriculture, and his Loi

---

[1] *La Croix*, 19 May 1960.   [2] *Forces Nouvelles*, 2 April 1960.
[3] *Forces Nouvelles*, 5 March 1960.   [4] JO (AN), 28 April 1960, pp. 517–18.
[5] ibid., p. 517.   [6] JO (AN), 4 May 1960, pp. 618–19 and 625–6.
[7] JO (AN), 28 April 1960, p. 518.
[8] Cf. Wahl in Beer and Ulam, *Patterns of Government* (2nd ed.), p. 447, and Yves Tavernier in RFSP, September 1962 and June 1963.

Complémentaire, based largely on CNJA proposals, was passed in August 1962. This law increased the powers and financial resources of the SAFERs, although not to the extent demanded by Debatisse and the majority of MRP.[1] The Fonds d'Action Sociale was given more money to help old peasants retire with adequate pensions. Producers' groups (SICA and others) were given the right to negotiate marketing agreements, thus breaking down some of the privileges of the middlemen.

All these reforms were supported by MRP speakers in the debate in July 1962, except that the majority of the party did not think sufficient time had been allowed for the debate or that the SAFER powers were adequate, and this led to an adverse vote.[2] But basically MRP, like the CNJA, favoured the structural reforms implemented by Pisani.[3] Such reforms take time to become effective, but the Pisani Charter, supported by Debatisse and the former JACists who had taken over FNSEA as well as CNJA by 1962, marked an important new development in French agriculture. The emphasis had been switched from price supports to structural reforms and long-term investment. FNSEA still supports the family farm, but recognizes the need for co-operative farming and organized marketing, preferring them to excessive individualism and 'Mélinian' protectionism. The 'rural revolution' has not been as dramatic as Wright implied in 1964,[4] partly because Pisani's successors, notably Edgar Faure, went back to cultivating the old peasant leaders and paying more attention to supporting prices than to reforming structures. But there has been a revolution in rural attitudes, and this revolution owes a great deal to the Christian Democrats (or at least Catholics) of JAC.

If the precise contribution of the Christian Democrats towards structural reform is difficult to assess, there can be no doubt that in two fields closely associated with agricultural modernization, namely mechanization and education, the Christian Democratic contribution was important. MRP advocated mechanization and agricultural training from the beginning. The mechanization programme was largely successful. Tractors increased from 37,000 in 1945 to almost 600,000 in 1958, and had surpassed 1,000,000 by 1964; combined harvesters numbered 250 in 1946 and 42,000 in

[1] See p. 150.   [2] See p. 149.

[3] Interview with Pflimlin, 3 April 1971. *Le Monde* suggested that another reason for MRP voting against Pisani was that the Christian Democrats did not like him as a man. Like Mendès-France, he was too outstanding a personality, too like a 'proconsular Radical', to appeal to MRP.

[4] G. Wright, *Rural Revolution in France*.

1958. But in 1968 there were still more horses than tractors at work in France and over 150,000 oxen were being used.[1] Today there may well be too many tractors, particularly in the south. It would be better to have more machinery co-operatives and fewer tractors, but peasants often prefer to own a tractor, even if it results in debt, than to share one. Although there were 9,000 machinery co-operatives in 1968, many more were still needed. As regards agricultural training, France still lags behind countries such as Holland and Denmark, although the gap has been narrowed since Pisani's reforms of 1962. The Christian Democrats helped to solve the problem by their support for the 1952 scheme for demonstration farms, of which there were 110 by 1960; and more important by their support of Centres d'Etudes Techniques Agricoles (CETA). CETAs were first established in 1945 by a wealthy northern farmer, Bernard Poullin, but the 'movement' was largely taken over by the young Catholic farmers of JAC. By 1962 there were over 1,000 CETAs, where young peasants could learn about cost accounting as well as about agricultural techniques.

One disappointment for the Christian Democrats has been the slow development of a European agricultural market. As early as 1948 Pflimlin had spoken of the advantages France could expect from a European agricultural market.[2] In 1955, as Faure's Minister of Finance, Pflimlin again spoke optimistically of the development of a European market,[3] and in the first debate on the Treaty of Rome Pierre Abelin was enthusiastic about the potential of the European agricultural market, provided such safeguards as a common external tariff were instituted.[4] In practice, however, neither the Common Agricultural Market nor the Green Pool fulfilled MRP's hopes. The latter, in fact, was a complete failure except in so far as it prepared French farmers psychologically for the Common Market.

The Green Pool was originally proposed by Pflimlin in a French Government Note sent to all members of the Council of Europe, together with Austria, Portugal and Switzerland, in March 1951.[5] Pflimlin referred to Schuman's press conference of 9 May 1950, when the Coal and Steel Community was proposed—'Europe will not be built all at once . . . it will be made by concrete achievements creating a *de facto* solidarity'. In Pflimlin's view agriculture should be the next stage in the functional integration of Europe. It was a

[1] Scargil, p. 26.   [2] *Aube*, 24 March 1948.   [3] *Monde*, 13 May 1955.
[4] JO (AN), 16 January 1957, p. 81.
[5] *Note sur l'Organisation des Marchés Agricoles Européens*, AP, 1951, pp. 558–60.

great social and economic industry affecting all Europe. Production was still insufficient for Europe's needs, and yet farmers could and would produce more if they knew that there was a guaranteed market for their products: 'this equilibrium between production and marketing cannot be realized within the context of individual European countries except by costly means, such as subsidies, or by unjustifiable ones, such as the destruction of excess produce'.[1] A European market, he argued, would lead to more rational production and ultimately to lower prices for the consumer. But, if these ends were to be achieved, it was essential that the European Agricultural Market (Green Pool) should be run by institutions similar to those of the Coal and Steel Community, for 'it is vital that the institutions responsible for the agricultural market can at all times assure the equilibrium of the market with the necessary flexibility and speed. If the institutions are only consultative, they will not have the means to resolve the problems which will arise.'[2]

The Council of Europe was asked to consider Pflimlin's proposals, and a committee was set up under René Charpentier of MRP, the President of the Agricultural Committee of the Consultative Assembly of the Council of Europe. Charpentier's Committee reported in December 1951, and, despite British disapproval of the Report, it was passed by 49 to 24 with 14 abstentions, thus achieving the necessary two-thirds majority. It was not surprising that the British opposed the Charpentier Report, for it was even more explicit than Pflimlin had been about the need for supranational institutions. Charpentier specifically proposed a High Authority similar to that of the Coal and Steel Community. (Although Pflimlin had hinted at the need for such an institution, he had never used the term High Authority.) Charpentier's arguments in favour of a Green Pool were similar to those of Pflimlin, principally that increased production and organized markets would ultimately benefit both farmers and consumers, but he admitted that the creation of a common agricultural market would be slow, because 'agriculture is a very long-term activity'.[3] Nevertheless, the High Authority must not lose sight of the ultimate aim of 'the unification and integration of the European agricultural markets'. It would have to fix common prices for agricultural products, orientate national production, train farmers, and ensure that a common external tariff was fixed in such a way that Europe would not be flooded with agricultural produce from other parts of the world. All these proposals foreshadowed the

[1] *Note sur l'Organisation des Marchés Agricoles Européens*, AP, 1951, pp. 558–60.
[2] ibid.   [3] AP, 1951, p. 562.

basic features of the Common Agricultural Policy developed in the 1960s under the Treaty of Rome. In one area, however, the Green Pool proposals were perhaps more realistic than later developments under the Common Agricultural Policy, because Pflimlin in particular was adamantly in favour of product-by-product integration rather than the rapid introduction of a common market for all products.[1]

The Consultative Assembly set up a working party to look into the Green Pool proposals in more detail and the Agricultural Ministers of the various countries met in Paris in March 1952, March 1953 and July 1954. But nothing came of the proposed European Agricultural Market. Pflimlin was probably right when he said that the initial mistake was to try to involve too many countries in the Green Pool, especially those like Great Britain, which were known to be against supranational developments.[2] Nevertheless, there were other reasons for the failure of the Green Pool. The French and Dutch disagreed about the products to be included in the common market. The Dutch favoured the inclusion of all as soon as possible; the French, supported by the Italians and Germans, wanted to start off with three or four products; the Belgians wanted a pilot scheme with wheat only, and, like the British, were unhappy about Charpentier's High Authority, which they thought was too powerful. With all these differences between the countries concerned, the Green Pool proposals died in 1954, when the Paris Conference of Agricultural Ministers decided that further discussions should continue within the framework of OEEC.

Although nothing came of the Green Pool, MRP did not abandon its interest in the development of a European Agricultural Market. In 1955 the MRP National Committee, after emphasizing the success of the European Coal and Steel Community, called for an Agricultural Community run on a similar basis.[3] Whilst the Treaty of Rome was being negotiated, MRP spokesmen contended that the Common Market would benefit French agriculture, provided prices and production were effectively controlled.[4] Moreover, as French prices were higher than those on the world market, it was essential that there should be a high external tariff, which would exclude world produce and allow the French farmer to benefit fully from the European market.[5] Like de Gaulle, MRP saw the Common Market

---

[1] *Note sur l'Organisation des Marchés Agricoles Européens*, AP, 1951, pp. 558–60.
[2] Interview with Pflimlin, 3 April 1971.   [3] *Forces Nouvelles*, 9 April 1955.
[4] JO (AN), 16 January 1957, speech by Pierre Abelin.
[5] JO (AN), 16 January 1957, speech by Pierre Abelin; cf. similar speech by

as a bargain between French agriculture and German industry, although, unlike de Gaulle, MRP was emotionally committed to European integration for other reasons.[1]

The first disappointment was that the Common Agricultural Policy did not begin to operate until 1962, and the main target prices were not fixed until July 1966. The target prices were set between 7 and 30 per cent above the lowest prices operating in the Six, but below the highest in the really inefficient areas of the Community. In general the prices were set too high, so that overproduction, particularly of cereals and dairy produce, has been a problem. In effect, the German taxpayer has subsidized inefficient French farmers, which might have been expected to satisfy the French agricultural community even if it has been expensive for the European Agricultural Guidance and Guarantee Fund. A major disadvantage of the system, however, has been that, whilst the efficient large-scale farmers of northern France have done extremely well out of the Common Market, the peasants of the south and west have found that prices are too low. Unfortunately they have not been low enough to encourage rapid restructuring. Moreover, agricultural production has increased throughout the Six, whilst demand has remained relatively stable, so that France has benefited less than might have been expected.[2] And the system whereby the Community buys excess produce at guaranteed prices (the intervention price) and then dumps it on the world market at much lower prices is extremely costly and wasteful. Overall, the common agricultural market has not solved France's agricultural problems in the way that MRP and other optimistically hoped it would in the 1950s.

In fairness to the French Christian Democrats it must be said that Pflimlin always maintained that strong supranational institutions were essential,[3] and that the Common Market has lacked institutional strength since the Luxembourg Crisis of 1965. Moreover, Charpentier, a strong advocate of the Common Market, said in 1960 that if France was going to take full advantage of the Common Agricultural Policy, she must put her internal marketing system right first:

it is essential to organize our fruit and vegetable market . . . to make sure that our slaughter-houses are more sanitary [the

René Charpentier in Council of Europe Consultative Assembly, 22 October 1956, *Monde*, 25 October 1956.

[1] See pp. 196–8.

[2] Cf. *Express*, 28 March 1971, 'Paysans au Secours', Pol Echevin, pp. 53–6.

[3] *Note sur l'Organisation des Marchés Agricoles Européens*, AP, 1951, pp. 558–60; and interview with Pflimlin, 3 April 1971.

Germans had been refusing French meat for sanitary reasons]; to institute a policy of quality; . . . and, above all, to improve the means of distribution of agricultural produce.[1]

Michel Cuperly mentioned the same weaknesses in an article in *Forces Nouvelles*, going on to say that producers must group together to organize their exports and make sure that their produce was tailored to the market, in particular with regard to quality. The Common Market, he argued, was no 'magic wand' which produced exports. Nevertheless, in the long term, advantages should accrue to France from the European Market.[2] And in 1971 Pflimlin remained optimistic about the future of the European agricultural market whilst admitting that it had not proved as advantageous to France as he had hoped.[3]

MRP was neither the most nor the least progressive of French political parties in its agricultural policy. No Christian Democrat was as outspokenly critical of protectionism and pressure groups as Mendès-France and his Minister of Agriculture, Roger Houdet.[4] On the other hand, the Christian Democrats were never as 'Mélinian' as the Peasants or as negative as the Communists. They were able to exert influence on agricultural policy both through their Ministers of Agriculture, Pflimlin and Valay, and through their various Ministers of Finance (Schuman, Buron, Pflimlin), whose decisions were frequently more important than those of the Ministers of Agriculture. The Christian Democrats' greatest contribution to agricultural change was their advocacy of planning, although it is true that they did not try to direct investment with sufficient selectiveness. In 1960 Michel Bosquet criticized agricultural policy since the war for its failure to improve the marketing system, its lack of emphasis on regional policy and selective investment, and for the 'derisory sums' spent on infrastructure, training and research.[5] All these criticisms could justifiably be levelled against MRP, although it must always be borne in mind that MRP had to work within coalition governments, that the agricultural pressure groups in the National Assembly were strong and well organized, and that, owing to the nature of agriculture, all reforms take a long time to become fully effective.

MRP could also be criticized for getting its priorities wrong and

---

[1] *Combat*, 4 March 1960.   [2] *Forces Nouvelles*, 31 December 1960.
[3] Interview with Pflimlin, 3 April 1971.
[4] E.g. Mendès-France, *Monde*, 11 February 1954; Houdet, *Monde*, 20 October 1954.
[5] *Express*, 28 January 1960.

for its somewhat naïve optimism about the European market. The party should no doubt have concentrated its attention on the home marketing system before advocating schemes such as the Green Pool. MRP certainly seems to have been rather carried away in its enthusiasm for agricultural 'Europe'. On the other hand, it must be conceded that both Pflimlin and Charpentier frequently maintained that the Common Agricultural Market would be ineffective without supranational institutions and a home market geared to exports. Finally, as regards structural reforms and agricultural training, more credit should be given to CNJA and FNSEA, the professional organizations taken over by ex-JACists, than to MRP as such. Nevertheless, if it is true to say that the agricultural revolution, which began in the early 1960s, would have been impossible without JAC support, it would be wrong to omit MRP's contribution to the psychological climate—in particular through their advocacy of planning and structural changes—which made the agricultural revolution possible.

Chapter 6

FOREIGN POLICY

In foreign, as in colonial, policy the French Christian Democrats were torn between nationalism and reconciliation. As a Resistance party MRP at first emphasized the former rather than the latter. In the immediate post-war period the party's foreign and colonial polices were essentially Gaullist, even after its break with the General in January 1946. France must re-establish herself as an independent world power; she must avoid subservience to either of the world blocs; Germany must be kept weak in order to maximize French influence in Europe; the French colonial empire must be kept intact to give France the population and resources to rival those of the USA, USSR and Great Britain. It was only when the illusory nature of these objectives became apparent that the Christian Democrats changed their tack to a policy of reconciliation. The change came first in foreign policy, when the development of the Cold War and the attitude of the three Big Powers exposed the unreality of French pretensions, in particular with regard to Germany. In colonial policy it took the defeat in Indo-China to bring France face to face with reality. At least it can be said of the Christian Democrats that they were willing to change with the times. Robert Schuman's Declaration of 9 May 1950 marked a definite break in MRP's foreign policy, as did the party's support for Defferre's Loi Cadre (1956) in colonial policy. Henceforth, reconciliation rather than nationalism predominated. The party had opted for Schuman rather than for Bidault.

This chapter will concentrate largely on MRP's European policy, and in particular on the German problem, because the party was interested primarily in Europe, where the Cold War was chiefly focused until the mid-1960s when the Far and Middle East took over as the main areas of conflict. MRP's final decline happened to coincide with the stabilization, if not the solution, of the outstanding European problems. By the policies it pursued in the Fourth Republic, MRP contributed as much as any French party to the present pattern of international relations in Western Europe. Georges Bidault and Robert Schuman ran the Quai d'Orsay for almost a decade after the Second World War. Although the Christian

159

Democrats advocated co-existence with the Russians, they welcomed the American presence in Western Europe. The twin pillars of their foreign policy were the Atlantic Alliance and European integration. They supported the former because they were firmly anti-Communist, and the latter because they believed it to be in the best interests of France, of themselves and of Europe. Although they soon abandoned their 'Third Force' arguments, placing France decisively in the Western camp, they wanted a Western Europe which could wield some influence in the Atlantic Alliance. They believed that this could best be achieved in the context of a closely integrated Western Europe. In the 1950s they had an almost naïve faith in the development of Community Europe, and although that faith was shaken by the failure of the European Defence Community and by de Gaulle's policies in the 1960s, it was never destroyed. MRP remained to the end the most 'European' of the French political parties.

MRP'S FOREIGN POLICY, 1944–8: THE GERMAN PROBLEM

Despite the 'European' attitude expressed in Gilbert Dru's Manifesto and MRP's commitment to the principles of the United Nations Charter,[1] Bidault's foreign policy from September 1944–July 1948 was completely in line with that of General de Gaulle. Three days after de Gaulle resigned the premiership in January 1946, *Le Canard Enchaîné* put the following words into Bidault's mouth: 'Now that de Gaulle has gone, *I* am going to be the Minister of Foreign Affairs'.[2] If *Le Canard* was hoping, or expecting, that Bidault would pursue a less nationalistic and intransigent foreign policy, it was mistaken.

Georges Bidault, a former history master steeped, like de Gaulle, in the glories of France's past and acutely conscious of the national weaknesses which in his view were primarily responsible for the Munich Settlement of 1938, was determined that France should play a strong and independent role in foreign policy. If she were going to play this role, she must mediate between Russia and America and oppose the re-emergence of a strong Germany. It was for these reasons that de Gaulle and Bidault went to Moscow in December 1944. The Franco-Soviet pact which followed did not result in a Soviet commitment to France's desires for a Rhine frontier and the

---

[1] Dru Manifesto, MRP docs, no. 1; and MRP Congr. 1945, Paris, motion on foreign policy.
[2] *Le Canard Enchaîné*, 23 January 1946.

dismemberment of Germany, nor did it even lead to Stalin asking for French representation at Yalta, but it did indicate France's wish to play a relatively independent role in foreign policy. In the following years this was clearly shown by Bidault's policy towards Germany.

In November 1945 Bidault announced at a press-conference that he was opposed to the revival of the old Germany; the German states should eventually be allowed to have their own governments, but there should be no central German government.[1] Bidault's ideas about Germany were spelt out in more detail between this date and the Moscow Conference of March 1947. In January 1946 he told the National Assembly that, although the three Great Powers were tending to try to bypass France, he was determined to ensure that Germany should be incapable of reviving her war potential; the coalmines of the Saar should be handed over to France, the Ruhr should be internationalized and its resources used 'for the benefit of humanity', the Reich should be disarmed 'militarily, economically and financially', and the Germans should pay appropriate reparations; he approved the weakening of Germany implicit in the Russian takeover of Germany's eastern territories.[2] He told *Le Monde* that the 'new Germany' should be deprived of the Ruhr and Rhineland; although he had no objection to economic contacts between Germany and the Ruhr and Rhineland, 'our view is that the Ruhr and Rhineland should be under international control. This implies the complete political separation of the Ruhr and Rhineland from Germany'.[3] Four months later he told a meeting at St Etienne that the separation of the Ruhr and Rhineland from Germany was the only way to keep Germany from 'her national industry: war'.[4]

Bidault did not achieve his objectives at the Paris conference of the Four in July 1946, which failed to reach agreement on the future of Germany, and by the Moscow Conference of April 1947 there were signs that France was moving away from its 'Morgenthau' theses on Germany. Bidault conceded that some degree of economic centralization was necessary if Germany was to recover from the economic chaos produced by the war, but he continued to advocate political decentralization; each German state should be allowed to draw up its own constitution, subject to Allied approval, and a weak Federal Diet with four representatives from each state should be set up, but 'the states should retain full competence in all fields except those specifically delegated by them to the central government.'[5] Moreover, he was still insistent that Germany should pay reparations, that steel

[1] *Monde*, 6 November 1945.   [2] JO (AN), 17 January 1946, pp. 78–82.
[3] *Monde*, 22 March 1946.   [4] *Monde*, 30 July 1946.
[5] *Monde*, 25 January 1947.

production should be limited, that the Ruhr should be under international control and the Saar incorporated into France.[1]

The Russians agreed with the French demand for reparations, but were prepared to accept the incorporation of the Saar into France only in exchange for a role in the international administration of the Ruhr. As the British and Americans were opposed to a Russian presence in the Ruhr—indeed Bevin already wanted the Ruhr to be integrated into Germany as the new state of North Rhine—Westphalia—Bidault came away from Moscow empty-handed. The Moscow Conference ended in deadlock and it was agreed to reconvene in London in December. But before the meeting in London, the situation changed dramatically with the American offer of Marshall Aid. In June 1947 Bidault told the National Assembly that France would accept the offer,[2] but, after a meeting in Paris between Bidault, Bevin and Molotov, Russia decided to reject Marshall Aid. The combination of the failure of the Moscow Conference, the decision on Marshall Aid and the departure of the Communists from the French Government (May 1947) (followed by the 'insurrectional' strikes of late 1947) inevitably brought France into the Western camp, consequently ending her 'independent' foreign policy, the success of which had depended on at least some degree of Russian support.

After the failure of the London Conference of the Four (December 1947) to reach any agreement about Germany, the three Western Allies decided to implement their own plans for the western zones of Germany at another London conference, the first session of which ran from 23 February to 9 March 1948. Bidault was still determined to do what he could to uphold the French theses on Germany. Prior to his departure for London he told the National Assembly that although France had failed in her attempt to act as a bridge between the Anglo-Saxons and the Russians, she would continue to press for some form of international control of the Ruhr and Rhineland and for the establishment of a decentralized system of government in Germany.[3] Events, however, rapidly conspired to weaken the French position. The Prague coup of late February, the Russian boycott of the Allied Control Commission in Germany (20 March) and the start of the Berlin Blockade (30 March) convinced the Americans and British of the need for rapid decisions about the future of West Germany, with or without French approval. The Americans and British favoured a federal state with a strong central government and the fusion of the French zone with the Anglo-

[1] *Monde*, 20 March 1947.   [2] JO (AN) 20 June 1947, p. 1250.
[3] JO (AN), 13 February 1948, pp. 741–47.

American Bizone, which had been set up in May 1947. The French had to give way over the proposals for the establishment of a centralized West German state, although they resisted fusing their zone economically with the Bizone until September 1948. More significantly from the French point of view, the Americans and British agreed to the setting up of the International Ruhr Authority and the continued economic integration of the Saar into France prior to a final agreement. The London Agreements were signed in June 1948, although another conference was held in December to institute the International Ruhr Authority, which was established in Düsseldorf in April 1949. The International Ruhr Authority was a concession to the French, as the Americans and British had been opposed to a body which would be able to intervene in the Ruhr economy after the setting up of the German Federal Government. Their opposition was soon justified, for the Social Democrats attacked the International Ruhr Authority as a *Diktat* and the Christian Democrats contended that it was inhibiting the development of the German economy.[1]

Schuman, who was still Prime Minister when the London Agreements were signed, said of them: 'They are not perfect, but we know that our safety depends on close union with those who have fought for the same ideal'.[2] This was a diplomatic way of saying that all the major tenets of Bidault's German policy had been rejected. A centralized German government with power to legislate and raise taxes had been accepted in principle. No special regime was established for the Rhineland. The industry of the Ruhr remained in German hands despite the International Ruhr Authority. The French National Assembly, not surprisingly, accepted the London Agreements only by a narrow majority, 296–287. All the MRP and Socialists voted for the Agreements, the acceptance of which depended on the Radicals who split, 26 for (including Queuille and Mendès-France) and 12 against (including Daladier).[3] In summing up the debate, Bidault said, 'We must struggle to build Europe, the sole means of reconciling Germany to European civilization . . . the London Agreements are a step towards this reconciliation.'[4] If it is true that the London Agreements were a step towards the reconciliation of Germany, it must also be admitted that that reconcilia-

---

[1] *Monde*, 10 January 1951. Schumacher called it a *Diktat*; Erhard was the chief CDU critic.

[2] JO (AN) 16 June 1948; p. 3592.

[3] ibid., p. 3611. All the Gaullists and Communists and some Conservatives voted against.

[4] JO (AN), 16 June 1948, p. 3570.

tion owed little to Bidault or MRP despite their vote accepting the London Agreements.

The replacement of Bidault by Schuman at the Quai d'Orsay in July 1948 marked the failure of Bidault's attempt to give France an independent foreign policy role, but it did not lead to an immediate change in French policy towards Germany. In November 1948 Schuman protested at the Anglo-American decision to hand back the Ruhr industries to the Germans, especially as the decision was announced without consulting France.[1] And a week later he said that insufficient powers had been conferred on the International Ruhr Authority; he feared that too much power had been handed over to the German authorities, and, with uncharacteristic hyperbole, remarked 'The Reich which has been reconstituted in London will evolve, as always, towards adventurism.'[2] Robert Rochefort has pointed out that Schuman had had too much experience of the Germans to be under any illusions about them,[3] and Schuman himself wrote 'One must recognize what history has taught us: Germany will never be satisfied. It is for this reason that there has been, and probably always will be, a German problem.'[4]

Nevertheless, Robert Schuman, born in Luxembourg as an exile from Lorraine and educated at various German universities, was temperamentally very different from Georges Bidault. Like Metternich, Schuman had the Rhinelander's cosmopolitan, pragmatic approach to politics. Although as a young man he regarded himself primarily as a Frenchman, he does not seem to have objected overtly to the German occupation of Alsace and Lorraine.[5] He was too steeped in German culture to be a Germanophobe. Although, as a devout Catholic, he deplored the excesses of Nazism, he had not, unlike Bidault, been an outspoken opponent of Hitler in the 1930s. Schuman was even an Under-Secretary of State for a few days in Pétain's Government, and, as such, his case came before the High Court at the Liberation; unlike so many of his fellow Ministers, he was acquitted (on 5 December 1945) owing to his later opposition to Pétain. In contrast, Bidault had 'the temperament of a peasant from the Massif Central, . . . he was determined to hold on to all the land he possessed and was distinctly xenophobic in outlook.'[6] Whilst Schuman had spent most of the war reading books, Bidault had been President of the National Resistance Council. It was the

---

[1] *Monde*, 12 November 1948.   [2] *Monde*, 18 November 1948.
[3] R. Rochefort, *Robert Schuman*, p. 236.
[4] R. Schuman, *Pour l'Europe*, p. 88.   [5] Rochefort, pp. 36–37.
[6] Interview with Corval, 7 February 1967.

difference between the reconciler and the resister, between the cosmopolitan and the nationalist.

The change of personalities at the Quai d'Orsay helped to give a new orientation to French policy, but in the same way as Schuman was more sceptical about reconciliation with Germany than has often been assumed, Bidault was more realistic about the need to reintegrate Germany into the European family than was apparent from his 'Gaullist' pronouncements of 1944–48. In March 1948 he agreed that German 'observers' should attend OEEC meetings,[1] and at the Hague Congress in May 1948 he spoke of the need to reintegrate a democratic Germany into Europe.[2]

France's changing attitude to Germany between 1948–50 owed less to personalities at the Quai d'Orsay than to the evolution of the international situation. The development of the Cold War made France dependent on her more powerful Western allies, who were determined not to repeat the errors of the Versailles settlement. Moreover, the Cold War changed French perspectives on security— Russia rather than Germany now appearing as the main threat—and at the same time France's membership of the Atlantic Pact (Treaty of Brussels setting up NATO, March 1949) strengthened her position vis-à-vis Germany. Schuman told the National Assembly that the Atlantic Pact complemented the Dunkirk Treaty of 1947 and the Brussels Treaty Organization of 1948: 'Today we have achieved what we strove for in vain between the two wars. The United States has recognized that there can be no security for America if Europe is in danger.'[3] When the Atlantic Pact was debated a few months later, MRP was almost unanimous in its support for it. Only Paul Boulet, a life-long pacifist, voted against it, whilst Charles d'Aragon and Abbé Pierre abstained on the grounds that the Alliance only crystallized the division of the two blocs.[4]

France's new confidence was reflected in a more generous approach to the German problem. Interviewed by Le Monde in August 1949, Schuman said 'Personally, I think that there can be no solution to the problems of Europe without the progressive integration of the new Germany into Europe; it is in the interests of France to reflect on how this may be done, and, when the time comes, to act with dynamism.'[5] Shortly afterwards Adenauer said that he hoped 'with all his heart for a better entente with France';[6] he suggested that such

---

[1] Monde, 17 March 1948. West Germany joined OEEC in October 1949.
[2] Monde, May 1948. The Hague Congress led to the setting up of the Council of Europe in 1949.
[3] JO (AN), 25 July 1949, p. 5251. [4] JO (AN), 25 July 1949, pp. 5231–3.
[5] Monde, 14 August 1949. [6] Monde, 5 November 1949.

an entente could start with closer economic co-operation, 'perhaps with an Anglo-French-German customs union.'[1] The way was clearly open for Schuman's famous initiative of 9 May 1950. Bidault's 'Gaullist' policy towards Germany had been abandoned, but Stalin did as much as Schuman to reconcile France and Germany.

THE EUROPEAN COAL AND STEEL COMMUNITY (ECSC)

'The road towards Europe reached a parting of the ways in 1950.'[2] A choice had to be made between *ad hoc* co-operation, such as that operating in OEEC and the Council of Europe, or a new initiative had to be taken to bring the European countries closer together. In Schuman's view a new initiative was essential for economic and political reasons. Although OEEC had done useful work in organizing the distribution of Marshall Aid and in freeing trade, the Western European economy had by no means recovered from the effects of the war; Marshall Aid was due to end in 1951, and Schuman believed that it was essential to pursue the reorganization and rationalization of European industry; he believed that such modernization could not be achieved within the loose framework of OEEC.[3] At the same time he was sceptical about the chances of the Council of Europe doing anything to draw the European nations closer together politically. After signing the Treaty setting up the Council of Europe (May 1949) Schuman told Pierre-Henri Teitgen, 'It is a worthwhile organization, but one cannot expect much of it. One cannot hope for much useful work from an organization of 13, 14 or 15.'[4] Schuman later wrote that 'Strasbourg [i.e. the Council of Europe] is the headlamp lighting the road to Europe, but . . . it lacks the authority of a body which can take majority decisions.'[5] Schuman would doubtless have agreed with Maurice Duverger's comment on the Council of Europe—'Talking about Europe is not building Europe.'[6]

Equally worrying for Schuman was the problem of Germany. Although France had abandoned her *revanchist* policies, there was still considerable bitterness between France and Germany. The latter was irked by the economic incorporation of the Saar into France as well as by the setting up of the International Ruhr Authority. Both of these unilateral Allied decisions tended to arouse German hostility and even nationalism, especially in the case of Schumacher, leader of the Social Democratic Party (SPD). Schuman,

1 *Monde*, 23 March 1950 and 4 April 1950.
2 Schuman, *Pour l'Europe*, p. 132.   3 Schuman, *Pour l'Europe*, p. 130.
4 Quoted in Rochefort, p. 265.   5 Schuman, p. 133.
6 *Monde*, 9 August 1949.

with his dual Franco-German background, was particularly anxious to avoid a repetition of the history of the 1920s.

On 9 May 1950 he produced what he himself called his 'bomb',[1] namely the proposal that 'all French and German coal and steel production be placed under a common High Authority, in an organization open to participation by other European countries.'[2] The idea of the European Coal and Steel Community was Jean Monnet's, but Schuman immediately adopted it. Fully aware that it was a revolutionary proposal and might well arouse hostility, he was determined to act decisively and fast. The French Cabinet knew nothing of the proposal until 3 May, and did not formally approve it until the morning of 9 May. Britain, Italy and the Benelux countries were not told about it until the early afternoon of 9 May. Adenauer, however, was consulted a few days before, as Schuman rightly recognized that he was the key figure; when Adenauer gave his approval 'in principle', Schuman decided to announce his proposal.[3] The reactions in Bonn, Washington and London were respectively 'enthusiastic', 'favourable' and 'cold'.[4] Italy welcomed the proposal, as did the Benelux countries after some initial hesitation. The Six countries which accepted the proposal for the Coal and Steel Community met in Paris in June 1950 to work out appropriate texts; the Treaty was signed in April 1951, and the Community began to operate in August 1952. The most revolutionary feature of the Coal and Steel Community was its High Authority, a supranational body of 'independent persons', chosen by member governments but responsible to the Community; their task was to modernize coal and steel production, develop the internal and external marketing of these products and improve the standard of living of the workers concerned. A Court was established to ensure that the Treaty was not infringed, and an Assembly was nominated by national Parliaments to keep an eye on the High Authority and, if need be, dismiss it by a two-thirds majority.[5]

The Declaration of 9 May 1950 was indeed a 'bomb' both in the

---

[1] Schuman, p. 166.   [2] *Monde*, 11 May 1950.

[3] F. Roy Willis, *France, Germany and the New Europe, 1945–67*, p. 88, says that Adenauer only heard about the ECSC proposal on the morning of its announcement, but Schuman, p. 166, says Adenauer's approval had been received before 9 May. Richard Mayne, one of Monnet's close collaborators, agrees with Schuman that Adenauer was told about the proposal in advance, but his formal approval of it was not received until the morning of 9 May: *The Recovery of Europe*, p. 180.

[4] *Monde*, 11 May 1950.

[5] For details about the institutions and working of ECSC, see William Diebold, *The Schuman Plan*, or H. L. Mason, *The European Coal and Steel Community*.

sense that it marked a *volte face* in French policy towards Germany and on account of its surpranational implications. But it should have come as no surprise to MRP, whose militants had been calling for decisive steps towards European integration since 1947. The foreign policy motion of that year's Congress declared that 'in order to ensure the security and prosperity of all the European nations it is essential to prepare from now on for a system of European federalism, based on respect for the diverse cultures of the European peoples'.[1] In his report on foreign policy at the 1948 Congress Marc Scherer said that the establishment of Benelux and OEEC and the signing of the Treaty of Dunkirk and the Brussels Pact were 'only partial initiatives, . . . we must aim at a European federation. If it is true that the federal idea has not been properly spelt out, and if there remain uncertainties as to the functioning of federalism in a European context, its implementation nevertheless remains the surest guarantee of peace in Europe'. In prophetic vein Scherer went on to propose that 'all essential resources such as the coal of the Rhine-Westphalia basin, should be held in common'. The first task, he said, was to build Western Europe, but in line with Christian Democratic doctrine he hoped that Europe would develop as a 'bridge' between East and West, not as a satellite of one of the two blocs.[2] After a short debate the Congress unanimously approved Scherer's report.

At Strasbourg in 1949 the slogan above the party platform was 'Construire l'Europe pour assurer la paix.' If these were vague words, those used by Maurice Schumann in his report on foreign policy were not: 'Europe needs federalism for its own security, . . . we are prepared to abandon part of our sovereignty for the common interest . . . Germany must be part of the new Europe . . . If England does not want to join us, we will build Europe on our own.'[3] And Robert Schuman, after defending the Atlantic Pact and arguing that France must work with her neighbours, including Germany, was given a standing ovation by the Congress.

It seems that MRP's militants adopted a 'European' stance more quickly than the party leadership. They were certainly ahead of Bidault, if not of Schuman, by 1948. Thus, it was not surprising that Schuman's proposal for a Coal and Steel Community was warmly welcomed at the MRP Congress at Nantes in May 1950, a fortnight after the historic declaration.

After praising Jean Monnet—'This is the first time that I have

1 MRP Congr. 1947, Paris.
2 MRP Congr. 1948, Toulouse; report on 'La Politique Extérieure'.
3 MRP Congr. 1949, Strasbourg; report on 'La Politique Extérieure'.

mentioned his name publicly: I no longer have the right to keep quiet about it. He was one of the principal initiators of the idea'— Schuman went on to justify his proposals. He spoke first of the economic advantages of choosing coal and steel; there were only about a thousand companies concerned, and they had similar types of management and workers; moreover, these industries were not subject to major climatic differences as, for example, was agriculture. But the main reason for choosing coal and steel was political; it would make war between France and Germany impossible. However, the Coal and Steel Community should not be seen only in a Franco-German context; it was also the first step towards a European federation and a way of strengthening the Atlantic Alliance through the modernization of two of Europe's basic industries. At the same time, however, Schuman emphasized that the Coal and Steel Community was not in any sense directed against Russia; he believed that 'co-existence between the two political and economic regimes is possible, but it is essential that we should respect each other'; by strengthening the Atlantic Pact, 'a purely defensive alliance', such respect was more likely to develop.[1] The party, as frequently happened over the years, gave Schuman a standing ovation, and his report was unanimously adopted.

The European Coal and Steel Community, in fact, aroused no qualms within MRP. Whereas a tiny minority had opposed the Atlantic Pact and a larger, and more vociferous, minority was to oppose the European Defence Community, the Coal and Steel Community met with approval from all sections of the party. In the debate in the National Assembly, which followed the Council of Europe's recommendation in favour of the Coal and Steel Community, Marc Scherer and Robert Schuman defended the proposals on behalf of MRP, and Bidault also spoke warmly of the proposed Community;[2] even if Britain refused to join it, 'Let us begin without Great Britain in order to convince her of the advanages of the Community.'[3] After the Treaty was signed in Paris on 4 April 1951, Maurice Schumann, on behalf of the MRP National Committee, welcomed it as 'a great date in our history'.[4] The Foreign Affairs Committee of the National Assembly approved the Treaty by 25

---

[1] MRP Congr. 1950, Nantes; report on 'La Politique Extérieure'.

[2] As Prime Minister Bidault had shown no interest in Monnet's proposal; it was for this reason that Monnet took it to Schuman. Willis, p. 95; Mayne, pp. 177–9.

[3] JO (AN), 14 January 1950, Scherer, pp. 7691–4; Schuman, pp. 7694–6; Bidault, pp. 7737–8.

[4] Monde, 20 April 1951.

votes to 18, all 7 MRP members voting for it.[1] And in the debate in the National Assembly (6–11 December 1951) no MRP deputy spoke against the Treaty. Alfred Coste-Floret, the MRP *rapporteur* of the Treaty, defended it primarily on the grounds that it 'should reinforce peace by the establishment of European institutions, by bringing to an end the antagonism of France and Germany and by integrating the industries of war'. He said that the High Authority should not be regarded as 'the board of a cartel'; on the contrary, its decisions had to be published and it could be overthrown by the Assembly. Meanwhile, the Court of Justice's role would be 'analagous to that of the Conseil d'Etat', and that of the Consultative Committee 'similar to that of the Economic Council'.[2] Robert Schuman maintained that 'the chief political objective is the improvement of Franco-German relations',[3] a theme which he later developed in the debate in the Council of the Republic, when he said that 'France and Germany will never again be able to wage war on one another.'[4] He regretted that Britain had refused to join the Coal and Steel Community, but asserted that it had the full support of Churchill and Eden. Finally, he believed that, whilst the Community would not be an economic panacea, it would stimulate investment and encourage the modernization of two key industries.[5] In the vote at the end of the debate all eighty-seven members of MRP voted for the Treaty of Paris. MRP's first 'European' initiative had been completely successful in so far as it had been unanimously supported by the party.[6]

THE EUROPEAN DEFENCE COMMUNITY (EDC)

The proposal for a European Defence Community (Pleven Plan, 24 October 1950) was much more controversial than that for the European Coal and Steel Community. MRP was regarded as *the* major proponent of EDC, but in fact MRP's attitude towards the Treaty was much more *nuancé* than has sometimes been implied.[7] Pierre-Henri Teitgen was the leader of the most partisan group of MRP advocates of EDC, but Robert Schuman's defence of the Treaty

---

[1] Besides MRP those who voted for the Treaty were 7 Socialists, 5 Radicals and 6 Conservatives (Independents and Peasants); those against were 9 Gaullists, 6 Communists, 2 Progressistes and 1 Conservative: *Monde*, 2 December 1951.

[2] JO (AN), 6 December 1951, pp. 8854–63.   [3] ibid., pp. 8894–8.

[4] JO (CR), 1 April 1952, p. 811.   [5] JO (AN), 6 December 1951, p. 8897.

[6] JO (AN), 13 December 1951, p. 9143. 377 voted for the Treaty of Paris (including 105 Socialists, 87 MRP, 71 Radicals, 73 Conservatives), and 237 voted against (including 97 Communists, 116 [out of 119] Gaullists, 1 Socialist, 19 Conservatives).

[7] E.g. Grosser, p. 319.

was often rather negative, whilst Georges Bidault reluctantly supported it as a military necessity; at the same time he made no attempt to conceal his opposition to the proposed European Political Community (EPC), an adjunct of EDC. Moreover, a significant minority led by André Monteil in the National Assembly and by Léo Hamon in the Council of the Republic, actively opposed EDC. Despite these doubts within the party, MRP pinned its hopes on EDC as a vital step towards European integration. The rejection of EDC was taken as a personal attack on the Christian Democrats, who never forgave Mendès-France for 'the crime of 30 August', although the rejection of EDC was not the fault of Mendès-France.

In discussing EDC and MRP's attitude to it, it is important to remember that the political scene, both internationally and internally, changed considerably between the original Pleven proposal of October 1950 and the rejection of the Treaty in August 1954. EDC was proposed at the height of the Korean War and in the wake of the worst defeat in French colonial history up to that time (at Caobang in Indo-China, when over 3,000 men were killed or captured by the Viet Minh). By August 1954 the international situation was much less tense. Stalin was dead; an armistice had been concluded in Korea; the war in Indo-China was over. Even more important, as far as EDC was concerned, was the evolution of French internal politics between 1950–54. In October 1950 the two most 'European' parties, MRP and SFIO, were in the Government; in August 1954 neither was. Moreover, the number of MRP and Socialist deputies had been cut from a total of over 270 to under 200 at the General Election of June 1951. It is true that the Communist representation had also been reduced (from 183 to 101), but at the same time the Gaullist RPF had greatly increased its number of deputies, and with 120 was the largest group in the National Assembly. The RPF split of 1952 and de Gaulle's dissolution of the RPF in 1953 did nothing to help the supporters of EDC; in foreign policy the Gaullists remained united in their opposition to the European Army.

EDC dominated French politics for four years. In Raymond Aron's opinion, it was 'the greatest ideological quarrel France has experienced since the Dreyfus Affair'.[1] Governments were made and unmade over the issue of EDC. Pinay was defeated over the budget in December 1952, partly because MRP had grown tired of his delaying tactics on EDC. René Mayer, a partisan of EDC, had to replace Schuman with Bidault at the Quai d'Orsay to get Gaullist support for his investiture in January 1953, but when he came out openly in favour of ratification, he was overthrown in a debate on fiscal policy,

[1] R. Aron and D. Lerner, *La Querelle de la CED*, p. 9.

when 71 out of 83 Gaullist deputies voted against him. In the governmental crisis of May–June 1953 Mendès-France failed to get invested, because a significant minority of MRP (37) refused to vote for him, although the Christian Democrats sympathized with his social and economic proposals; he had refused to commit himself to the ratification of EDC. Bidault, on the other hand, failed to get invested (by only one vote) because a significant minority of Gaullists (17) refused to vote for an EDC supporter, albeit a lukewarm one, although they agreed with the rest of Bidault's programme. Laniel was eventually accepted as Prime Minister by both Christian Democrats and Gaullists on the grounds that the ministerial crisis must be ended, although his vagueness over EDC satisfied neither side. Finally, in February 1955, Mendès-France was defeated over his Tunisian policy, with which MRP agreed, partly because the Christian Democrats had not forgiven him for 'the crime of 30 August'.

EDC was a direct result of the Korean War which began in June 1950. The Americans believed that the invasion of South Korea was a Communist probe to test the determination of the West to defend itself globally. In these circumstances it was vital for Europe to organize its defences, and this entailed the rearmament of West Germany. It was pointed out that there were 175 divisions on the Russian side of the Iron Curtain and only 10 on the Western side. Acheson, Bevin and Schuman met in New York in September 1950, and Acheson, with Bevin's approval, proposed the formation of an autonomous German army. Schuman, who ten months previously had told Le Monde that 'Germany will never be rearmed or included in the Atlantic pact',[1] not surprisingly opposed Acheson's demand. The final communiqué of the conference, however, noted that the three foreign ministers had discussed the possibility of 'German participation in an integrated force for the defence of European freedom'.[2] Schuman returned to Paris convinced that the Americans intended to rearm Germany with or without French support. This was the origin of the Pleven Plan of 24 October 1950 proposing 'the creation, for the common defence of Europe, of a European army linked to the political institutions of a united Europe.'[3] The Pleven Plan was a back-handed attempt to rearm Germany without quite admitting it. The proposal for EDC had the semantic advantage of substituting 'a German contribution to European defence' for

[1] Monde, 16 November 1949; in the debate on the Atlantic Pact, Schuman had said 'The reconstitution of German military forces is out of the question', JO (AN), 25 November 1949, p. 6351.

[2] RIIA, Documents, 1949–50, p. 334.   [3] JO (AN), 26 October 1950, p. 7219.

'German rearmament', and 'German divisions in a European army' for 'the German Army'.

The Pleven Plan was difficult to implement technically as well as politically. This led to a delay of nineteen months between the original proposal and the signing of the Treaty in May 1952. In the first phase of negotiations between October and December 1950 no progress was made because the Americans wanted German units of at least 5,000 men, whilst Jules Moch, the French Minister of Defence, refused to consider units of more than 1,000 men. After his failure to get agreement on the small unit, Moch turned against EDC. In the second phase of negotiations between January–August 1951 there were two negotiating teams. The one in Bonn eventually agreed that there should be twelve German divisions in the European Army. The one in Paris failed to come to a decision about the appropriate institutional machinery for EDC. The third phase of negotiations ran from September 1951 to May 1952, eventually producing the EDC Treaty. Again there were negotiations in both Bonn and Paris. In the former the so-called Contractual Agreements were worked out; on the ratification of EDC the Occupation Statute and High Commission were to be abolished, although the occupation troops were to remain in Germany as NATO forces. It had already been agreed at an Atlantic Council meeting in Lisbon in February 1952 that Germany would not join NATO. In Paris the EDC Treaty had meanwhile been drawn up. The basic national military unit was to be the division; integration would occur only at the corps level, i.e. there was to be 'high level' not 'low level' integration; there were to be 14 French, 12 German, 12 Italian and 5 Benelux divisions; the military headquarters would be fully integrated; member countries could withdraw troops for overseas duties with the permission of the Commissariat, which would in all normal circumstances grant it. The institutional machinery consisted of the Commissariat of nine members (two each from France, Germany and Italy, one each from the three Benelux countries); the Commissariat was to be the 'supranational' body of EDC, but in numerous cases it could act only with the consent of the national representatives on the Council of Ministers, the second main organ of EDC; the EDC Assembly would be the same body as the ECSC Assembly except that France, Germany and Italy were to appoint three extra members each; the Assembly would receive an annual report from the Commissariat, and could force it to resign by a two-thirds majority. Finally, the ECSC Court would also become the Court of EDC.[1]

The Contractual Agreements were signed in Bonn on 26 May 1952

[1] For full details of the 132 clauses of the EDC Treaty see *Monde*, 10 May 1952.

and the EDC Treaty in Paris on the following day. Immediately afterwards Acheson, Eden and Schuman signed a tripartite declaration, by which the Americans and British guaranteed to intervene if Germany attempted to secede from EDC. The Treaty had finally been signed, but, as Fauvet wisely commented, 'to sign is not to ratify'.[1] The controversy over EDC was to rage for another two years and three months.

There were four debates on EDC, although there was never a proper ratification debate.[2] In the October 1950 debate on Pleven's original proposal only three members of MRP did not vote for Pleven[3]; in the first proper debate on EDC (February 1952) 81 out of 88 MRP voted for the Treaty,[4] and in the second debate (November 1953) 83 out of 88 voted for it[5]; in the so-called ratification debate of August 1954, 80 out of 86 MRP were still in favour of the Treaty.[6]

The cold voting figures indicate why MRP was regarded as the most 'European' party in the National Assembly, but they do not convey the passions aroused for and against EDC even in this most 'European' party, nor the varying degrees of support shown by the defenders of the Treaty. Within MRP there were at least four different attitudes towards it. The out-and-out partisans were led by Pierre-Henri Teitgen; they supported EDC from the beginning, worried least about conditions (such as the need for a settlement of the Saar problem before ratification) and were enthusiastic advocates of the European Political Community (EPC). Next to the extreme partisans was a group whose views reflected those of Robert Schuman. They were entirely in favour of European integration, but would have preferred economic and political steps to be taken before attempting military integration. But when the course of events forced them to act first in the military sphere, they decided to make the best of a

[1] *Monde*, 27 May 1952.

[2] On 27 August 1954 General Aumeran put down a *motion préalable* to reject the Treaty without debate; MM. Delbez and Chupin, partisans of EDC, then put down a *motion préjudicielle*, the effect of which would have been to postpone the ratification debate, as those in favour of EDC realized they were now in a minority. But Aumeran insisted on his *motion préalable*, and in accordance with the rules of the National Assembly it had to be put before the *motion préjudicielle*. Aumeran's *motion préalable* was carried by 319–264, i.e. EDC was rejected by this margin.

[3] Bessac and Bonnet voted against; Couston abstained. The pro-EDC vote was 343–225.

[4] Aubin, Billiemaz, Bouret, Denis, Elain and Monteil voted against; Couston abstained. The pro-EDC vote was 327–287.

[5] Aubin, Denis and Bouret voted against; Monteil and Billiemaz abstained. The pro-EDC vote was 275–244.

[6] Aubin, Denis and Bouret voted against; Couston, Monteil and Billiemaz abstained. The anti-EDC vote was 319–264.

bad job. By 1953–54 they were often as enthusiastic about E D C at least in their public statements, as the Teitgen group. Then there were those who, like Bidault, were lukewarm supporters of the Treaty. They were opposed to the E P C and they insisted that problems such as the status of the Saar should be solved before ratification; their approach was logical rather than impassioned—if Germany had to be rearmed it would be better to have a semi-integrated German army than a completely independent one. Finally, there was a small group of outright opponents of E D C, led by Monteil in the National Assembly and Hamon in the Council of the Republic. They, too, were 'Europeans',[1] but they believed that German rearmament would exacerbate the division of Europe and encourage *revanchist* tendencies in Germany.

The arguments used by the various supporters of E D C often overlapped, but certain differences of emphasis can be detected. The strongest advocates of the Treaty were usually those who had a mystical faith in Europe; often they were amongst the most anti-Communist members of the party. Pierre-Henri Teitgen, notorious for his passionate approach to politics, proposed the creation of a 'European Army for a United Europe'[2] in the Council of Europe three days before Churchill made a similar proposal in August 1950 and a month before Dean Acheson asked for the rearmament of Germany. In the debate on Pleven's original proposal (October 1950), Teitgen tried to brush aside any fear which might be felt about the revival of German militarism:

The problem of German rearmament is a false problem, . . . the German units will be integrated . . . there will be no question of the revival of the German High Command or the emergence of a new Wehrmacht. If Germany has to be defended, why should other Europeans have to lay down their lives for the Germans? . . . What we are proposing to Germany is not revived militarism, but Europe.[3]

At the 1953 Congress Teitgen emphasized that the Russians only understood strength; the best way to move towards *detente* was for Western Europe to strengthen itself through the establishment of E D C prior to negotiations with Russia.[4] Moreover, he saw no evidence that the Russians were becoming more interested in peaceful co-existence—'I am not saying that the U S S R is preparing for

[1] The principal opponents, André Monteil, Henri Bouret, André Denis and Léo Hamon had all voted for E C S C.
[2] *Monde*, 10 August 1950.   [3] J O (A N), 25 November 1950, pp. 7203–8.
[4] M R P Congr. 1953, Paris; debate on foreign policy.

war, but she gives the impression that she is. Why is she producing three times as much military material now as in the last year of the War?'[1]

Teitgen, of course, advocated the building of Europe for reasons other than defence. In what *Le Monde* described as an 'impassioned' defence of EDC, he told the MRP National Committee that EDC was an essential step towards European integration: 'the months pass and people talk of the risk of ratifying EDC. *I* see a great opportunity: let us take the risk so as not to miss the opportunity.'[2] Another strong defender of EDC was François de Menthon, who told the 1953 Congress that the delay in the ratification of EDC was encouraging the growth of nationalism; if nationalism were allowed to flourish, it would ruin all chances of a united Europe:

> These are decisive hours for Europe . . . the European Defence Community is a fundamental element in the whole economic and political development of Europe. Its failure will undoubtedly shatter the whole edifice of united Europe, which MRP has striven to build for seven years . . . We are engaged in a double combat, against the spirit of Munich and against Maurrassian nationalism.[3]

Menthon, like other strong partisans of EDC, was an enthusiastic advocate of the European Political Community (EPC). Paul-Henri Spaak's original EPC proposal of 29 May 1952 had been rejected by the Assembly of the Council of Europe by 47–42, but Robert Schuman, still France's Foreign Minister in 1952, took it up, and he and Alcide de Gasperi, the Italian Prime Minister, persuaded the ECSC Council of Ministers to agree to the ECSC Assembly (plus 9 co-opted members and 13 observers) elaborating 'a project for a European Political Community' in accordance with Article 38 of the EDC Treaty. The ECSC Council of Ministers made their decision on 10 September 1952 and the so-called *Ad Hoc* Assembly set to work on drafting the EPC Treaty, completing their work in March 1953. The draft proposed a Senate of 87 chosen by the national parliaments, a Chamber of 268 elected by universal suffrage, and an Executive Council, whose president would be chosen by the Senate. The Council could be overthrown by the Senate or censured by the Chamber, in each case by a two-thirds majority. There was also to be a European Supreme Court, a consultative Economic and Social Council and a Council of National Ministers. Despite the direct election of the Chamber and the apparent power of EPC's bicameral parliament, many prerogatives remained in the hands of the Council

[1] *Monde*, 6 January 1953.   [2] *Monde*, 20 January 1953.
[3] MRP Congr. 1953, Paris; report on 'La Politique Extérieure'.

of National Ministers, whose unanimous agreement would have been required on almost all matters concerned with foreign policy. In some ways the EPC Treaty foreshadowed the Treaty of Rome by laying down objectives such as 'a common market amongst member states based on the free movement of goods, capital and persons' and 'the co-ordination of the policy of member states in monetary, credit and financial matters'.[1]

At the 1953 MRP Congress Menthon insisted that as soon as EDC had been ratified the Six should move on to the signature and ratification of EPC. In fact, EPC was dead even before EDC. Two months before the MRP Congress Bidault had already made it clear that he was opposed to EPC.[2] In August 1953, when the Six foreign ministers met to discuss the draft treaty, Bidault argued that too much supranational power was vested in the EPC Executive Council, and that the treaty would have to be redrafted. The redrafted version should have been discussed by the Foreign Ministers in 1954, but after the rejection of EDC, EPC was also shelved. Arguably European federalists such as Teitgen and Menthon made a mistake in linking EPC so closely with EDC. As a result EPC was never considered on its own merits and it was inevitably dropped at the same time as EDC.

Robert Schuman and Alfred Coste-Floret were the most prominent MRP politicians who were at first rather doubtful about EDC but later moved into the camp of the out-and-out partisans. There can be little doubt that Schuman was a reluctant enthusiast for EDC. On several occasions in 1949 he had said that there could be no question of Germany being rearmed.[3] Ten years after the rejection of EDC Schuman made it clear in his book, *Pour l'Europe*, that the economic and political integration of Europe ought to have preceded the attempt at military integration.[4]

Commenting on the original Pleven proposal of October 1950, Jacques Fauvet said that, although Schuman rather than Pleven was primarily responsible for the EDC proposal, he (Schuman) had not *chosen* to propose the military integration of Europe, but had been forced into the military sphere by American pressure for German rearmament.[5] Interpellated[6] by Debré in the Council of the Republic in November 1950, Schuman was careful to point out

[1] *'Ad Hoc' Assembly, Draft Treaty Embodying the Statute of the European Political Community*, Strasbourg, 1953, p. 54; see Willis, pp. 159–61, for a useful discussion of EPC.

[2] *Monde*, 11 March 1953.   [3] See p. 172.   [4] Schuman, p. 35.

[5] *Monde*, 25 October 1950.

[6] To interpellate was to question ministerial policy by means of a critical motion followed by a debate and vote.

177

that E D C was acceptable only if it were linked to E C S C as part of a general movement towards a united Europe. Moreover, any notion of an independent German army was 'inconceivable . . . It would be incompatible with our previous commitments . . . There will be no German army unless it is fully integrated into a European army.'[1] A month later he assured the National Assembly that 'under no circumstances will German units be at the disposal of the German Government.'[2] Despite his desire for Franco-German reconciliation, Schuman's experience of the Germans made him doubt the wisdom of German rearmament, and this weakened his whole defence of E D C.

In the 1952 debate on E D C, Schuman defended the proposed Treaty as a means for reconciling France and Germany and building Europe, but he could not conceal his doubts about the feasibility of an integrated army: 'The idea is grandiose and original and cannot be attacked as a concept. It is up to you to decide whether it can be realized in practice.' He went on to say that General Eisenhower believed it could work, but he failed to put forward any arguments countering those of Jules Moch who contended that E D C would be militarily 'ineffective'.[3]

Probably the most decisive evidence of Schuman's uncertainty about the practicality of E D C was the eight-month delay between the signing of the Treaty in May 1952 and its submission to the National Assembly for examination in January 1953, a delay which, in Raymond Aron's view, 'has never been satisfactorily explained'.[4] If one accepts Jacques Fauvet's contention that 'in 1952 or 1953 the Treaty would have been ratified if it had been submitted to the National Assembly',[5] Schuman's indecision can in the last analysis be explained only on the ground that he doubted whether E D C was a practical proposition. Schuman's official explanation was that the Treaty could not be submitted until an *exposé des motifs* had been worked out by the Six, but, as Fauvet has pointed out, the *exposé* added nothing to the substance of the Treaty. It is true that the internal political situation was hardly conducive to a ratification debate. De Gaulle, Daladier, Herriot and Auriol were outspoken opponents of the Treaty, but Fauvet believes that, despite their opposition, a decisive initiative in favour of ratification would have succeeded in 1952 when a sufficient number of Socialists would have

[1] JO (CR), 16 November 1950, pp. 2973–6.

[2] JO (AN), 12 December 1950, p. 8930.

[3] Schuman speech, JO (AN), 11 February 1952, pp. 573–6; Moch speech, ibid., p. 617.

[4] Aron and Lerner, p. 7.   [5] ibid., p. 29.

voted for EDC to ensure the passage of the Treaty even if the Gaullist dissidents had left the Pinay Government. Schuman had acted with great decision over ECSC. The only satisfactory explanation for his indecision over EDC lies in the fact that he lacked, not political courage, but political conviction as to the practicality of EDC.

Although it is impossible to be precise about numbers, it is probable that the supporters of Schuman, i.e. those who were enthusiastic advocates of European integration but had some doubts about EDC, were the largest group in MRP. A typical member of this group was Alfred Coste-Floret. Reporting on foreign policy at the 1952 Congress, he described EDC as the second step towards the building of Europe (the first being ECSC):

> It is not certain that the second step is as happy as the first. The Schuman Plan was a clearly drafted and carefully limited abandonment of national sovereignty. The Pleven Plan, however, implies the abandoment of sovereignty on a quite different scale, because a national army is the instrument and means of a national policy. France did not wish the problem to be posed in this way, but the American Secretary of State put it on the agenda by proposing a German national army in September 1950. France found herself isolated . . . Pleven made his proposal to get France out of an impasse . . . But if we declare ourselves in favour of the European Army in order to prevent the renaissance of the Wehrmacht, we are not prepared to accept any European Army. It must be one in which the forces are properly integrated, and which is under adequate political control, . . . Moreover, we must have an Anglo-American guarantee to intervene in the event of German secession.[1]

Speakers such as Coste-Floret were more inclined to express doubts before their own supporters than in the National Assembly. In the debates of February 1952 and November 1953 Coste-Floret gave no indication that he had any doubts about EDC. On the former occasion he said that a vote against EDC would solve nothing; Europe would be no nearer to unification and the Americans would simply rearm Germany unilaterally.[2] On the latter he criticized General Aumeran for calling the Europe of the Six 'Little Europe': 'United Europe will have a population almost as large as that of the United States . . . It will make possible the growth of economic prosperity and social justice . . . It will also be an essential factor in the security of France'. He wanted to see Britain closely associated with the Six, and the implementation of the proposed Political Community. He main-

[1] MRP Congr. 1952, Bordeaux; report on 'La Politique Extérieure'.
[2] JO (AN), 12 February 1952, pp. 648–50.

179

tained that the Saar problem was simply being used as an excuse by those who were unwilling to ratify EDC.[1]

Other typical members of the Schuman group were Robert Lecourt, who advocated ratification of EDC in the November 1953 debate but only on the ground that there was no alternative,[2] and Jean Lecanuet, who told the 1954 Congress that 'A European army would not have been first on our list of priorities; it is not our fault that peace requires vigilance. It is the fault of the Soviet Union, which has tried to oppose ECSC as much as EDC.' 'In any case', he argued, 'EDC is but one step towards united Europe . . . We must move forward in other sectors, such as agriculture and transport.'[3] In another report at the 1954 Congress Etienne Borne summed up the arguments of the Schuman group: 'We regard EDC as the most reasonable solution to the problem of European defence; nevertheless, we favour it not as a *primary* objective, but as a means to the construction of a united Europe.'[4]

In divisions in the National Assembly those members of MRP who thought like Schuman inevitably voted for the European Defence Community, but it is clear that many of them were unhappy about the ground on which they had been forced to fight the second battle for a united Europe. Nevertheless, their mystical faith in 'Europe' kept them going, even though they had doubts about the practicality of EDC.

Unlike Robert Schuman, Georges Bidault lacked any mystical faith in 'Europe'. Bidault was instinctively against EDC as a semi-supranational organization, but logically in favour of it as the only practical way of rearming Germany without creating an independent German army. His attitude was summed up in the words, 'We have to make Europe without unmaking France' ('faire l'Europe sans défaire la France').[5] He was therefore opposed to EPC, to all intents and purposes sabotaging the proposed treaty in August 1953,[6] and at the same time very insistent that France should have the right to withdraw troops for use in the French Union as and when required.

In the February 1952 debate Bidault, who was Deputy Premier and Minister of Defence, argued that he was in favour of EDC, because the alternative was an independent German army; moreover a vote against EDC was a vote for American withdrawal; those who opposed EDC were supporting the Communists. Bidault then introduced one of those historical parallels of which he was so fond. Europe must

[1] JO (AN), 17 November 1953, pp. 5206–7.   [2] ibid., pp. 5632–4.

[3] MRP Congr. 1954, Lille; report on 'La Politique Extérieure'.

[4] ibid., report on 'Le Sens de Notre Engagement Politique'.

[5] JO (AN), 6 March 1953, p. 167.   [6] See p. 182.

unite to defend herself or her fate would be like that of Greece when confronted by Philip of Macedon. Nevertheless, despite his defence of ED C, Bidault contended that there must be certain conditions: no German troops should be recruited until the Treaty had been ratified, national contingents should only be integrated progressively into the European Army, and the political institutions of ED C should be such that it might be possible for Britain to participate in them.[1]

After this initial, and rather negative, defence of ED C, Bidault remained remarkably quiet about the European Army for several months. He made no reference to it at the 1952 Congress, and Fauvet commented in October 1952 that Bidault had been 'very discreet' about ED C for a long time. Nevertheless, Fauvet argued, it could not be assumed that Bidault was opposed to ED C; indeed he had only recently spoken in favour of it in the Foreign Affairs Committee. But his defence of ED C owed nothing to enthusiasm for the Treaty as such; rather it was due to his belief that it was futile to negotiate with the Russians except from a position of strength, and in so far as ED C strengthened Western Europe, it would contribute towards peace and *détente*.[2]

Within a few months, however, Bidault had changed his tack, for in July 1953 he maintained that the non-ratification of ED C was no reason for rejecting the Russian proposal for a summit meeting. The outcome of the Russian proposal was the Berlin Conference (January 1954), which failed to reach any solution to the problems of Germany and Austria, and the Geneva Conference (May–July 1954), which achieved a compromise peace in Indo-China. Philippe Devillers and Jean Lacouture have examined the suggestion that Molotov may have persuaded Bidault to drop ED C in exchange for the Russians exercising diplomatic pressure in favour of a negotiated solution in Indo-China, but they found no evidence to substantiate this theory.[3] Indeed, the most likely explanation for Molotov's violent attack on Bidault, *after* the basic features of a negotiated solution for Indo-China had been worked out, is that Molotov had decided it would be preferable to conclude a settlement with Mendès-France, who was known to be sceptical about ED C, than with Bidault, who, at least in public, continued to advocate ratification.

Although one major reason for the replacement of Schuman by Bidault at the Quai d'Orsay in January 1953 was that the Gaullists regarded Bidault as no more than a lukewarm supporter of ED C, Bidault made it clear on various occasions in 1953 that he favoured ratification of ED C *provided* certain conditions were fulfilled. In

[1] JO (AN), 13 February 1952, pp. 684–6.   [2] *Monde*, 23 October 1952.
[3] Lacouture and Devillers, *La Fin d'une Guerre*, pp. 200–5.

February he promised the other five foreign ministers that France would ratify the treaty if two French protocols were accepted.[1] These protocols required British 'links' with EDC in the form of a guarantee to keep troops on the Continent and the 'participation' of the British in the political machinery of EDC.[2] The second of these conditions presupposed the dilution of the supranational character-istics of the EDC institutions, and, as such, was in line with Bidault's general aversion to loss of French sovereignty, an aversion which was demonstrated again in the autumn with his attack on the pro-posed EPC. In his investiture speech in June (when he failed to become Prime Minister by one vote) Bidault added another condi-tion, namely a satisfactory settlement of the Saar problem.[3] In view of the fact that the people of the Saar had voted two to one for the autonomist, Hoffmann, in the December 1952 Election, i.e. for the 'Europeanization' of the Saar, Bidault's condition looked like an-other delaying tactic, and was later criticized as such by Alfred Coste-Floret.[4]

Bidault's basic position in 1953–54 was that EDC ought to be ratified because German rearmament was inevitable, but that the supranational aspects of the Treaty should be minimized. In March 1953 he told the National Assembly that there could be no question of France 'selling out' over EDC, but

France, whilst entering EDC and confirming her commitment to the progressive integration of Europe, intends to maintain her role as a world power . . . We have to make Europe without unmaking France. Making Europe does not entail the disappearance of France; on the contrary, it means putting France at the head of the Community as its initiator and inspirer.

He went on to say that he would prefer further steps towards economic rather than political integration, a scarcely veiled criticism of EPC although he did not specifically mention the draft treaty. Moreover, it was essential that France should be able to use her troops in the French Union if required: 'We speak on behalf of 120 million people, . . . We must pursue two objectives which are not contradictory: the consolidation of the French Union and the construction of Europe.'[5] There can be little doubt that Robert Schuman, in sentiment, if not literally, would have put the last phrase the other way round. For Schuman, Europe came first, the

[1] *Monde*, 27 February 1953. [2] *Monde*, 20 February 1953.
[3] JO (AN), 9 June 1953, p. 2990. [4] JO (AN), 17 November 1953, p. 5206.
[5] JO (AN), 6 March 1953, pp. 1667–9.

French Union second. This was the fundamental difference between his position and that of Bidault.

Bidault continued to hedge his support for EDC with so many conditions that it seems questionable whether he would ever have asked the National Assembly to ratify the Treaty. The answer would seem to be that Bidault had become convinced of the need to ratify EDC, but that it must be *his* version of the Treaty, not the one which had been signed in May 1952. It may well be that this was the only realistic approach to take by late 1953 or early 1954. If there was to be a majority for EDC, it required the support either of a significant number of Socialists or of Conservatives. The supranational appeal of EDC failed to attract the support of more than half the Socialists. So the only hope of getting EDC through the Assembly was to convince the Right that the Treaty did not infringe national sovereignty too much. This seemed to be Bidault's strategy in late 1953, when he told both the Council of the Republic and the National Assembly that German rearmament was inevitable owing to Germany's geographical position; EDC was the best way to rearm and control Germany, but France must be free to defend the French Union, and Britain must be closely associated with EDC—'the protocols we are preparing will establish closer political and military links between Britain and the Continent than ever before.'[1]

Bidault's version of the Treaty would have been so hedged around with protocols and escape clauses that its 'European' (i.e. supranational) characteristics would have been virtually non-existent. And Britain would never have agreed to associate herself with the institutions of EDC unless they had been inter-governmental rather than supranational. It is also clear that France, by insisting on her right to withdraw forces for service overseas, was opening the way to secession, or at least partial withdrawal, by other members. In the last resort Bidault's EDC would not have been unlike Western European Union (WEU), the inter-governmental organization which was set up in place of EDC.

Although the vast majority of MRP supported EDC owing to their basic enthusiasm for European integration, whilst others, like Bidault, supported it as the best of a bad lot of alternatives, there was a small group of active opponents within the party. Most of these opponents were also 'Europeans' in the sense that they favoured European integration, but they did not believe either that

[1] JO (CR), 29 October 1963, p. 1687; for National Assembly debate see JO (AN), 17–20, 24 and 27 November 1953. Bidault was taken ill during his speech in the Assembly (20 November 1953) and it was mostly read out by Maurice Schumann.

the time was ripe for military integration or that EDC would do anything to promote European security; on the contary, by provoking the Russians, it would reduce the chances of peaceful co-existence and *détente*.

The main argument of the MRP opponents of EDC was that military integration should be one of the last, not one of the first, steps to European integration. In the EDC debate of February 1952, when André Monteil was one of six interpellators,[1] he said that he agreed with General Juin that to attempt military before political integration was to put 'the cart before the horse',[2] a contention which had previously been made by Henri Bouret in the MRP National Committee.[3] At the 1953 Congress M. Besson, a delegate from Yonne, said that 'the militants are 100 per cent behind the European idea, but we do not want a military Europe'; he suggested that it would be better to pursue the 'Dutch-French proposal for a common agricultural market and forego the idea of a European army.'[4] Jean Seché, president of the Equipes Ouvrières of Seine, agreed with Besson: 'We do not advocate an armed Europe, but a political Europe, an economic Europe, a social and cultural Europe.'[5] And Monteil repeated that he was 'for Europe but against EDC, . . . EDC means a Europe of the helmet and the barracks.'[6]

It was argued that EDC would both offend the Russians and encourage a revival of German militarism. André Denis insisted that every effort should be made to solve the German problem by negotiation; if these efforts failed, then, but only then, should the Six threaten to ratify EDC.[7] Léo Hamon, speaking immediately after Robert Schuman at the 1953 Congress, pointed out that Schuman had said that war with the Russians was 'improbable', but that EDC was necessary: 'Surely there is a contradiction here? Our whole policy is based on the hypothesis of open, probable and imminent aggression by the Russians. But, if this aggression is 'improbable', why provoke the Russians with EDC?'[8] In the same debate Denis argued that twelve or fifteen German divisions would reduce the chances of peace by frightening the Russians; EDC would thus be counter-productive as regards the security of Western

---

1 The other five were Fajon (PCF), Daladier (Rad.), Cot (Progressiste), Billotte (RPF) and Aumeran (Ind.). Fauvet commented that the list of interpellators showed the widespread doubts about EDC existing in all parties, including the SFIO, although there was no Socialist interpellator on this occasion. *Monde*, 12 February 1952.

2 JO (AN), 11 December 1952, p. 586.   3 *Monde*, 29 January 1952.

4 MRP Congr. 1954, Lille; debate on foreign policy.   5 ibid.

6 ibid.   7 *Monde*, 25 October 1952.

8 MRP Congr. 1953, Paris; debate on foreign policy.

Europe.[1] And Seché said that France should try to negotiate with the Russians in the changed atmosphere of the 'Malenkovian era'; France should say to the Kremlin, 'If you pursue a policy of international *détente*, we will abandon EDC, but if you do not make any moves towards *détente*, we will increase our efforts to implement EDC.'[2]

The opponents of EDC were not only worried about the reaction of the Russians to a German army, they also expressed other doubts about the wisdom of German rearmament: 'Do not believe that the juridical barriers put up by our negotiators will bar the revival of German militarism', said Monteil in the February 1952 debate. He warned that the Italian army was weak and those of Benelux small; France had overseas commitments, so that soon the Germans would dominate the European Army: 'Do not forget that the German army of the 1920s developed out of a tiny kernel, . . . the European army will soon be another Wehrmacht.'[3] Bouret pointed out that the German commitment to recover the eastern territories would transform the Atlantic Alliance from a defensive to an aggressive organization even if, strictly speaking, the Germans were not in NATO.[4] And Denis warned that EDC could lead to an arms race between the two Germanies, which could result in the other EDC members being dragged into a German civil war.[5]

Another argument used against EDC was that it was an American organization. Denis told the 1953 Congress that he was all in favour of a 'politically and economically united Europe, but not of a Europe, which will be a pawn in the hands of the Pentagon',[6] and Monteil told the National Committee that 'Europe ought not to become the battering-ram for America's "roll-back" policy.'[7] Monteil also resented the fact that in NATO the United States and Great Britain 'will be able to wield the influence given to them by an independent army, but France will only have the weight given to her by an impersonal contribution to an integrated army.'[8] Hamon, too, occasionally expressed an almost Gaullist resentment against the Anglo-Americans; after telling the MRP National Committee that France was still a world power, he said that 'Europe cannot be built at the expense of France, the French Union and peace.'[9]

In spite of lively opposition at the 1952 and 1953 Congresses,

[1] MRP Congr. 1953, Paris; debate on foreign policy.   [2] ibid.
[3] JO (AN), 11 February 1952, pp. 585–9.
[4] MRP Comité National, *Monde*, 29 January 1952.
[5] MRP Congr. 1953, Paris; debate on foreign policy.   [6] ibid.
[7] *Monde*, 20 October 1953.   [8] JO (AN), 11 February 1952, p. 586.
[9] *Monde*, 20 October 1953.

MRP remained more committed to EDC than any other party. The Christian Democrats never forgave Mendès-France for 'the crime of 30 August', although Mendès-France had no alternative but to propose a modified version of EDC. He had asked Bourgès-Maunoury (for EDC) and General Koenig (against) to work out a compromise. When they failed to agree, he put forward his own suggestions for modifying the Treaty. The essential point was his proposal that for a provisional period member-states should have the right to act without the Commissariat's consent in matters affecting their national interests. Although this removed the supranational element from EDC, the Gaullist members of the Government (Koenig, Lemaire and Chaban-Delmas) resigned; nothing short of the total abandonment of EDC would have satisfied them. The five other countries of course could not possibly accept Mendès-France's 'dilution' of the Treaty, especially as Germany, Belgium and Holland had already ratified it, and when the Six met in Brussels in August 1954 there was deadlock. At the end of the month the National Assembly decided to postpone the ratification debate until the Greek Kalends; EDC was dead. The final irony was that, with the London and Paris Agreements establishing Western European Union (WEU), the National Assembly in effect accepted the original American proposal of 1950.

The majority of MRP voted against WEU in the National Assembly and for it in the Council of the Republic, a *volte face* which Poher tried to justify on the grounds that,

If the London and Paris Agreements had come before the Council of the Republic when Mendès-France was still Premier, we would have voted against them, because Mendès-France believes in a European organization built on the basis of associated nations, . . . but Edgar Faure sees the Agreements in a much more European light, interpreting them quite differently from Mendès-France.[1]

Poher failed to explain what he meant by the phrase 'much more European', except to remark that Faure 'wishes to move forward with the building of Europe avoiding all dogmatism'. With these words Poher attempted to sweep under the carpet the true facts about MRP's most dishonest parliamentary performance in the Fourth Republic. For the defeat of WEU would have led to the isolation of France, with the USA and Great Britain relying wholly on Germany. Yet the most convinced Europeans and Atlanticists, led by Menthon and Teitgen, made speeches whipping up all the anti-Germanism they had condemned for years, and cast their votes

[1] MRP Congr. 1955, Marseilles; report on 'La Politique Extérieure'.

against the Treaty, something which they could never have done if they had not been able to rely on the patriotism and responsibility of the Mendésist majority (whom at other times they accused of fellow-travelling) to take the odium of 'voting for the Wehrmacht'. Arguably it was the most immoral and irresponsible performance of the whole régime, and it was the work of the most moralizing and self-righteous party. Robert Schuman, Pierre Pflimlin and Paul Coste-Floret were amongst the few honourable exceptions.[1]

MRP's attitude to Mendès-France over EDC and WEU was quite irrational. Even if Mendès-France had come out openly in favour of EDC, there would no longer have been a majority for the Treaty in the National Assembly by the summer of 1954.[2] Yet in the Cold War atmosphere still prevailing in 1954 some form of German rearmament was inevitable. Whilst MRP behaved like *un enfant gâté*, Mendès-France acted pragmatically and logically. But in fairness to the Christian Democrats, it must be admitted that the failure of EDC was a genuinely traumatic experience for them. The 'European party' had put all its eggs in one basket and the fall of that basket seemed to symbolize the failure of MRP. In a remarkably frank report at the 1954 Congress, Etienne Borne said

The building of Europe is the one great new idea in a world constantly threatened by nationalism and imperialism . . . Europe represents a hopeful opening in international relations . . . We are the party of Europe. Europe is our way of denying a return to the past. It is our revenge, and quite legitimately so, for the failures and difficulties experienced in our social policy.[3]

MRP, the new 'party of the Fourth Republic', had been unable to

[1] There were two important votes on WEU. On 23 December 1954 the National Assembly voted against ratifying the Treaty by 280–259. 61 out of 85 MRP joined the Communists, two-thirds of the Gaullists and one-quarter of the Socialists in voting against the Treaty; 16 MRP, including R. Schuman, P. Pflimlin and P. Coste-Floret, abstained, whilst the small Mendésist group, led by R. Buron, A. Monteil and J.-J. Juglas, voted for it. This vote naturally caused considerable consternation in Washington, London and Bonn, and Mendès-France, after making use of a procedural device (a minor alteration to the Treaty), insisted on a further vote (a confidence one this time) on 29 December. Despite Adenauer's appeals to his fellow Christian Democrats of MRP to vote for the Treaty, 52 members of the party followed G. Bidault, M. Schumann and P.-H. Teitgen in voting against it; a dozen others abstained, but R. Schuman, P. Pflimlin, P. Coste-Floret, J. Fonlupt-Esperaber and H. Meck joined the MRP Mendésists in voting for the Treaty. JO (AN), 23 December 1954, pp. 6862–3, and 29 December 1954, pp. 6958–60.
[2] Aron and Lerner, pp. 40–5; Grosser, p. 318.
[3] MRP Congr. 1954, Lille; report on 'Le Sens de Notre Engagement Politique.'

prevent a return to the habits and practices of the Third Republic between 1946–51. The failure of *la Révolution par la loi* was the party's first major defeat. When Mendès-France arrived on the scene and started to slay one or two of the domestic dragons which had hitherto always defeated MRP, they found it unforgivable—he was showing up their own past failings. When into the bargain he 'attacked' *their* concept of Europe, they found it even more intolerable, for Europe had become a surrogate for MRP's failures at home (although this is vigorously denied by former party leaders).[1] It was, as Borne said, 'our way of denying a return to the past'. The defeat of EDC implied just such 'a return to the past'. Nationalism had triumphed over supranationalism. MRP's hope of playing an important role in a Christian Democratic Europe had been shattered.

THE EUROPEAN ECONOMIC COMMUNITY (EEC) AND MRP'S EUROPEAN POLICY AFTER 1954

Having burnt their fingers over EDC, MRP adopted a more sober approach towards the European *relance*, which led to the establishment of the European Economic Community (Common Market) and Euratom (Treaties of Rome, 25 March 1957), but Edelgard Mahant, in her otherwise excellent thesis on the attitude of the French and German political parties to the EEC negotiations,[2] probably exaggerates the retrogessive effect of the EDC rebuff on MRP. It is true that MRP at first tended to press for further specialized communities in sectors such as agriculture and transport rather than for the more comprehensive Common Market advocated by the Benelux countries and the Spaak Committee, but there is ample evidence that MRP appreciated the advantages of far-reaching economic integration from an early stage in the Brussels negotiations. The party did not simply swing round to the proposed Common Market as a result of the Suez debacle, although Suez certainly had a catalytic effect on MRP's attitude to the *relance*. On the other hand, MRP's whole approach to the *relance* was marked by pragmatic realism, as was clearly shown by Robert Schuman's final speech in the Common Market ratification debate of July 1957.

The *relance* owed its impetus to the Benelux countries, led by Johan Willem Beyen, the Dutch Foreign Minister, and Paul-Henri Spaak, the Belgian Foreign Minister, who drew up a memorandum

[1] E.g. Poher, interview, 24 March 1970; Lecourt, interview, 22 June 1970; Pflimlin, interview, 3 April 1971.
[2] Edelgard Mahant, *The French and German Political Parties and the Common Market Negotiations, 1955–57* (Ph.D. Thesis, London, 1970).

in April 1955, calling for comprehensive economic integration. This was followed by the Messina Conference of the Foreign Ministers of the Six in June 1955, which set up an inter-governmental Committee under Spaak to study the steps which should be taken to achieve the comprehensive integration of the Western European economies under common institutions. The Spaak Committee held its first session in Brussels in July 1955, producing its final report in April 1956. The Spaak Report called for the establishment of the Common Market and Euratom. The first part of the Report, on the Common Market, was the most important. It proposed the elimination of customs barriers between the member states and the free movement of capital and labour. The Common Market would entail the elimination of non-tariff barriers to competition; it would include agriculture; investment and readaptation funds would be set up to help backward regions and to retrain workers. The Spaak Report was accepted by the Foreign Ministers at Venice in May 1956, although France found its sections on agriculture and the overseas territories unsatisfactory. Nevertheless, Spaak was invited to preside over a conference to negotiate two treaties, one setting up a Common Market, the other Euratom. The Conference began work in Brussels in June 1956, and after difficult negotiations, in which the French theses on agriculture and overseas territories were largely accepted, the Treaties instituting the European Economic Community and Euratom were signed in Rome on 25 March 1957.

MRP's attitude to the *relance* was at first cautious. In April 1955 the National Committee proposed the establishment of further specialized communities in sectors closely related to the ECSC, in particular transport and energy.[1] In the same month Beyen, the Dutch Foreign Minister, was proposing his much more grandiose scheme for a Common Market. MRP explained its minimalist approach in the next number of *Forces Nouvelles*: 'The first task is to re-establish a European atmosphere in order to revive confidence which has been shaken by the defeat of EDC. Concrete and precise initiatives, which are immediately realizable, must restore coherence and authority to the organization of Europe.'[2] MRP also reacted cautiously to the Messina communiqué (July 1955). René Plantade, Editor-in-Chief of *Forces Nouvelles*, did not even mention the Common Market in his report on the Messina conference, whose results were said to be 'meagre',[3] and Jacques Mallet argued that the primary aim of the *relance* should be the strengthening of ECSC,

---

[1] *Forces Nouvelles*, 9 April 1955.
[2] *Forces Nouvelles*, 23 April 1955; cited in Mahant, p. 111.
[3] *Forces Nouvelles*, 11 June 1955; cited in Mahant, p. 112.

followed by the setting up of atomic energy, transport and overseas investment pools.[1] In March 1956 the National Committee called for 'the creation of Euratom' but only for 'a start on work for the Common Market'.[2] Yet the Spaak Committee had already been at work in Brussels for eight months and was to produce its final report a month later (April 1956). On the basis of the above evidence, Edelgard Mahant concludes:

> Thus, from the time of the Messina Conference until the Suez crisis (which began in June 1956) MRP clung to the old functionalist idea on which the Coal and Steel Community had been based. It advocated the creation of Euratom and other specialized communities which it hoped would gradually lead to the transfer of authority to common institutions.[3]

Mrs Mahant goes on to say that in July 1956 Jean-Marie Louvel agreed that the Common Market was probably more important than Euratom,[4] and that in September Robert Schuman said the two communities should be established together:[5] 'Thus MRP abandoned its own policy of specialized communities and came to support the Government's policy of more wide-ranging integration in the form of the Common Market.'[6]

Although it is true that MRP was slow to make specific references to the Common Market, the party's underlying belief in European integration remained unchanged,[7] and there is evidence to show that MRP was not as slow to grasp the full implications of the *relance* as Mrs Mahant suggests. At the 1955 Congress Alain Poher called for the integration of transport, energy, taxation and social services; this extension of economic, fiscal and social integration would require 'the urgent establishment of new institutions, responsible to a democratic Assembly and subject to the jurisdiction of a Court of Justice.'[8] Robert Schuman and Robert Lecourt both spoke in favour of the European *relance*, and although neither referred specifically to a 'common market', it is clear that they, like Poher, were in favour of far-reaching steps to integration, going well beyond the

---

[1] *Forces Nouvelles*, 9 July 1955; cited in Mahant, p. 112.

[2] *Forces Nouvelles*, 31 March 1956; cited in Mahant, p. 113.

[3] Mahant, p. 113.

[4] JO (AN), 6 July 1956, p. 3336; cited in Mahant, p. 113.

[5] *Bulletin des Presse und Informations der Bundesregierung*, 19 September 1956; cited in Mahant, p. 113.

[6] Mahant, p. 113.

[7] See J. Fauvet, *Monde*, 24 May 1955.

[8] MRP Congr. 1955, Marseilles; report on 'La Politique Extérieure'.

establishment of a limited number of specialized communities.[1] At the May 1956 Congress, which took place a month after the publication of the Spaak Report, Schuman welcomed the proposed Common Market and Euratom. After outlining the weaknesses of the traditional inter-governmental organizations, the Council of Europe, OEEC and WEU, and describing the Coal and Steel Community as a successful but limited operation, he called for the setting up of the Common Market, 'a genuine economic union, implying the harmonization of legislation, technology and taxation, together with the reorganization of firms and the retraining of workers.'[2]

The Suez crisis and the invasion of Hungary gave a boost to MRP's European enthusiasm, with speakers like Jacques Mallet, Maurice-René Simonnet and Alfred Coste-Floret contending, quite unconvincingly, that if 'Europe' had existed, France and Britain might not have had to climb down over Suez, and the Russians might somehow have been deterred from invading Hungary.[3]

MRP, however, had other motives for supporting the *relance*, quite unconnected with 'third force' foreign policy arguments. The party continued to see Franco-German reconciliation as an underlying motive for European integration. Robert Schuman told the 1956 Congress that there was a danger of Germany relapsing into neutralism if the *relance* failed; this, he said, would be 'the end of united Europe'.[4] Other MRP spokesmen feared that if Germany were denied Europe, she might turn to the East, especially if the Social Democrats, who were expected to win the 1957 Election, came to power.[5]

Not surprisingly, in view of the nature of the Treaty of Rome, MRP's main motives for supporting it were economic and social. Teitgen told the National Assembly that Europe had been the world's banker in 1910, but 'today, in spite of recent economic growth, she is losing ground to the USA and USSR'; the only way for Europe to close the gap was to develop a unified market, which would allow large-scale investment, long production runs and expenditure on advanced technology.[6] In the ratification debate of July 1957 Pierre Abelin, the MRP *rapporteur* of the National Assembly's Economic Affairs Committee, developed the themes outlined by Teitgen in January; in particular, he was optimistic about the

[1] MRP Congr. 1955, Marseilles; debate on foreign policy.
[2] MRP Congr. 1956, Montrouge; report on 'La Politique Extérieure'.
[3] *Forces Nouvelles*, 29 September 1956 (Mallet); ibid., 30 March 1957 (Simonnet); *Politique Etrangère*, December 1956 (Coste-Floret).
[4] MRP Congr. 1956, Montrouge; report on 'La Politique Extérieure'.
[5] *Forces Nouvelles*, 20 October 1956 and 13 April 1957.
[6] JO (AN), 15 January 1957, pp. 12–13.

191

prospects for French agriculture, as the Six had opted for a protectionist agricultural market in accordance with French wishes[1]; he hoped the common agricultural policy would quickly be elaborated in detail.[2] Jean-Marie Louvel, reporting on behalf of the Finance Committee, concentrated on France's lack of energy resources, a factor which had had a particularly adverse effect on her balance of payments; he hoped the problem would soon be resolved by the exploitation of oil in the associated territories (principally Algeria) and by the development of Euratom.[3]

MRP also laid great emphasis on social policy. For this reason Teitgen disapproved of a 'free market economy'; to ensure that the economic advantages of the Common Market resulted in higher living standards for the masses, he advocated a powerful role for the Economic and Social Committee and considerable funds for the Investment Bank and Readaptation Fund.[4] In view of the feeble role allotted to the Economic and Social Committee and the limited funds set aside for the Investment Bank, it was not surprising that Abelin criticized both institutions in the ratification debate.[5]

MRP was insistent that the French overseas territories should be closely associated with the Common Market. Louvel told the National Assembly that it was a question of 'solidarity' between Europe and Africa. It was essential to guarantee the overseas territories suitable market outlets, long-term contracts and adequate prices. If these objectives were to be achieved, it would be necessary to establish a relatively high common external tariff and a system of community preferences.[6] In February 1957 the MRP National Committee claimed that 'only the association of Europe and Africa will allow the economic and social development of Algeria and Black Africa by means of greater investment',[7] and Jacques Menditte told the 1957 Congress that the close association of the African territories with the Common Market would prevent them from going neutralist and thus falling under the influence of one of the blocs.[8] The Germans were reluctant to concede the French demands for a special relationship with the overseas territories, partly because they had their own traditional trade links in South America and partly because they did not want to get associated with 'colonialism'. In the end they agreed to a compromise, which was much nearer to the

[1] In the January 1957 debate Abelin had insisted on the importance of a protected agricultural market, JO (AN), 16 January 1957, p. 81.

[2] JO (AN), 3 July 1957, pp. 3176–9.   [3] ibid., pp. 3183–5.

[4] ibid., 15 January 1957, p. 13.   [5] ibid., 3 July 1957, p. 3179.

[6] ibid., 17 November 1957, p. 116.   [7] *Forces Nouvelles*, 23 February 1957.

[8] MRP Congr. 1957, Biarritz; report on 'La Politique Extérieure'; and see Teitgen, JO (AN), 6 July 1957, pp. 3363, for similar argument.

French position than to their own; the French and Belgian overseas territories were to be associated for a period of five years, after which a new convention would be negotiated. Teitgen did not conceal his delight that Germany would be contributing 200 million dollars over five years to the (largely) French overseas territories.[1]

MRP was not happy about the institutional structure of the European Economic Community or of Euratom, but their criticisms were rather restrained; the memory of the abortive European Political Community lingered on. Robert Schuman had told the 1956 Congress that 'a European authority with real powers of decision'[2] was needed, and Teitgen said that the Common Market would be no more than a 'heavy lorry with a two horse-power engine'; the Council of Ministers was too powerful in relation to the other institutions, and unanimity was required too frequently.[3] Poher would have liked to have seen an Assembly elected on the basis of universal suffrage and endowed with real powers of control,[4] a proposal repeated many times by MRP spokesmen in the 1960s. But Teitgen was wise enough to admit that 'the failure of EDC taught us some lessons', and that, although it would be necessary to strengthen the institutional machinery of the Communities by stages, at least only one Assembly had been established for them[5] (at one time there had been talk of three assemblies). In explaining MRP's vote Robert Schuman also discussed the Treaties in a very pragmatic manner:

In spite of what others may say, we are no longer fanatical Europeans. Certainly we believe in Europe, but not as a simple, infallible panacea . . . After ratification constant efforts will be needed to implement the Treaties and to carry through the processes of readaptation and harmonization . . . The EEC will be a continuous creation, an immense task.

He went on to say that he believed in the dynamic effect of integration; the institutions could be adapted as economic harmonization progressed.[6]

In the Common Market debate of January 1957 all the MRP deputies voted for the principle of the market (except Buron who was absent on leave),[7] and in the ratification debate of July 1957 the party voted unanimously for the Treaties of Rome instituting the

---

[1] JO (AN), 6 July 1957, p. 3365.
[2] MRP Congr. 1956, Montrouge; report on 'La Politique Extérieure'.
[3] JO (AN), 15 January 1957, p. 11.
[4] MRP Congr. 1955, Marseilles; report on 'La Politique Extérieure'.
[5] JO (AN), 6 July 1957, p. 3362.   [6] ibid., 9 July 1957, pp. 3476–7.
[7] JO (AN), 22 January 1957, p. 239. The vote was 322–207 in favour.

Common Market and Euratom.[1] MRP had recovered its European 'soul' after the debacle of EDC, but it was a chastened MRP which voted for the 1957 Treaties. The party's conviction about the advantages of European integration had not been shaken by the events of August 1954, but it had lost some of its naïve faith in the possibility of achieving a United States of Europe by one or two quick steps. What remained of its faith in Europe was to be severely tested in the 1960s.

In the early years of the Fifth Republic, MRP, in company with all the French political parties, had to concentrate primarily on Algeria. So long as national unity was required, MRP stood by de Gaulle, but Alain Poher made it clear at the 1961 Congress that the Christian Democrats were fundamentally opposed to the General's European (and economic and social) policy.[2] By a strange paradox the Common Market might not have survived if de Gaulle had *not* come to power in 1958, for de Gaulle alone had sufficient political weight to obtain a common agricultural policy tailored almost entirely to the interests of France. Yet, despite this Gaullist achievement, MRP was opposed to de Gaulle's European policy for two main reasons. The party disagreed both with the General's anti-Americanism and with his concept of Europe.

Although MRP advocated European integration, it did not want it at the expense of the Atlantic Alliance. MRP professed doctrinal opposition to the development of blocs, but when the existence of blocs became a reality in 1947, the party had had no hesitation in choosing the Western side. It favoured co-existence, but not if that meant neutralism or a defenceless Western Europe. Lecanuet told the 1960 Congress that it was necessary to strengthen the Atlantic Alliance at the same time as building Europe. De Gaulle, on the other hand, by determining to build a 'European Europe', based on a French nuclear strike force (the *force de frappe*), was jeopardizing both Europe and the Alliance: 'De Gaulle proposes to replace the system of Atlantic deterrence with a national force capable of deployment at any time in any place. We are aware of the grandeur of this ambition, but we are totally opposed to this policy of prestige.'[3] The foreign policy motion of the Congress demanded the 'political construction of Europe' and the strengthening of the Atlantic Alliance, 'the fundamental guarantee of Western security',[4] and in 1962 the Congress asserted that 'only a Community Europe,

[1] JO (AN), 9 July 1957, p. 3495. The vote was 340–236 in favour.
[2] MRP Congr. 1961, Royan; report on 'La Politique Extérieure'.
[3] MRP Congr. 1960, Evian; report on 'La Politique Etrangère'.
[4] ibid.

as a partner of the United States in NATO, can assure the cohesion of the free world.'[1] After MRP had left the Government in May 1962 over de Gaulle's European policy, Pflimlin told the MRP Federation of Haute Savoie that the Atlantic Alliance and NATO, 'its indispensable military instrument', were fundamental to the security of Western Europe; the Alliance contrasted with America's withdrawal from Europe in 1919, a withdrawal which had been followed by European weakness and another war within twenty years:

> The American alliance will remain for a long time the essential foundation of our security, . . . that does not mean to say that we decline responsibility for our own defence. Indeed, we have a right to demand a greater role in making decisions affecting our security. But . . . an American withdrawal would constitute a mortal danger for our country.[2]

Pflimlin saw the *force de frappe* as the symbol of de Gaulle's determination to break up the Atlantic Alliance; at the same time it would encourage nationalism, whose revival would reduce the chances of uniting Europe,[3] a theme which was repeated by Théo Braun in his report on European policy at the 1963 Congress, which passed a motion condemning 'a purely national *force de frappe*'.[4]

Nevertheless, MRP's attitude to the *force de frappe* was rather indecisive. In so far as the project brought France a certain amount of national prestige, and perhaps technological advantage, MRP was inclined to support it; in so far as it was anti-'European' and anti-American, it was inclined to oppose it. Thus Marie-Madeleine Dienesch and Paul Rivière argued that MRP should not support the 1962 Socialist censure motion on the *force de frappe* on the ground that the Pierrelatte nuclear complex would do more good to France than harm to Europe, and Henri Dorey, President of the MRP group in the National Assembly, and Maurice-René Simonnet, Secretary General of MRP, argued that Pierrelatte should be converted into a European nuclear project instead of being wound up.[5] With an amendment to this effect, 33 out of 57 MRP voted for the Socialist censure motion on 16 July. The motion received only 206 out of the necessary 241 votes, but proportionately this was more than the 207 out of the necessary 268 votes received in the 1960 censure motion

---

[1] MRP Congr. 1962, Dijon.   [2] *Monde*, 22 May 1962.
[3] *Monde*, 13 July 1962; also MRP Congr. 1965, Vichy; report on 'La Politique Extérieure'.
[4] MRP Congr. 1963, La Baule; report on 'L'Europe'.
[5] MRP National Committee meeting 11 July 1962; *Monde*, 13 July 1962.

on the *force de frappe*, when 21 MRP had voted for the motion.[1] In spite of his criticism of de Gaulle's foreign policy Pflimlin did not vote against the Government in the *force de frappe* censure motions, although he did vote against it in the October 1962 censure motion which led to the defeat of the Pompidou Government.[2] The explanation is that Pflimlin, a member of the 'Gaullist' wing of MRP, was prepared to go a long way in his support of the General, even to the extent of not voting against the *force de frappe*, although he was critical of it. Pflimlin would accept almost any of de Gaulle's polices except those which were in direct conflict with the Atlantic Alliance, as in the case of France's withdrawal from NATO in 1966, or in direct conflict with MRP's concept of Europe, as in May 1962.

It was in their concept of Europe that the Christian Democrats really clashed with the Gaullists. The differences between the two sides came to a head with de Gaulle's press conference of 15 May 1962 when he insisted that Europe could only be built on the basis of national states; those who believed in a federal Europe were living in a dream world of stateless people who wanted to speak 'Esperanto or Volapük'. Within twenty-four hours MRP's five Ministers had resigned from the Government. A week later Pflimlin contrasted his view of Europe with that of de Gaulle.

Pflimlin began by saying that at least de Gaulle had abandoned his original formula of 'Europe des Patries' in favour of 'Europe des Etats'. But, in practice, there was not much difference between the two, except that in the latter case regular meetings between Heads of State were envisaged. However, 'Europe of the States is nothing new. It takes us straight back to the Congress of Vienna and the "Concert of Europe", which our grandfathers talked about. It lasted only so long as the musicians refrained from hitting each other over the head with their instruments.' Instead of the 'Europe of States' Pflimlin proposed a 'Europe of Peoples', 'that is a Europe in which the people can participate through their elected representatives'. How was this to be achieved? Pflimlin said that the first steps towards a democratic European Community had already been taken by the authors of the Treaties of Paris and Rome. It remained now to implement the Treaty of Rome and develop the institutions of the Community. He was not averse to 'a transitional period of inter-governmental co-operation, preparing the way for a true political

---

[1] Robert Schuman and Paul Coste-Floret joined the party's progressive wing, led by Bernard Lambert and Nestor Rombeaut, in voting for the 24 October 1960 censure motion. When the vote went up to 33 on 16 July 1962 the most notable addition was Maurice-René Simonnet, MRP's Secretary General.

[2] See p. 241.

Community', but de Gaulle had excluded any development towards such a Community, because he was opposed for all time and in all circumstances to majority decisions being taken by Community organs. But 'the truth of the matter' said Pflimlin 'is that political union has no future if it is subject to the rule of unanimity, . . . Our partners are hardly likely to be attracted by an engagement which holds out no promise of an eventual marriage.'[1]

Jean Seitlinger, a Moselle deputy and Secretary General of Nouvelles Equipes Internationales, the European Christian Democratic Liaison group, developed the same theme at the 1962 MRP Congress. He distinguished between 'two schools', one which proposed 'a Europe of States, based on the simple, traditional form of inter-governmental co-operation,' the other 'a Europe of Peoples, proposed by men like Robert Schuman, . . . entailing the abandonment of some degree of sovereignty for the sake of the Community as a whole'. If a Europe of Peoples were to become a reality, 'the European Parliament must be elected by universal suffrage, the executives must be fused, and more power must be transferred to the Community institutions'. Moreover, it was essential to widen the Community; he hoped that the negotiations for British entry would succeed, provided Britain was prepared to commit herself to 'the development of Community Europe',[2] a condition which was also made by Pflimlin in his speech earlier in the month.[3] On many occasions in the 1960s MRP was to advocate British entry. André Monteil criticized de Gaulle for his unilateral decision to keep Britain out of Europe in 1963,[4] and even Maurice Schumann, the most Gaullist of the Christian Democrats, said 'In the long run there can be no Europe without Britain, for Britain showed herself to be part of Europe in 1940.'[5]

Issues such as British entry and the future of the European Parliament were in reality only the tip of the iceberg as far as MRP's criticism of de Gaulle's European policy was concerned. The Christian Democrats' real fears lay much deeper and were concisely summarized by Pflimlin at MRP's last Congress. Firstly, de Gaulle's concept of a 'European Europe', by which he meant an anti-American Europe, would do nothing to bring about European unity: on the contrary, de Gaulle's policy was alienating Germany and preventing Britain from joining Europe. At the same time, the Gaullist concept

---

1 *Monde*, 22 May 1962.
2 MRP Congr. 1962, Dijon report on 'La Politique Etrangère'.
3 *Monde*, 22 May 1962.
4 MRP Congr. 1963, La Baule; debate on 'L'Europe'.
5 *Monde*, 17 January 1966.

of national independence was reawakening 'national passions, . . . This is the paradox of present French policy. It aims to achieve European unity on principles which are the negation of co-operation and unity'.[1] Although MRP was almost dead by the mid-1960s, the party's 'Europeanism' continued to attract many Frenchmen, as was shown by Lecanuet's unexpected success at the Presidential Election of December 1965.[2] However, the problem was that the Christian Democrats had little else to offer to the electorate except 'Europeanism'. It was one thing to protest against de Gaulle's European (and other) policies in the first round of a Presidential Election; it was quite another to vote for a small, rather conservative, centre party at a General Election.

MRP's European policy had evolved from a nationalistic, 'Gaullist' position in the immediate post-war period through a naïvely supranationalistic phase in the mid-1950s to pragmatic support for Community Europe in the 1960s. MRP was, of course, not just 'European' in some vague, idealistic sense. The Christian Democrats were 'European' because they believed that a united Europe would benefit France, particularly French agriculture, and because they realized that Christian Democracy had no future in France, but might well have a decisive role to play in some future European federation. However, they were well aware that the United States of Europe had become a very long-term prospect. Indeed, Robert Schuman in the last years of his life was becoming increasingly doubtful whether it would be possible to revive the necessary political will to achieve a federal Europe; he believed that de Gaulle had rekindled the fires of nationalism to such an extent that it would be difficult to douse them down again.[3] Perhaps Schuman's fears were those of an old man who had, as it were, got to the verge of the Promised Land and then had had to retreat into the desert. The events of the late 1960s and early 1970s would tend to indicate that Schuman was over-pessimistic. And, even if Europe is still far from the federation advocated by Schuman, Adenauer and de Gasperi, the fact that it (or at least Western Europe) has developed means of co-operation, which go far beyond the traditional inter-governmental methods, owes much to the Christian Democrats of Europe, and not least to those of France.

1 MRP Congr. 1965, Vichy; report on 'La Politique Etrangère'.
2 See pp. 251–3.
3 Interview with Poher, 24 March 1970.

Chapter 7

COLONIAL POLICY

There are many mysteries which history will have to explain. Why did MRP defend a form of colonialism which was contrary to all its traditions? The war in Indo-China, the repression in Madagascar, the *coup de force* in Morocco, . . . in each case MRP was not only involved but played a leading role. (J.-M. Domenach, *Esprit*. November 1967)

MRP's colonial policy was, as Domenach suggests, strangely contradictory. Louis Aujoulat's Report at the 1945 Congress contained many advanced economic and social proposals for the French Union (the name soon to be adopted by the former empire); the Overseas Labour Code of 1952 owed much to MRP; Robert Buron and Jean-Jacques Juglas, both members of the progressive wing of MRP, were Mendès-France's successive Ministers of Overseas France;[1] another MRP liberal, Pierre-Henri Teitgen, was Minister of Overseas France in Edgar Faure's Government, which conceded full independence to Tunisia and Morocco; MRP supported Defferre's Loi Cadre of 1956 which led directly to the independence of Black Africa in 1960; almost the whole of MRP supported de Gaulle's Algerian policy—indeed it was the only thing that kept them in the Government from 1960–62. And yet, Christian Democratic politicians, in the persons of Paul Coste-Floret and Jean Letourneau, cannot escape responsibility for dragging France further into the morass of Indo-China; Pierre de Chevigné 'pacified' Madagascar with a scorched earth policy which probably caused 100,000 deaths between 1947–49[2]; and Georges Bidault, supported by Maurice Schumann, agreed to the deposition of the Sultan of Morocco in January 1953, an action which was as politically dishonourable as it was inept.

In a way it was ironical that MRP became so heavily involved in the problems of decolonization, for unlike the Radicals and Conservatives, and to a lesser extent the Socialists, MRP had no vested interests in the old empire. The Christian Democrats knew almost

---

[1] Though both temporarily lost the party whip for entering the Mendès-France Government.

[2] *Esprit*, April 1950, p. 594.

nothing about overseas France, and yet Indo-China became an MRP fief, Socialist influence being largely eliminated during the Generals' Affair of 1950–51. For five-and-a-half of the seven-and-a-half years of the war, MRP Ministers were responsible for Indo-China;[1] the party held the Ministry of Foreign Affairs (which was also responsible for relations with Morocco and Tunisia) without a break until the last month of hostilities;[2] and at various times ran the Ministries of Defence and War.[3] In addition, seven of the twelve Ministers of Overseas France in the Fourth Republic were Christian Democrats; and they ran the Ministry at the rue Oudinot for a total of almost six years out of a possible twelve.[4]

MRP's colonial policy was based on a mixture of idealism and quasi-federalism, which, in practice, all too often resembled old-fashioned paternalism. MRP made a break with the pre-war doctrine of assimilation, but was opposed to anything comparable to dominion status for former colonies. Instead the party advocated 'progressive federalism', i.e. the maximum economic, social and political progress compatible with a federal structure of which France was clearly the head. As the Catholic Church believes in national Catholic churches within a unified structure under the control of the papacy, so MRP favoured a family of nations and territories within the unified structure of the French Union. But, as with the Catholic Church, there could be no question of secession. Paris was to be to the French Union what Rome is to the Catholic Church, both spiritual home and supreme authority.

In the sordid world of practical politics MRP soon found that its idealism became tainted, that not everyone agreed that the highest calling in life was to be a Frenchman. Gradually, MRP's colonial

[1] Coste-Floret, Minister of Overseas France, November 1947 to October 1949. Letourneau, Minister of Overseas France, October 1949 to June 1950. Minister with Special Responsibility for Indo-china, July 1950–May 1953.

[2] Bidault, September 1944 to July 1948 (except for Blum's one-month Government in December 1946); Schuman, July 1948 to December 1952; Bidault, January 1953 to June 1954.

[3] Coste-Floret, Minister of the Army, January to November 1947; Teitgen, Minister of the Armed Forces and National Defence, November 1947 to July 1948; Bidault, Minister of National Defence, August 1951 to February 1952; Chevigné, Minister of State for War, July 1951 to June 1954.

[4] Apart from Coste-Floret and Letourneau (note 1 above), MRP Ministers of Overseas France were Pflimlin, March 1952 to June 1953; Buron, June 1954 to January 1955; Juglas, January to February 1955; Teitgen, February 1955 to January 1956; Colin, May to June 1958. Other Ministers of Overseas France were Moutet (Soc.) 1946–7; Mitterrand (UDSR), July 1950 to August 1951; Jacquinot (Ind.) August 1951 to June 1954, except for Pflimlin's interlude under Pinay in 1952; Defferre (Soc.) January 1956 to June 1957; Jaquet (Soc.), June 1957 to May 1958.

policy became more pragmatic and progressive, a process retarded by the party's right wing, accelerated by its left wing, and compromised all along the line by the exigencies of practical politics.

In fairness to MRP it must be conceded that decolonization was the most difficult problem the Fourth Republic had to tackle. Indeed it proved to be the Spanish ulcer of that Republic, which in other fields achieved so much. Jean Lacouture, the Le Monde journalist and North African expert, once pointed out that France in effect lost the war, although she came out on the winning side. In contrast to Britain, therefore, she could not afford to be generous in 1945. She had to prove herself after the humiliation of 1940, and the only way she could do this was by consolidating the French Union with its 120 million inhabitants.[1] Moreover, France had scarcely begun to recover from the war in Europe when the first colonial struggle began in Indo-China at the end of 1946. But, even without the psychological problem created by the defeat of 1940 and the practical problem of a 'premature' colonial war, France would have encountered greater difficulties than Britain in decolonizing owing to the very different colonial traditions of the two countries.

Since the Durham Report of 1840 Britain had always contended that her long-term objective was some form of self-government for her colonies. The French colonial tradition, on the other hand, emphasized the Jacobin concept of 'la République une et indivisible'. France would 'assimilate' her overseas subjects; they would eventually have the same economic, social and political rights as citizens in the Métropole, but independence or dominion status was not even a long-term objective. Thus, although France adhered to the Atlantic Charter, whose third principle emphasized the right of all peoples to choose the form of government under which they wanted to live, and although she signed the United Nations Charter, which laid down that independence was the inevitable and only morally desirable goal of colonization, she also, in the persons of General de Gaulle and René Pleven, signed the Brazzaville recommendations (January 1944), which proclaimed a quite different objective.

Whereas the aims of the work of civilization accomplished by France in her colonies rule out all idea of autonomy and all possiblity of development outside the French Empire; [therefore] the eventual constitution, even in the far-off future, of self-government in the colonies is out of the question.[2]

[1] Interview with Lacouture, 7 February 1967.
[2] La Conférence de Brazzaville, Janvier-Février 1944 (Ministère des Colonies, Paris, 1945), p. 32.

201

It is true that the Brazzaville Conference also proposed generous economic and social policies, but in the post-war world in which 'independence' increasingly became *the* magic word for colonial peoples, the Brazzaville recommendations, devoid as they were of political content, appeared obsolete before they could be implemented.

Three trends may be analysed in MRP's colonial thinking. Paul Viard, Dean of the Algiers Law School and MRP spokesman on colonial affairs on the first Constitutional Committee of 1945–46, was an outspoken assimilationist. He argued that French greatness and a French Union firmly controlled by Paris were inseparable. His ideas were rejected by the Constitutional Committee and, in time, by the vast majority of MRP, but they remained important, representing as they did the thinking of the MRP Right throughout the period of decolonization.[1]

Louis Aujoulat was the early spokesman of the MRP liberals. In his report on Colonial Policy at the 1945 Party Congress he envisaged major social and economic reforms throughout the Empire. He recommended a large-scale educational programme, improved medical services (including mobile medical teams ready to fly to any part of the world), the legalization of trade unions and a labour code. Economic planning would be essential to implement this social programme, 'not an overall plan, but individual plans worked out for each colony or group of colonies'. The political policy outlined for the colonies was much less progressive. Aujoulat preferred association to assimilation, except for French departments such as those of Algeria which were to be fully integrated with the mother country, but some partners were to be more equal than others: the overseas territories should be represented in an Assembly of the Community but it would be wise to limit their representation. Each of the overseas territories should have territorial and local assemblies, but only at the local level would they be fully controlled by natives. The territorial assemblies should not be sovereign: 'they should act only within specified areas ... laid down by the law.'[2] In other words, the French National Assembly would decide the powers of the territorial assemblies.

Aujoulat's recommendations of 1945 went no further than those of the Brazzaville Conference of 1944, but during 1946 Aujoulat seems to have realized that the logical conclusion of his progressive

---

[1] For details about Viard's proposals to the first Constitutional Committee, see Wright, *The Reshaping of French Democracy*, pp. 148–9.

[2] MRP Congr. Paris, December 1945; report on 'La Politique Coloniale'.

economic and social ideas was a liberal political structure for the French Union. Aujoulat now proposed an Assembly of the French Union, whose membership was to be in direct proportion to the population of the respective territories, i.e. there would be more 'native' than 'Metropolitan' members in the new Assembly, which would have legislative authority in matters specifically concerned with the Union. Aujoulat also stated that he was in favour of a High Council of the Union 'with definite authority',[1] although he failed to say exactly what he meant by this. He suggested, too, that the President of the French Union should be elected by the Union. These proposals would, as he rightly said, lead to 'a fundamental revision of our political system'.[2] If a French Union with political organs of this type had come into being, its history might have been very different. As it was, the Assembly of the French Union was virtually powerless; the High Council did not meet until 1951; and the President of the French Union was the President of France. In these circumstances it was not surprising that Morocco and Tunisia boycotted the institutions of the French Union from the start.

Aujoulat did not propose a confederation or a 'Commonwealth' but, without ever being very specific, he seemed to be advocating a quasi-federal structure in which the various member states could wield some definite influence. André Colin, the first Secretary General of MRP, and Georges Le Brun-Kéris, one of the party's experts on Black Africa, later claimed that the vast majority of MRP favoured Aujoulat's more progressive ideas.[3] There is no reason to dispute this claim, because the more liberal members of MRP could hardly oppose Aujoulat's economic and social proposals, whilst his political proposals were too vague to upset the party's right wing. Moreover, imprecise though they were, Aujoulat's proposals were certainly a good deal more radical than those being expressed by General de Gaulle a year later: 'The Union must be French, which means that the authority, I repeat authority, of France must be exercised decisively . . . in the fields of public order, national defence, foreign policy and economics.'[4]

The amalgam of MRP conservative and liberal colonial thinking was Bidault's idea of 'progressive federalism',[5] as opposed to the

[1] *Aube*, 11 April 1946.   [2] ibid.
[3] Interview with Colin, 18 October 1966; interview with Le Brun-Kéris, 14 October 1966.
[4] *Aube*, 16 May 1947 (speech at Bordeaux).
[5] Philippe Devillers has rightly pointed out that, although Bidault coined the phrase 'progressive federalism', he did not himself attempt to practise it. He remained an assimilationist in all but name. Nevertheless, the phrase remains

left-wing idea of immediate federalism. Three federal organs were to be created in Paris—the President, High Council and Assembly of the French Union—but the French Government was to decide how much autonomy should be granted to the various states of the Union. The more advanced ones were to become Associated States with a considerable degree of internal autonomy.[1] The less advanced would remain under direct French administration, either as Departments[2] or Overseas Territories.[3] The left-wing native bloc in the Overseas Committee (of the Second Constituent Assembly), led by Ferhat Abbas, was opposed to Bidault's proposals and managed to obtain some minor concessions, but overall Bidault's plan was accepted, because he managed to win over the Socialists when he threatened to resign (20 September 1946), the Socialists preferring a rather rigid French Union to another constitutional crisis. It seemed worthwhile to concede to Bidault's wishes in return for minimum interference with the rest of the Constitution, especially as the Radicals, led by Herriot, and the Gaullists also favoured a centralized French Union.[4]

Bidault got his way. A French Union with decisive guarantees of French sovereignty came into being.[5] The question was how far the French Government would 'federalize' the Union, and whether the result would be a close-knit federation from which secession would be impossible, or a loose association of states joined to the mother country only by economic and cultural ties. Theories may mean very little in politics, but in France, perhaps, they count for more than in most countries. It seemed promising that MRP had shown signs of being willing to adapt its theory, the party having expressed both

an adequate description of the position adopted by the majority of MRP. Interview with Devillers, 5 December 1967.

[1] Apart from Vietnam, Laos and Cambodia, which became Associated States in 1950, the nominally independent protectorates, Morocco and Tunisia, were theoretically Associated States, but they showed little interest in acquiring a status which did nothing to reduce their dependence on Paris.

[2] This status applied to the Algerian departments and to four West Indian and Indian Ocean territories. They were administered by the Ministry of the Interior.

[3] This status applied to all the other former colonies, which were now represented in Parliament and administered by the Ministry of Overseas France.

[4] Cf. JO (AN Constit.), 27 August 1946, p. 3334, for Herriot's views. Also P. M. Williams and M. Harrison, *De Gaulle's Republic*, p. 23.

[5] The French Union clauses adopted in the Second Constitutional draft in September 1946 gave much greater emphasis to French sovereignty than those in the first draft—cf. François Borella, *L'Evolution Politique et Juridique de l'Union Française Depuis 1946* (Thèse, Nancy, 1957); and interview with Alain Dutheillet de Lamothe, 26 April 1967.

liberal and conservative views. It now remained to be seen what its leaders would do when they had the power to act as well as to talk.[1]

MRP'S COLONIAL POLICY IN PRACTICE

Rather than attempting a global analysis of French decolonization, case studies will be made of the protectorates (Indo-China, Morocco and Tunisia), Black Africa and Algeria. As far as MRP was concerned the Indo-China episode was particularly important, partly because MRP was so intimately involved in the implementation of Indo-China policy, and partly because the Geneva Agreement of 1954 marked the end of the period in which MRP's colonial policy was controlled by the right wing. Thereafter the liberals predominated and the influence of Bidault and his friends withered away. The cases of Morocco and Tunisia, where MRP pursued both reactionary and progressive policies, illustrate the tensions produced by this transitional phase. In Black Africa and Algeria, on the other hand, the liberal wing held sway throughout.

INDO-CHINA, MOROCCO AND TUNISIA

The first stage in the tragic history of French decolonization began in 1946, 12,000 miles away in Indo-China, whose five constituent parts, Tonkin, Annam, Cochin-China, Laos and Cambodia, had become part of the French Empire in the 1880s.[2] With the Japanese surrender at the end of the Second World War, Northern Vietnam (Tonkin and Northern Annam) had been occupied by Chinese Nationalist forces and Southern Vietnam (Southern Annam and

[1] Throughout any discussion of colonial policy it should, of course, be remembered that power often lay not in Paris but with the colonial administrations who frequently disobeyed or ignored instructions from Paris. Cf. Williams and Harrison, *De Gaulle's Republic*, p. 22, 'Ministers in Paris were generally well-intentioned, often liberal, rarely blind or reactionary. But time and again they were too weak to impose their will upon a local administration, often supported by settlers in the colony and by powerful politicians and business interests in the capital'; and see also Robert Schuman's complaints about the 'independent' actions of Residents General in Morocco and Tunisia during his four years of responsibility for these protectorates (1948–52), *La Nef*, March 1953, pp. 7–9.

[2] Cochin-China was legally a colony, whilst the other four were protectorates. The main problem centred on Vietnam (Tonkin, Annam, Cochin-China), where nationalism was more advanced than in Laos and Cambodia. The first Indo-China War (like the second) was fought mainly in Vietnam, and for convenience the word Vietnam is frequently used in the following pages when, strictly speaking, the phrase Indo-Chinese Union or Associated States (after 1950) should be used.

Cochin-China) by British. General de Gaulle appointed Admiral d'Argenlieu High Commissioner of Indo-China in August 1945, and by March 1946 the French had taken over from the Chinese in the North as well as from the British in the South. But the most important event in Indo-China in the winter of 1945–46 was that Ho Chi Minh, after declaring Vietnam's independence in September 1945, set up a provisional Government in Hanoi. When the French returned to Hanoi in March 1946 they were faced with a *de facto* Government, which had carried through what amounted to a social and economic revolution since September 1945.[1]

In these circumstances France could either attempt to work out a new relationship with her former Indo-Chinese colonies or try to restore the old one by force. After negotiations with Ho Chi Minh at Fontainebleau in the summer of 1946, France opted in effect for the latter. War actually broke out owing to the decision of a French colonel (against the orders of General Leclerc, the Commander-in-Chief) to bombard Haiphong as a reprisal in November 1946. But the atmosphere which had produced the outbreak of war owed much to the intransigence of Bidault, the French Prime Minister in the summer of 1946. He had told Max André, the MRP chief negotiator at Fontainebleau, that there could be no question of conceding the word 'independence' to Ho Chi Minh, because this would be the first step towards the disintegration of the French Union.[2] Ho Chi Minh patched up a *modus vivendi* at the end of September, but he realized that he would come under severe criticism from his more extreme supporters for his failure to extract the word 'independence', and a few days later he told the American journalist, David Schoenbrun:

It will be a war between an elephant and a tiger. If the tiger ever stands still, the elephant will crush him with his mighty tusks. But the tiger will not stand still . . . He will leap upon the back of the elephant, tearing huge chunks from his side, and then he will leap back into the dark jungle. And slowly the elephant will bleed to death. That will be the war of Indo-China.[3]

Jean Sainteny believes that a deal could have been done with Ho Chi Minh in 1946, arguing that Ho was both moderate in his demands and more nationalist than Communist.[4] In fact, with the Communists still in the French Government and therefore opposed to the

---

[1] For details see Philippe Devillers, *Histoire du Vietnam, 1940–52*, pp. 180–207.
[2] Interview with André, 3 October 1966.
[3] D. Schoenbrun, *As France Goes*, p. 234.
[4] J. Sainteny, *Histoire d'une Paix Manquée, Indochine 1945–47*.

secession of French territory, and with MRP having won more votes than any other party at the June election, Ho Chi Minh could hardly have come to Paris at a worse time. Bidault, conservative though he was, accurately reflected Gaullist, Radical and even Communist (as well as MRP) colonial thinking in the summer of 1946. France was just recovering her self-respect after the years of humiliation; she could hardly be expected to agree to secession from her new Union of a Hundred Million Frenchmen. When Ho Chi Minh told *Franc-Tireur*[1] that all that he wanted was 'one word, independence', he was asking for the one thing which no French Government would have conceded at that time.

Ironically, the word 'independence' was to be conceded (although not granted) within eighteen months of the outbreak of war. But by then Ho Chi Minh, who had been welcomed in Paris as a Head of State in 1946, was *persona non grata*. France had opted instead for Bao Dai,[2] the former Emperor of Annam, a decision which owed much to MRP. The so-called Bao Dai solution was the brainchild not of MRP but of Admiral d'Argenlieu, but it was MRP who adopted it and tried, amidst increasing Socialist doubts, to make it work.

The Bao Dai solution was first proposed in January 1947, but was not fully implemented until three years later when the French National Assembly (in January 1950) finally ratified the various agreements made with Vietnam, Cambodia and Laos in 1949. The three-year delay was sufficient to destroy what little credibility Bao Dai possessed. In December 1947 the Schuman Government matched its tough domestic policies by announcing that there could be no question of negotiations with the Communist-led Viet Minh. In the same month Bollaert, the High Commissioner who had replaced d'Argenlieu, signed a preliminary agreement with Bao Dai near Dalat. This was followed by the Along Bay Protocol of June 1948, which was an important landmark because the word 'independence' was used for the first time. However, any possible goodwill which might have resulted from this concession was destroyed when Paul Coste-Floret, the MRP Minister responsible for Indo-China, immediately told the National Assembly that 'independence' excluded

---

[1] *Franc-Tireur*, 15 August 1946.

[2] Bao Dai. Born 1913, adopted son of Emperor Khai Dinh, whom he succeeded in 1925; educated in France, returned Annam 1932. During war first supported Vichy regime of Admiral Decoux, then Japanese after *coup* of March 1945. Abdicated to become Ho Chi Minh's adviser after revolution of September 1945; deserted to Hong Kong, where first approached by French in 1947. Married to a Catholic, which strengthened Socialist suspicions that he was an MRP protégé, e.g. Paul Rivet, JO (AN), 10 March 1949, p. 1517, and Marius Moutet, interview, 20 October 1966.

diplomacy, a national army and the status of Cochin-China (still nominally a colony).[1] The main reason for this apparent *volte face* was doubtless Gaullist pressure, for the General had said in September 1947 that anyone responsible for the loss of French territory would in due course have to explain his actions before the High Court (i.e. face impeachment).[2] The MRP leaders, as always, had their eyes on their electorate, which Edmond Michelet once claimed was 90 per cent Gaullist.[3]

The immediate result of the French Government's apparent *volte face* was that Bao Dai refused to return to Vietnam until the independence protocols had been accepted by the National Assembly. This did not occur until March 1949, and Bao Dai did not return until the following month. By the Elysée Agreement of March 1949, ratified by the National Assembly in January 1950, France solemnly recognized the 'independence' of Vietnam, Cambodia and Laos. But, even now, 'independence' was hedged around with conditions: the new Associated States could have diplomatic relations only with the Vatican, India, Siam and China; the French Army could still move freely throughout Indo-China; and French personnel (businessmen, teachers, missionaries) were given special concessions.

The Elysée Agreement, then, did not concede enough, nor did it come soon enough, for the victory of the Chinese Communists in 1949, followed by Mao Tse Tung's recognition of Ho Chi Minh's Government in January 1950, added a new dimension to the Indo-China War. Henceforth it was seen as part of the general war against Communist aggression, and the Americans started to aid the French instead of criticizing them as colonialists. At the end of 1950 Mendès-France told the National Assembly that France must choose between a massive military effort and negotiations with the enemy.[4] In fact Jean Letourneau, who had replaced Coste-Floret at the rue Oudinot in October 1949, chose neither. He refused to send conscripts to the unpopular *sale guerre*, nor did he contemplate direct American intervention because this would have reduced French influence in Vietnam (and, in any case, was out of the question so long as the United States was involved in Korea). On the other hand, he resolutely refused to consider negotiations with Ho Chi Minh.[5] Instead he continued with the second phase of the Bao Dai solution,

1 JO (AN), 8 June 1948, p. 3290.

2 Lacouture, *Ho Chi Minh*, p. 151; *Monde*, 11 January 1967. The shift to the Right of French Governments after the break-up of tripartism in May 1947 was, of course, also an important contributory factor, see p. 230.

3 Interview with Michelet, 25 April 1967.

4 JO (AN), 22 November 1950, p. 8004.

5 ibid., 27 January 1950, p. 592; ibid. 19 February 1952, p. 6670.

based on the building up of a Vietnamese national army and the extension of Vietnamese independence. Although certain minor concessions were made towards the latter, e.g. the handing over of hospital administration to the Vietnamese, François Borella has shown that Letourneau, in his dual capacity as French Cabinet Minister and High Commissioner in Indo-China, exercised a greater degree of administrative power in the Associated States than had ever been exercised by previous High Commissioners.[1] France's decision to devalue the Indo-Chinese piastre unilaterally in May 1953, contrary to the Agreements of 1950, showed the flimsy nature of Vietnamese independence, and it was not surprising that the Governments of all three Associated States began to talk about seceding from the French Union as the only means of achieving complete independence. By the end of 1953 it was clear that France had lost political control of Indo-China. Dien Bien Phu and the Geneva Treaty of 1954 only confirmed what had already happened. France could no longer resist the tide of decolonization.

The war in Indo-China was important for MRP because it brought the party face to face with the realities of the colonial situation. Only independent nations could enter the United Nations, hence the appeal of the word 'independence'. With the United States and the Soviet Union both agreed on the desirability of decolonization, the old colonial powers had no alternative but to grant independence or to use force on a large scale to prevent it. Like de Gaulle, the Christian Democrats gradually trimmed their sails when faced by the colonial wind of change. The importance of the removal of Bidault from the Quai d'Orsay in June 1954 and the signing of the Indo-China peace treaty in Geneva a month later was that together they marked the end of the period in which MRP had been dominated by its right wing in colonial policy. From the mid-1950s MRP, with the exception of the steadily declining Bidault faction, consistently supported progressive colonial policies.

This was a complete reversal of what had gone before. Hitherto the Bidault philosophy had predominated. The essence of that philosophy, if philosophy is the right word, was summed up by Pierre Corval, one of MRP's liberals, who said that Bidault had the mentality of a peasant of central France, who had inherited a certain amount of land and had no intention of surrendering a square inch of it: 'as time passed Bidault became more and more conservative . . .

---

[1] Borella, p. 216 ff. After the death of de Lattre de Tassigny, who had been both High Commissioner and Commander-in-Chief in Indo-China, Letourneau took over the office of High Commissioner (January 1952), a post which he held until May 1953.

he was the most reactionary of them all.'[1] Bidault's policy of not surrendering any French territory applied as much to North Africa as to Indo-China. W. S. Lee has shown how Bidault consistently took a less liberal line on Tunisia than Robert Schuman had done.[2] In this he was supported by his Minister of State, Maurice Schumann, who seems to have been easily swayed by the settlers' lobby. The reactionary Hauteclocque was replaced as Resident General by Voizard in June 1953, but this did not imply a more liberal policy; indeed, Bidault appointed Voizard against the advice of Faure, Mitterrand and Teitgen,[3] all regarded as progressives in colonial policy. Voizard, it is true, introduced important administrative reforms early in 1954, but these did not decrease French control over the Tunisian executive. The reorganized municipal and *caidat* councils did not satisfy the nationalist party, the Neo Destour. Bourguiba, the most moderate of France's colonial opponents, criticized the Bey for approving the reforms, and from March 1954 armed attacks on the French became more frequent.[4]

It was the same story in Morocco. In January 1951 General Juin, the Resident General, had wanted to depose the Sultan who was demanding reforms leading to a measure of independence, but Robert Schuman, supported by Jules Moch, the Socialist Minister of National Defence, refused to accept this. Juin's successor, General Guillaume, soon found himself at loggerheads with the Sultan. When the latter refused to sign various decrees eroding his own authority and outlawing the nationalist party, the Istiqlal, Guillaume determined to depose the Sultan. He did so with the support of El Glaoui, the Pacha of Marrakesh, and of Bidault on 20 August 1953. Although at the time Bidault denied any foreknowledge of the deposition, he privately admitted to Georges Hourdin, a pre-war colleague on *L'Aube*, that he had authorized it.[5] Twelve years later Bidault publicly admitted that he had given orders for the deposition of the Sultan.[6] Shortly after the deposition, François Mauriac described Bidault's North African policy as a betrayal of Christian Democracy. Bidault and Maurice Schumann, he claimed, had supported (or at least had not restrained) Generals Juin and Guillaume and M. Boniface, the settlers' leader. There was no

---

[1] Interview with Corval, 7 February 1967.

[2] W. S. Lee, *French Policy and the Tunisian National Movement* (Oxford D.Phil. 1963), p. 90 ff.

[3] ibid., p. 439.   [4] ibid., pp. 455–9.

[5] Interview with Hourdin, 6 June 1967. Hourdin went straight to the Quai d'Orsay on hearing of the deposition, and Bidault, in the presence of his *chef de cabinet*, flew into a rage and admitted his responsibility.

[6] *Resistance, the Political Autobiography of Georges Bidault* (1965), p. 185.

difference between the policies advocated by Martinaud-Déplat in the National Assembly and those carried out by Bidault and Schumann.[1] In Morocco and Tunisia, as in Indo-China, Bidault was in favour of some measure of internal administrative autonomy, but he had no intention of permitting a degree of independence which would allow any of the (former) colonial territories to run their own foreign policy or to choose whether or not they wished to remain within the French Union. Bidault pursued his policies with a logic and ruthlessness which led by way of Démocratie Chrétienne and his self-exclusion from MRP to his presidency of the OAS Resistance Council after the arrest of Salan in 1962. But by that time Bidault had been repudiated by his own party which, with one or two exceptions,[2] had opted for a very different course.

Even before the end of the war in Indo-China, an MRP liberal wing had emerged, but it was only in relation to North and Black Africa that the liberals became the dominant force within the party.

As early as the 1951 Congress Kenneth Vignes and André Peretti were advocating the conciliation of nationalism in Tunisia and Morocco.[3] And, even before that, André Denis, Paul Boulet, Charles d'Aragon and Abbé Pierre had called for a negotiated peace in Indo-China.[4] But the years 1953–54 marked the turning-point in the fortunes of the liberals. At the 1953 Congress Robert Buron, Léo Hamon, André Denis and Henri Bouret all advocated negotiations with Ho Chi Minh, and for the first time Congress passed a motion demanding 'a peaceful solution' to the war. Vague though this was, it was an advance on all previous motions. Meanwhile, the 1953 Congress also condemned in the strongest possible terms the policy of intimidation in North Africa, proposing instead reforms leading to complete internal autonomy in Morocco and Tunisia.[5] Later in 1953 MRP criticism of Bidault's Indo-China policy was more

[1] *Observateur*, 15 October 1953. Martinaud-Déplat, the right-wing Radical leader, was the chief spokesman of the North African lobby in the National Assembly.

[2] Very few members of MRP joined Bidault's right-wing breakaway party, Démocratie Chrétienne; see pp. 226–7.

[3] MRP Congr. 1951, Lyon; debate on Coste-Floret's report on 'La Politique Coloniale'.

[4] Boulet, d'Aragon and Abbé Pierre all resigned from MRP in 1950, largely because they were against the Atlantic Alliance. Denis was expelled in 1954 for opposition (amongst other things) to EDC. For their criticisms of Indo-China policy see JO (AN), 28 January 1950, p. 684 ff. and ibid., 19 October 1950, p. 7020 ff.

[5] MRP Congr. 1953, Paris; motion voted after Kenneth Vignes's report on 'L'Union Française'. *Monde*, 26 May 1953, referred to the enthusiastic applause which greeted liberal statements on Morocco and Tunisia.

pronounced than ever before. Henri Bouret contended that now that the Associated States had expressed their wish to leave the French Union there was no point in French forces remaining in Indo-China. The only logical solution was to negotiate with Ho Chi Minh for a peaceful withdrawal.[1] André Monteil and André Denis spoke in a similar vein,[2] and at the end of the debate nine MRP joined the Socialists, Communists and Mendésist Radicals in voting against the Government, whilst four others abstained.[3] Seven of the nine who voted against the Government had previously supported Charles Lussy's Socialist motion demanding immediate negotiations, whilst five other members of MRP had abstained when this motion was defeated by 313–248.[4] These figures were repeated in the debate of 5 and 9 March 1954 (resulting from interpellations demanding an immediate cease-fire), when ten members of the party voted against the Laniel Government.[5] Thus, by late 1953–early 1954 almost one-seventh of MRP's deputies were prepared to ignore the party whip in deference to their liberal convictions.

It was the same story in North Africa. After blindly following the reactionary policies of Robert Schuman,[6] Georges Bidault and Maurice Schumann in the early 1950s, MRP opted for a more liberal approach from 1954 onwards. It is true that MRP brought down Mendès-France's Government in a confidence vote on Tunisian policy in February 1955, but Alfred Coste-Floret made it quite clear that MRP was in favour of the liberal policy which had begun

[1] JO (AN), 27 October 1953, pp. 4575–6.

[2] ibid., pp. 4580–1 and 4613–14.

[3] The nine were MM. Aubin, Billiemaz, Bouret, Buron, Denis, Fouyet and Monteil, and Mmes Lefebvre and Poinso-Chapuis; JO (AN), 27 October 1953, p. 4635. The four abstainers were Barangé, Couston, Elain and Le Sciellour.

[4] The seven were the same as the nine in note 3 above, except that Buron and Poinso-Chapuis were amongst the five abstainers (the other three being Barangé, Elain and Le Sciellour); JO (AN), 27 October 1953, p. 4629.

[5] Those who voted against were Aubin, Billiemaz, Bouret, Buron, Couston, Fouyet, Gau, Monteil, Reille-Soult and Mme Lefebvre; JO (AN), 9 March 1954, p. 788.

[6] Robert Schuman has sometimes been described as a liberal over North Africa, and in theory he was one. At Thionville in June 1950 he said that France's aim was 'to lead Tunisia towards independence, which is the final goal for all territories of the French Union', and his La Nef article of 1953 (see p. 205, note 1) also indicated his goodwill and moderation. But, in practice, Schuman, who was always much more interested in Europe than in North Africa, conceded to pressure from the Right. Thus, on 19 July 1950 he retracted his Thionville remarks, substituting 'internal autonomy' for 'independence'. And later in 1951 he allowed Maurice Schumann to draft the famous Note of 15 December which emphasized the definitive nature of the link between France and Tunisia, thus preparing the way for the violence of the next four years.

with Mendès-France's visit to Tunis at the end of July 1954. Since then Boyer de La Tour, Voizard's successor as Resident General, had declared an amnesty for all rebels who handed in their arms. Bourguiba had been transferred from prison to house arrest, and the 1938 decree abolishing the Neo Destour had been repealed. Having praised the Mendès-France Government for all the steps it had taken in Tunisia (except for its permitting Bourguiba to act as spokesman for the Bey's Government when he was not officially in it), Coste-Floret quite brazenly told Mendès-France that MRP would not support the Government, because in a vote of confidence a party had to take into account the whole of a Government's policy and not just part of it.[1] As Daniel Mayer pointed out, Coste-Floret's arguments were somewhat hypocritical.[2] True though this was, they also reflected the general opinion in MRP which was determined to get rid of Mendès-France because of EDC but at the same time approved the Government's North African policy. Not surprisingly, 21 members of MRP (out of 87) voted with Mendès-France on 4 February 1955, but they could not save his Government which went down by 319–273.[3]

The reforms begun by Mendès-France were completed by his successor Edgar Faure, who signed a Convention granting complete internal autonomy to Tunisia (2 June 1955). MRP had already shown at its 1955 Congress that it was in favour of the new policy. Robert Lecourt, Jacques Fonlupt-Esperaber, Kenneth Vignes and Pasteur Lagravière all advocated the continuation of liberal policies in Tunisia and Morocco, and the Congress demanded 'progressively greater participation by Arabs in public affairs and the administration'.[4] After internal autonomy had been granted to Tunisia, Maurice Schumann (somewhat ironically in view of his earlier policy as Minister of State responsible for Morocco and Tunisia) maintained that the achievement of internal autonomy was the logical result of 'the path which we have followed for so long'. He contended that past difficulties had been caused by Tunisian intransigence rather than by French unwillingness to talk (a doubtful contention), but he was prepared to let bygones be bygones, and MRP would vote for the Conventions granting internal autonomy.[5] On 8 July 1955 no members of MRP, not even Bidault, joined the forty-four die-hard

[1] JO (AN), 4 February 1955, pp. 755–8.   [2] ibid., p. 756.
[3] Strictly speaking 11 MRP and 10 IOM (affiliated to MRP). The MRP deputies who voted for Mendès-France were Bouret, Buron, Denis, Fonlupt-Esperaber, Guissou, Hutin-Desgrées, Juglas, Lenormand, Monteil, Reille-Soult, Thiriet. 3 MRP abstained—Elain, Aubin, Abbé Gau; JO (AN), 5 February 1955, p. 782.
[4] MRP Congr. 1955, Marseilles; motion on colonial policy.
[5] JO (AN), 7 July 1955, pp. 3697–702.

213

colonialists like Martinaud-Déplat, Frédéric-Dupont and General Aumeran who voted against the Conventions.[1] And sixteen months later the policy of Mendès-France and Faure, supported by the vast majority of MRP, reached its logical conclusion when Tunisia and Morocco joined the United Nations as fully independent states.

Morocco had, in fact, taken the final steps to independence even more rapidly than Tunisia. When Edgar Faure succeeded Mendès-France as Prime Minister in February 1955, Mohammed V, the deposed Sultan of Morocco, was still in prison in Madagascar, and terrorism persisted in Morocco itself, culminating in the murder of a wealthy liberal settler, Jacques Lemaigre-Debreuil, in June. (The extreme right was probably responsible, possibly in collusion with the police.) The Faure Government decided to clean the Augean stables by asking Gilbert Grandval (a Gaullist, who had been French Commissioner in the Saar) to reconcile the two sides. Without specifically advocating the return of Mohammed V, Grandval proposed the abdication of Ben Arafa, Mohammed V's elderly uncle who had replaced him in 1953, and the establishment of representative government. He warned that action should be taken before 20 August, the anniversary of the Sultan's abdication. It was not, and massacres duly occurred. Grandval resigned, being replaced by Boyer de La Tour. Meanwhile, General Catroux had been sent to discuss the situation with the deposed Sultan in Madagascar. On 1 October the deadlock was broken when Ben Arafa abdicated. Six weeks later Mohammed V returned to Morocco in triumph.

Between 6 and 8 October 1955 the National Assembly debated the Government's Moroccan policy. At the end of the debate every member of MRP, except Bidault, voted for Faure's policy.[2] Robert Lecourt, the main MRP speaker, said that for too long there had been double-talk about the creation of 'a Franco-Moroccan community', but in practice there had been no proper dialogue between the two sides. France had been wrong to assume that nationalists were necessarily her enemies. He supported the new policy of discussing matters with the representatives of all shades of opinion in Morocco, and he maintained (rather unconvincingly) that the reduction of

[1] JO (AN), 8 July 1955, p. 3780. The Conventions were approved by 538–44.

[2] ibid., 8 October 1955, p. 4985. The vote was carried by 452–136. Bidault joined representatives of the extreme right such as Pierre André, General Aumeran, Frédéric-Dupont and Martinaud-Déplat in voting against Faure's policies. Bidault argued that France was precluded from negotiating with a collegiate Moroccan Government by the Treaty of Algeciras, which had laid down that the sole representative of Morocco was the Sultan. He also condemned a policy which might lead to the restoration of the deposed Sultan. Mohammed V; ibid., p. 4955.

direct French influence in Morocco would actually increase French sovereignty in the French Union as a whole, because the new relationship of friendship would augment France's moral authority.[1]

A month after the debate on Morocco, the Sultan and Christian Pineau, the Socialist Foreign Minister, began negotiations which led to Moroccan independence in March 1956 (the communique spoke of France and Morocco as 'equal and sovereign states'), followed by the Treaty of Alliance and Friendship of May 1956 and Morocco's entry into the United Nations in November. MRP's attitude to these developments was shown by the enthusiastic approval of Pierre-Henri Teitgen's Report, *Pour Sauver l'Afrique Française*, at the 1956 Congress,[2] and the fact that Bidault alone refused to vote for the ratification of the Treaty of Alliance and Friendship (28 May 1956) which granted Morocco independence.

BLACK AFRICA

The French Union, as defined in Chapter VIII of the Constituion of the Fourth Republic, consisted both of Associated States[3] and of Overseas Departments and Territories. The Overseas Departments were the French West Indies and Réunion.[4] The Overseas Territories consisted of Black Africa[5] and Madagascar. French policy towards Black Africa was relatively enlightened, and with the exception of Madagascar, where the 1947 revolt was harshly suppressed, decolonization was achieved peacefully. Pierre de Chevigné, the MRP High Commissioner in Madagascar in 1947–48, certainly ruled with an iron fist, but the Madagascar episode was an aberration as far as MRP was concerned. The party's sympathetic and progressive approach to the problems of Black Africa was typified by their attitude to the 1952 Labour Code and the 1956 Loi Cadre.

[1] JO (AN), 8 October 1955, pp. 4963–4.

[2] The Report was concerned mainly with Black Africa, but began by praising the recent steps in Morocco and Tunisia, which, Teitgen claimed, had produced 'l'indépendance dans l'interdépendance', MRP Congr. 1956, Montrouge.

[3] For definition, see p. 204, note 1.

[4] Algeria was also divided into Departments, but was legally part of Metropolitan France.

[5] French Black Africa comprised fourteen colonies which were grouped into two territories, each under a Governor-General. The two territories were French West Africa (Mauritania, Senegal, Guinea, the Ivory Coast, Dahomey, Sudan, Upper Volta and Niger) and French Equatorial Africa (Gabon, Congo, Oubangui-Chari, Chad, Togo and Cameroun). In 1958 all except Guinea chose to enter the French Community and in 1960 the remaining thirteen became independent. All have retained their former names except the Sudan which became Mali and Oubangui-Chari which became the Central African Republic.

215

The two most important attempts to implement the economic and social recommendations of the Brazzaville Conference were the laws of April 1946 setting up the Fonds d'Investissement pour le Développement Economique et Social (FIDES) and of December 1952 enacting a Labour Code for the overseas territories. Until 1946 the colonies had been obliged to finance their development out of their own resources. But from then on they were allowed to receive help from metropolitan France. This aid was distributed through FIDES in the light of the needs of the various overseas territories, and, as Robert Delavignette has pointed out, the Labour Code of 1952 could not have been implemented without the economic development brought about by FIDES.[1] The new Labour Code extended the forty-hour week, minimum wages, collective bargaining, factory inspectors and family allowances throughout the overseas territories, and there can be no doubt that the Code owed much to MRP.[2]

Joseph Dumas was its *rapporteur*, and the debate of November 1952 was dominated by MRP and IOM[3] speakers. Indeed none of the other parties seems to have shown much interest in the Labour Code, for MRP alone took up all its allotted time in the debate,[4] and a large number of deputies did not bother to vote (the bill was carried by 353–1, the one vote against being cast by General Aumeran of the extreme right). Pierre Pflimlin, the Minister of Overseas France in Pinay's Government, welcomed the bill, emphasizing in particular the importance of the inspectorate which would see that the Labour Code was implemented.[5] Pflimlin's Minister of State, Louis Aujoulat, said that the Labour Code was the 'fulfilment of the promise made by France during the war' (i.e. at Brazzaville).[6] He hoped the Code would bring about real social progress in the overseas territories, and emphasized that such a Code had become essential in order to protect the growing number of urban natives.[7] Jean-Jacques Juglas, the MRP President of the Overseas Committee from 1946–55, also hoped that the Code would encourage social progress, whilst Paul Coste-Floret said that it showed 'the entire world the true characteristics of Republican France, ... Liberty, Equality and Fraternity.'[8] Léopold Senghor, Abbas Gueye, Mamadou Konaté and Mamba Sano, all members of IOM, also spoke in favour of the new Labour

---

[1] Robert Delavignette, 'French Policy in Black Africa', in *Colonialism in Africa, 1870–1960*, ed. L. H. Gann and P. Duignan, p. 258.

[2] *Monde*, 4 February 1953. Article by N. Jacquefont.

[3] The Indépendants d'Outre Mer were affiliated to MRP.

[4] *Monde*, 4 February 1953.   [5] JO (AN), 22 November 1952, p. 5548.

[6] ibid., p. 5462.   [7] ibid., p. 5485.   [8] ibid., p. 5469.

Code, the essence of their comments being summed up by Abbas Gueye who said that 'from now on we are going to be treated on the same terms as the workers of France'.[1]

If the Labour Code of 1952 did no more than fulfil the promises of Brazzaville, the Loi Cadre of 1956 went far beyond anything promised at Brazzaville and perhaps even beyond the legal provisions of the 1946 Constitution.[2] For, thanks to the liberal implementation of the Loi Cadre, the fourteen territories of French Black Africa received complete internal autonomy in 1957. When de Gaulle granted legal independence in 1960, he did little more than crown the edifice erected by Defferre.

Gaston Defferre, Guy Mollet's Socialist Minister of Overseas France, and Houphouet-Boigny of the Rassemblement Démocratique Africain[3] were the men chiefly responsible for the Loi Cadre of June 1956 and the implementing decrees of November. Universal suffrage on a common roll was extended to all the overseas territories, whose territorial assemblies were given complete control of internal affairs. The territorial assemblies elected governments which were presided over by French governors, but the real power was now in the hands of the African ministers. France retained control over foreign and monetary policy; in all other areas the territories became self-governing.

Although the Loi Cadre has justifiably been referred to as the Loi Defferre, MRP deserve some credit for it, because Defferre's predecessor at the rue Oudinot, Pierre-Henri Teitgen, did much of the preparatory work for the Loi Cadre,[4] and in the main debate on it (29 January–3 February 1957) MRP was unanimous in its support for the Loi. Pierre-Henri Teitgen argued that it was anomalous that the territorial assemblies could only deliberate, whilst all decisions were taken by the Governor and his civil servants; he wanted to see the territorial assemblies responsible for everything except foreign and monetary policy.[5] Robert Buron wanted to see the proposed territorial governments responsible to the territorial assemblies and not to the French governors.[6] Léopold Senghor (IOM), like Buron, showed

---

[1] JO (AN), 22 November 1952, p. 5471.   [2] Cf. Williams and Harrison, p. 30.
[3] Until 1950 the RDA, whose sole aim was independence, had been associated with the PCF. Thereafter it left the orbit of the Communist Party to join the UDSR, regarded as a progressive party in colonial matters (Pleven and Mitterrand were amongst its leaders).
[4] Cf. 'Pour Sauver l'Afrique Française', special number of *Forces Nouvelles*, July 1956, especially pp. 21–32, in which Teitgen both agreed with Defferre's proposals and claimed that many of them had already been put forward by himself, a claim supported by AP, 1957, p. 37.
[5] JO, 29 January 1957, pp. 363–4.   [6] ibid., 30 January 1957, pp. 396–7.

217

himself to be more federalist in approach than Houphouet-Boigny or Defferre,[1] who stuck to a more Jacobin approach, no doubt partly out of political conviction but partly also on account of the 1946 Constitution which seemed to rule out the possibility of dividing sovereignty within the French Union. At the end of the debate MRP, including Georges Bidault, voted unanimously for the Loi Cadre.[2]

Jean-Jacques Juglas later claimed that MRP felt a particular affinity with Black Africa.[3] And it is true that the Christian Democrats were naturally interested in countries where Catholic missionaries had been relatively successful (unlike North Africa), but it was also easier to advocate liberal policies in territories which had fewer natural resources than North Africa or Indo-China and where settler influence was almost non-existent. With the exception of Madagascar, MRP's record with regard to Black Africa was one of which the party could be proud.

ALGERIA

MRP's enlightened approach to the problems of Black Africa (and to those of Morocco and Tunisia after 1954) was reflected in their attitude to Algeria. Indeed, if one considers the whole period of the Algerian war (November 1954 to March 1962), MRP could claim to have been as liberal as any party except the Communists. The fluctuating attitude of the Socialists owed much to the party's electoral connections with minor civil servants both in Algeria and France (the poor whites being the most reactionary class in Algeria), and that of the Radicals and Conservatives to their financial interests in North Africa. The Socialists in particular were faced with a dilemma over Algeria. Whilst out of office (prior to January 1956 when Mollet became Prime Minister) they had been much more progressive than MRP in campaigning against the war, but after the settlers' violent demonstrations of 6 February 1956, Mollet decided to send conscripts to Algeria whilst at the same time proposing the *triptyque* (cease-fire; elections three months later; negotiations with representatives of all the Algerian people). But once terrorism spread into the city of Algiers, the Socialists opted for special powers (Robert Lacoste) and repression (occupation of the Kasbah by

[1] JO, 29 January 1957, p. 372.

[2] I.e. for the November decrees implementing it. The vote was 301–151 in favour. In the original vote on the Loi Cadre, 26 June 1956, MRP had also voted unanimously for the bill, which was carried by 470–105. There was no full-scale debate on this occasion, but Buron had pledged MRP's support for the Loi Cadre.

[3] Interview, 2 December 1966.

Massu's paratroopers). And after Mollet's fall (June 1957) the Socialists were reduced to rather feeble calls for reform. MRP's attitude to Algeria appeared to be less contradictory, principally because MRP did not participate in the Mollet government although in general they supported it. MRP's liberal wing was no larger than that of the Socialists, but, as with the Socialists over Indo-China from 1951–54, it gave the impression that it was because the Christian Democrats could be more critical when out of office.

Algeria was by far the most difficult of France's colonial problems. The Gordian Knot was eventually cut. But the price was heavy: a republic was buried, the army's morale was destroyed, and political strife reached a nadir of bitterness. The intractability of the problem resulted less from Algeria's juridical links with metropolitan France than from its close proximity to France (unlike Indo-China or Black Africa), the size of its European population (over a million, i.e. five times as many as in Tunisia and four times as many as in Morocco) and their comparatively deep roots (Algeria had been colonized in the 1830s, whereas the rest of North Africa and Indo-China were acquired over half a century later).

Prior to de Gaulle's return to power in 1958, MRP insisted that Algeria must remain French, but it must be a 'new Algeria' with greater political, social and economic opportunities for the Arabs. The reports of Joseph Dumas and Pierre-Henri Teitgen at the 1955 and 1956 Congresses proposed major economic and social reforms and were enthusiastically received by the delegates. Georges Le Brun-Kéris frequently advocated greater political devolution in the form of a three-tier 'federal' system, with authority divided between Paris, Algiers and Algerian local assemblies. MRP supported Mollet's *triptyque*. A minority of the party openly criticized Lacoste's use of special powers and the army's abuse of them. The vast majority favoured Bourgès-Maunoury's Loi Cadre of August 1957 and were sceptical about the mutilated version finally accepted by the National Assembly in January 1958. And in the penultimate governmental crisis of the Fourth Republic MRP refused to support Bidault's bid for the premiership, opting instead for the progressive Pflimlin.

Although MRP (up to the spring of 1958) emphasized that Algeria and France were one country, the Christian Democrats also pointed out that economic, social and political reforms were essential. Pierre-Henri Teitgen told the 1956 Congress that anyone who suggested handing over Algeria should be impeached;[1] André Colin told the 1957 Congress that 'History has created an indis-

[1] MRP Congr. 1956, Montrouge; report entitled 'Pour Sauver l'Afrique Française'.

219

soluble link between the destinies of Algeria and France';[1] and Georges Le Brun-Kéris told the 1958 Congress that if France surrendered Algeria, she would be giving up 'one quarter of the nation'; moreover the Soviet Union would move in to pick up the pieces.[2] If MRP's leaders had not progressed beyond statements such as these, Georges Bidault would never have had to leave the party. But in fact these intransigent statements were counterbalanced by a series of constructive criticisms and proposals for reform.

Teitgen told the 1956 Congress that Algeria had been run since the Second World War by a 'heartless oligarchy, who are ruled by the profit motive . . . and scornful of the six million Arabs who are living at subsistence level',[3] and Buron condemned the 'deplorable racism of the French in North Africa';[4] Boisdon, Jacobson and Vignes all emphasized that social and economic misery were at the heart of the Algerian problem; without major reforms in these areas no political solution could be expected.[5] Moreover, a prominent minority did not hesitate to criticize the Army and police for using third-degree methods. Fonlupt-Esperaber told the 1955 Congress that 'some of our police are using torture as freely as the Gestapo used it against our friends in the Resistance';[6] Pasteur Lagravière emphasized that such methods were self-defeating, destroying Arab confidence in the French.[7] And when Robert Lacoste's special powers came up for renewal in 1957, Menthon criticized the use that had been made of them, and together with twelve other Christian Democrats abstained.[8] At the 1958 Congress both Buron and Mme Lefebvre were insistent that Lacoste must be excluded from any future government, and Le Brun-Kéris euphemistically said that 'too many things have been done which ought not to have been done.'[9]

1 MRP Congr. 1957, Biarritz; report on 'La France d'Outre Mer'.

2 ibid., 1958, St Malo; report entitled 'Sauver l'Afrique du Communisme'.

3 ibid., 1956, Montrouge; report entitled 'Pour Sauver l'Afrique Française'.

4 ibid., debate on Teitgen's report.

5 ibid., 1957, Biarritz; debate on Colin's report on 'La France d'Outre Mer'.

6 ibid., 1955, Marseilles; debate on Dumas' report on 'La France d'Outre Mer et l'Algérie'.

7 ibid.

8 Menthon's speech, JO (AN), 19 July 1957, pp. 3775–7; the vote in favour of renewed special powers was carried by 280–183. The original special powers act, giving the Minister responsible for Algeria 'the power to take all necessary measures to restore law and order', had been passed on 16 March 1956 by 455–76 with all members of MRP voting for it.

9 MRP Congr. 1958, St Malo; report and debate on 'Sauver l'Afrique du Communisme'.

But MRP did not just sit on the fence criticizing the Government. Teitgen (at the 1956 Congress) and Colin (1957) both emphasized MRP's support for Mollet's *triptyque*.[1] MRP including Bidault, voted for the Loi Cadre for Algeria in January 1958.[2] Under this Law, which was to have been implemented by decree, the Algerian departments were to have been grouped into territories, each with its own assembly for local affairs; two years later these assemblies were to have elected a federal assembly, from which in turn a federal council responsible for internal affairs would have been elected; Arabs were to have been given full political rights in the elections for the territorial assemblies.[3] The Loi Cadre was not unlike that which had been passed for Black Africa in 1956. But it had come too late, a point which was emphatically made by Le Brun-Kéris at the 1958 Congress when he said 'The Right must bear a terrible responsibility for delaying the Loi Cadre'.[4]

By the end of the Fourth Republic MRP had not been able to make any substantial contribution to the solution of the Algerian problem, but the party had not been afraid to criticize the excesses of the settlers and of the security forces nor to advocate progressive political reforms even if no one had yet uttered the word independence. But MRP had now made a complete break with the traditional Right and were on the verge of shedding their own right wing in the person of Georges Bidault.

The last MRP Congress attended by Bidault was at Biarritz in 1957. Already it was clear that his views on Algeria were out of line with those of the rest of the party; indeed, only two federations, those of Indre-et-Loire and Deux-Sèvres, still supported Bidault.[5] Not surprisingly perhaps, Bidault was at pains to persuade the delegates that he was not in disagreement with MRP's Algerian policy. But although he professed to agree with the liberalism of André Colin's report, he went on to say that 'true liberalism' would be shown by France's determination to carry out her 'civilizing mission' in Algeria. He said that there was no evidence that the army had used excessive force in cold blood, and pointed out that the Resistance had not always behaved in a gentlemanly fashion when friends had been killed by the enemy. He reminded the delegates of 1940: it had been

[1] MRP Congr. 1956, Montrouge; report entitled 'Pour Sauver l'Afrique Française'; MRP Congr. 1957, Biarritz; report on 'La France d'Outre Mer'.
[2] JO (AN), 28 January 1958, p. 340. The Loi Cadre was carried by 315–231.
[3] JO (Lois et Décrets), 6 February 1958.
[4] MRP Congr. 1958, St Malo; report entitled 'Sauver l'Afrique du Communisme'; the Loi Cadre had originally been put before the National Assembly by Bourgès-Maunoury on 12 August 1957.
[5] *Monde,* 30 May 1957.

right to say no then, and it was still right to say no to the surrender of French territory. He favoured reforms but there could be no question of federalism or independence.[1] Although Bidault received a standing ovation after this speech, there was clearly a growing gulf between his own intransigence and the rest of the party's determination to learn from past mistakes and adapt themselves to the era of decolonization. The gulf widened in February 1958 when Bidault defended the French bombardment of Sakhiet (in Tunisia), whilst Teitgen expressed grave concern about the incident.[2] A month later Bidault found himself completely isolated at a meeting of the MRP National Committee,[3] and after the fall of Gaillard in April (engineered by Bidault and his *Algérie française* friends[4]) the same Committee voted 25–0 with three abstentions against supporting Bidault for the premiership. Bidault remarked that he would 'rather mourn the Fourth Republic than *Algérie française*'.[5] He did not attend the MRP Congress in May 1958 and the break was complete.

The problem of Algeria was aggravated further by the fact that France's professional army, defeated in 1940 and humiliated in 1954, was determined to make a last stand in Algeria. The professional soldiers were as contemptuous of the rich *gros colons* of Algeria as of the politicians in Paris. Many of them respected their courageous Arab opponents and genuinely wanted to integrate them into a new and egalitarian French Algeria. Moreover, if the politicians 'ratted' over this last bastion of overseas France, their own way of life would be at an end. Hence they were prepared to abandon the tradition of *la grande muette*, their historic non-involvement in politics. In 1958 they successfully followed de Gaulle's defiant example of 1940, but their attempted encore in 1961 ended in complete failure. Soldiers of integrity, like Generals Challe and Massu, got involved with *Algérie française* extremists like Lagaillarde whose racism they despised. Others of less integrity, like General Salan, went further, ending up as leaders of the OAS thugs. And they did all this in the name of the honour of the army. It may have been tragic, but it was not surprising that the soldiers got right out of their depth in the *dessous* of Algeria, for over the years experienced politicians such as Mendès-France, Mitterrand, Mollet and de Gaulle all made completely contradictory statements about how the problem should be solved. De Gaulle's

[1] MRP Congr. 1957, Biarritz; debate on 'La France d'Outre Mer'.

[2] JO (AN), 11 February 1958, pp. 676–81.

[3] *Monde*, 18 March 1958.

[4] Soustelle (Gaullist), Duchet (Cons.) and Morice (Rad.). Although Bidault had voted for the Loi Cadre, he regained his reputation as a hard-liner by responding to the Algerian settlers' demand for Gaillard's blood.

[5] *Monde*, 22 April 1958.

saving grace was that he had the political authority, though only just, to impose a solution.

Although de Gaulle returned to power in 1958 as a result of the army revolt in Algiers, his attitude to decolonization had changed considerably since the immediate post-war period, when he had been an uncompromising defender of the French empire. Pragmatism was one of the General's characteristics, and by the early 1950s he seems to have realized that France would have to change her attitude to her former colonies; perhaps, after all, she should opt for something like the British Commonwealth. *Algérie Française* Gaullists like Soustelle certainly miscalculated the General's attitude when they helped to bring him back to power in 1958. It is now clear that de Gaulle's overriding objective was to liquidate the Algerian affair so that he could concentrate on foreign policy. After becoming Prime Minister in June 1958, de Gaulle went to Algiers and told the settlers 'Je vous ai compris', but it was soon apparent that although he understood their attitude, he did not sympathize with it. No *Algérie française* politician was at first asked to join his Government, although Soustelle became Minister of Information (not, as he had hoped, Minister of the Interior) *after* the Socialist party conference had expressed its support for de Gaulle in July 1958. Instead Algerian 'liberals' like Pflimlin and Mollet were asked to join the Government, whilst Pinay was given the Ministry of Finance to reassure the Conservatives. The unexpectedly large number of conservative Gaullists elected to the National Assembly in November 1958 made de Gaulle's position more difficult, but after being elected President in December he astutely appointed Michel Debré, both a Gaullist *inconditionnel* and a supporter of *Algérie française*, as Prime Minister. Events were soon to show that for Debré devotion to the General counted for more than enthusiasm for Algeria. Pinay was retained at the Ministry of Finance and, for the rest, civil servants such as Couve de Murville or Algerian liberals such as Buron were asked to make up the Government. Meanwhile the army was mollified by conciliatory statements, whilst leaders of the revolt were quietly 'promoted' out of the way (Salan, for example, received a sinecure as military Governor of Paris).

In 1959 de Gaulle prepared the way for an Algerian settlement with two important initiatives. On 16 September he proposed that the Algerians should have the right to self-determination, and in December he announced that members of the Community (the former French Union) could choose to become independent whilst remaining within the Community. Clearly Algeria could not be permanently excepted from this 'Commonwealth' of free and

223

independent nations. In France the Right reacted adversely to the self-determination offer, but Bidault's attempt to form a Rassemblement pour l'Algérie Française fizzled out when only 23 deputies (none of them MRP) censured Debré in October (441 voted for him and 88, including 1 MRP,[1] abstained). In Algeria the extremist settlers, supported by a few soldiers, tried to repeat *le treize mai*, but de Gaulle stood firm and 'the week of the barricades' (24–30 January 1960) came to nothing. After the revolt had collapsed, de Gaulle went to Algeria to reassure the army, but his dismissal of Soustelle in February indicated that he had no intention of being deflected from his policy of self-determination. For several months, however, there was no progress, for the FLN continued to insist that nothing short of total independence would satisfy them, whilst de Gaulle's remarks frequently suggested that he had become more intransigent. However, the deadlock was broken on 4 November with de Gaulle's renewed offer of self-determination and his announcement of a referendum on the issue. In January 1961 he received a three to one majority for his self-determination policy.[2] Two months later the army again attempted to browbeat the Paris Government into changing its Algerian policy, but de Gaulle took up special powers (Article 16), the conscripts in Algeria refused to follow the professional soldiers, and the French people demonstrated their disapproval of the army revolt. Ironically the abortive army *coup* provided de Gaulle with the breakthrough for which he had been searching, for the FLN now realized that the alternative to de Gaulle's offer might be something much worse, namely an OAS or army take-over in Algeria. Negotiations between the French Government and the FLN began in May 1961, but looked like breaking down until de Gaulle unilaterally gave up France's claim to Saharan oil (5 September). During the winter of 1961–62 OAS terrorism reached a crescendo, but with the French Government and FLN both determined on an agreement, the outcome of the Evian talks early in 1962 was almost inevitable. The war ended on 18 March and the secession of Algeria was overwhelmingly approved at the referendum of 8 April.[3] The long nightmare was at last over.

During the second phase of the Algerian war (1958–62) MRP was remarkably united behind de Gaulle in spite of the tortuous course

[1] Roger Devemy.

[2] 15,200,000 for de Gaulle's policy; 5,000,000 against. The No vote was inflated by Communists and Left Socialists voting against the General on the ground that they wanted immediate, direct negotiations with the FLN; they were not opposed to self-determination as such.

[3] 17,500,000 for; 1,750,000 against; over a million spoiled ballot papers. The Communists voted Yes, so the 1,750,000 against were nearly all extreme right.

he sometimes appeared to be following. Indeed, Algeria was the only thing which kept MRP in the Government after 1960, for the Christian Democrats were very critical of the Gaullist style of government (*pouvoir personnel*), and in particular of the General's European policy. But they realized the seriousness of the Algerian problem, which was no longer situated primarily in Algeria itself, but turned on the risk of military subversion and civil war in metropolitan France. In these circumstances MRP accepted that de Gaulle must be left a free hand in Algeria, for it was certain that no one else had the authority to deal with the problem. Moreover, by 1961 the vast majority of MRP thoroughly approved of the way the President's policy was evolving, and one of their leaders, Robert Buron, was a member of the French negotiating team at Evian.

Thus, it was not surprising that MRP had little to say about Algeria at their Congresses between 1959–62. On each occasion they did little more than reaffirm their trust in de Gaulle. In 1959 Charles Bosson restricted himself to saying he was pleased that de Gaulle's policy was similar to that outlined by Pflimlin.[1] In 1960 Simonnet condemned 'the week of the barricades', and Pflimlin and Buron made strong defences of the Government's policy;[2] the Congress confirmed its support for de Gaulle's policy as outlined in the self-determination speech of 16 September 1959 and the 10 November offer of negotiations with the FLN. In 1961 Lecanuet again defended the policy of self-determination and hoped that the Evian talks would lead to peace.[3] And in 1962 Teitgen and Colin welcomed the Evian Agreement and pledged MRP's support for de Gaulle's Algerian policy, now concentrated on the struggle with the OAS and the renewal of friendship with Algeria, in spite of the fact that MRP had left the Government ten weeks previously.[4] It was the same story in the National Assembly. In the debate of October 1959 Simonnet compared de Gaulle's self-determination offer of 16 September to his speech of 18 June 1940; on both occasions de Gaulle had made a historic challenge, and now as then the Christian Democrats were on his side.[5] In June 1961 Dorey said that MRP understood 'the agonies of the French Algerians', but their difficulties could be solved only by negotiation; he condemned the violent methods of both OAS and FLN and hoped that the Evian talks would

[1] MRP Congr. 1959, Paris; report on 'La Politique Générale'.
[2] ibid., 1960, Evian; report and debate on 'La Politique Générale'.
[3] ibid., 1961, Royan; report on 'La Politique Générale'.
[4] ibid., 1962, Dijon; debate on 'La Politique Générale'. For MRP's departure from Pompidou's Government, see p. 196.
[5] JO (AN), 15 October 1959, pp. 1797–9.

H   225

lead to a peaceful solution.[1] In November 1961 Paul Coste-Floret and Nestor Rombeaut both complained about the inadequate time allowed for discussion of Algeria in the National Assembly but approved the general outlines of de Gaulle's policy and voted for the Algerian military credits.[2] In March 1962 Simonnet, on behalf of the MRP group, approved the Evian Agreement and looked forward to an era of co-operation between Algeria and the whole European Community.[3] And, in line with their general policy, MRP called for a Yes vote at the referenda of 8 January 1961 and 8 April 1962.

The one major exception was Georges Bidault, who had launched a new party, Démocratie Chrétienne, on 1 July 1958. His declared aim was to build a broad-based Christian Democratic party like the German CDU. Ironically he said that the new party would support both de Gaulle and *Algérie française*—the contradiction between the two not being fully apparent until September 1959. Only two members of MRP attended the press conference at which Démocratie Chrétienne was launched (Louvel and Bichet), and the party was at once condemned by MRP's liberal Secretary General, Maurice-René Simonnet.[4] Although 13 of the 57 MRP deputies elected in November 1958 stood on MRP-Démocratie Chrétienne tickets, Bidault's following in the National Assembly (among MRP) was limited to a tiny group of *Algérie française* supporters, notably Alfred Coste-Floret and Roger Devemy. Démocratie Chrétienne never got off the ground as a party, because Bidault was not only isolated in MRP but also suspect in the eyes of the extreme right who had never forgiven him for his stance against Vichy. After de Gaulle's self-determination speech of 16 September 1959 Bidault joined the Conservative Duchet in setting up the Rassemblement pour l'Algérie Française. In the October debate on Algeria he made a short speech condemning de Gaulle for making an unconstitutional offer to surrender Algeria, but no members of MRP joined the twenty-three extreme right deputies who voted against the Government on 15 October.[5] At the MRP Congress of 1960 four delegates spoke out against negotiations with the FLN (none of them deputies[6]), but the party overwhelmingly voted for de Gaulle's policy as outlined on 16 September 1959. Only Roger Devemy and Alfred Coste-Floret

[1] JO (AN), 29 June 1961, p. 1361.

[2] ibid., 8 November 1961, p. 4026 (Coste-Floret), p. 4035 (Rombeaut).

[3] ibid., 21 March 1962, pp. 517–19.   [4] *Forces Nouvelles*, 6 July 1958.

[5] Bidault's speech, JO (AN), 15 October 1959, p. 1818. In the vote of confidence, carried by 441–23 with 88 abstentions, Devemy abstained. The rest of MRP voted for Debré, ibid., p. 1830.

[6] Schmitt (Seine), Guermont (Calvados), Morenne (Seine-et-Marne) and Vierling (Moselle).

came out in favour of a No vote in the referendum of January 1961, and not even they joined Bidault in speaking against de Gaulle's policy in the Algeria debate of June 1961.[1] In November 1961 ten right-wing members of MRP did vote against the Algerian military credits, ostensibly on the ground that Debré had allowed insufficient discussion of the Algerian problem,[2] but only Alfred Coste-Floret attended the launcing of the Comité de Vincennes when Bidault and his friends gave their overt approval to the OAS. At the Comité's meeting in the Mutualité there were loud cheers each time Salan's name was mentioned (Salan was by now leading the OAS). Not surprisingly, the Comité was outlawed by the Government six days later (22 November). Bidault remained within the pale of legality until the Evian Agreement of March 1962, after which he identified himself wholly with the OAS with his launching of the second 'National Resistance Council' in company with other *Algérie française* fanatics like Jacques Soustelle and Colonel Argoud. With a warrant out for his arrest, Bidault at first lived incognito in Switzerland and in 1963 went into exile in Brazil, from where he returned to Brussels in 1967.

After Bidault joined the OAS, Etienne Borne wrote an article in which he condemned Bidault for his betrayal of Christian Democratic principles. But it was an article written as much in sadness as in condemnation. Borne reminded his readers of Bidault's courage in the Resistance and of his mastery of the written and spoken word, but, he concluded, 'Georges Bidault is above all the victim of Georges Bidault'. Over-confident in his own ability, he had refused to listen to others. Over-knowledgeable about history—or at least his version of it—he had come to equate Algeria in 1962 with Alsace-Lorraine in 1871, the Evian Agreement of 1962 with the Armistice of 1940, and de Gaulle of 1958–62 with Pétain of 1940–44. Two events in particular had embittered Bidault: his rejection by the National Assembly on the eve of success at Geneva in 1954 and MRP's refusal to support his bid for the premiership after the fall of Gaillard in April 1958. On the second occasion MRP had chosen Pflimlin instead, and so partly in order to spite Pflimlin Bidault had opted for de Gaulle

[1] There was no vote at the end of the debate, not because Article 16 was in operation, but because the Right realized that they were too unpopular and numerically weak to attempt to censure the Government.

[2] The credits were voted by 332–138, JO (AN), 8 November 1961, p. 4076. Bidault again condemned de Gaulle for acting unconstitutionally by proposing the 'amputation' of France; he also contended that there would have been no need for the OAS if de Gaulle had not broken his promises, ibid., pp. 4014–17. Amongst the ten MRP who voted against the credits were right-wingers such as A. Coste-Floret, C. Bonnet, R. Devemy and J.-M. Commenay, ibid., p. 4076.

in the crisis of May. But de Gaulle in turn chose Pflimlin not Bidault—'Georges Bidault had made a major miscalculation; he had himself been duped, and his bitterness knew no end.'[1]

Whilst Bidault was pursuing the murky path which led to his presidency of the illegal OAS 'National Resistance Council', his former colleagues of MRP closed ranks behind Pflimlin, Teitgen, Buron and Simonnet in supporting General de Gaulle. As has been seen, there was a small *Algérie française* group, notably Roger Devemy, Christian Bonnet, Jean-Marie Commenay and Alfred Coste-Floret, who followed their leaders with sullen resignation and occasional rebelliousness (as with Devemy's abstention in the debate which followed de Gaulle's speech of 16 September 1959 and the refusal of ten right-wingers to vote for the military budget in November 1961), but only Coste-Floret resigned from MRP in protest against the Evian Agreement.

Between 1958 and 1962 the Christian Democrats consistently supported de Gaulle's Algerian policy, although they criticized the General for his unwillingness to let the National Assembly debate Algeria properly. MRP's enlightened and realistic Algerian policy contrasted sharply with their Indo-China policy, which had been characterized by a stubborn refusal to come to terms with post-war nationalism. By the mid-1950s, however, the Christian Democrats, with the exception of Bidault, had learnt from past mistakes. Certainly in the case of Algeria they showed considerable moral courage in attacking the barbaric methods of the French security forces and of the OAS, and they displayed both courage and wisdom in supporting the progressive and pragmatic policy initiated—even if timidly—by Mollet and completed by de Gaulle.

CONCLUSION

A survey of MRP's colonial policy indicates that the party did not always 'defend a form of colonial policy which was contrary to its traditions' (J.-M. Domenach). Indeed, the party's liberal policies towards Black Africa and, for most of the time, towards Morocco, Tunisia and later Algeria amount to a convincing refutation of Domenach's contention. Nevertheless, it cannot be denied that the Christian Democrats, almost in spite of themselves, were associated with policies which were contrary to their 'traditions' in Indo-China and, spasmodically, in North Africa. It is, therefore, legitimate to ask why this 'betrayal' occurred.

In the case of Indo-China there seem to have been three funda-

[1] *France-Forum*, March 1962.

mental factors.[1] Firstly, Indo-China was 12,000 miles away and most people took no interest in the war until after 1950. Secondly, the Viet Minh was a Communist-led organization, and after 1950 the war was part of the strategic 'hot' war against Communism. Whereas it was not difficult for MRP liberals to advocate concessions to the nationalist (but non-Communist) Neo Destour and Istiqlal, it was almost impossible for a Catholic party in the Cold War atmosphere of the early 1950s to advocate concessions to a nationalist movement which was also Communist. Thirdly, MRP was in Government without a break until 1954. It would have been very difficult for MRP deputies to have abandoned their leaders in midstream, especially when the leaders were experiencing such difficulties with their chosen policy, the Bao Dai solution.[2] Bidault and Letourneau constantly assured their supporters that the war was being won and that Bao Dai was on the verge of success. It was only with the invasion of Laos in 1953 that the hollowness of Letourneau's claims was exposed. But up to that time MRP remained basically loyal to its leaders, and the most important single reason for this was probably, as Léo Hamon once claimed, that 'all parties are sentimental . . . MRP was sentimental in its attitude to Georges Bidault.'[3] This 'sentimental' attitude to Bidault, based on memories of the Resistance, began to break down with the deposition of the Sultan of Morocco in 1953, but was not finally destroyed until Bidault's extreme *Algérie française* position became apparent in the late 1950s.

Other factors also contributed to the ineffectiveness of the MRP liberals prior to 1954. They lacked leadership. Robert Buron was thought to be 'clever, but rather emotional'.[4] Léo Hamon, as a Councillor of the Republic, was out of the mainstream of politics. Kenneth Vignes was a member of the Assembly of the French Union, and therefore without influence. The one man who might have provided leadership was Robert Schuman, but he had his eyes on the Rhine and not the Mekong. He was prepared to advocate 'American' policies in Indo-China in return for United States pressure in favour of EDC and European integration. He was prepared to withdraw his promise of 'independence' for Tunisia in exchange for the 'European' support of the Conservatives led by Pinay, a tactic which, incidentally, did not work because Schuman was ousted from the

[1] For a full discussion of MRP's policy in Indo-China, see R. E. M. Irving, *The MRP and French Policy in Indo-China, 1945–54* (Oxford D.Phil., 1968).
[2] This point was strongly emphasized by P.-H. Teitgen, interview, 5 December 1967. Teitgen himself was a good example of a man whose liberalism only became fully apparent after the Indo-China débacle.
[3] Interview with Hamon, 1 December 1966.
[4] Interview with Lacouture, 7 February 1967.

Quai d'Orsay under Conservative-Gaullist pressure in January 1953.

Nor did the political situation as a whole favour the liberals prior to 1954. The end of tripartism in 1947 brought the Socialists and MRP, both theoretically liberal over colonial policy, under increasing Radical, Conservative and Gaullist pressure. And, although the 1951 Election strengthened the Third Force coalition, the coalition moved to the Right when twenty-seven dissident Gaullists voted for the investiture of Pinay in March 1952. The replacement of Schuman by Bidault at the Quai d'Orsay in January 1953 was a defeat both for the partisans of EDC and for the advocates of liberal colonial policy, but eighteen months later Mendès-France's accession to power inaugurated a new era in colonial policy, not so much in Indo-China (Bidault had already agreed to peace terms similar to those accepted by Mendès-France) as in North Africa. Mendès-France, with his customary realism, saw that the advanced colonial territories would have to move more rapidly towards independence. And, despite MRP's hatred of Mendès-France, the Christian Democrats agreed with the realism he showed over Tunisia. It was, therefore, not surprising that after the overthrow of Mendès-France, MRP pursued colonial policies in North and Black Africa which were more in line with the altruism and realism so often expressed at party Congresses but so frequently ignored by the party leaders up to 1954.

Chapter 8

CHRISTIAN DEMOCRACY IN THE FIFTH REPUBLIC

The Fifth Republic has witnessed the decline and fall of MRP and the emasculation of the Centre parties which had played such an important role in the Fourth Republic. MRP soon found itself on the horns of a dilemma. On the one hand the Christian Democratic leaders and militants were totally opposed to Gaullist foreign policy, both in its anti-'European' and anti-American manifestations; and they were equally critical of the whole style of government, epitomized by the phrase *pouvoir personnel*, i.e. de Gaulle's habit of governing 'autocratically' and 'technocratically' without paying due attention to the views of the National Assembly and the interest groups. On the other hand the Christian Democratic electorate preferred Gaullism to any alternative whenever a clearcut choice had to be made. But if the MRP leaders had accepted Gaullism in deference to their electorate's views, they would have had to abandon quite genuine principles on which they differed from the Gaullists.

Once the UNR had established itself as *the* Gaullist party, i.e. by 1962, MRP could no longer compete with it. At the General Election of November 1962 MRP lost 700,000 voters (30 per cent of its 1958 electorate) and one-third of its deputies. The experiences of 1947 and 1951 had been repeated. The Christian Democrats were quick to realize that MRP as such had no future, the party in 1963 (at the La Baule Congress) voting unequivocally to merge itself into some new political grouping, but they were slow to grasp the significance of the development of a large moderate conservative party (the UNR). For the Christian Democrats refused to believe that the new Gaullist party could outlast the General. Had not the old RPF disintegrated within two years of the 1951 Election? After his unexpected success at the 1965 Presidential Election, Jean Lecanuet founded the Centre Démocrate, proclaiming that 'the French will gather in the Centre',[1] but, as Jean Charlot has shown, this was to misunderstand the nature and political orientation of the new Gaullist party.[2] Whereas the RPF had been founded by, and was led by, General de Gaulle, the

[1] *Monde*, 7 and 21 December 1965.
[2] Jean Charlot, *The Gaullist Phenomenon*, especially chapter 1.

231

UNR was founded *in spite of* de Gaulle, who did not want to be associated with any political party in 1958. Although de Gaulle's attitude had changed by 1962, when he endorsed candidates of the UNR, the very different circumstances in which the UNR had come into being meant that the party developed a life and structure of its own, limited though they were in the early days. Long before the Lille Congress of 1967, when the UDR (successor to the UNR) decided to improve its structure and increase its membership, it was clear that this new moderate conservative party would be unlikely to disintegrate as the RPF had done. More serious for the Christian Democrats was the fact that the Gaullist party had entrenched itself firmly in the French Centre, claiming that it was the party of all Frenchmen except Communists. It was easy enough for Lecanuet to contend (perhaps justifiably) that 'deep down France is Centrist'.[1] His problem was how to woo the Centre electorate away from Gaullism.

Given the limited number of potential Centre voters, the establishment of a viable new Centre party was bound to be difficult. The way to the Right was barred by the relative success of Giscard d'Estaing's Independendent Republicans, and was in any case rejected by a majority of MRP leaders and militants, if not by the Christian Democratic electorate.[2] The only alternative was an opening to the Left, but the fundamental problem here was the existence of the Communist party. The Christian Democrats refused to consider merging themselves into any organization which might make a deal with the Communists. Having rejected any collaboration with either Gaullists or Communists, Lecanuet really could not afford to break with the Socialists as well. But this is precisely what he did in 1965, when he and Fontanet helped to scuttle Gaston Defferre's Democratic and Socialist Federation (the proposed left-of-centre party open to all except Communists). The collapse of Defferre's Federation may have been a watershed in the history of the Left in France, for it is just conceivable that a French 'Labour Party' might have got off the ground at a time when the Communist party was only just beginning to emerge from the ghetto into which it had confined itself since 1947. Perhaps, on the other hand, Duverger was right to contend that the Gaullists could never have been effectively challenged either by the Communist or the non-Communist Left in isolation: a pact between the two was the *sine qua non* of electoral success.[3]

[1] *Monde*, 7 March 1967.
[2] Cf. M.-C. Kessler, 'Giscard d'Estaing et les Républicains Indépendants', RFSP, 1965, pp. 940–57.　　　　　　　　　[3] E.g. RFSP, 1964, pp. 33–51.

As far as the Christian Democrats were concerned, all their difficulties in the late 1960s and early 1970s stemmed from the collapse of Defferre's Federation in 1965. Some former MRP militants, e.g. Bernard Lambert, joined the tiny left-wing Parti Socialiste Unifié (PSU). Others were active in Robert Buron's Objectif 1972 (Objectif Socialiste after November 1971), which was in close liaison with the new Socialist party. The right wing, led by Fontanet, broke away from the Centre Démocrate to join Duhamel's Centre Démocratie et Progrès (CDP), which entered the Gaullist majority after the election of Pompidou as President in June 1969. Meanwhile Lecanuet and Abelin continued to talk of an opening to the Left, but the Centre Démocrate had destroyed any possibility of being considered a party of the Left both by the policies it professed and by the candidates it endorsed at the 1967 and 1968 General Elections. In November 1971 Lecanuet joined Servan-Schreiber's Reform Movement, whose object was to bring together those Centre parties which were allergic to contacts with either Communists or Gaullists. However, the political future of a liaison group consisting of the rump of the old Christian Democratic party and a hotch-potch of right-wing Radicals was obviously extremely limited in view of the fact that many Radicals and nearly all the Socialists had already declared themselves to be in favour of the development of some kind of Popular Front. *Volentes nolentes* the Christian Democrats appeared to have no future except as a ginger group within the Gaullist majority.

MRP'S ELECTORAL PERFORMANCE AND ATTITUDE TO THE GAULLIST REGIME

Before discussing the MRP and CD role in the attempted realignment of parties in the Fifth Republic, the electoral performance and general political attitude of the Christian Democrats must be briefly analysed.

General de Gaulle's return to power in 1958 did not at first affect MRP adversely, but, when the party became increasingly apprehensive about the development of the regime, its voters began to desert it. The turning point came in 1962 when MRP decided to oppose the direct election of the President (October 1962 referendum), the penalty for this decision being paid at the General Election of November 1962, from which MRP never recovered.

Although de Gaulle's return to power entailed the resignation of MRP's President, Pierre Pflimlin, as Prime Minister, the Christian Democrats did not hesitate to support the General. 71 out of 74

MRP deputies voted for de Gaulle's investiture on 1 June 1958. The only important dissenting voice was that of Menthon, who disputed the democratic legitimacy of a Government which had come to power as a result of violence in Algiers'.[1] MRP entered de Gaulle's Government, with Pflimlin as Minister without Portfolio, Bacon as Minister of Labour and Buron as Minister of Public Works. Paul Coste-Floret, Teitgen and Menditte were members of the Constitutional Committee, all three voting for the Committee's draft on 14 August. The MRP National Committee, which had endorsed de Gaulle's Government by 115–6,[2] voted for the new constitution by 121–12, although Robert Schuman expressed doubts about the possible abuse of Article 16 by de Gaulle's successors.[3] MRP thus campaigned for an affirmative vote at the constitutional referendum of 28 September 1958, a decision which doubtless helped the party to retain most of its voters at the November General Election. Surprisingly MRP's National Committee even accepted the new electoral system (single member constituencies with two ballots),[4] although the party had been strongly in favour of proportional representation (PR) throughout the Fourth Republic. PR, at least as organized until 1951,[5] had tended to benefit the larger parties, but in 1958 MRP acknowledged (as it had failed to do in the bitter electoral discussions of 1951) that it was no longer a mass party. As it turned out, the electoral system made very little difference. Indeed Georges Dupeux calculated that MRP did slightly better under it than it would have done under the old PR system (57 seats instead of 53).[6] MRP had expected to do rather badly in small (rural) constituencies and suffer from second ballot alliances. In fact, the first did not happen, as the Christian Democratic deputies proved to be

[1] Lacaze and Mme Lefebvre also voted against. De Gaulle was invested by 329–224; JO (AN), 1 June 1958, p. 2593.

[2] *Monde*, 17 June 1958.

[3] ibid., 9 September 1958. Article 16 lays down that 'When the institutions of the Republic, the independence of the nation, the integrity of its territory or the execution of its international commitments are gravely and immediately threatened and the regular functioning of the constitutional public authorities is interrupted, the President of the Republic takes the measures required by these circumstances after official consultation with the Prime Minister and the Presidents of the assemblies as well as with the Constitutional Council. He informs the nation of these measures by a message. These measures must be inspired by the will to assure to the constitutional public authorities, within the shortest possible time, the means of fulfilling their tasks. The Constitutional Council is consulted on these measures. Parliament meets automatically. The National Assembly cannot be dissolved during the exercise of exceptional powers.'

[4] *Monde*, 14 September 1958.

[5] For details see Williams, Appendix VI, pp. 504–8.   [6] Chapsal, p. 360.

more firmly entrenched in the rural areas than they had themselves realized. Nor did the second happen in 1958, for at that time MRP could still make second ballot alliances with the Socialists in some areas. But it did happen at every subsequent election, when all the Centre parties found themselves under considerable pressure from the big political groupings to their Right and Left.

With 2,270,000 votes at the first ballot in 1958 (11 per cent of votes cast), MRP came within 100,000 votes of its 1956 poll. The electorate had increased by just under a million since 1956, so that MRP's share of the registered electorate was fractionally down (8·3 per cent compared with 8·8 per cent), but overall the party did better than might have been expected, given the fact that it had to compete with the Gaullist UNR.[1] It is difficult to draw precise conclusions about the Christian Democratic vote in 1958, because the official electoral statistics do not distinguish between MRP and Démocratie Chrétienne voters,[2] and it is clear that Bidault's Démocratie Chrétienne, supported by men like Tixier-Vignancour, attracted a certain number of extreme right electors who would never have voted for MRP. Moreover, the UNR was too new a party to have established itself as *the* Gaullist party in 1958. Some MRP voters doubtless thought their own party was as Gaullist as the UNR.[3]

MRP did, in fact, suffer at the hands of the UNR, expecially in Alsace and in parts of Brittany, where André Colin and André Monteil were defeated at the second ballot, but the party made unexpected gains amongst trade unionists in Loire-Atlantique, where Nestor Rombeaut was returned, and amongst peasant activists in Finistère, where Bernard Lambert was returned. Of the old Fourth Republic parties, MRP came out of the Election second

[1] Full results of first ballot, November 1958 General Election:

Registered electorate	27,736,491	
Votes cast	20,994,797	
Abstentions	6,241,694	(22·9% reg. elect.)
Spoiled papers	652,889	(2·3% reg. elect.)
Communists	3,907,763	(14·3% reg. elect.; 19·2% votes cast)
SFIO	3,193,786	(11·7% reg. elect.; 15·7% votes cast)
Extreme Left	261,738	(0·9% reg. elect.; 1·2% votes cast)
Radicals	1,503,787	(5·5% reg. elect.; 7·3% votes cast)
MRP	2,273,281	(8·3% reg. elect.; 11·1% votes cast)
Gaullists	4,165,453	(15·2% reg. elect.; 20·4% votes cast)
Independents	4,502,449	(16·5% reg. elect.; 22·1% votes cast)
Extreme Right	533,651	(1·9% reg. elect.; 2·6% votes cast)

[2] See p. 226 on Bidault's attempt to launch Démocratie Chrétienne as a new, broad-based Christian Democratic party in the summer of 1958.

[3] F. Goguel, RFSP, 1963, p. 302.

best. The Conservatives (Independents and Peasants) gained over a million votes (4,500,000 compared with 3,250,000 in 1956), but the Radicals and Communists lost about 1,500,000 votes each, and, although the Socialists held their poll at just over 3,000,000, they were relatively less successful than MRP, because SFIO candidates were standing in over 90 per cent of constituencies, whilst there were MRP candidates in only just over half the constituencies. However, MRP's 'success' in 1958 should not be exaggerated. The party made almost no impression outside the traditional bastions of moderate conservatism, to which it had been confined since 1951.

The vast majority of MRP, as has been shown above,[1] supported de Gaulle's Algerian policy, but between 1959 and 1962 the party became increasingly critical of almost every other aspect of the General's policy. Pierre-Henri Teitgen was a leading critic of the evolution of the régime towards presidentialism and technocracy; men like Simonnet, Blin, Lambert and Rombeaut were constant critics of the economic and social policies of the Debré and Pompidou Governments; and the party was united in its opposition to de Gaulle's attacks on 'Europe' and the Atlantic Alliance.

Although MRP participated in the Debré Government, it soon became apparent that the party and militants were by no means unconditional supporters. Robert Lecourt was the Minister responsible for relations with the Community (the former colonies); Robert Buron remained at the Ministry of Public Works and Paul Bacon at the Ministry of Labour, whilst Joseph Fontanet became a junior Minister responsible for Industry and Commerce. But there were portents of things to come in the abstention of nine MRP deputies, mainly members of the party's left wing, in the vote on Debré's governmental programme,[2] and in the MRP National Committee's criticism of Pinay's deflationary measures of December 1958, which had entailed a considerable cut-back in public expenditure.[3]

MRP's special Congress at Clichy in January 1959 was mainly concerned with changing the party statutes, but the final motion insisted that the social gains of the past must not be sacrificed. At the full Congress in May Alain Poher expressed grave doubts about the Government's economic and social policies. He conceded the necessity of restrictions on consumption until the balance of payments had been put right, but denounced the attacks being made on the

1 See chapter on Colonial Policy, pp. 218–8.
2 The abstainers were Blin, Cassez, Charpentier, P. Coste-Floret, Dutheil, Lambert, Raymond-Clergue, Rieunaud, Thibault, JO (AN), 16 January 1959, p. 90. The vote was carried by 453–6.
3 *Monde*, 6 January 1959.

Common Market and demanded more support for agriculture and a 'substantial increase in family allowances'.[1] In the subsequent debate Louis Bour of the Seine Federation insisted on the necessity of selective investment in housing in spite of the country's economic difficulties, and Nestor Rombeaut demanded investment in regions such as Loire-Atlantique which were suffering particularly high unemployment. Bacon, however, succeeded in reassuring the Congress that none of the social gains of the Liberation would be sacrificed and that deflationary measures were a necessary short-term expedient.[2] At the same Congress Teitgen expressed doubts about the Government's European policy, and Pflimlin said that, although he had no objection to de Gaulle handling the Algerian question, he did not like the way that so many lesser matters were being decided by technocrats instead of by parliamentarians.[3] But, in comparison with the years 1960–62, MRP criticisms of the Government were still relatively muted in 1959.

The first major clash came in March 1960, when de Gaulle refused to call a special session of the National Assembly to discuss the agricultural crisis, although a request for such a session had been signed by over half the deputies of the National Assembly in accordance with Article 29 of the Constitution. The MRP National Committee, whilst confirming its support for de Gaulle's Algerian policy, maintained that the General's failure to comply with the Constitution was a threat to democracy, and that 'however great the prestige of the Head of State, he ought to abide by the laws of the State'.[4] At the party Congress at Evian, Teitgen came out strongly against the regime:

We are no longer living under a régime which can, strictly speaking, be called democratic. . . . The Fifth Republic is like a train drawn by a powerful locomotive, behind which is a tender called the UNR. This poor tender, unconditionally linked to the locomotive, thinks it is pushing it, when all it is doing is to provide the necessary fuel! And right at the back of the train there is a guard's van. It is said that the Government and a Prime Minister, who is the guard, are inside. Also in this train, behind the tender, is the MRP carriage, with Maurice Schumann looking gleefully out of one window and Simonnet anxiously out of another. . . . But, take care! This train could well be heading for an abyss. Therefore, I would like to see

1 MRP Congr. Paris, 1957; report on 'La politique economique et sociale'.

2 ibid., Debate on economic and social policy.

3 ibid. Teitgen in report on 'La Démocratie Moderne'; Pflimlin in debate on foreign policy.

4 *Monde*, 15 March 1959.

the MRP carriage loosen its bonds to the locomotive and tender so that it is not dragged into the abyss with them.[1]

Teitgen was warmly applauded for his metaphor but Robert Lecourt took him up on it, warning that there was a bloody dispute going on at the points ahead, and that, so long as this was so, MRP should stick with the train: 'It is only on account of Algeria that we have accorded a special degree of confidence to General de Gaulle'.[2] The Congress's final motion condemned both 'unconditional loyalty to one man' and 'systematic opposition', whilst insisting that, although MRP had authorized some of its members to participate in the Government, the party could not accept responsibility for all the policies of the Government. Amongst the Government policies rejected by MRP were those adopted towards the Atlantic Alliance and European integration.[3] In the context of the former the most important issue was that of the *force de frappe*, roundly condemned by Robert Schuman and Pierre-Henri Teitgen at the National Committee meeting of October 1960.[4] Although MRP was far from happy about the *force de frappe*, no members of the party signed the October 1960 censure motion criticizing it; but 21 out of 58 MRP voted for the motion on 24 October.[5]

By 1961 it was apparent that Algeria alone was keeping MRP in the Government. Apart from Alfred Coste-Floret and Roger Devemy (and, of course, Bidault, who was no longer in MRP), the Christian Democrats opted for an affirmative reply at the January referendum, which in essence gave de Gaulle a free hand to negotiate a cease-fire with the Algerian rebels. The MRP National Committees of February and October and the National Congress at Royan in May all expressed support for de Gaulle's Algerian policy. Otherwise 1961 was a year of growing tension between MRP and the Government. At the National Committee meeting in February Simonnet criticized the Government for its failure to discuss its policies in the National Assembly.[6] At the party Congress in May Teitgen called

[1] MRP Congr. 1960, Evian; debate on Simonnet's report on 'La Politique Générale'.

[2] ibid.

[3] ibid., motion passed after debate on Lecanuet's report on foreign policy.

[4] *Monde*, 11 October 1960.

[5] Blin, C. Bonnet, Burlot, Cassez, Charpentier, Commenay, P. Coste-Floret, Delrez, Devemy, Dutheil, Gabelle, Lambert, Laurent, F. Mayer, Raymond-Clergue, Rieunaud, Rombeaut, R. Schuman, Seitlinger, Thomas, Ulrich; JO (AN), 25 October 1960, p. 2762. It should be noted that this group included both the extreme right of the party over Algeria (Bonnet, Commenay, Devemy) and progressives like Lambert and Rombeaut.

[6] *Monde*, 28 February 1961.

the use of Article 16 an 'amputation of democracy', although Pflimlin defended de Gaulle's use of the Article, 'provided its application is limited in time and scope'.[1] By September MRP had joined the Socialists, Communists and many Conservatives in outright condemnation of the continued use of Article 16.[2] MRP was also becoming more critical of Debré's methods of Government. One of the reasons for the estrangement between Debré and Robert Lecourt, culminating in the latter's dismissal from the Government on 24 August 1961, was that Lecourt was becoming increasingly irritated by Debré's failure to consult his senior colleagues.[3] Debré would have liked to have replaced Lecourt with Maurice Schumann, but the MRP leaders refused to let Schumann enter a Government 'in which there is no dialogue'.[4]

When the MRP National Committee met in October, Bosson, Guyomard and Quincey demanded the withdrawal of the MRP Ministers, but on the advice of Pflimlin, Colin and Simonnet, who argued that the Algerian problem must be solved first, the demand was rejected by 64–24.[5] The hardening of MRP's attitude was further demonstrated two months later when 23 out of 57 MRP voted a Socialist-Radical censure motion on Debré's policies.[6] *L'Année Politique* commented that the year 1961 had seen MRP 'take its distance from a Government with which it is in disagreement on everything except Algeria'.[7]

The year 1962 was an important turning-point in the history of MRP as in that of France as a whole. The Algerian war ended in April, direct election of the President was introduced in October and the Gaullists won a decisive electoral victory in November. The MRP Ministers resigned from Pompidou's Government in May, and the Christian Democrats moved from conditional support of the Government to conditional opposition, and, in so doing, unwittingly

---

[1] MRP Congr. 1961, Royan; debate on 'La Politique Générale'.

[2] E.g. Simonnet, *Forces Nouvelles*, 22 September 1961. De Gaulle gave up the use of Art. 16 on 30 September 1961.

[3] *Forces Nouvelles*, 27 August 1961; confirmed in interview with Lecourt, 22 June 1970.

[4] *Forces Nouvelles*, 27 August 1961.   [5] *Monde*, 10 October 1961.

[6] Blin, Burlot, Charpentier, Commenay, P. Coste-Floret, Delrez, Devemy, Domenech, Dutheil, Gabelle, Lambert, Mahias, F. Mayer, Raymond-Clergue, Rieunaud, Rombeaut, R. Schuman, Seitlinger, Simonnet, Thibault, Thomas, Trellu, Ulrich; JO (AN), 15 December 1961, p. 5727. (199 voted the censure motion out of the required 276.) It should be noted that 18 of the above also voted against the *force de frappe* on 24 October 1960 (see p. 238, note 5), which suggests that the vote indicated general opposition rather than specific opposition on that issue.

[7] AP, 1961, p. 171.

began the destruction of the old MRP. By the mid-1960s it was clear that Christian Democracy was dead as a political force in France unless MRP could merge itself into some new political formation.

MRP had no difficulty in approving the Algerian cease-fire (referendum of 8 April), although Alfred Coste-Floret, a founder member of MRP, finally resigned from the party when the MRP National Bureau unanimously advocated an affirmative reply at the referendum.[1] However, when de Gaulle replaced Debré with Pompidou on 14 April, MRP decided to enter the Government only after a four-hour debate in the National Committee, which showed that the party was very divided in its attitude to the Gaullist regime. Simonnet and Blin argued that MRP should not join the Government until Pompidou had shown that he would not bypass Parliament as Debré had done; Teitgen was against joining a Government which had not announced its programme; Rombeaut objected to a Government headed by a banker. But Pflimlin argued that MRP would have more influence on the Government from within than from outside. He was supported by Maurice Schumann and about two-thirds of the National Committee (the vote was secret), but MRP entered the Government with certain conditions, namely that steps must be taken towards further European integration, that Parliament must be allowed to play a greater role in the functioning of the regime, and that there must be progress in social, family and agricultural policies.[2] Having laid down these conditions, Pflimlin accepted a senior Government post as Minister responsible for Co-operation with Overseas Territories; Buron returned to the Ministry of Public Works and Bacon to the Ministry of Labour; Fontanet became Minister of Health, and Schumann was delegated to the Prime Minister with special responsibility for regional policy. MRP's reticence towards the Pompidou Government, however, was immediately shown when twenty-one deputies abstained in the vote on the Government's programme.[3] This was more than twice as many as had opposed Debré's 'investiture' in January 1959.[4] And within a month the MRP Ministers had left the Government in protest at

---

[1] *Monde*, 28 March 1961.   [2] ibid., 17 April 1961.

[3] Barniaudy, Blin, Cassez, Charpentier, Mme de la Chevrelière, P. Coste-Floret, Commenay, Delrez, Devemy, Domenech, Dubuis, Dutheil, Ihuel, Lambert, F. Mayer, Raymond-Clergue, Rieunaud, Rombeaut, Thomas, Trellu, Ulrich; JO (AN), 28 April 1962, p. 833. Again it was the hard core of anti-Gaullists who refused to vote for Pompidou. 17 of this group had already voted against the *force de frappe* on 24 October 1960 and 16 against Debré on 15 December 1961. They cut right across the party, from the *Algérie française* wing (Commenay, Devemy) to the progressives (Lambert, Rombeaut)

[4] See p. 236.

de Gaulle's derisory remarks about Europe made at his press conference of 15 May.[1]

The Party Congress at Dijon in June emphasized its approval of the resignation of the MRP Ministers, but Simonnet rejected systematic opposition to the Government. MRP hoped to make capital out of opposing the régime, but had to keep an eye on its electorate, which might be critical of Debré or Pompidou but was certainly not anti-Gaullist. MRP's more critical approach became apparent in July when four members of the party signed a censure motion for the first time, forming a 'European entente'[2] with the Socialists and many Radicals and Conservatives against the *force de frappe*. Although the censure motion of 15 July received only 206 of the 241 votes required, a majority of MRP (32 out of 57) voted for it.[3]

MRP's rather indecisive posture as an opponent of Gaullism became more apparent over the issue of the direct election of the President in the autumn of 1962. Ten MRP deputies signed the censure motion of 2 October,[4] and 50 out of 57 voted it on 5 October, thus helping to bring down the Pompidou Government.[5] But at the same time Paul Coste-Floret emphasized that MRP was voting the censure motion not because all members of the party were opposed to the direct election of the President, but because de Gaulle had acted unconstitutionally by announcing a referendum to change the Constitution without first consulting Parliament.[6] Coste-Floret had himself advocated a full Presidential régime with proper separation of powers and direct election of the President at the 1962 MRP Congress,[7] and he simply repeated his view in the National Assembly on 4 October. Significantly he added that MRP's condemnation of de Gaulle's methods did not necessarily mean that the party would

[1] See p. 196. [2] André Laurens in *Monde*, 13 July 1961.

[3] Barniaudy, Barrot, Blin, Bosson, Burlot, Charpentier, Commenay, P. Coste-Floret, Delrez, Devemy, Diligent, Domenech, Dorey, Dutheil, Fourmand, P. Gabelle, Ihuel, Lambert, Laurent, Lux, F. Mayer, Méhaignerie, Orvoën, Raymond-Clergue, Rieunaud, Rombeaut, R. Schuman, Seitlinger, Simonnet, E. Thibault, Thomas, Trellu; JO (AN), 16 July 1962, p. 2528. For the first time moderates like Bosson and Dorey voted against the Government, although the majority of the 32 had already registered their disapproval of the Gaullist regime; 19 of them had voted against the *force de frappe* on 24 October 1960; 21 had censured Debré on 15 December 1961; and 17 had abstained on the vote on Pompidou's governmental programme on 28 April 1962.

[4] Barniaudy, Blin, Burlot, Charpentier, Devemy, Fréville, Gabelle, Laurent, Raymond-Clergue, Ulrich.

[5] All except Mme de la Chevreliére, Davoust, Halbout, Le Guen, Lenormand, Rivière, M. Schumann; JO (AN), 4 October 1962, pp. 3268–9. 280 voted the censure motion; only 241 votes were required.

[6] JO (AN), 4 October 1962, pp. 3215–17.

[7] MRP Congr. 1961, Dijon.

vote No at the referendum on 28 October. In fact the MRP National Committee of 7–8 October voted 110–23 for a negative response at the referendum, but refused to join an alliance of opposition parties. MRP, with its eye on its electorate, was clearly deeply divided once again, with Pflimlin and Schumann supporting de Gaulle, and Simonnet, Teitgen and Colin opposing him.[1] Had it not been for the success of the censure motion of 4 October, the vote in the National Committee would doubtless have been much closer. Certainly, in electoral terms, MRP's National Committee committed a major blunder in calling for a negative vote at the referendum, for Georges Dupeux later estimated that no more than one-tenth of MRP and Conservative voters followed their leaders' call for No.[2] In a sense, as Dupeux pointed out, the MRP electorate voted 'logically'. Told to vote Yes in September 1958 they could not see why they should not also vote Yes in October 1962.[3]

Moreover, the MRP voters repeated their 'logic' at the General Election of November 1962, Dupeux calculating that 48 per cent of MRP's 1958 voters transferred their votes to the UNR or abstained.[4] At the first ballot MRP obtained 1,666,000 votes (6·1 per cent of the registered electorate, 9·1 per cent of votes cast), but eleven MRP candidates were standing under the label MRP-Ve République and they received 190,000 votes. Excluding the MRP-Ve République vote, the Christian Democrats won only 5·3 per cent of the registered electorate compared with 8·3 per cent in 1958. At the second ballot

[1] *Monde*, 9 October 1961.   [2] RFSP, 1964, p. 69.

[3] 28 October 1962 referendum on direct election of the President: Yes—13,150,516 (62·3 per cent of votes cast, 46·7 per cent of the registered electorate); No—7,974,538 (37·8 per cent of votes cast, 28·3 per cent of the registered electorate); abstainers—6,490,915 (23 per cent of the registered electorate).

[4] RFSP, 1964, p. 62.

Full results of first Ballot, 1962 General Election:

Registered electorate	27,535,019	
Voters	18,931,733	
Abstentions	8,603,286	(31·0% reg. elect.)
Spoiled papers	601,747	(2·1% reg. elect.)
Communists	3,992,431	(14·4% reg. elect.; 21·7% votes cast)
Extreme Left	449,743	(1·6% reg. elect.; 2·4% votes cast)
SFIO	2,319,662	(8·4% reg. elect.; 12·6% votes cast)
Radicals	1,384,498	(5·0% reg. elect.; 7·5% votes cast)
MRP	1,635,452	(5·9% reg. elect.; 8·9% votes cast)
UNR-UDT (Gaullists)	5,847,403	(21·2% reg. elect.; 31·9% votes cast)
RI (Gaullists)	798,092	(2·8% reg. elect.; 4·4% votes cast)
Independents	1,742,523	(6·3% reg. elect.; 9·6% votes cast)
Extreme Right	159,682	(0·5% reg. elect.; 0·9% votes cast)

For above statistics and remaining statistics in the next two paragraphs, see F. Goguel, *Le Référendum d'Octobre et les Elections de novembre 1962*, pp. 306–432.

many MRP voters clearly decided to vote 'usefully', i.e. for the UNR, for the MRP vote declined by 280,000 whereas the UNR vote went up by 1,500,000. The attraction of Gaullism for MRP voters was further emphasized by the fact that the MRP-Ve République vote rose by almost a quarter (44,000) at the second ballot. Altogether 38 MRP deputies were elected, of whom 7 were returned on MRP-Ve République tickets, including such leading members of the party as Maurice Schumann and Marie-Madeleine Dienesch.[1]

MRP and the Conservatives were the two major victims of the Gaullist advance of November 1962. As in the October 1946 referendum and the June 1951 General Election, MRP was deserted by a considerable number of its electors when opposing General de Gaulle. The party was swept aside at the second ballot in traditional areas of Gaullist and moderate conservative strength, such as Alsace and the Moselle region of Lorraine; it lost two of its three seats in Nord (Maurice Schumann alone surviving); it suffered from the Gaullist advance in Brittany, and its young peasant and trade union leaders such as Lambert and Rombeaut were amongst the twenty deputies who were not re-elected; the party even lost its Secretary General, Simonnet, in Drôme. For Simonnet, who had played a leading role in bringing MRP into opposition, the election was a bitter blow, for at the Dijon Congress (1962) he had predicted a major MRP electoral advance. His strategy had been proved wrong and he resigned from the Secretary Generalship in April 1963.

The fundamental reason for MRP's defeat was stated quite simply by François Goguel, who described the MRP electorate as 'the most susceptible [of all French voters] . . . to the attractions of Gaullism'.[2] The lesson of 1962 was that MRP *alone* could not stand against de Gaulle. If it tried to do so, much of its electorate deserted it. MRP clearly had no future unless it became once again *le parti de la fidélité*, allying itself with the UNR, or merged itself into some new political formation to the left of centre. The next few years saw the Christian Democrats agonisingly trying to reappraise their role in French politics.

THE CHRISTIAN DEMOCRATS AND PARTY REALIGNMENT: FROM THE LA BAULE CONGRESS (1963) TO THE PRESIDENTIAL ELECTION (1965)

The Christian Democrats' determination to realign themselves

[1] 11 MRP and 4 MRP-Ve *République* candidates were elected at the first ballot, and 20 and 3 respectively at the second.

[2] F. Goguel, *Le Référendum d'Octobre et les Élections de Novembre 1962*, p. 311.

politically did not suddenly begin at La Baule in 1963,[1] but the Congress of that year was nevertheless the most important single step towards realignment, for MRP, in an unwonted gesture for a political party, voted to merge itself into some new political formation of 'démocrates à vocation majoritaire'.[2] MRP's first chance to demonstrate the likely orientation of the Christian Democratic part of this new formation presented itself with Defferre's abortive Presidential candidature (18 December 1963–25 June 1965). The Defferre initiative showed that the Christian Democrats were more divided than ever before. In a sense the failure of Lecanuet's Centre Démocrate was foreshadowed by the failure of Defferre, even if the Christian Democratic divisions were temporarily papered over by Lecanuet's relatively successful Presidential bid in 1965.

The Congress at La Baule and the Defferre initiative showed that the Christian Democrats were divided into four political families, three in opposition to Gaullism and one in support of it. The opponents were: the Defferrists (Left Centre) who favoured a realignment with the moderate Left; the 'Democrats' (Right Centre) who favoured a realignment with the traditional Right; and the Autonomists who advocated constructive opposition but did not believe that the time was ripe for merging MRP into a new political party. The 'Gaullists', on the other hand, had a simple objective—to rejoin the majority at the earliest opportunity. The divisions between these groups were never rigid. Pflimlin sometimes advocated a Gaullist approach, whilst at others he seemed more at home with the Right Centre. Teitgen was essentially an Autonomist, but was often to be found upholding the theses of the Left Centre. Lecanuet was inclined to use the language of the Left Centre whilst acting like a member of the Right Centre. In spite of the success of the Defferrists at the Vichy Congress in 1965, the 'Democrats', led by Lecanuet and Fontanet, were always the biggest single group in the party. The two smaller groups, the Autonomists (whose chief representatives were Simonnet and Teitgen) and the Gaullists (led by Maurice Schumann and more tentatively by Pflimlin) were generally less vocal than the Defferrists and 'Democrats', but the Gaullist group, despite its small size in the party, remained influential on account of its considerable electoral support.

[1] E.g. at the end of 1958 the Rassemblement des Forces Démocratiques (RFD) had been founded by Roger Lavialle, Rémy Montagne, Michel Debatisse, Bernard Lambert, Théo Braun and Nestor Rombeaut, in an attempt to encourage contacts between MRP, Socialists, Radicals and *forces vives* (trade unions, etc.). The MRP leaders, however, refused to support RFD and it disintegrated in 1959.
[2] MRP Congr. 1963, La Baule; final motion.

The differences between the various groups emerged at the Congresses of La Baule (1963) and Le Touquet (1964) and in the subsequent arguments. At La Baule Joseph Fontanet, the new Secretary General, introduced one of the most important reports made at an MRP Congress.[1] He began his speech by telling the delegates that the development of a majority party had changed the political situation in France irrevocably. It was, therefore, essential to develop an opposition majority party. After rejecting Duverger's thesis that no viable opposition party could be established without the Communists, he called on the Christian Democrats to merge themselves into a new political party. This new party could not just be an amalgam of the old parties, which had lost favour with the electorate and whose traditions precluded the possibility of their working together as a modern majority party. Instead all Catholics and non-Catholics, together with the *forces vives* of the peasant organizations, trade-unions and political clubs, must come together to form a new political party, which could challenge the Gaullists. The Communists alone would be excluded from this new party, and they would eventually 'die' in isolation. In a sense Fontanet was doing no more than reviving the old Christian Democratic dream of a Centre party from which only the extreme right and extreme left would be excluded, but his speech was warmly welcomed by a party which was smarting under the electoral defeat of 1962. In the enthusiasm of the Congress Fontanet's *résolution d'orientation* was passed unanimously in spite of the fact that Pflimlin, representing the Right, and Mme Lefebvre, representing the Left, expressed doubts about the political realism of Fontanet's analysis.

Pflimlin wondered whether the SFIO, owing to pressure from its Left, would ever consent to joining 'this new democratic party of tomorrow'. He contended that MRP's future lay with the majority, whose social, economic and European policies could be changed under pressure from the Christian Democrats.[2] At the Le Touquet Congress Maurice Schumann, the most Gaullist of the Christian Democrats, developed this theme even more forcibly. He proposed that MRP should join the majority at once whilst retaining its own identity.[3] Pflimlin did not speak at Le Touquet, significantly leaving the Congress before Fontanet's report on general policy. Later Pflimlin refused to support Lecanuet's Centre Démocrate,[4] and he

[1] MRP Congr. 1963, La Baule; report on 'L'Orientation du Mouvement'.

[2] ibid., 1963, La Baule; debate on Fontanet's report.

[3] ibid., 1964, Le Touquet; debate on Fontanet's report on 'La Politique Générale'.

[4] *Monde*, 25 August 1966.

abstained in the Presidential Election of 1965, whilst Maurice Schumann voted for de Gaulle.[1] The MRP Gaullists carried their conviction to its logical conclusion at the 1967 General Election, when Maurice Schumann, Charles de Chambrun, Emile Bizet, Augustin Chauvet and Marie-Madeleine Dienesch all received the investiture of the UDR. Pflimlin, whose Gaullism was always more *nuancé* than Schumann's, refused to stand in 1967 or 1968 but joined Duhamel's new party, the CDP, when it entered the majority in July 1969.[2]

The Autonomists were a smaller group than the Gaullists, but Teitgen, who at times supported the opening to the Left, wondered whether Fontanet's proposed merger of MRP was not premature. Colin (who later joined the Centre Démocrate) and Simonnet expressed similar doubts at the National Committee meeting of October 1964.[3] Three years later, when the National Bureau decided to stop publishing *Forces Nouvelles* and sell the old MRP headquarters in the rue de Poissy, Teitgen told *Le Monde* that MRP was not dead—'it is only taking a siesta'.[4]

The majority of MRP, however, agreed with Fontanet that the future of the party lay in some new political formation. But the Defferre initiative soon showed that the majority was fundamentally divided. The Right Centre, led by Lecanuet and Fontanet, based its hopes on the evolution of the Comité des Démocrates.[5] After the 1962 General Election, MRP, which could have formed its own parliamentary group, had shown its interest in evolving a new political formation by constituting the parliamentary group, Centre Démocratique, with Pleven's friends and a few Conservatives.[6] The Comité des Démocrates was closely linked with the parliamentary group Centre Démocratique. Formed in April 1963 as a study group, the Comité's leaders were Joseph Fontanet and Jean Lecanuet of MRP, Maurice Faure and Jacques Duhamel of the Radical party, Pierre Baudis and Antoine Pinay of the Independents, and Théo Braun of the CFTC. On the initiative of Maurice Faure the Socialists were invited to send observers, and Chandernagor attended the Comité's first meeting in this capacity, whilst three others joined

---

[1] *Express*, 17 January 1966.   [2] See pp. 262–4, for details about the CDP.
[3] *Monde*, 21 October 1964.   [4] *Monde*, 29 September 1967.
[5] Strictly speaking, the Comité d'Etudes et de Liaison des Démocrates.
[6] The group Centre Démocratique consisted of 38 MRP, 2 MRP *apparentés*, 7 Conservatives (Independents) and 7 Entente Démocratique. The last named was a small group led by René Pleven, who was perhaps more of a Christian Democrat than anything else. Over the years he had belonged to various parliamentary groups, his flexibility being facilitated by his membership of a tiny party, the UDSR.

the Comité early in 1964. However, the National Bureau of the SFIO forbade Socialists to attend meetings of the Comité in May, and henceforth it was dominated by politicians of the Right. Their political orientation was shown in 1965 when such well-known reactionaries as Frédéric-Dupont, Dides, Tardieu and Lafay received the support of the Centre at the municipal elections, whilst the Comité tried to get Pinay to stand as a Presidential candidate in September before opting for Lecanuet.

In these circumstances it was surprising that the MRP Congress at Vichy (May 1965) ever agreed, albeit conditionally, to support Defferre's Presidential bid. The two most important factors which led to this decision were the determination of MRP's Defferrists (the Left Centre) and the very real anti-Gaullism of the party leadership. In addition, the Comité des Démocrates had proved relatively unsuccessful. Thus, although Fontanet continued to regard it as the basis for a new opposition party, he had decided that the new party could not be established in time for the 1965 Presidential Election; instead, its first battle would be at the General Election of 1967. Finally, although the leaders were reticent about committing themselves to a Socialist candidate, they were prepared to go quite a long way with Gaston Defferre, who had publicly stated that the old stumbling block of *laïcité* should be forgotten by both sides.[1]

The crucial factor, however, in producing the pro-Defferre vote at the Vichy Congress was the determination of the party's Left Centre. An opinion poll of 1963 had shown that less than a quarter of MRP's militants favoured a *travailliste* (i.e. 'Labour party') solution, and that more than half favoured a Centre formation of the type advocated by Lecanuet.[2] And in May 1964 only 13 per cent of MRP voters said that they would vote for Defferre in a Presidential Election (62 per cent said they would vote for de Gaulle and 25 per cent were undecided).[3] Nevertheless at Vichy the MRP Left Centre reaped its reward—illusory though it proved to be—after two years of hard lobbying.

At the La Baule Congress Francine Lefebvre, the former Paris deputy and a leader of the Equipes Ouvrières, had insisted that if MRP were going to merge itself into some new political formation it must do so in company with the Socialists.[4] Mme Lefebvre, however, failed in her bid for election to the National Bureau, indicating the dominance of the Right Centre at this point. After

[1] *Monde*, 23 May 1964 and 8 June 1964.
[2] RFSP, 1963, p. 722, note 15.   [3] ibid., 1964, p. 510.
[4] MRP Congr. 1963, La Baule; debate on Fontanet's report on 'La Politique Générale'.

the official announcement of Defferre's candidature, Fontanet said it was too early for MRP to take up a position for or against it,[1] but the Young Christian Democrats at their Congress in January 1964 gave an enthusiastic welcome to Defferre's initiative.[2] Meanwhile, various Christian Democratic personalities were waging a campaign in favour of Defferre. Amongst the more important were two deputies, Armand Barniaudy and Jean Moulin, the Secretary General of the CFTC, Eugène Descamps, and the Editor-in-Chief of *Forces Nouvelles*, Jean-Pierre Prévost.[3]

At the end of 1964 the supporters of Defferre were still a minority in MRP. The National Committee meeting of October showed that the party was deeply divided, the final motion emphasizing that, although MRP was not *a priori* opposed to Defferre's candidature, it still regarded the Comité des Démocrates as 'the basis for all necessary realignments'.[4] In the early months of 1965 the Defferrists gained ground, partly as a result of internal quarrels in the Bouches-du-Rhône SFIO over electoral alliances for the March municipal elections in Marseilles. A group of anti-clerical rebels broke with Defferre to ally with the Communists, and Defferre therefore moved closer to the Centre, fighting the second round of the election with the support of MRP and CNI.[5] When he announced the Fédération Démocrate et Socialiste on 8 May 1965 he attacked the Communists and Gaullists, appealing to all 'from Socialists to Christian Democrats' to join him in setting up 'a political formation capable of winning a majority'.[6] On 13 May he met the leaders of the Comité des Démocrates, who published a rather vague communiqué sympathizing with Defferre's attempt 'to simplify French political life',[7] but on the next day Camille Laurens announced that the CNI, although remaining in the Comité des Démocrates, would not participate in Defferre's Fédération Démocrate et Socialiste.[8] Jean-Pierre Prévost of *Forces Nouvelles*, on the other hand, welcomed Defferre's proposal: 'The creation of a new party capable of winning a majority ought to be pursued . . . Gaston Defferre's proposal constitutes a useful step in this direction.'[9]

It was in these circumstances that MRP held its Vichy Congress (27–29 May 1965). Defferre appeared to have moved nearer to the

[1] *Monde*, 15 January 1964.   [2] ibid., 14 January 1964.
[3] *Express*, 18 October 1964.   [4] *Monde*, 21 October 1964.
[5] ibid., 13 April 1965. (Defferre had in fact also allied with MRP and CNI in 1959.)
[6] ibid., 9–10 May 1965.   [7] ibid., 15 May 1965.
[8] *Journal des Indépendants*, 17 May 1965. In any case, Defferre did not want the Independents.
[9] *Forces Nouvelles*, 18 May 1965.

Centre and important MRP personalities such as Robert Buron and Pierre-Henri Teitgen had joined men like Jean Mastias, leader of the Equipes Jeunes, and Jean-Pierre Prévost in supporting Defferre. Nevertheless, the committed Defferrists of the Left Centre were never a majority in MRP despite the fact that the Vichy Congress declared itself to be 'interested in' Defferre's proposed Fédération Démocrate et Socialiste and 'ready to study how it should be set up'.[1] The Congress thus followed Lecanuet and Fontanet, who had opted for a tentative Yes, and rejected Pflimlin's advice to boycott an organization which might come under Communist influence. The tentative Yes was, in fact, almost tantamount to a No owing to the three conditions laid down by Abelin in his report on General Policy. Firstly, there must be no attempt at 'satellization' by the SFIO; the Socialists would have to agree to merge themselves fully into the new organization. Secondly, there must be no question of any contacts with the Communists at present or in the future. Finally, the main emphasis within the new party must be on the word 'Democratic', not 'Socialist'.[2]

All now depended on the SFIO June Congress. The Socialists, like the Christian Democrats, came out in favour of the Defferre proposal, but their final motion was also hedged with conditions. In particular, it referred to the need to integrate private schools into the State system, a concession to Mollet, who had insisted on some reference to *laïcité*, and the Socialists also expressed their wish to see the Communists 'reintegrated into French political life'.[3] Although MRP and SFIO had both declared themselves in favour of Defferre's initiative, it was not surprising that when a committee of sixteen (4 SFIO, 4 MRP, 4 Radicals and 4 representatives of the political Clubs) met on 15 June they failed to come to any agreement over their attitude to the Communists and over the old problem of *laïcité*. The committee of sixteen adjourned *sine die*, and Defferre drew his conclusions by withdrawing his candidature on 25 June.

With the hindsight of history the surprising thing is not that Defferre failed, but that he got as far as he did. His candidature had not been proposed by the parties but by the Clubs and in *L'Express*;

[1] Final motion of MRP Congr. 1965, Vichy.

[2] The conditions were outlined in Abelin's report and included in the final motion in favour of Defferre's proposals.

[3] For an analysis of the SFIO's attitudes to Defferre, see P. M. Williams 'De Gaulle's challenger', *Parliamentary Affairs*, Summer 1964. The Defferre candidature is also discussed in some detail in RFSP, 1964, pp. 505–26 and RFSP, 1965, pp. 67–86. The best analysis of the reasons for the failure of Defferre is contained in an article by Jean Gros, 'La Fédération de Gaston Defferre', *Esprit*, September 1965, pp. 326–41.

he was, therefore, always rather suspect in the eyes of the party leaders. Neither Mollet nor Fontanet, the two key men, really wanted the Defferre candidature, Mollet owing to his commitment to the old SFIO, whose existence was threatened by the proposed Fédération Démocrate et Socialiste,[1] Fontanet owing to his wish to develop a new centre party out of the Comité des Démocrates and because he realized that the MRP electorate, whatever the militants might say, would not vote for a new party in which Socialists would inevitably play a leading part. Lecanuet later said as much when he claimed that the real problem for MRP was not Defferre but the SFIO: 'Our electorate was always more to the Right and suspected that the SFIO, under electoral pressure from the Communists, would try to draw the Federation to the Left.'[2] Neither Lecanuet nor Abelin thought that the problem of *laïcité* was a crucial factor in Defferre's failure,[3] although it was certainly a major sticking point for Mollet; he, too, had to keep an eye on his electorate.

As far as the Christian Democrats were concerned, the Defferre initiative was important because it brought to a head the fundamental divisions within MRP. The Gaullists, led by Schumann, and the conservatives, led by Pflimlin, were opposed both to Defferre's Fédération Démocrate et Socialiste and to Lecanuet's proposed anti-Gaullist Centre party. The Autonomists did not want to see MRP merged into a new formation, although they advocated constructive opposition. The Left Centre, who had supported Defferre, refused to accept the failure of the Fédération Démocrate et Socialiste, eight members of the party signing a declaration regretting Defferre's failure and proposing another attempt to constitute a 'Labour party'.[4] One of their leaders, Jean-Pierre Prévost, was sacked from the editorship of *Forces Nouvelles* a week later.[5] The Right Centre had triumphed, but it was a Pyrrhic victory, whose hollowness became apparent in 1966 when Jean Mastias and the Equipes Jeunes criticized Lecanuet's new Centre Démocrate[6] and Buron resigned from MRP to found Objectif 1972, the aim of which was to initiate in due course a political formation of the type proposed

[1] Cf. *Monde*, 9 October 1965. Early in 1964 Mollet had said in Puy de Dôme, 'Guy Mollet will support the Defferre campaign 100 per cent provided Gaston Defferre supports the policies of the SFIO 100 per cent', *Monde*, 23 February 1964.

[2] Interview with Lecanuet, 8 July 1970.

[3] Interviews with Lecanuet and Abelin, 8 July 1970.

[4] *Monde*, 22 June 1965. The eight signatories were Prévost, Buron, Mme Lefebvre, Teitgen, Mastias, Barangé, Farine and Byé.

[5] Prévost had been Editor-in-Chief since February 1961.

[6] *Monde*, 3 March 1966.

by Defferre.[1] Even before it got off the ground, the Centre Démocrate's chances of success were thus extremely limited.

THE CENTRE DÉMOCRATE AND ITS RIVALS IN THE FRENCH CENTRE

The Centre Démocrate (CD) was the direct result of Lecanuet's successful candidature at the Presidential Election of December 1965, although it had been mooted for at least two years before it came into being. But it soon became apparent that it was one thing for Lecanuet to have rallied a protest vote at the first round of a Presidential Election and quite another to mould it into a viable political force. Lecanuet had succeeded in putting de Gaulle *en ballottage*,[2] but the election had also shown the limitations of Lecanuet's electoral base despite his optimistic remarks of 10 December when he announced the impending creation of the CD.

After Pinay's refusal to stand as a Centre candidate (24 September 1965) Lecanuet had announced that he would stand as a 'democratic, social and European candidate'.[3] He resigned his post as President of MRP to show his desire 'to look beyond the present political formations'.[4] At first Lecanuet was virtually unknown nationally, but he was young (45), good-looking and articulate, distinct advantages in the first French election in which television played an important role. Lecanuet, like Mitterrand, criticized *pouvoir personnel*, technocratic government and the *force de frappe*, but, unlike Mitterrand, who was somewhat constrained by the Communist Party, Lecanuet could lay great emphasis on the need for further steps towards European integration, criticizing de Gaulle for boycotting the institutions of the Common Market and implying that the boycott was aggravating the agricultural crisis.

Lecanuet polled $3\frac{3}{4}$ million votes (15·8 per cent of those cast) at the first ballot,[5] thus apparently vindicating his claim that there was

[1] *Monde*, 19 October 1966; and see, p. 255, note 1, for more details about Objectif 1972.

[2] A second round was necessary unless one candidate got over 50 per cent of the votes cast (de Gaulle got 44 per cent—see p. 252, note 1). In the second round only the two leading candidates after the first round can stand.

[3] *Monde*, 28 October 1965.   [4] ibid.

[5] Presidential Election, 5 and 19 December, 1965:

First Ballot		% Electorate Votes Cast
Registered electorate	28,233,167	
Votes cast	24,001,961	
Abstentions	4,231,206	14·9
Spoiled papers	244,292	0·9
Valid votes	23,757,669	84·2

a large unrepresented Centre electorate, which had no desire to vote for de Gaulle or for a candidate of the Left supported by the Communists. This Centre electorate, he contended, would in future be able to find its political home in his proposed new party, the Centre Démocrate.[1] In the first flush of enthusiasm which followed the ballot of 5 December, this seemed a reasonable assumption, but an analysis of the Lecanuet vote shows that it was based on doubtful premises.

François Goguel concluded that the Lecanuet electorate 'coincided almost exactly with that of the traditional right',[2] a conclusion which is open to detailed criticism, for Philip Williams found that in some parts of the Catholic west, notably Mayenne, Lecanuet did best amongst young Catholics of leftish tendency.[3] Nevertheless, all the Departments where Lecanuet received more than 18 per cent of the vote figured in Goguel's 1951 map of traditional right Departments.[4] The Lecanuet vote was also confined to areas of satisfactory religious practice[5] and to Departments with a higher proportion engaged in agriculture than the national average.[6] Goguel, therefore, deduced that Lecanuet should be regarded more as a candidate of the Right than of the Centre, and that the likelihood of the Centre Démocrate making any real impact outside 'agricultural regions of Catholic tradition'[7] was somewhat limited. Moreover, despite Lecanuet's $3\frac{3}{4}$ million votes, he had not come out top in any Department, although

Continued

First Ballot		% Electorate	Votes Cast
De Gaulle	10,386,734	36·8	43·7
Mitterrand	7,658,792	27·1	32·2
Lecanuet	3,767,404	13·3	15·8
Tixier-Vignancour	1,253,958	4·4	5·3
Marcilhacy	413,129	1·5	1·7
Barbu	277,652	1·0	1·2
Second Ballot			
De Gaulle	12,643,527	44·8	54·5
Mitterrand	10,553,985	37·4	45·5

RFSP, 1966, pp. 226 and 239.

For detailed discussion of 1965 Presidential Elections, see P. M. Williams, 'The French Presidential Election of 1965', *Parliamentary Affairs*, Spring 1966; D. B. Goldey, 'Organization and Results', *Political Studies*, June, 1966; François Goguel, 'L'Election Présidentielle Française de Décembre 1965', RFSP, April 1966.

[1] *Monde*, 10 December 1965.　　[2] RFSP, 1966, p. 235.

[3] E.g. in Sablé-sur-Sarthe (Mayenne); P. M. Williams, unpublished research on 1965 Election.

[4] Goguel, *Géographie*, p. 121; and RFSP, 1966, p. 235.　　[5] ibid., p. 175.

[6] RFSP, 1966, p. 236; seven departments with more than double the national average, two with about 50 per cent more, one with 25 per cent more.

[7] ibid., p. 236.

he had beaten Mitterrand into third place in six Departments of western France (Manche, Calvados, Orne, Mayenne, Maine-et-Loire and Vendée), two in the east (Bas-Rhin and Haut-Rhin) and one in the Massif Central (Haute-Loire). Even in his best Department, Mayenne, Lecanuet obtained less than a quarter of the votes of the registered electorate, and in twenty-eight Departments (almost one-third of the total) he got less than 12 per cent. The combined de Gaulle-Lecanuet vote was very similar to the Yes vote at the October 1962 referendum.[1] Thus, although Lecanuet had attracted enough votes to put de Gaulle *en ballottage*, there was no real evidence that numerically or politically he had broken out of the traditional bastions of moderate conservatism.

Lecanuet's vote consisted of the hard core of the old MRP and CNI, together with disenchanted Gaullists and discontented Catholic peasants. The vast majority of these voters returned to de Gaulle on 19 December, although a significant minority, especially of discontented peasants, probably followed Lecanuet's ambiguous advice to abstain.[2] The most important result of the Presidential Election was the success of Mitterrand as the candidate of the united Left. Those members of the SFIO who had advocated an opening to the Left seemed to have been vindicated. It was clear that Mitterrand's Fédération de la Gauche Démocrate et Socialiste (FGDS), set up on 15 September 1965, and supported by the Radicals as well as by the Socialists, was likely to be the chief long-term beneficiary of the Presidential Election and that any revival of 'Defferrism' was improbable in the near future. Lecanuet would thus be blocked on his Left and dependent on a volatile Centre Right electorate which had already shown that it was not averse to flirting with Gaullism. In these inauspicious circumstances the Centre Démocrate was set up in January 1966, and its first National Convention was held at Lyon in the following April.

Lecanuet's aim was to form a Centre party opposed both to Gaullism and Communism. He hoped to rally the Defferrist wing of the SFIO, the Faure wing of the Radical party, the Independents who were opposed to Giscard d'Estaing, and all of the old MRP. From the start he ran into difficulties from within the CD itself and from

---

[1] RFSP, 1966, p. 235.

[2] Lecanuet advised his electorate not to vote for de Gaulle, but refused to tell them to vote for Mitterrand, doubtless realizing that, as in the October 1962 referendum, the majority would disobey. A number of committed 'Europeans' (notably Jean Monnet and Pierre Uri), who had supported Lecanuet in the first round, came out in favour of Mitterrand in the second. But the influence of such 'intellectuals' on the Lecanuet electorate was probably very limited; cf. Jean Ranger in RFSP, 1966, p. 183.

its opponents to Left and Right. Moreover, as Raymond Barrillon pointed out, he was attempting to fulfil his grand design with only one positive policy, the furtherance of European integration; for the rest, he had nothing to offer except anti-Communism and anti-Gaullism.[1] Lecanuet's first difficulties were internal. The old MRP Left criticized the Centre Démocrate from the beginning. At their Congress in January 1966 the Equipes Jeunes under Jean Mastias said they would have preferred a new Defferre alliance of the non-Communist Left to the CD.[2] Félix Lacambre, leader of Action Catholique Ouvrière, criticized the conservative membership of the Comité Directeur set up in January 1966,[3] and Lacambre and Georges Delfosse, a former assistant Secretary General of MRP and leader of the Equipes Ouvrières, refused to attend the first CD National Convention in April.[4] Georges Suffert, a left-wing Catholic who had been a prominent supporter of Defferre's Presidential bid, maintained that the vast majority of MRP militants were opposed to Lecanuet's CD and favoured a new *rassemblement* of Christian Democrats, Socialists, Radicals and non-Gaullist Independents.[5] Etienne Borne would have preferred a Defferre type party, but said that if he had to choose between Lecanuet's CD and Mitterrand's FGDS he would opt for the former.[6] Lecanuet, in fact, also professed to be in favour of a Defferre solution, provided, of course, that the FGDS was prepared to give up all contacts with the Communists:[7] he even offered to work out a governmental programme with Mitterrand on this basis.[8] But after the success of the united Left at the Presidential Election of 1965 this was clearly not practical politics. And later in

---

[1] *Monde*, 23 April 1966, and 17–18 July 1966. Pierre Viansson-Ponté made the same point, *Monde*, 14 September 1966.

[2] The Congress voted 372–46 with 112 abstentions for a new Defferre type party; *Monde*, 1 April 1966.

[3] *Express*, 20 February 1966. The first Comité Directeur consisted of *President*, Jean Lecanuet (MRP); *Vice Presidents*, Maurice Faure (Rad.), Bertrand Motte (CNI); *Secretary General*, Théo Braun (MRP, ex-CFTC); *Members*, Pierre Abelin (MRP), Paul Alduy (Rad.—Rassemblement Démocratique), Edmond Barrachin (CNI senator), Pierre Baudis (CNI), Edouard Bonnefous (UDSR senator), André Colin (MRP senator), Bernard Cornut-Gentille (without affiliation), Jacques Duhamel (Rad.—Rassemblement Démocratique) Guy Ebrard (Rad.), André Fosset (MRP senator), François Japiot (CNI), Jacques Ménard (CNI senator), Rémy Montagne (ex-Rassemblement Démocratique), Pierre Pflimlin (MRP), Paul Pillet (MRP), Paul Ribeyre (CNI senator), Jacqueline Thome-Patenôtre (Rad. senator), Pierre Fauchon (*avocat*), Paul Bouju (*professeur*), Albert Genin (former Sec. Gen. of FNSEA); *Forces Nouvelles*, 3 February 1966.

[4] *Monde*, 26 April 1966.   [5] *Express*, 13 March 1966.
[6] *Forces Nouvelles*, 15 April 1966.   [7] *Monde*, 27 April 1966.
[8] ibid., 16 May 1966.

1966 Lecanuet received another blow from amongst his potential supporters, when Robert Buron, supported by Jean Mastias and Jean-Pierre Prévost, resigned from MRP and founded Objectif 1972 as a liaison organization to rally those who favoured a non-Communist left-wing federation.[1] To make matters worse, Pflimlin, who attended the Lyon Convention, criticized the CD for its anti-Gaullism and refused to join the new Comité Directeur.[2] Later in the year he decided not to stand at the 1967 General Election.

The CD also suffered from the new orientation of the Radical party, which had elected René Billères as its President in October 1965 in place of Maurice Faure, and had subsequently joined the FGDS.[3] Maurice Faure had been a Vice President of the first Comité Directeur of the Centre Démocrate, but was forced to resign from it in February 1966, together with two other Radical members, Mme Thome-Patenôtre and Guy Ebrard, when the Radical Party Bureau pointed out that they were breaking one of the party rules which forbade membership of two 'political movements'.[4] Lecanuet revived the Comité des Démocrates as a liaison organization purely for the sake of 'associating' Faure and his friends with the CD,[5] a

[1] *Monde*, 19 October 1966. The aim of Objectif 1972 was 'another majority . . . under the banner of socialism for modern times', *Monde*, 12 November 1966. Buron said that Objectif 1972 was neither a party nor a club, but 'a welcoming organization (*structure d'accueil*) for the many democrats who regretted the failure of Gaston Defferre's attempted regroupment of 1965', ibid.; and Jean-Pierre Prévost called it 'a new laboratory for left-wing ideas', *T.C.* 7 December 1967. Objectif 1972 held four National Conventions (December 1967, December 1968, March 1970, November 1971). At the last of these it changed its name to Objectif Socialiste. Its aims, however, did not change; it refused to join the Socialist party, as advocated by several delegates, remaining instead 'une structure d'accueil et de formation', *Monde* 16 November 1971. The only left-wing militants who could not join Objectif Socialiste were Communists, although Buron did not rule out the possibility of future electoral alliances with the PCF, *Nouvel Obs.* 22 March 1971.

[2] The Comité Directeur co-opted at Lyon consisted of *President*: Jean Lecanuet; *Sec. General*: Théo Braun; *Assistant Sec. Generals*: Denis Baudouin, Christian Legrez; *Members*: seven deputies—P. Abelin, P. Coste-Floret, J. Fontanet, R. Montagne, P. Pillet (all MRP or Groupe Centre Démocratique), P. Baudis (CNI), J. Duhamel (ex-Rad.); eight senators—A. Colin, A. Fosset (MRP), R. Barrachin, J. Ménard, J. Rastoin (all CNI), R. Blondelle (Paysan), E. Bonnefous (ex-UDSR), P. Ribeyre (unaffiliated); there were also seven farmers, three lawyers and ten others representing trade unions, employers' organizations, civil servants and the young. For full details see *Monde*, 26 April 1966.

[3] In typical Radical fashion the Congress (October 1965) recommended electors to vote for Mitterrand whilst 'recognizing the value of Lecanuet's candidature'; *Monde*, 26 October 1965.

[4] Art. 2 of Radical party statutes, *Monde*, 12 February 1966.

[5] *Monde*, 17 February 1966.

manoeuvre which could not conceal the fact that the CD had already moved perceptibly to the Right. Faure attended the CD Convention at Lyon and told the delegates that he was 'a good friend and close neighbour of the Centre Démocrate',[1] but in the General Election of March 1967 he was ignominiously forced to join the FGDS between ballots or risk losing his seat. Although the Comité Directeur elected at Lyon contained Jacques Duhamel (ex-Radical) and Edouard Bonnefous (ex-UDSR), it was, as Barrillon pointed out, essentially a conservative body in which Independents and members of the MRP Right Centre predominated.[2]

To add to Lecanuet's difficulties Giscard d'Estaing, who had been dismissed from the Ministry of Finance in January 1966, decided to organize the Républicains Indépendants (RI) as a party. The RI *rassemblement*, originally set up in November 1962, consisted of those Independents who, as Gaullists, had been refused the endorsement of the CNI in 1962 and a number of Giscard's personal friends, notably de Broglie and Jacquinot. The RI had remained within the majority, but published a newspaper of its own, *La France Moderne*.[3] Giscard, no doubt to the surprise of Pompidou, reacted to his dismissal by announcing the establishment of the RI as a party which would remain within the majority but keep its distance from it ('Oui, mais' . . .). By June 1966 the RI was in existence as a new party, but it was apparent that if Giscard were going to do well at the 1967 General Election he would have to capture a considerable part of the Lecanuet electorate of December 1965. Giscard made it clear that he was aiming to do just that by declaring that the RI was 'liberal, centrist and European'.[4] In a television programme in February 1966, Giscard said that he was aiming to win centre voters to his version of Gaullism.[5] He specifically told *Combat* in April that he hoped to see defections from the CD to the RI.[6] And at a press conference in July he said that his objective was to place himself 'at the point where moderate opinion and Christian Democratic ideas meet'.[7] By April 1966 there were already signs that Giscard was a real threat to Lecanuet, for in a SOFRES opinion poll 38 per cent said that they thought Giscard had more political future than Lecanuet, whilst 31 per cent thought he had less (31 per cent had no opinion).[8]

[1] *Monde*, 26 April 1966.   [2] ibid.

[3] Changed to *La France Moderne, Libérale, Centriste et Européenne* in April 1966. Although rather a mouthful, the new title indicated that Giscard was out to poach the Lecanuet electorate.

[4] *France Moderne*, April 1966, pp. 6–7.   [5] *Monde*, 16 February 1966.

[6] *Combat*, 18 April 1966.   [7] *Monde*, 3–4 July 1966.   [8] RFSP, 1967, p. 73.

Lecanuet was well aware of the threat posed by Giscard's RI. He talked of Giscard's 'difficult attitude', contending that he was 'more suited to financial juggling than to the definition of a coherent policy, . . . he is trying to benefit at the same time by his personal loyalty to de Gaulle and by criticizing his policy'.[1] At the Lyon Convention in April 1966 Lecanuet attacked Giscard for claiming to be a 'European' whilst supporting de Gaulle's policies which were destroying the unity of Europe.[2] Lecanuet claimed that the CD was quite different from the RI, not only because he was a genuine 'European' whereas Giscard was not, but because the CD was aiming to change Gaullism 'from outside', whilst the RI was attempting the impossible, i.e. to change Gaullist policies from inside the majority.[3]

Despite his manifest difficulties, both within the CD and on account of his electoral rivals to Right and Left, Lecanuet optimistically claimed that the CD would win enough seats at the 1967 General Election to enable it to act as arbiter in the National Assembly; the CD would be so strong that it would not even have to consider acting as a 'hinge group' (groupe charnière) within the majority.[4] The electorate, however, decided otherwise, revealing the underlying weaknesses of the CD.

THE GENERAL ELECTIONS OF 1967 AND 1968

According to the official figures published by the Ministry of the Interior, the CD received 2,864,272 votes at the first ballot in March 1967 (12·8 per cent of votes cast). In 1962, in a much smaller turnout the combined MRP–CNI vote had been 3,069,872 (16·7 per cent of votes cast). Even allowing for the fact that Goguel estimated the true CD vote at 3,017,447 in 1967 (owing to 150,000–odd CD votes being wrongly attributed to 'others'), the Centre suffered a severe defeat. The Gaullists advanced by just under 2 per cent in 1967 compared with 1962 and the combined Left by 0·7 per cent (PCF 0·6 per cent, FGDS 0·1 per cent), but the CD fell back by 2·6 per cent.[5]

---

[1] *Monde*, 8 March 1966. [2] ibid., 25 April 1966.
[3] *T.C.*, 7 July 1966. [4] *Forces Nouvelles,* 23 September 1966.
[5] *1967 General Election, first ballot.*

Electorate	28,291,838	
Abstentions	5,404,687	(19·1% of reg. elect.)
Votes cast	22,887,151	
Spoiled papers	494,834	(1·7% of reg. elect.)
Valid votes cast	22,392,317	(79.1% of reg. elect.)
Comms	5,029,808	(22·5% of votes cast)
P.S.U.	506,592	(2·7% of votes cast)
Left Federation	4,207,166	(18·8% of votes cast)

I

A combination of factors was responsible for the CD's failure. The electorate clearly preferred the apparent discipline and stability offered by the Right or Left to the 'Fourth Republican' non-commitment of the Centre. The Gaullists were united under the umbrella of Pompidou's Comité d'Action pour la Ve République, which had agreed that Gaullists, whether UDR, UDT or RI, would not stand against each other, even at the first ballot (apart from a few dissident Gaullists, who stood without the support of Pompidou's Comité, the agreement was kept). On 20 December 1966 the PCF and FGDS had also made a national agreement to withdraw in favour of the best placed candidate of the Left at the second ballot,[1] and similar pacts were later made with the PSU, although the PSU refused to incorporate itself into the FGDS as the Socialists and Radicals had done. With one or two exceptions the Left stuck to its agreements with remarkable discipline.

In contrast Lecanuet refused to make any official alliances, although he announced that in constituencies where his candidates had no chance of success at the second ballot, they would be withdrawn to ensure the defeat of Communists or Gaullists.[2] There were also one or two cases where the CD and Tixier-Vignancour's ultra-conservative ARL had unofficial alliances, e.g. in the 15th and 16th *arrondissements* of Paris where the CD did not oppose candidates supported by the ARL, whilst the mayors of Saint-Cloud and Nice stood with the dual support of CD and ARL.[3] Lecanuet optimistically hoped that discontented Gaullists, appreciative of his opposition to the General, and discontented Socialists and Radicals, upset by the FGDS–PCF agreement of 20 December, would vote for the CD.[4] This was to misunderstand the mood of the electorate at a time when most Frenchmen preferred the cohesion and discipline offered by the Left and Right. By sitting on the fence the CD did

1967 General Election, first ballot—continued

Gaullists	8,453,572	(37·7% of votes cast)
Dissid. Gaullists	105,544	(0·5% of votes cast)
CD	3,017,447	(13·5% of votes cast)
Others	878,472	(3·9% of votes cast)

Source: Ministry of Interior figures with modifications made by F. Goguel, RFSP, 1967, pp. 436–8.

[1] Normally this meant the candidate with the largest number of votes, but in fifteen cases the Communist withdrew in favour of a Federation candidate even when he had received a larger poll. This was a concession to the fact that it was easier to unite opposition round a non-Communist candidate. If the PCF had made more such concessions, the Gaullist majority in the National Assembly could have been wiped out.

[2] *Monde*, 20 February 1967.   [3] RFSP, 1967, p. 432.

[4] *Forces Nouvelles*, 23 September 1965; *Combat*, 21 February 1966.

not create the impression that it could form the basis of a viable majority; for those with memories of the past, the CD, by leaving its options open until after the election and by talking of a *rassemblement* in the Centre, looked all too like a party of the Fourth Republic. Lecanuet's position was also weakened by his failure to find a safe constituency for himself (in the end he did not stand) and by the background of some of his candidates. Viansson-Ponté remarked that the CD's endorsement of Frédéric-Dupont, the darling of the *concierges* of the 7th *arrondissement* but a well-known figure of the extreme right, could hardly be expected to appeal to the 'Defferrist' electorate.[1] Giscard d'Estaing commented that it was ironical that the CD was supporting several 'candidates of reaction', as it had done at the 1965 municipal elections.[2] And André Fosset, an MRP Senator, resigned when the CD gave its unofficial blessing to Jacques Soustelle by refusing to oppose him in Lyon.[3]

Another factor which worked against the CD was the new electoral law of November 1966 by which candidates were eliminated at the first ballot if they did not receive 10 per cent of the registered electorate; this was a much stiffer hurdle than the 5 per cent of votes cast which had applied in 1958 and 1962.[4] Altogether 151 of the 382 CD candidates were eliminated by the 10 per cent rule,[5] and only 27 were elected (René Pleven at the first ballot, the remainder a week later). The electoral geography of the CD was, as Goguel has pointed out, very similar to that of MRP in the second half of the Fourth Republic[6]—considerable strength in Brittany, rather less in Alsace, and fragmented support in a line running from Haute-Savoie to Basses-Pyrénées. However, two important differences were apparent: the CD received less support than MRP in the areas of traditional Christian Democratic strength, but did surprisingly well in some traditional Radical fiefs, notably in Gers and, to a lesser extent, in Pyénées Orientales, doubtless owing to the fact that certain prominent notables had received the investiture of the CD.[7] Between the two ballots there were no official negotiations between

[1] *Monde*, 16 February 1967.   [2] *Nouvel Obs.*, 2 February 1967.   [3] ibid.

[4] For example, Jean Chelini was eliminated in the second constituency of Marseilles where he got 7,634 votes out of a registered electorate of 81,372. This was only 3,604 votes fewer than Emile Loo, the SFIO-Federation candidate, who eventually won the seat at the second ballot. The election of Loo was, incidentally, a good example of the discipline of the Left; cf. R. E. M. Irving and A. MacLeod, 'The Legislative Elections of March 1967 in the Second Constituency of Marseilles', *Parl. Affairs*, Summer 1967, pp. 222–33.

[5] *Monde*, 7 March 1967.   [6] RFSP, 1967, p. 445.

[7] MM. Brocas and Montesquiou in Gers and M. Alduy in Pyrénées-Orientales, ibid., p. 446.

the CD and Gaullists or the CD and the Left. Lecanuet left it to CD candidates to advise their voters about their choice at the second ballot: on no account should they vote for a Communist, and preferably not for a Gaullist. In certain areas, however, notably Rhône and Isère, CD candidates were withdrawn to the advantage of the Gaullists, a tacit *quid pro quo* for Gaullist withdrawals in Savoie and Loire.[1] At the second ballot the CD vote plummeted (1,660,000 fewer votes than at the first; in 1962 the Centre had lost almost 900,000 votes between ballots), but the remarkable feature of the second ballot at the 1967 Election, when compared with the 1962 and 1968 General Elections and the 1965 Presidential Election, was that more Centre voters cast their ballots for candidates of the Left than for Gaullists. There appear to have been three main reasons for this.[2] Firstly, the 1967 Election took place in 'normal' conditions (for the first time since 1945 France was neither fighting nor in the immediate aftermath of a war), and, after the Gaullist advance at the first ballot, there seemed to be a danger of a huge Gaullist majority after the second; Centre voters could thus vote for the Left, even for Communists, without there being any risk of a Popular Front Government. Secondly, the really Gaullist part of the Centre electorate had already abandoned Lecanuet before the first ballot. A dozen former MRP deputies, including Maurice Schumann, Marie-Madeleine Dienesch and Charles de Chambrun, had never joined the CD and were endorsed by the Comité d'Action pour la Ve République. Finally, a considerable number of the 1,250,000 Tixier-Vignancour electors of December 1965 voted not for Tixier's ARL on 5 March 1967 but for the CD (the ARL polled less than 200,000 votes); on 12 March the more embittered members of the extreme right, in particular the North African refugees in south-east France, voted, as Tixier had advised, for FGDS candidates (and perhaps sometimes even for Communists).

Lecanuet's CD thus failed to make the desired breakthrough. Indeed, although boosted by extreme right votes,[3] the CD did even worse than the Centre in 1962, itself a very bad year for MRP and Independents. Despite Lecanuet's insistence that France was 'centrist at heart' and that a majority could be found between the Gaullists and Communists, the electorate seemed to prefer bipolarization. The events of May–June 1968 indicated the fragility of the 'Popular Front' alliance, but the Election of 1968, which will not be discussed

---

[1] RFSP, 1967, p. 451.   [2] ibid., pp. 459–60.
[3] Votes which will tend increasingly to go to the Gaullist party as the memory of Algeria fades.

at any length here owing to its abnormality,[1] gave little comfort to the man who had always said that the PCF–FGDS alliance was artificial, for Lecanuet's Centrists lost almost a million votes[2] (2,290,000 compared with 3,017,000 at the first ballot in 1967), whereas the total loss of the combined Left (PCF-FGDS-PSU) was only 646,994 (9,096,672 compared with 9,743,566 at the first ballot in 1967).[3] Despite the 'great fear' the percentage of votes cast for the combined Left was down by only 2·4 per cent compared with a 5·2 per cent decline in Centre votes. Moreover, although the Left and the Centre both disintegrated after the turmoil of the summer of 1968, the Left appeared to be recovering its unity by the early 1970s, whereas the Centre, or at least the Centre as envisaged by Lecanuet, was weaker than ever.

THE FRENCH CENTRE AFTER THE GENERAL ELECTIONS OF 1967 AND 1968 AND THE PRESIDENTIAL ELECTION OF 1969

In April 1967 the parliamentary group Progrès et Démocratie Moderne (PDM) was set up. It consisted of the 27 CD deputies elected in March, together with 14 others from a variety of political backgrounds. The heterogeneity of the group is indicated by the fact that 13 had formerly been in MRP (led by Pierre Abelin); 10 had been Independents (led by Bertrand Motte); 11 had been

---

[1] For a detailed discussion of the events of May and June and the General Election which followed, see D. B. Goldey, 'The Events of May and the French General Election of June 1968', *Parl. Affairs*, Autumn 1968, pp. 307–37, and Spring 1969, pp. 116–33. On the Election see also François Goguel, 'Les Elections Législatives des 23 et 30 Juin 1968', RFSP, 1968, pp. 837–53.

[2] Standing as Centre Progrès et Démocratie Moderne (CPDM).

[3] *1968 General Elections, first ballot figures.*

Electorate	28,171,635	PCF	4,435,357 (20·0% of votes cast)
Abstentions	5,631,892	PSU	874,212 (3·9% of votes cast)
Voters	22,539,743	Federation	3,654,003 (16·5% of votes cast)
Spoiled papers	401,086	Rest of Left	133,100 (0·6% of votes cast)
Valid votes	22,138,657	CPDM	2,290,165 (10·3% of votes cast)
		Gaullists	10,201,024 (46·0% of votes cast)
		Others	550,796 (1·4% of votes cast)

Comparison with 1967 first ballot

PCF	− 594,451	(−2·4%)
PSU	+ 367,620	(+1·7%)
Fed. and rest of Left	− 420,063	(−1·7%)
CPDM and other moderates	+1,195,055	(−5·2%)
Gaullists	+1,642,968	(+7·8%)
Others	− 54,679	(−0·2%)

Source: RFSP, 1968, p. 840.

Radicals of various sorts (their most prominent figure was Jacques Duhamel); 3 had been in the UDSR with René Pleven; and 4 others, led by the former Gaullist Minister Pierre Sudreau, had had no previous party affiliation.

The 1968 General Election reduced the PDM group to 31 (it had fought the Election as CPDM[1]), and a year later, after the Presidential Election, two-thirds of the PDM, led by Duhamel and now calling themselves Centre Démocratie et Progrés (CDP), joined the majority, with Duhamel, Pleven and Fontanet entering the Government. After July 1969 the division between the majority and the opposition ran through the middle of the PDM group. Lecanuet's CD remained in opposition, although spurned by the new Socialist party which came into being in July 1969 under Alain Savary and widened its compass in June 1971 when François Mitterrand took over as First Secretary[2]. Meanwhile, Duhamel's CDP continued to try to attract the remaining CD deputies into the majority,[3] whilst Servan-Schreiber hoped that his new Reform Movement would ensure that Lecanuet's followers would remain in the opposition.[4]

The electoral defeats of 1967 and 1968 only brought into the open the obvious weaknesses of the Centre. Internal dissensions continued in the CD. Within a month of the 1967 Elections André Fosset had written an open letter to Le Monde criticizing the CD for its drift to the Right,[5] and Jules Peneau, the leader of the Equipes Ouvrières in Loire-Atlantique and a CD candidate in March, resigned from the party for the same reason;[6] in June the former CFTC official, Théo

[1] Centre Progrès et Démocratie Moderne.

[2] Most of those who joined the Socialist party after the Epinay unity conference (June 1971) came from a political club background. They included left-wing Christian Democrats like Robert Buron and perhaps as many as half of the members of Objectif 1972 (most of the remainder being members of the PSU); Monde 13 November 1971. Shortly after the Epinay conference, Mitterrand opened discussions with the Communists and Radicals with a view to fighting the 1973 Elections together. No approach was made to the CD; Combat 26 June 1971.

[3] Monde, 5 October 1971.

[4] After a meeting at St Germain-en-Laye (3 November 1971), attended by Jean-Jacques Servan-Schreiber, President of the Radical party, Jean Lecanuet, President of the CD, André Morice, President of the Centre Républicain, and Emile Müller, President of the Parti de la Démocratie Socialiste, Servan-Schreiber announced the establishment of a Reform Movement of anti-Communist opposition parties. In practice, as Barrillon pointed out (Monde, 5 November 1971), Servan-Schreiber was opting for the Centre Right with all the electoral problems implied by such a choice. Moreover, many Radicals were not happy about the choice, Monde, 7–8 November 1971. See p. 264, for the CD's reaction to the Reform Movement.

[5] Monde, 24 April 1967.   [6] ibid., 12 April 1967.

Braun, resigned as Secretary General of the CD (he was replaced by Abelin). But, just as the CD seemed to be consolidating itself unashamedly as a Right-Centre party, Lecanuet opted for outright opposition to the Government.[1] This immediately raised difficulties with members of the PDM group, notably Duhamel and Motte who were already considering the possibility of entering the Gaullist majority on the right terms.[2] Within four months of the Election it was found necessary to set up a Comité d'Entente Centriste to resolve differences between the supporters of Lecanuet and Duhamel. By the autumn there was an open rift between the two factions. Only ten of the PDM followed Lecanuet's advice to vote for the censure motion of 10 October (which received 207 of the 244 votes required), and Duhamel and Fontanet refused to attend the CD's second National Convention at Nice in November 1967. At the Convention the strongly anti-Gaullist faction, led by Lecanuet and Abelin, triumphed, but in so doing they opened up a split with Motte's Independents, which was only papered over by a timely intervention by Lecanuet who had to appeal for more votes so that Motte would not lose his post as a Vice-President of the CD.[3]

The Events of May and June 1968 helped to draw the Centre together again, although it was noticeable that it was Duhamel who made all the running by organizing the CPDM to fight the Election and by coming out decisively against the 'anarchists' of May, even although he was not yet ready to join the majority. Despite the fact that the Centre fought the June Election with its back to the wall, the old differences soon reappeared in the PDM group. Goguel distinguished four 'political families' after the 1968 Election: those former Radicals and UDSR who had always refused to ally with the extreme left (Duhamel, Montesquiou and Pleven); the MRP group (Abelin, Bosson and Fréville); a small number of former Socialists, who, like the Radicals of the Centre, had refused any dealings with the PCF (led by Boutard); and a group without previous political affiliation (Sudreau and his friends).[4]

Lecanuet continued to profess optimism. He foresaw the possibility of defections from 'the large and incoherent Gaullist majority' and welcomed the disintegration of the PCF-FGDS alliance.[5] He hoped that the French people would rally to the Centre, the only place where 'genuine dialogue' was possible.[6] But, even at its

[1] E.g. *Monde*, 20 October 1967; *Combat*, 16 October 1967.
[2] *Combat*, 16 October 1967.
[3] *Monde*, 21 November 1967; Barrillon commented that, although the practice of appealing for more votes to ensure the election of a platform nominee had often been used at Radical Congresses, he had never heard of MRP using it.
[4] RFSP, 1968, p. 849.   [5] *Monde*, 22 October 1968.   [6] ibid.

weakest, the non-Communist Left showed no inclination to rally to Lecanuet. And the Centre finally split when Duhamel, who had been condemned by Lecanuet for his failure to call for an unequivocal No at the April 1969 referendum,[1] opted for Pompidou rather than Poher at the second ballot of the Presidential Election. Thereafter the split in the Centre seemed to be unbridgeable. The vast majority of the PDM group followed Duhamel, Fontanet, Pleven and Motte into the majority, forming the new Centre party, CDP.

In 1971 about 25 of the 31 members of the PDM group were claimed by the CDP and 10 by the CD;[2] ironically, although Duhamel and Lecanuet were at loggerheads and the CDP was in the majority whilst the CD remained in the opposition, a certain amount of cross-voting went on and the boundary between the CDP and CD within PDM was not entirely clear even amongst the deputies themselves. Lecanuet was determined to continue in opposition, ruling out any possibility of joining the majority, at least until after the 1973 General Election.[3] The CD's third National Convention (January 1970) had expressed the hope that the Socialist friends of Chandernagor and the Radical followers of Servan-Schreiber would join Lecanuet, but the CD Convention of October 1971 refused to give a positive response to Servan-Schreiber's offer of such an alliance.[4] However, a fortnight later, Lecanuet, in another *volte face*, decided that the CD would, after all, participate in Servan-Schreiber's Reform Movement. Lecanuet contended that no 'genuine reforms' could be expected from the Gaullist majority, so that, despite the Government's broadly acceptable attitude to European integration, the CD would continue its role as 'constructive opposition', henceforth in company with the Servan-Schreiber Radicals. But of course the old problem of attracting a sufficient number of electors remained as intractable as ever.

In the long run the CD appeared to have no future except within the Gaullist majority unless a major split occurred in the UDR or the Communists went back into their ghetto. The peaceful transfer of power from de Gaulle to Pompidou in 1969 and the restructuring of the Gaullist party after the Lille Congress of 1967 made it unlikely that the UDR would suddenly disintegrate, although the effect of a severe electoral setback could not be ascertained. Likewise, although the French Communist Party remained more hidebound and conservative than its Italian counterpart, its leaders were well aware

[1] *Monde*, 18 February 1969.
[2] Interview with Mlle Nicole Hébert (Duhamel's Secretary), 7 July 1971.
[3] *Monde*, 25 May 1971.   [4] ibid., 23 October 1971.

that its electoral alliances with the non-Communist Left had worked to its advantage since 1962. In these circumstances the PCF seemed likely to continue its glacial advance towards the new Socialist party in the hope that one day the two parties would form the basis of a Popular Front government. The closer the two major parties of the Left moved, the more likely it was that the Reform Movement would collapse and that Lecanuet's followers would move into the Gaullist majority.

Conclusion

Christian Democracy appears to be a spent force in France, but the historical balance-sheet is by no means wholly negative. By their splendid Resistance record the Christian Democrats proved that Catholics (at least those of the Left and Centre) could be loyal Republicans. By their support for nationalization, economic planning and the welfare state they showed that Catholics could be as interested as Socialists in economic and social justice. And like the Socialists, they were prepared to put the Republic before their party in the difficult years between 1947 and 1951 when political democracy seemed to be threatened by the extreme right (Gaullists) and extreme left (Communists). After committing major blunders in Indo-China and Morocco, they faced up to the realities of post-war nationalism, contributing in no small measure to solving the problems of Black Africa and Algeria. In Europe they preached reconciliation and integration after a bout of Germanophobia in the immediate post-war period.

But Christian Democracy in France flattered only to deceive. The artificiality of MRP's 5,000,000 poll (25 per cent of votes cast) in 1945–46 soon became apparent. Many Conservatives voted MRP because their own parties were in disarray after collaborating with Vichy; they had no love for the social-reforming Christian Democrats, but they had even less for the Socialists and Communists. MRP, *le parti de la fidélité*, was also presumed to have the tacit support of General de Gaulle, but the Christian Democrats refused to follow him into opposition in January 1946, and he broke with them by rejecting the Constitution of the Fourth Republic in October 1946 and by founding the RPF in April 1947. Thereafter many MRP voters of 1945–46 followed the General's banner, whilst others went over to the reviving Conservative parties. In the municipal elections of October 1947 MRP's vote was cut to 10 per cent (compared with 25 per cent a year before), and at the General Election of 1951 MRP's poll was down to 2,500,000 (12·5 per cent of votes cast). The 1956 figure was similar, but half of the MRP deputies elected in 1951 and three-fifths of those elected in 1956 came from traditionally conservative departments, principally in the west and north-east. *Nolens volens* MRP had become a regional and 'confessional' party. The militants remained left-wing, but the electorate was largely conservative.

Some Christian Democrats, notably Francisque Gay the founder of *L'Aube*, argued that MRP should have left the Government after

266

the breakdown of tripartism in 1947, which resulted in the parliamentary pendulum swinging to the Right and the virtual abandonment of *la révolution par la loi*. But this was to ignore MRP's commitment to political democracy and the Republic. Gay also contended that MRP had come to power too quickly in 1945. In consequence the MRP leaders, who had had no parliamentary experience, lost touch with their backbenchers and militants. The leaders refused to discuss their policies, relying instead on the loyalty learnt by their followers in Catholic Action and in the Resistance. As a result the Movement suffered from intellectual stagnation, and the disillusioned militants failed to fulfil their allotted task as political educators.[1]

But although there was an element of truth in all these criticisms, MRP's real problem lay elsewhere. At no time in the Fourth or Fifth Republic did the Christian Democrats succeed in coming to a satisfactory working arrangement with the Socialists, their natural left-of-centre partners. Yet after MRP had been cut to size in 1951, the survival of Christian Democracy as a viable political force depended on such an agreement. It is true that the Christian Democrats and Socialists got on without undue friction in the tripartite phase (1944–47), but even before its end Guy Mollet, an ardent *laïc*, had become the leader of the Socialist party in place of Léon Blum, who had been prepared to extend the hand of friendship to the Christian Democrats. On the other hand the *practical* effect of the change from Blum to Mollet was less dramatic than might have been expected, for Mollet was quite prepared to co-operate with MRP, not least in getting himself re-elected mayor of Arras every six years. Nevertheless, after the Communists left the government in May 1947, the Socialists came under increasing pressure from their Left, whilst the Christian Democrats had to keep an equally wary eye on the Gaullists to their Right. Schuman's conservative financial policy in 1947–48 widened the gap between MRP and the Socialists, and in February 1950 the Socialists left the Government in protest at Bidault's fiscal policy. After bringing down the Bidault Government four months later, the Socialists agreed to take office under Pleven (July 1950–February 1951), but relations with MRP deteriorated again owing to differences over Indo-China, culminating in the Generals' Affair of 1950–51.

However, it was not until after the 1951 General Election that relations between the two parties reached their nadir. The Gaullists had insisted on bringing up the old and contentious issue of subsidies for Catholic schools, partly on account of electoral promises but

1 F. Gay, *Les Démocrates d'Inspiration Chrétienne à l'Epreuve du Pouvoir (mémoire confidentiel)*, (1951), especially pp. 10–11, 31–6.

mainly in order to drive a wedge between the Socialists and Christian Democrats. Once MRP had been shown to be little more than the junior partner of the RPF, the Gaullists could claim that a vote for MRP (rather than for RPF) was wasted. The Barangé Law of 1951 had the desired effect, for the Christian Democrats could not vote against a measure supported by their electorate, whilst the Socialists could not betray their historic role as defenders of *laïcité*. The schools question remained 'the Maginot line between the Right and the Left' (Suffert). But, in spite of the fury of the 1951 battle, all hope that the 'line' could be breached did not disappear, for within two or three years no Socialist mayor (i.e. almost no Socialist deputy) would have dreamt of repealing the Barangé Law, which brought far more credits to State schools than to Catholic schools. So the Barangé Law, damaging though it was in 1951, did not really alienate the parties permanently. And although the Socialists were in opposition from 1951 to 1955, many MRP militants (as well as leaders like Pierre-Henri Teitgen and François de Menthon) hoped that a new MRP-SFIO 'alliance' could be forged.

The Gaullist split of 1952 made such an 'alliance' theoretically possible, for when the twenty-seven dissident Gaullists decided to vote for the Conservative Pinay in March, MRP could have joined the Socialists in opposition. If they had done so, a left-of-centre Mendésist coalition might have been formed (Socialists, MRP, left-wing Radicals and a few Gaullists). The 1952 MRP Congress showed that the militants would have supported such a coalition, because they hated Pinay's social and economic policies. In December 1952 it was an MRP revolt which led to the fall of Pinay. And in the ministerial crisis of the summer of 1953 three-fifths of MRP supported Mendès-France's bid for the premiership. But MRP did not go into opposition in 1952, because the party leaders wanted to press on with European integration in the form of EDC, and Pinay, whatever his other faults, was a committed 'European'. Mendès-France, on the other hand, refused either to support or condemn EDC, although he queried its practicality. MRP's doubts about Mendès-France's 'Europeanism' persisted in 1953, and were apparently confirmed in 1954 with the rejection of EDC during his premiership. The 'crime of 30 August' only added salt to the wound inflicted by Mendès-France's attacks on Bidault during the Geneva conference in the summer of 1954. MRP got its revenge by helping to overthrow Mendès-France in 1955 and by opposing the Mollet-Mendès-France Republican Front at the General Election of 1956. But, in the opinion of men like Francisque Gay and Robert Buron,[1] MRP's

[1] Gay, *Combat*, 16 July 1954; Buron, interview, 23 December 1966.

attitude to Mendès-France showed complete lack of judgment. In its determination to destroy Mendès-France, MRP sowed the seeds of its own destruction, for it lost all credibility as a left-wing party. The irony of the situation was summed up by Raymond Barrillon: 'MRP and the Socialists realize their mutual need for co-operation, and it is wanted by the MRP militants, . . . but the only possible bridge is Pierre Mendès-France, and he is totally unacceptable to MRP.'[1]

MRP and the Socialists had a final chance to reach an agreement at the time of Defferre's presidential initiative of 1963–65. During the first five years of the Fifth Republic the two parties had been drawing closer together again. Several of MRP's new deputies in 1958 were trade unionists and peasant activists, and the internal reforms of 1959 helped to 'democratize' the party. Moreover, the Debré Educational Law of 1959 (although it caused the usual bitterness) removed—at least superficially—one of the traditional bones of contention between MRP and SFIO. Both parties were very critical of de Gaulle's European policy and of his style of government in general. They supported him only over Algeria. MRP's 'failure' at the 1962 election (when one-third of its seats were lost) made party realignment all the more necessary, and the La Baule Congress voted for such realignment. But with whom? As has been seen, there were small groups of MRP Gaullists and Autonomists, but the majority of the party was divided into 'Democrats' (Right Centre) and Defferrists (Left Centre). The former was always a larger group than the latter, but the 1965 Congress nevertheless opted for Defferre's 'big' Federation (stretching from the Socialists to the Christian Democrats by way of the Radicals). The determined lobbying of the Defferrists and the very real anti-Gaullism of the majority of MRP were responsible for this unexpected result. But the conditions laid down by both MRP and SFIO made it unlikely that the Defferre Federation would ever get off the ground. MRP wanted the SFIO to wind itself up and merge (like MRP) into a decisively anti-Communist Federation. The Socialists insisted that the SFIO should remain intact and that the Federation should commit itself to *laïcité*. In these circumstances agreement was impossible.

Having broken with the Socialists, the Christian Democrats had only two alternatives: to go it alone in the Centre or to join the Gaullist majority in the hope of influencing it from inside. Lecanuet opted for the first alternative, launching the Centre Démocrate after his relatively successful presidential bid of 1965, but the Left Centre refused to join him and at the General Election of 1967 the majority

1 *Monde*, 24 May 1955.

269

of the Right Centre preferred de Gaulle (or Giscard d'Estaing) to Lecanuet. Fontanet, the other leader of the Centre Démocrate, drew his conclusions and joined the Gaullist majority in 1969. If Christian Democracy had any future in France, it appeared to be as a ginger-group within the Gaullist UDR which had already acquired many of the characteristics of the moderate, conservative German CDU.

With the hindsight of history, it is clear that the French Christian Democrats missed three great opportunities to develop as a left-of-centre party or 'federation': in 1945 when Léon Blum was prepared to extend the hand of reconciliation to the Catholic Resisters; in the mid-1950s when a Mendésist coalition might have emerged; and in the mid-1960s when Defferre proposed his 'big' federation. These opportunities were missed for a variety of reasons connected with the complexities of French politics and the jealous individualism of the parties, which in turn merely reflected the divisions of the French people. But the two major reasons why Christian Democracy failed to develop as a social-reforming Movement were the schools question and the conservatism of the party leadership. The Christian Democrats and Socialists could not agree to sink their differences over *le problème scolaire*. The wounds of one hundred and fifty years of history could not be healed in one generation. Meanwhile, as the leaders were 'educated into the responsibilities of power' (and the attractions of office), they quietly abandoned MRP's left-wing principles. Schuman was said, as Finance Minister, to worship a graven image, the currency; Bidault, as Prime Minister, quarrelled with the Socialists not over clericalism or colonialism, but on a trade union issue; Pflimlin was no reactionary (especially over Algeria), but he was far from progressive in home affairs; Lecanuet would not hear of including the word Socialist in the title of Defferre's Federation. The leaders could always count on the support of their conservative electorate, and normally—though by no means always—on the loyalty and discipline of the parliamentary party. The progressive views of the militants could thus be safely ignored. And so, partly of their own volition and partly on account of the unfavourable political climate, the Christian Democrats gravitated to the Right of the political spectrum where they had little or no chance of fulfilling their original aims.

Bibliography

French Christian Democracy can, of course, be understood only in the context of the general historical, political, social and economic development of France since the Revolution of 1789, and more especially since the advent of the Third Republic in 1875. It is appropriate, therefore, to divide this bibliography into two parts. The first is a general bibliographical essay on books which are particularly useful for an understanding of French politics (using that word in its broadest sense), and the second is a detailed list of books, articles and primary sources essential for the study of Christian Democracy.

PART I

The most useful historical introductions in English are Gordon Wright, *France in Modern Times* (Rand McNally, 1960); D. W. Brogan, *The Development of Modern France, 1870–1939* (Hamish Hamilton, 1940); A. Cobban, *A History of Modern France* (3 vols, Penguin, 1965); David Thomson, *Democracy in France Since 1870* (Oxford University Press, 5th edn. 1969). For politics in the Third Republic see especially J. E. C. Bodley, *France* (Macmillan, revised edn 1902); A. Siegfried, *Tableau des Partis en France* (Grasset, 1930); A. Thibaudet, *Les Idées Politiques de la France* (Stock, 1932); F. Goguel, *La Politique des Partis sous la IIIe République* (Seuil, 1946); Alain, *Le Citoyen Contre les Pouvoirs* (Sagittaire, 1925). There are several useful books on the politics of the Fourth Republic, but both French and English-speaking scholars are in general agreement that the outstanding study is Philip M. Williams, *Crisis and Compromise: Politics in the Fourth Republic* (Longmans, 1964). Other important books are: Gordon Wright, *The Reshaping of French Democracy* (New York, 1948); J. Fauvet, *De Thorez à de Gaulle: les Forces Politiques en France* (Le Monde, 1951); J. Fauvet, *La IVe République* (Fayard, 1959); F. Goguel, *France under the Fourth Republic* (Ithaca, 1952); H. Lüthy, *The State of France* (Secker and Warburg, 1955); Georgette Elgey, *La République des Illusions, 1945–51*, and *La République des Contradictions, 1951–54* (Fayard, 1965 and 1968); Duncan MacRae, *Parliament, Parties and Society in France, 1946–58* (Macmillan, 1967); R. Priouret, *La République des Députés* (Grasset, 1959); D. Schoenbrun, *As France Goes* (Gollancz, 1957); A. Siegfried, *De la IIIe à la IVe République* (Grasset, 1956); and *De la IVe à la Ve République* (Grasset, 1958);

271

D. Pickles, *French Politics: the First Years of the Fourth Republic* (Oxford University Press, 1953); A. Werth, *France, 1940-1955* (Robert Hale, 1956); S. Hoffman *et al.*, *France, Change and Tradition* (Gollancz, 1963). On both the Fourth and Fifth Republic see J. Chapsal, *Le Vie Politique en France depuis 1940* (Presses Universitaires de France, 2nd edn 1969), and Philip M. Williams, *Wars, Plots and Scandals* (Cambridge University Press, 1970). On the Fifth Republic the most useful introductions are Philip M. Williams and Martin Harrison, *Politics and Society in de Gaulle's Republic* (Longmans, 1971); John Ardagh, *The New France* (Penguin, 1970); F. Goguel and A. Grosser, *La Politique en France* (Colin, 1964); P. Viansson-Ponté, *Histoire de la République Gaullienne* (2 vols, Fayard, 1970-71). See also J. S. Ambler, *The Government and Politics of France* (Houghton Mifflin, 1971); Malcolm Anderson, *Government in France—an Introduction to the Executive Power* (Pergamon, 1970); P. Avril, *Politics in France* (Penguin, 1969); H. W. Ehrmann, *Politics in France* (Little, Brown, 1968); R. C. Macridis and Bernard Brown, *The de Gaulle Republic* (Dorsey, 1960); L. G. Noonan, *France: the Politics of Continuity in Change* (Holt, Rinehart and Winston, 1970); D. Pickles, *The Fifth French Republic* (Methuen, 3rd edn 1965); E. R. Tannenbaum, *The New France* (Chicago University Press, 1961); P. Viansson-Ponté, *Bilan de la Ve République: les Politiques* (Calmann-Levy, 1967) and *Après de Gaulle Qui?* (Seuil, 1968); N. Wahl, *The Fifth Republic* (New York, 1959); Philip M. Williams and Martin Harrison, *De Gaulle's Republic* (Longmans, 2nd edn 1962); Philip M. Williams, *The French Parliament, 1958-67* (Allen and Unwin, 1968). De Gaulle's *Memoirs* and a biography of de Gaulle, such as A. Werth, *De Gaulle* (Penguin, 1965) or J. Lacouture, *De Gaulle* (Hutchinson, 1970), are also indispensable reading.

Amongst the more specialized books on post-war France the following are particularly useful. On political parties: M. Einaudi, J. M. Domenach and A. Garosci, *Communism in Western Europe* (New York, 1951); J. Fauvet, *Les Partis Politiques dans la France Actuelle* (Le Monde, 1947) and *Histoire du Parti Communiste Français* (2 vols, Fayard, 1964-65); Annie Kriegel, *Les Communistes Français* (Seuil, 1968); Charles A. Micaud, *Communism and the French Left* (Weidenfeld and Nicolson, 1963); D. Ligou, *Histoire du Socialisme en France, 1881-1961* (Presses Universitaires de France, 1962); Harvey G. Simmons, *French Socialists in Search of a Role, 1956-67* (Cornell University Press, 1970); Peter J. Larmour, *The French Radical Party in the 1930s* (Stanford University Press, 1964); Francis de Tarr, *The French Radical Party from Herriot to Mendès-France* (Oxford University Press, 1961); E. R. Tannenbaum, *The Action*

Française (Chicago University Press, 1962); Ed. John McClelland, *The French Right* (Cape, 1970); R. Rémond, *The Right Wing in France* (University of Pennsylvania Press, 1966); S. Hoffman, *Le Mouvement Poujade* (Colin, 1956); J. Charlot, *The Gaullist Phenomenon* (transl. from French; Allen and Unwin, 1971); M. Duverger, *Political Parties* (Methuen, 3rd edn 1964).

On Elections see *Cahiers de la Fondation Nationale des Sciences Politiques* for detailed studies of each general election since 1956; Peter Campbell, *French Electoral Systems and Elections since 1789* (Faber, 2nd edn 1965); F. Goguel, *Géographie des Elections Françaises sous la IIIᵉ et la IVᵉ République* (Colin, 1970); A. Lancelot, *L'Abstentionnisme Electoral en France* (Colin, 1968); J. Meynaud and A. Lancelot, *La Participation des Français à la Politique* (Presses Universitaires de France, 1965); Philip M. Williams, *French Politicians and Elections, 1958–69* (Cambridge University Press, 1970). On social structure and pressure groups see Georges Dupeux, *La Société Française, 1789–1960* (Colin, 1960); M. Duverger (ed.), *Partis Politiques et Classes Sociales* (Colin, 1955); H. Ehrmann, *Organized Business in France* (Princeton University Press, 1957); W. R. Fraser, *Education and Society in Modern France* (Routledge and Kegan Paul, 1968); J. E. S. Hayward, *Private Interests and Public Policy: the Experience of the French Economic and Social Council* (Longmans, 1966); Val R. Lorwin, *The French Labour Movement* (Harvard University Press, 1954); J. Fauvet and H. Mendras, *Les Paysans et la Politique dans la France Contemporaine* (Colin, 1958); H. Mendras, *Sociologie de la Campagne Française* (Presses Universitaires de France, 1965); J. Meynaud, *Les Groupes de Pression* (Colin, 1958) and *Nouvelles Etudes sur les Groupes de Pression* (Colin, 1962); Yves Tavernier, *La F.N.S.E.A.* (Colin, 1965); Gordon Wright, *Rural Revolution in France* (Oxford University Press, 1964); J. S. Ambler, *The French Army in Politics: 1945–62* (Ohio State University Press, 1966); J. Planchais, *Une Histoire Politique de l'Armée, 1940–67* (Seuil, 1967); F. Nourissier, *The French* (transl. from French; Knopf, 1968). On economic change and planning see A. Sauvy, *Histoire Economique de la France entre les Deux Guerres* (Paris, 1965); Pierre Bouchet, *Economic planning: the French Experience* (Praeger, 1964); J. and A.-M. Hackett, *Economic Planning in France* (Allen and Unwin, 1963); Charles Kindleberger, *Economic Growth in France and Britain* (Harvard University Press, 1964); PEP, *Economic Planning in Britain, France and Germany* (Allen and Unwin, 1968); A. Shonfield, *Modern Capitalism* (Oxford University Press, 1965); OECD Reports on France.

On foreign and colonial policy the following books are particularly useful: A. Grosser, *La IVe République et sa Politique Extérieure* (Colin, 1961) *La Politique Extérieure de la Ve République* (Colin, 1965); Erling Bjøl, *La France devant l'Europe* (Munksgaard, 1966); F. Roy Willis, *France, Germany and the new Europe* (Oxford University Press, 2nd edn 1968); Simon Serfaty, *France, de Gaulle and Europe* (John Hopkins, 1968); R. Aron and D. Lerner, *La Querelle de la C E D* (Colin, 1956); P. Manin, *Le R.P.F. et les Problèmes Européennes* (Presses Universitaires de France, 1966); M. Couve de Murville, *Une Politique Etrangère, 1958–69* (Plon, 1971); F. Borella, *L'Evolution Politique et Juridique de l'Union Française depuis 1946* (Nancy, 1957); P. Devillers, *Histoire du Vietnam, 1940–52* (Seuil, 1952); H. Grimal, *La Décolonisation, 1919–65* (Colin, 1966); J. Lacouture, *Cinq Hommes et la France* (Seuil, 1961); J. Lacouture and P. Devillers, *La Fin d'une Guerre, Indochine 1954* (Seuil, 1960); W. S. Lee, *French Policy and the Tunisian National Movement* (Oxford D.Phil., 1962); R. Le Tourneau, *Evolution Politique de l'Afrique du Nord, 1920–1961* (Colin, 1962); W. G. Andrews, *French Politics and Algeria: the Process of Policy Formation, 1954–62* (Appleton, Century, Crofts, 1962); D. Pickles, *Algeria and France: from Colonialism to Cooperation* (Methuen, 1963).

PART II

This section consists of books, articles and other source material on Christian Democracy and related subjects (e.g. Catholic Action, Catholic trade unions, etc.). Books by prominent Christian Democrats are also included. The best bibliographies on the themes in this section are to be found in W. Bosworth, *Catholicism and Crisis in Modern France* (Princeton University Press, 1962); J. Chelini, *La Ville et l'Eglise: Premier Bilan des Enquêtes de Sociologie Urbaine* (Cerf, 1958); M. P. Fogarty, *Christian Democracy in Western Europe, 1820–1953* (Routledge and Kegan Paul, 1957); and R. Rémond (ed.), *Forces Religieuses et Attitudes Politiques dans la France Contemporaine* (Colin, 1965). For a detailed list of MRP publications see Jean Charlot, *Répertoire des Publications des Partis Politiques Français, 1944–67* (Colin, 1970), pp. 144–77. The Reports of all the MRP Congresses can be read on microfilm at the Fondation Nationale des Sciences Politiques, Paris (or at Nuffield College, Oxford), and there are MRP and CD archives at 207 Boulevard St Germain, Paris. The following newspapers and periodicals are also essential sources for the study of Christian Democracy: *L'Aube* (1935–40; 1944–51; MRP daily); *Forces Nouvelles* (1944–67; MRP

weekly, then fortnightly); *Terre Humaine* (1950–57; Christian Democratic monthly); *France-Forum* (1957; Christian Democratic/
Centrist monthly); *Démocratie Moderne* (1967; Centrist weekly);
La Croix (moderate Catholic daily); *Témoignage Chétien* (Left
Catholic weekly); *Carrefour* (Right/Gaullist weekly); *Etudes* (Jesuit
monthly); *Esprit* (impossible to categorize, but basically progressive
Catholic). *Le Monde, Le Nouvel Observatuer* (formerly *L'Observateur*
and *France-Observateur*) and *L'Express* all contain much useful
information and comment. MRP's internal propaganda such as
MRP à l'Action (for militants) and *Action Fédérale* (for federation
leaders) also bear some study; for a full list of such material see
Charlot, *Répertoire des Publications des Partis* (cited above).

G. ADAM. *La C.F.T.C., 1940–58* Colin, 1964

G. ALMOND. 'Political Ideas of Christian Democracy', *Journal of Politics*,
November 1948

S. H. BARNES. 'The Politics of French Christian Labour', *Journal of Politics*,
February 1959

G. BIDAULT. *Resistance: the Political Autobiography of Georges Bidault* Weidenfeld and Nicolson, 1967

— *Le Point* Table Ronde, 1968

L. BITON. *La Démocratie Chrétienne dans la Politique Française* Giraudeau et
Cie, 1953

L. BODIN. 'La Presse Catholique en France, ses Patrons, ses Inspirateurs',
France Observateur 5 May 1955

J. E. C. BODLEY. *The Church in France* Macmillan, 1906

E. BORNE. *De Marc Sangnier à Marc Coquelin* Toulouse, 1953

W. BOSWORTH. *Catholicism and Crisis in Modern France* Princeton University
Press, 1962

B. BROWN. 'The Decision to Subsidise Private Schools', in Brown and Christoph,
Cases in Comparative Politics Dorsey, 1964

J. BUR. *Laïcité et Problème Scolaire* Bonne Presse, 1959

R. BURON. *Le Plus Beau des Métiers* Plon, 1963

— *Les Dernières Années de la IVᵉ République* Plon, 1968.

M. BYÉ, *et al. Le MRP—Cet Inconnu* Editions Polyglottes, 1961

Cahiers de la Fondation Nationale des Sciences Politiques—for Christian Democratic voting see *Cahiers* on Elections

R. B. CAPELLE. *MRP and French Foreign Policy* Praeger, 1963

L. V. CHAIGNEAU. *L'Organisation de l'Église Catholique en France* Spes, 1955

J. CHELINI. *La Ville et l'Église: Premier Bilan des Enquêtes de Sociologie Religieuse Urbaine* Cerf, 1958

A. COUTROT. 'L'Élaboration d'une Décision Législative sous la Ve République:
la Loi Scolaire de Décembre 1959', RFSP, June 1963

A. COUTROT and F. DREYFUS. *Les Forces Religieuses dans la Société Française*
Colin, 1965

CHRISTIAN DEMOCRACY IN FRANCE

R. CORNILLEAU. *Souvenirs et Témoignages* Rennes, 1959

L. CROUZIL. *Quarante Années de Séparation, 1905–45* Didier, 1946

A. DANSETTE. *Histoire Religieuse de la France Contemporaine* 2 vols, Flammarion, 1952

— *Destin du Catholicisme Français, 1926–56* Flammarion, 1957

M. DARBON. *Le Conflit entre la Droite et la Gauche dans le Catholicisme Français, 1830–1953* Toulouse, 1953

R. DELAVIGNETTE. *Christianity and Colonialism* (trans. J. Foster) New York, 1964

— 'French Colonial Policy in Black Africa', in *Colonialism in Africa* (eds Gann and Duignan) Cambridge University Press, 1960

A. DELMASURE. *Les Catholiques et la Politique* La Colombe, 1960

A. DERRO. *L'Épiscopat Français dans la Mêlée de son Temps, 1930–54* Bonne Presse, 1955

JACQUES DUQUESNE. *Les Catholiques Français sous l'Occupation* Grasset, 1966

J.-B. DUROSELLE. *Les Débuts du Catholicisme Social en France, 1822–70* Presses Universitaires de France, 1951

M. EINAUDI and F. GOGUEL. *Christian Democracy in Italy and France* University of Notre Dame Press, 1952

Esprit. Special numbers on 'La Question Scolaire' (March 1949 and February 1958); on 'Mounier' (December 1950); on 'Politique et Religion' (March 1958)

M. P. FOGARTY. *Christian Democracy in Western Europe, 1820–1953* Routledge and Kegan Paul, 1957

J. P. GAULT. *Histoire d'une Fidélité: Témoignage Chrétien* Editions du Témoignage Chrétien, 1952

F. GAY. *Pour un Rassemblement des Forces Democratiques d'Inspiration Chrétienne* Bloud et Gay, 1935

— *Les Démocrates d'Inspiration Chrétienne à l'Épreuve du Pouvoir* Bloud et Gay, 1950

B. GEORGES. *Problèmes du Catholicisme Français* Paris, 1953

G. HOURDIN. *La Presse Catholique* Fayard, 1957

J. HOURS. *La Doctrine de la Démocratie Chrétienne* Colin, 1952

R. E. M. IRVING. *The MRP and French Policy in Indochina, 1945–54* Oxford D.Phil., 1968

La Nef. Special numbers entitled 'Tableau des Partis Politiques' (April 1951) and 'Problèmes du Catholicisme Français' (January 1954)

A. LATREILLE and R. RÉMOND. *Histoire du Catholicisme en France, Période Contemporaine* Spes, 1962

A. LATREILLE and A. SIEGFRIED. *Les Forces Religieuses et la Vie Politique: Le Catholicisme et le Protestantisme* Colin, 1951

G. LE BRAS. *Etudes de Sociologie Religieuse* Presses Universitaires de France, 1957

V. LEMIEUX. *Le MRP dans le Système Politique Français. Sociologie d'un Destin* Thesis, Paris, 1960

J. LENOIR. *Essai sur la Démocratie Chrétienne et ses Fondements Philosophiques* Monte Carlo, 1954

G. LEPOINTE. *Les Rapports entre l'Église et l'État en France* Presses Universitaires de France, 1960

G. LEVARD. *Chances et Perils du Syndicalisme Chrétien* Fayard, 1955

J. MADAULE. *Les Chrétiens dans la Cité* Sagittaire, 1946

J. MAÎTRE. *Le Fonctionnement de la Presse Catholique en France* Paper presented to round table conference of *Association Française de Science Politique*, 1957

J. MARITAIN. *Humanisme Intégral* Aubier, 1936

— *Christianisme et Démocratie* Hartmann, 1953

— *L'homme et l'Etat* Presses Universitaires de France, 1953

F. MAYEUR. *L'Aube: Étude d'un Journal d'Opinion* Colin, 1966

L. V. MEJAN. *La Séparation des Églises et de l'État* Presses Universitaires de France, 1959

R. MEGRINE. *La Question Scolaire en France* Presses Universitaires de France, 1960

M. MERLE. *Les Églises Chrétiennes face à la Décolonisation* Colin, 1965

H. DE LA MONTAGNE. *Histoire de la Démocratie Chrétienne de Lamennais à Georges Bidault* Amiot-Dumont, 1948

M. MONTUCLARD. *Conscience Religieuse et Démocratie, la Deuxième Démocratie Chrétienne en France, 1891–1902* Seuil, 1965

E. MOUNIER. *Le Personnalisme* Presses Universitaires de France, 1949

E. PEZET. *Chrétiens au Service de la Cité: de Léon XIII au Sillon et au MRP* Nouvelles Editions Latines, 1965

PRELOT-LAURENT. *Manuel du Parti Démocrate Populaire* Paris, 1928

P. PFLIMLIN and R. LEGRAND-LANE. *L'Europe Communautaire* Plon, 1966

J. RAYMOND-LAURENT. *Les Origines du MRP* Editions du Mail, 1947

— *Le Parti Démocrate Populaire, 1924–44* Le Mans, 1966

R. RÉMOND. *Forces Religieuses et Attitudes Politiques dans la France Contemporaine* Colin, 1965

— *Lamennais et la Démocratie* Presses Universitaires de France, 1948

— 'Laïcité et Question Scolaire dans la Vie Politique Française sous la IVe République', in *Laïcité* (volume published by Presses Universitaires de France after colloque at Nice, 1960)

— 'Droite et Gauche dans le Catholicisme Français', RFSP, September 1958

— 'Evolution de la Notion de Laïcité entre 1919 et 1939', *Cahiers d'Histoire* no. 4, 1959

— 'Les Catholiques et les Elections', in *Le Référendum de Septembre et les Elections de Novembre 1958* Colin, 1960

— 'L'ACJF et l'Evolution des Structures Sociales', *La Vie Intellectuelle* February 1948

G. RENARD. *Pour Connaître le Sillon* Paris, 1966

R. ROCHEFORT. *Robert Schuman* Cerf, 1968

H. ROLLET. *Sur le Chantier Social: l'Action Sociale des Catholiques en France, 1870–1940* Lyon, 1955

— *L'Action Sociale des Catholiques en France, 1871–1914* 2 vols. (Vol. 1 1871–1901, Boivin, 1947; Vol. II, Desclée de Brouwer, 1958)

— *Albert de Mun et le Parti Catholique* Boivin, 1949

277

M. SANGNIER. *L'Esprit Démocratique* Paris, 1906

— *Discours* Paris, 1910

St Antony's Papers (Chatto and Windus)—*The Right in France*, especially articles by David Schapiro, 'The *Ralliement* in the politics of the 1890's', and Malcolm Anderson, 'The Right and the Social Question in Parliament'

P. H. SIMON. *De la Démocratie* Paris, 1945

Index

Principal references are shown in italics

Abbas, Ferhat, 204
abbés démocrates, 33, 35, 38
abbreviations, list of, 17–18
Abelin, Pierre, 69, 114, 118, 120, 145,
    153, 191, 233, 249, 250, 261, 263
ACGF (Action Catholique Générale,
    Femmes), 62, 80
ACGH (Action Catholique Générale,
    Hommes), 62, 80
ACJF (Association Catholique de la
    Jeunesse Française):
    founding of, 40, 79
    organization of, 63
    PDP and, 42, 49, 50
    end of, 79
ACO (Action Catholique Ouvrière), 79,
    254
Action Catholique Générale, Femmes
    (ACGF), 62, 80
Action Catholique Générale, Hommes
    (ACGH), 62, 80
Action Catholique Ouvrière (ACO), 79,
    254
Action Française:
    activities of, 20
    attacks on Christian Democrats, 42,
        48
    hatred of Popular Front, 25
    hierarchical view of society, 56
Action Libérale Populaire (ALP), 33
Action Rurale, 86
Adenauer, Konrad, 165–6, 167, 198
AFC (Associations Familiales Catho-
    liques), 80
Affre, Archbishop, 29
AGPB (Association Générale des Pro-
    ducteurs de Blé), 141–2
agriculture, *138–58*:
    alcohol lobby, 145
    Amicale Parlementaire Agricole, 146
    Common Agricultural Market, 138,
        139, 153–7, 158
    Common Agricultural Policy, 155,
        156–7
    Communist policy, 139, 157
    conservatism in, 139, 145

agriculture—*contd.*
    de Gaulle's contribution to common
        policy, 194
    effect of Common Market, 156
    effects of First World War, 141
    exports, 139, 143
    Green Pool, 139, 153–5, 158
    High Authority for Market, 154, **155**
    history of the problem, 140–3
    in inter-war years, 141–2
    in 19th century, 140–1
    in the depression, 142
    Loi Complémentaire, 149–52
    Loi d'Orientation, 150–1
    marketing system, 140
    Ministry of, 13, 138
    MRP *see* MRP
    Napoleonic inheritance laws, 140, **142**
    National Association for Migration
        and Rural Settlement, 149
    number of farms, 148
    parcellement, 140, 142
    percentage of population engaged
        in, 141, 148
    plans for mechanization, 139, 142–3,
        152–3
    polyculture, 140
    pressure groups, 139, 145, 157
    prices, 142, 154, 156
    production, 139, 143
    protection of, 141, 143, 145, 157
    reforms, 140
    remembrement, 142, 143, 144–5,
        149–50
    resettlement, 149
    restructuring, 139–40, 149, 152
    size of farms, 148
    the two agricultures, 140
    tractor revolution, 143, 152–3
    under Tanguy-Prigent, 142–3
    under Vichy, 142
    wages, 142, 146, 148–9
    see also AGPB, CETA, CGA, CGB,
        CNAA, CNJA, CUMA, FASASA,
        FAV, FNSEA, FORMA, JAC,
        SAFER, SICA

279

EEC (European Economic Community) —*contd.*
  establishment of, 188
  history of, 188–9
  institutional structure, 193
  Investment Bank and Readaptation Fund, 189, 192
  Messina Conference, 189, 190
  MRP policy *see* MRP
Einaudi, M., 47*n*, 52*n*, 64*n*, 65*n*, 66*n*, 67*n*, 76*n*, 83*n*, 84*n*, 124*n*
election(s):
  1876, 22
  1902, 23
  1924, 42
  1928, 44
  1932, 45
  1936, 45
  1967, 257–60
  1968, 260–1
  cantonal, 87, 88
  Council of the Republic, 87, 88
  maps, 92–4
  municipal, 87, 89–90, 150
  see also CD, MRP, PDP electoral performance, Presidency
electoral system:
  Law of 1966, 259
  under the Fifth Republic, 234–5
  see also proportional representation
Elysée Agreement, 208
EPC (European Political Community):
  Bidault's opposition to, 171, 175, 177
  considered by ECSC, 176–7
  draft constitution, 176–7
  effect of failure of, 193
  Menthon's policy, 176–7
  shelving of, 177
  supranational authority, 177
  Teitgen's policy, 174
équipes *see* MRP specialised teams
Equipes Jeunes, 99, 249, 250, 254
Equipes Ouvrières, 99, 130, 184, 247, 254, 262
Equipes Rurales, 151
Ere Nouvelle, L', 29
Esprit, 58, 84
Euratom, 188, 189, 190, 192, 193, 194
Eure, Department of, MRP Federation in, 96

Europe:
  Community Europe, 194–5, 198
  de Gaulle's concept of, 194, 196–8
  'European Europe', 194, 197–8
  Europe des Etats, 196, 197
  Europe des Patries, 196
  Europe of Peoples, 196–7
  Europeanism of the Christian Democrats, 198
  federal, 196, 198
  MRP concept of, 194, 196–8
  Pflimlin's concept of, 196–7
  political community of, 196–7
European:
  Defence Community *see* EDC
  Economic Community *see* EEC
  Federal Union, 47
  Parliament, 12, 197
  Political Community *see* EPC
  see also MRP foreign policy
Eveil Démocratique, L', 38, 39
Events of May–June 1968:
  CFDT reaction, 127–8
  effect on Centre, 263
  effects on industrial policy, 127, 128
  electoral effects of, 260–1, 263
Evian Agreement, 224, 225, 226, 227, 228
Express, L', 98, 134, 249–50

factory legislation, 26, 33
  see also industrial policy
Fallous Law, 22
family:
  allowances, 47, 59, 61
  as a natural social group, 61
  as a 'natural structure of society', 58
  as basic unit of society, 34
  associations, 34, 47, 61, 62, 80
  defining of rights, 67
  doctrine of the, 61–2
  education, 67
  insurance schemes, 34
  MRP view of *see* MRP social policy
  PDP view of, 47
  policy, housing as part of, 129
FASASA (Fonds d'Action Sociale pour l'Amélioration des Structures Agricoles) 149, 152
Fascism, Christian Democracy and, 11–12, 47–8

K   289